D1002268

Systematic Fieldwork
Volume 2

Systematic

In collaboration with:

Judith Abbott
Julie Ahern
Martha Ann Austin
Mark Bauer
Kenneth Y. Begishe
Paul Bugos
Steven Cobb
Richard Davidian
Lawrence Fisher
Kathleen Gregory
Mitsuru Hamamoto
Deborah Bouck Higgins
Kim Hirschman
Madelyn A. Iris
Rebecca Kolberg
Richard Levine
Gladys Levis-Pilz
Laura Linhart
Michael Low
Timothy McKeown
Frank Pasquale
Norris Minnick
Judith A. Remington
Eleanore Retzler
Alisu Schoua
Julie Spiegel
Jeff Ward
Derek Werner
Margaret Zacharias

Fieldwork

Volume 2

Ethnographic Analysis and Data Management

Oswald Werner
G. Mark Schoepfle

SAGE PUBLICATIONS
The Publishers of Professional Social Science
Newbury Park Beverly Hills London New Delhi

For June and Lisa

Dedicated to our parents
Julius Mathew Werner (1897-1975) and **Bella Toth Werner** (1905-1984)

and

Gordon Marcus Schoepfle and **Ester Schoultheis Schoepfle**

For information address:

SAGE Publications, Inc.
2111 West Hillcrest Drive
Newbury Park, California 91320

SAGE Publications Inc.
275 South Beverly Drive
Beverly Hills
California 90212

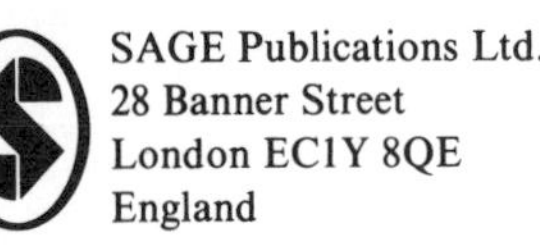

SAGE Publications Ltd.
28 Banner Street
London EC1Y 8QE
England

SAGE PUBLICATIONS India Pvt. Ltd.
M-32 Market
Greater Kailash I
New Delhi 110 048 India

Printed in the United States of America

Library of Congress Cataloging-in-Publication Data

Main entry under title:

Werner, Oswald.
Systematic fieldwork.

Bibliography: p.
Includes index.
1. Ethnology—Field work. 2. Ethnology—Methodology.
3. Interviewing in ethnology. I. Schoepfle, G. Mark.
II. Ahern, Julie. III. Title.
GN346.W47 1987 306′.072 85-26152
ISBN 0-8039-2853-X (v. 2)

Contents

List of Figures

Preface and Acknowledgments

Volume 1, *Systematic Fieldwork: Foundations of Ethnography and Interviewing,* sets the stage for Volume 2: *Ethnographic Analysis and Data Management*. Although Volume 2 can stand on its own as an exposition of data management and analysis, it is truly the culmination of this work.

The backbone of this book is the MTQ theory of lexical/semantic relations and the lexical/semantic fields that the relations comprise. Every method and every technique must provide an affirmative answer to the following question: Can we justify it in our theoretical framework? Our theoretical orientation may be seen as the first steps toward a theory of ethnography.

In the past, ethnography has been seen primarily as a more or less systematized method for acquiring ethnographic data. Here we assert that ethnographies must supersede mere technique. The cognitive sciences furnish many new insights into the workings of our main "instrument"—the human perceptual and cognitive capacities and capabilities. These insights must be taken into account if we are to understand the ethnographic process.

But the ethnographic process is even more complex. The human "instrument" gathers data from other human "instruments," each equipped with the same cognitive and perceptual capacities and capabilities. Only our respective cultural knowledge, which every social group accrues over time, makes us significantly different.

The task of ethnography is to use ourselves and our consultants' (informants') cognitions to understand their cultural biases better. The most difficult task for the ethnographer is always to keep his or her ethnocentrisms under control while exploring the ethnocentrisms of the natives. Concurrently we must think of native ethnocentrism in terms of the particular language we use for the interpretation of their native view.

In the first volume (see flowchart of chapters in Figure A) we explore the epistemology of ethnography, the impact of the personal equation of the ethnographer, preparation for fieldwork and field relations, the interview with its concomitant problems, and especially the problem of translation.

In this volume we turn to the processing of acquired data. Data acquisition, especially through interviewing, and data analysis do not necessarily follow each other in a simple sequence. The best procedure is iterated data aquisition: intelligent placement of the data in a data base, their analysis, the contribution of analyses to further data acquisition, and so on. An important aspect of analysis is to uncover holes in the acquired structure of our consultants' knowledge. We cannot fill these holes if we postpone analysis until after our return from the field.

Many times in the following page we reiterate that formal analysis does not depend on formal, structural interviewing. We prefer indirect questions and free-form interviewing, more akin to conversations with the natives than formal interviews. Only our preference for tape recording formalizes the interviewing process. However, conversations rarely (if ever) exhaustively fill the boundaries of any cultural domain. Conversational interviews should therefore be followed by structural questioning, used to round out and to tie up loose ends. Again the process may be seen as iterative, alternating between periods of free and open acquisition of new data through indirect questioning and conversations and structured interviewing intended to complete the coverage of native knowledge systems.

We are often asked if ethnoscience methodology, as we present it in these two volumes, is all there is to ethnography. The answer is, "Of course, not!" We have to separate the craft of ethnography from the art. The craft can be taught. Art can be taught—up to a point—and practice is an important dimension of becoming a good artist. But great art is ultimately dependent on the talent of the artist.

For many applications of ethnography a master craftsman-ethnographer is all that is required. These volumes address the problem of becoming such a master craftsman. For the novice we address a second crucial problem: how to get started. For example, although taxonomies are hardly the be-all and end-all of ethnographic description, taxonomies of the stage, props, actors, and activities are a good place to start an ethnography. Later, when the skills of the apprentice have matured, the master ethnographer may adapt his or her working style to fit the task.

There is another point to be made. Our cognitive ethnoscience methodology is lexicographic in spirit—at least on the lowest level. However, lexocography quickly expands to linked lexical items (better, naming units) that form networks of propositions. Nevertheless, our interpretations of meanings are always close to the surface—near the face value of words and phrases. There is a good reason for this. Only surface, face value meanings are relatively free of ambiguity or multi-layered intentions. The deeper we dig, the more equivocal our interpretations become, the less likely we are to find a reliable compass to guide our way.

Quite to the contrary, it is not that these areas of ambiguity are unimportant in human affairs or ethnographies. But before we can imaginatively interpret deeper meanings we must understand and exhaust the meanings nearer the surface on which more profound understandings seem to rest. Even then, the deeper the meaning, the more obscure the intentions, and the less sure we are we have found the "real thing."

In other words, there is no substitute for hard ethnographic work. Interpretive ethnographers, who believe that they can enter deep understandings before they have fully explored the meanings contained in lexical/semantic fields and a wide variety of lexical/semantic relations, only delude themselves. They may produce great works of self-centered art, which will likely prove useless to anyone interested in developing practical solutions so vital to some of life's problems.

A few people remain to be acknowledged since the completion of the manuscript and the decision to publish this book in two volumes. Al Goodyear, formerly of Sage Publications, masterminded the two-volume approach. We learned a lot from each other in the process. We also appreciated his patience, good humor, and lunches at the Drake.

We are delighted that Mitch Allen has returned to Sage. He and Lois Smith shepherded our book through completion. They have always been encouraging and persistent. We are most grateful for their help.

Derek Werner has again edited the minor revisions that became necessary as a consequence of splitting one large book into two smaller volumes. Ray Walsh did much of the remaining mechanical production. Our families' patience, especially our wives', has been tried by the inevitable delays. We are grateful to all of them, far more than we can express in this preface.

Evanston, Illinois
Albuquerque, New Mexico, and
Gallina, New Mexico

—Oswald Werner
G. Mark Schoepfle

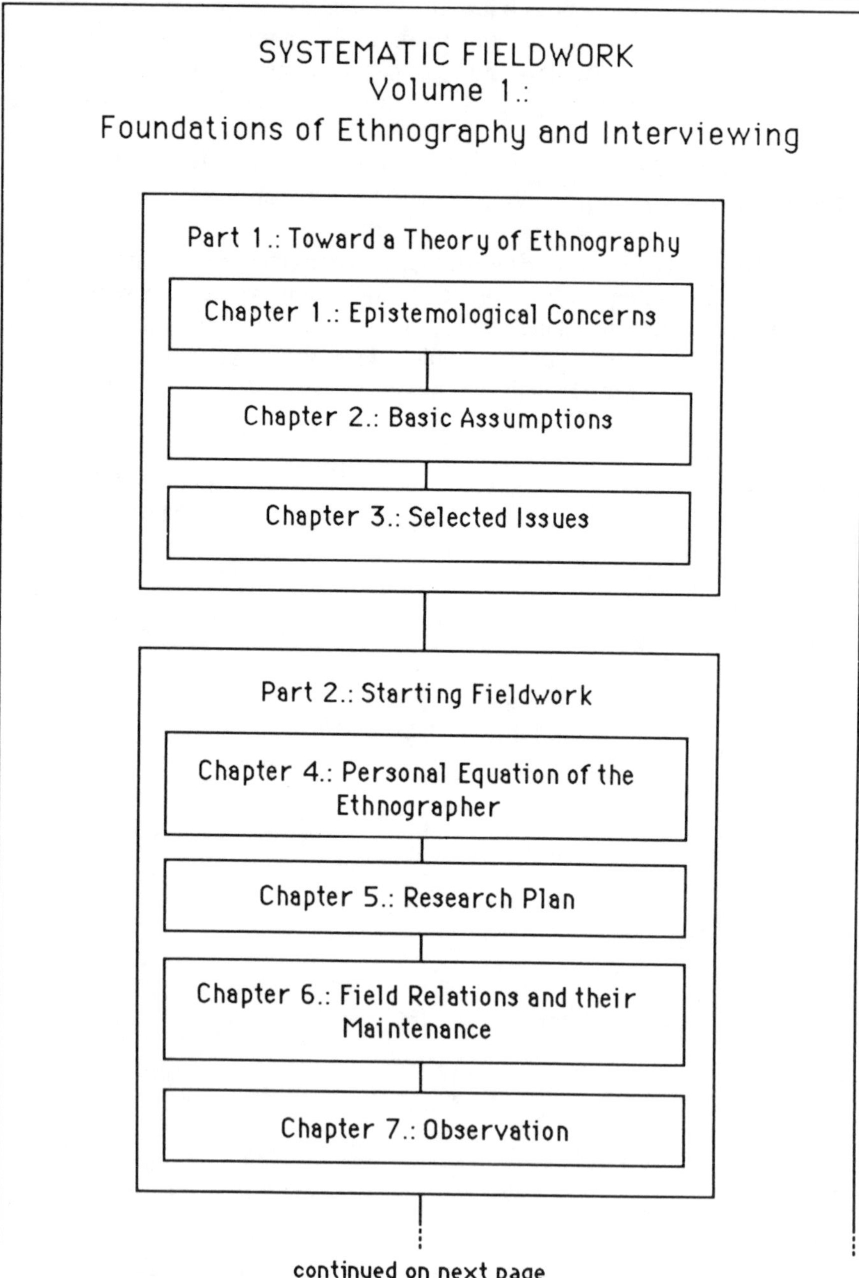

continued on next page

Figure A Flowchart of Volumes, Parts, and Chapters

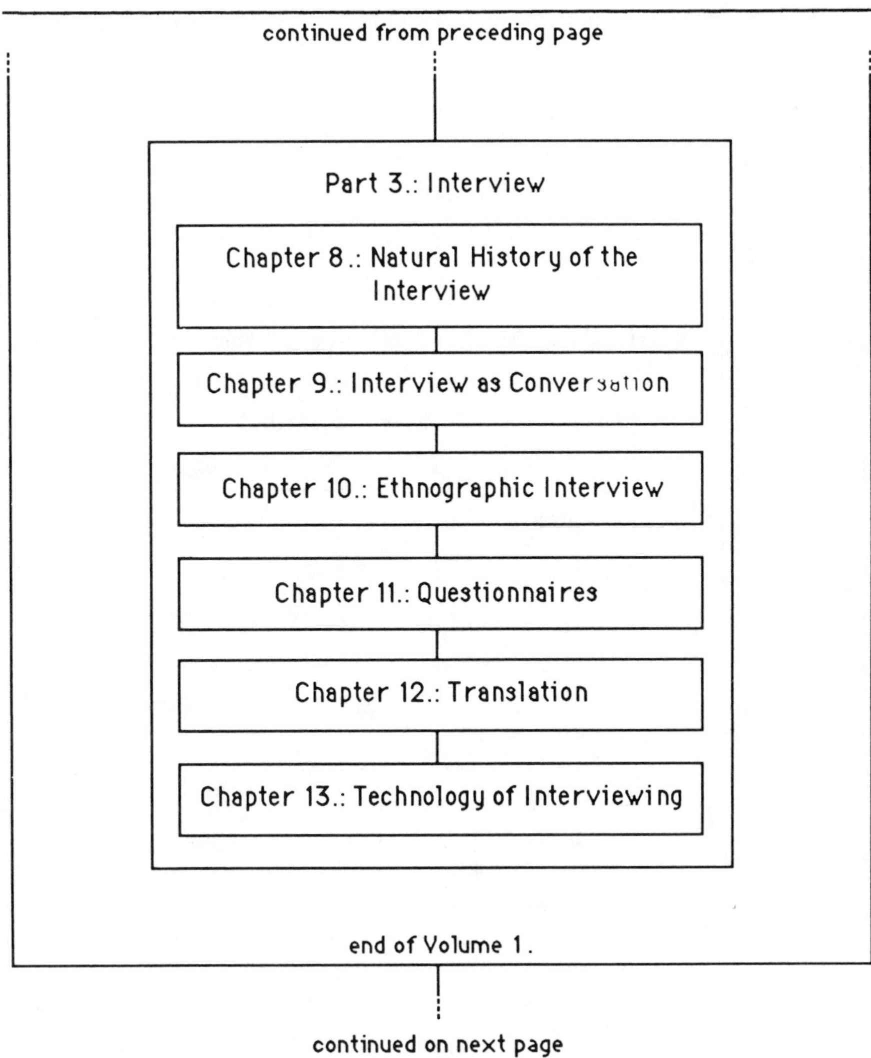

Figure A Continued

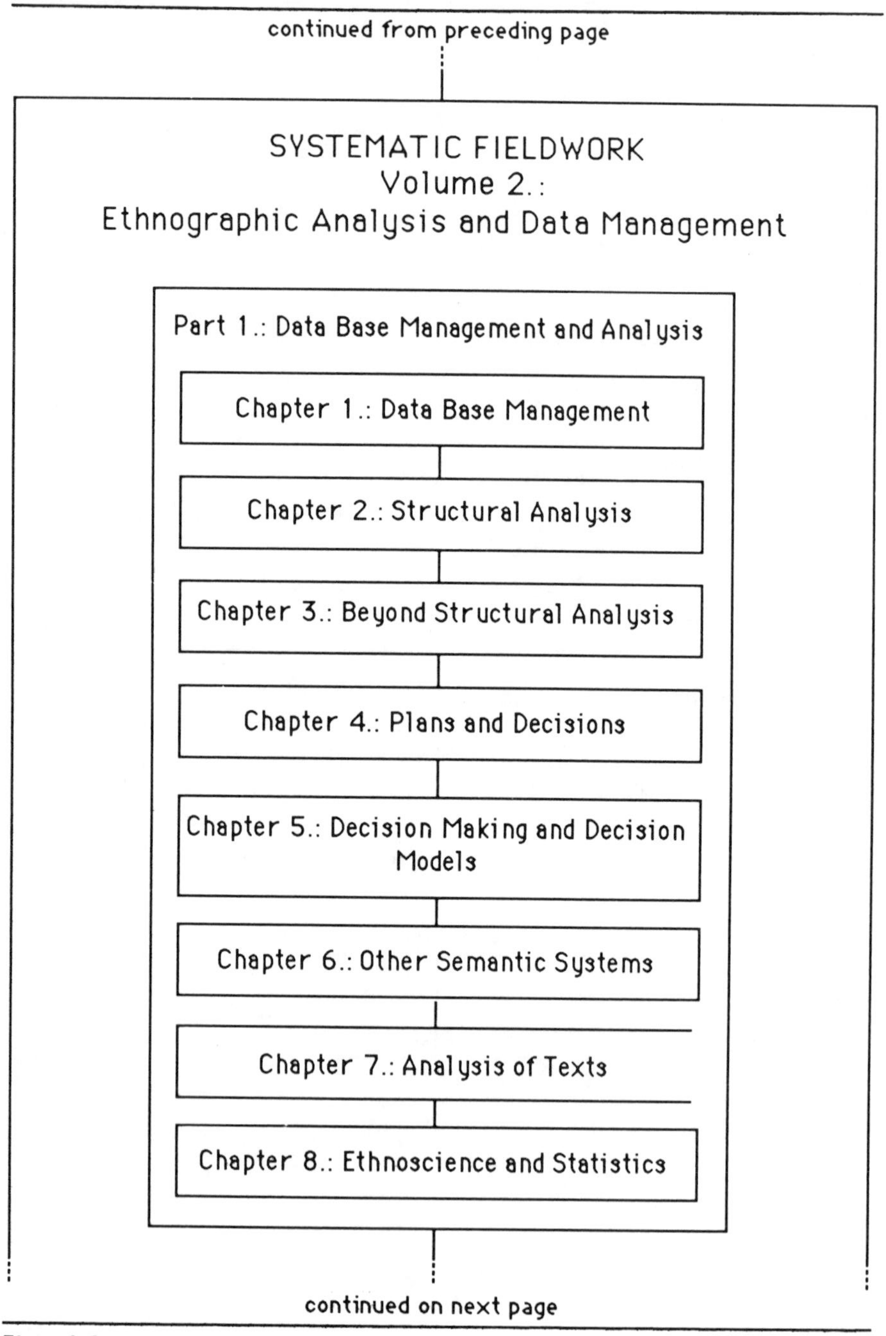

continued from preceding page
SYSTEMATIC FIELDWORK
Volume 2.:
Ethnographic Analysis and Data Management
Part 1.: Data Base Management and Analysis
Chapter 1.: Data Base Management
Chapter 2.: Structural Analysis
Chapter 3.: Beyond Structural Analysis
Chapter 4.: Plans and Decisions
Chapter 5.: Decision Making and Decision Models
Chapter 6.: Other Semantic Systems
Chapter 7.: Analysis of Texts
Chapter 8.: Ethnoscience and Statistics
continued on next page

Figure A Continued

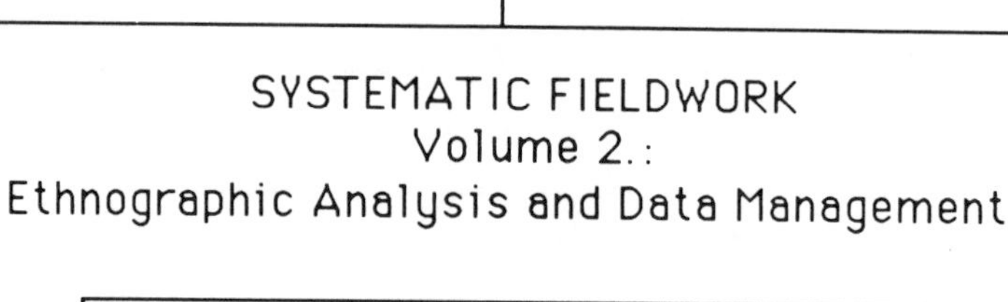

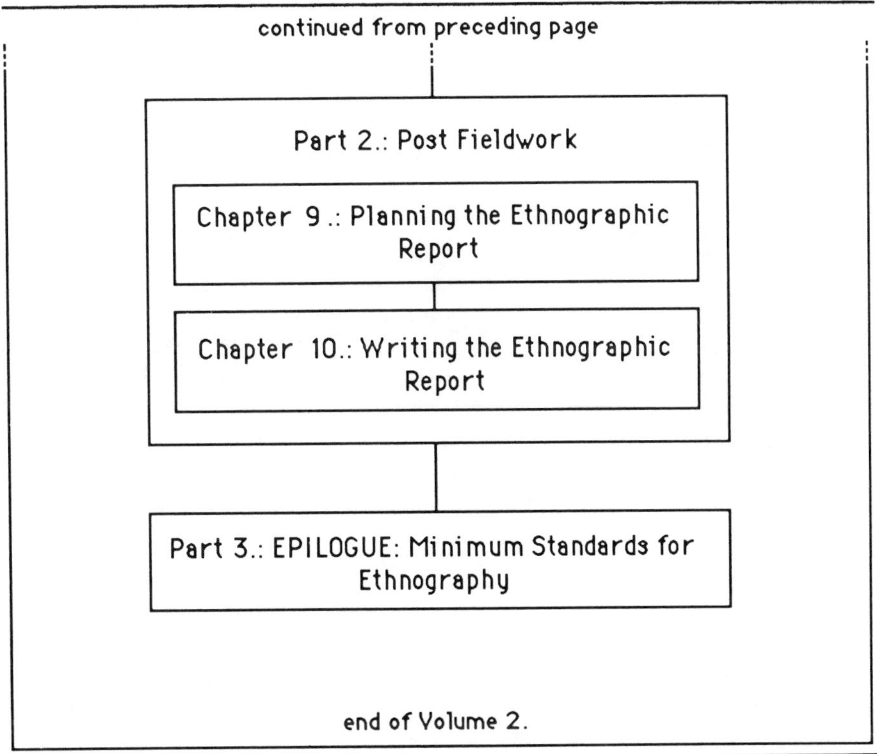

Figure A Continued

Introduction

We consider the management of ethnographic data—usually texts—part of analysis. This should not detract from the fact that a sound ethnographic data management system should be in place before collection of data begins. Once data are collected and managed properly, analysis in the narrow sense of the word can begin.

Before beginning this volume on data base management and ethnographic analysis, we must review and discuss a few fundamental issues. This discussion will further an understanding of what is involved in ethnographic analysis.

1 DESCRIPTION

An ethnography is first a description. It is a text (words in sentences set down on paper) that discusses a social group or a knowledge system (the encyclopedic approach) and makes the claim that it bears a close resemblance to the life in the group or to the knowledge in a social system.

In some applied work, perhaps with increasing frequency, no finished product or ethnography emerges at the end. Instead the ethnographer inserts his or her findings into the social system as the ethnographic process unfolds. This form of intervention is a powerful tool for influencing a social system, by necessity, in cooperation with the natives.

Unfortunately few, if any, applications of the ethnographic process for intervention have been recorded in sufficient detail. The genre is ripe for an ethnography of ethnography. It is too easy to rely simply on previous successes. We need more descriptions of the use of the ethnographic process for intervention into a social system. The resulting ethnography should follow the same principles of analysis described in this chapter.

2 TRANSLATION

Ethnography is also translation. This is easily seen in ethnographies brought home from distant places. These ethnographies were constructed from the lives of natives who speak a language very different from that of the ethnographer or the readership of the ethnography. Translation is therefore necessary to render an image of a drastically different way of life in an idiom familiar to readers.

The need for translation is less obvious when we apply ethnographic methods to groups or knowledge systems closer to home. Yet translation it is nevertheless.

This can be seen more clearly in the ethnoscience paradigm than in any other ethnographic form. The life of a group or the nature of a knowledge system is described from an internal view, as often as possible in the words of the natives. Over time any group develops a unique knowledge system, its own culture, which then manifests itself in the specialized use of language. Translation is required to understand these new meanings whether they belong to Bushmen or American auto workers.

In Volume 1, Section 12.3 we discuss ethnographic translation. The characteristic of this type of translation is the abundance of translator's notes. Whereas literary translation usually attempts to minimize translator's notes, in ethnographic translation any native text must be richly annotated with explanations of the cultural significance of any item in the text that could be misconstrued or simply missed by a reader outside the native culture.

One approach to compiling a maximal set of translator's notes involves compiling a bilingual dictionary. Such a dictionary can serve as translator's notes to any text composed in the native language of our consultants. A good dictionary must be applicable to any native text that may turn up. That is, it must provide thorough coverage of the lexical resources of the two languages involved. Ideally, coverage is 100%. Many factors make that ideal unattainable. But, at least in principle, 100% coverage is the goal. This relative completeness of coverage has consequences that we will discuss in detail below.

3 EXPERT SYSTEMS[1]

An ethnography can be seen as an expert system—a data base to which anyone interested in the lives of the natives can refer. As does a reliable encyclopedia, this data base can provide appropriate answers. Computerized expert systems can do more than just present retrievals of desired information. Such systems can additionally deduce new information based on old premises, much like human beings. Such devices can draw conclusions from existing knowledge that have never before been made and thus create information that de facto was not in the data base before.

It is important to realize that an ethnography viewed as an encyclopedia, or as an expert system, is another way of seeing ethnography as a method for 100% coverage of cultural knowledge. Looking at an expert system as a generative device that creates new information out of old can result in coverage that exceeds the initial 100% input of knowledge.

4 SKETCH

An ethnography is ideally a high-fidelity sketch, a photograph rather than an impressionistic painting, of a culture. Any sketch is an abstract of reality. That is, to be readable, any ethnographic sketch must be less rich than the ethnographic reality that gave rise to it.

During a one-year ethnographic expedition a good ethnographer may collect easily 3,000 pages of transcription and journal entries. An ethnography drawn from this data base rarely exceeds 300 pages. Contained in this 1:10 reduction is the sketchlike nature of an ethnography. A 1:10 reduction, incidentally, seems to constitute a pragmatic universal. In magazine article writing or filmmaking a ratio of 1:10 of collected data to final presentation seems well accepted.

A reduction in detail brings to mind a map analogy. However, although a map allows for radical reduction—even a good hiker's map requires reduction on the scale of 1:25,000—ethnographic maps approximate a reduction nearer 1:10. With the exception of folk maps, maps also employ uniform scales. If a map's reduction is 1:25,000, that implies that this scale applies uniformly to the entire area covered by the map.

Ethnographies do not have uniform scales of reduction. Some areas may be relatively neglected (requiring considerable reduction); other areas of interest may be elaborated (requiring minimal reduction). We have described in Volume 1, Section 1.1 many different types of ethnographies with different emphases. Any area of emphasis can be seen as an area of elaboration; any deemphasis (explicit or implicit), a reduction in the scale of the sketch. This feature of uneven elaboration and reduction encountered in ethnographic accounts makes the work of cross-cultural comparativists exceedingly difficult. One ethnography may concentrate on how birth is given (Jordan 1980), the other on economics (Bohannan and Bohannan 1968). Although birth of people and economic considerations are important to both, the first skimps on economy and the second on birth. Two ethnographies rarely cover the same topics with equal thoroughness.

5 REDUCTION

The key question of ethnographic analysis therefore becomes, Is there a way systematically to reduce ethnographic complexity? In other words, we pose the following problem: In mapping it is the landscape that is reduced to a map. More appropriately, the raw data of mapping are aerial photographs, already a radical reduction on the order of 1:15,000 (roughly 10 cm on film equal 1,500 meters, or about one mile on the ground). Common topographic maps are 1:75,000, or a 1:5 reduction of aerial photographs. A map is the analog to an ethnography. What is the analog to the aerial photographs?

The life of natives as it unfolds before the ethnographer is the "ground." Obviously, the ethnographer's interviews and journal entries are the raw data from which an ethnography emerges. These items are the analog to the aerial photographs. The methods of analysis introduced in this section are analogous to the principles of mapmaking. Our subject matter in this volume therefore includes analytical techniques that allow us to reduce the complexity of our interviews and journal entries to manageable levels.

The principles of mapmaking are well systematized; the reduction of raw ethnographic data to ethnographies is not. There are two steps involved in ethnographic reduction of complexity: First, we reduce raw textual data to known structures. This can be viewed as a step toward the creation of expert knowledge systems and requires 100% coverage in at least selected cultural domains. The second step is a systematic reduction of these structures into abstracted forms (in many, though not all, cases into subtrees, for example).

5.1 Sketch of Lexical/Semantic Relations

Theoretically, we distinguish two types of relations upon which both volumes of *Systematic Fieldwork* rest. First, there are subpropositional (or subsentence) relations; second, all others. We presented a commonsense derivation of the two atomic subpropositional relations M and T in Volume 1 (see Section 2.3). Here we will use a quicker but more abstract procedure.

Reichenbach (1942) introduced a theory of functions for the representation of sentences. An intransitive sentence, "Jane understands," can be represented by Understands(Jane), or u(j). A transitive sentence is treated analogously, but the number of arguments in parentheses increases. That is, "Jane understands algebra" becomes u(j,a). Reichenbach (1947) claims that, for example, the first sentence u(j) could be represented α(u,j) but that this is unnecessary because α is a constant. Our claim is that α is not a constant. It can assume two values: the relationship of modification M and of taxonomy T. M is reflexive ((a)M(a) exists), asymmetrical ((a)m(b) is not equal to (b)M(a)). These characteristics also apply to taxonomy T. However, T is transitive (If (a)T(b) and (b)T(c), then (a)T(c)), whereas M is not.

A new taxon (species) is created by adding new attributes (differentiae) to an old taxon (genus) via M. If interpreted this way, every declarative sentence may be seen as building a new taxonomy: Knowing the topic of a sentence[2] means that its genus in known. The comment is new information that attaches to the topic and thus creates a new taxon. We represent this graphically in Figure 1. It follows from this figure that if the number of differentiae (C) approaches the empty set (no attributes), then the relation of taxonomy reaches its limiting case—the relation of synonymy. At this point the relation becomes symmetrical: If (A)T(B) and (B)T(A), then and only then (A)S(B), where S stands for the relation of synonymy.

For practical elicitation, the taxonomic frame is usually "(B) is a (kind of)(A)." However, "All (B) are (A)" and several other manifestations of the relation in sentence form are also acceptable. The taxonomic question frame in English often uses the emphatic optional clause of "kind of"; that is, "What kind of (A) are there?"

The question frame for the M relation is most simply a request for a folk definition—say, "What does (B) mean?" The response is usually a paragraph symbolized in Figure 1 by (C). If (C) is analyzed into its simple constituent sentences, each acting as an independent attribute or modifier (differentiae), then the graphing convention can be generalized as shown in Figure 2. If we assume that almost all folk definitions (answering the question, "What does (B) mean?") are open ended—that is, have no upper limit or no longest definition exists—

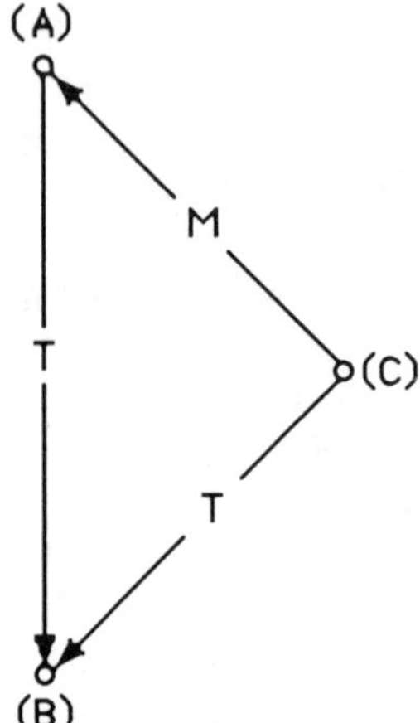

NOTE: The genus (a) is modified by attributes (C) (differentiae). This process creates taxon (B), the new species.

Figure 1 Basic MT Triangles

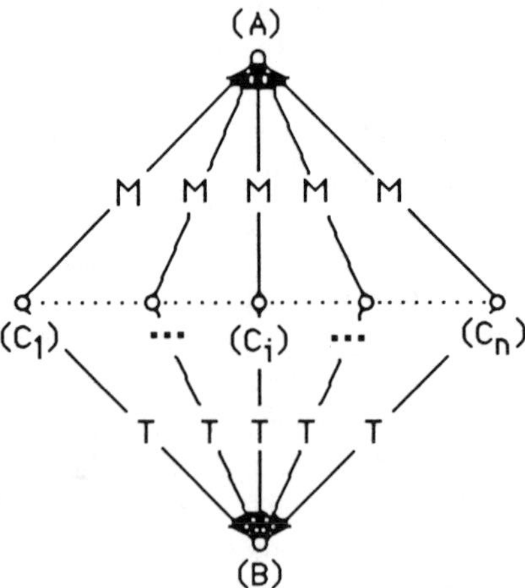

Figure 2 Generalization of MT Triangles

then we can represent Figure 2 in even more general form (Figure 3). The triangles symbolize the fact that the number of independent attributes (predicates) is indeterminate.

Our next illustration (Figure 4) shows how we envision the organization of the entire lexicon—or better, the entire system of enyclopedic knowledge—including knowledge of social organization. Note that the links form a network of propositions rather than just a network of lexical items.

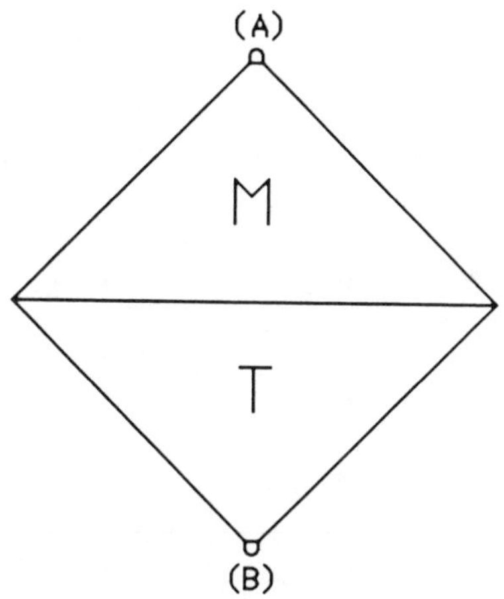

Figure 3 Generalization of MT Triangles

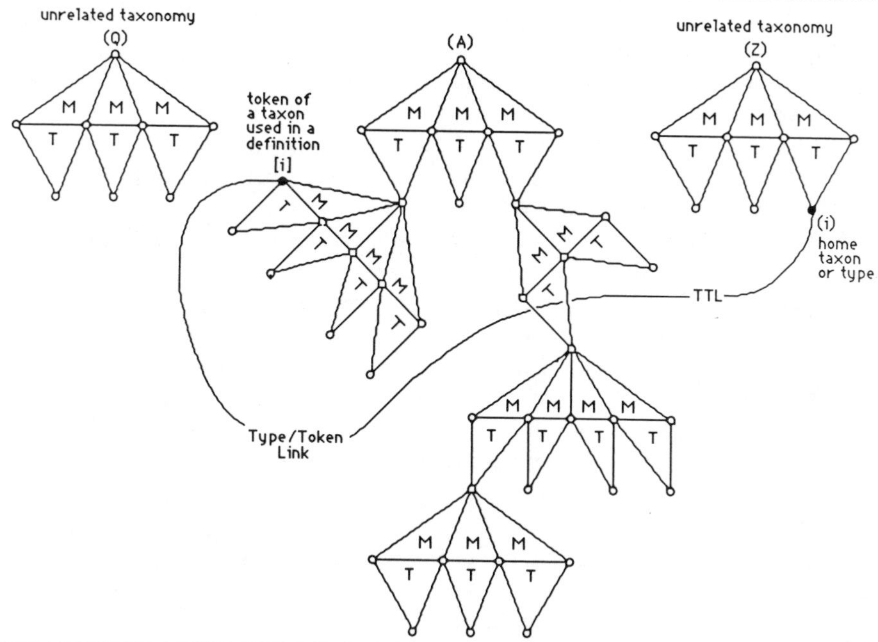

Figure 4 Lexical/Semantic Fields

The derivation we have presented so far is the subpropositional MT schema, yet it remains incomplete. Most sentences in ethnographic texts express complex relations. All known complex relations can be derived from M and T. The canonical formula for the largest family of complex relations is presented below. Other families of complex relations may exist, but they remain as yet unknown.

(B) T((name of complex relation)M((preposition)M(B)))

Examples of complex relations are "(B) is a part of (A)" (where "part" is the name of the relation and "of" is the preposition), "(B) is the cause of (A)," "(B) is used for (A)," "(B) is required for (A)"; even relations with complex names that have an internal structure of their own: "(B) is a land use rights holder to (A)" (Hutchins 1980). In this sentence (B) represents a list of names of Trobriand Islanders and (A) a list of named garden plots.

Very few complex relations can be organized into hierarchies of large lexical/semantic fields. The ones that can be so organized, such as the part/whole relation, are the exception rather than the rule. Most complex relations form only isolated links within other lexical/semantic fields.

The MT schema alone fails to account for all texts and must be supplemented by the relation Q (queueing or sequence), which represents all serial orders in time and space. Thus we have (Monday)Q(Tuesday)(Q = "is followed by"). More important Q is the relation for representing the hierarchic lexical/semantic fields of activities, or Verbal Action Plans. In the next illustration (Figure 5) we show a very simple plan for "getting up" in the morning. Please note that we employ the *inverse* of the graph representations used for T and M. Previously, nodes represented concepts and arrows the relations between those concepts. Nodes now represent the Q relation and arrows are labels for activities.

In this volume we consistently use MT and Q to justify theoretically all aspects of ethnographic fieldwork. In short, the MTQ schema consistently provides the theoretical basis for all problems of ethnographic fieldwork. These ideas are elaborated in Volume 1, *Foundations of Ethnography and Interviewing*. A few loose ends, elaborated in the two volumes of *Systematic Fieldwork,* remain.

The Q relation ("and then") forms a bridge between subpropositional and proposition/logical relations. It is closely related to C conjunction (logical "and"), which also forms a bridge between propositional and subpropositional relations: Although "And" can link sentences "S and S" ("John went to the store and Jill went up the hill"), it can also link items within sentences, as in "The church is between the blue *and* the red skyscrapers." This sentence cannot be reduced to the conjunction of two sentences.

Other logical relations are disjunction D ("or"), negation N, and implication F ("If . . ., then . . ."). The relation of implication may be extended by modal operators.

The role of quantification in this schema remains unaccounted for. It is related to M but seems simultaneously to differ from it. Further work is needed to incorporate this important aspect of language into the theory.

We will see later in this volume that contexts can be viewed as high-level attributes, attached by the M relation to (sometimes) long segments of discourse. Similarly, we view conditions for deciding on a course of action (decision criteria) also as high-level attributes. More information on these topics may be found in the specific sections of this volume.

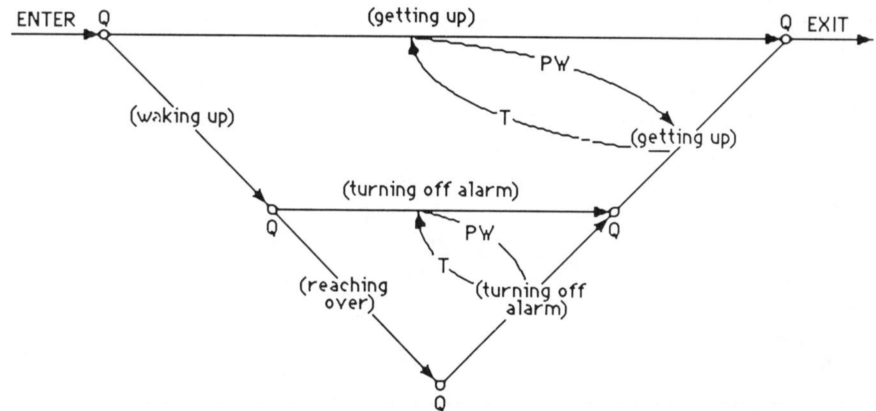

NOTE: Plans may use the same labels on different levels of specificity. Note also that although the sequential relation is Q, the relation between subplans and their superplans is part/whole. Occasionally a subplan dominates its superplan taxonomically. This apparent paradox is explained in Chapter 3.

Figure 5 Simple Verbal Action Plan

These structures account for an almost 100% coverage of ethnographic texts (transcriptions and journal entries). By "almost 100%" we mean that a few residual structures remain unanalyzable. Though a tremendously rigorous demand for analytical success, 100% coverage remains our ultimate goal. Unfortunately, no known short-cuts exist. Only after a systematically exhaustive analysis of all texts can we proceed to the second step of reducing, again systematically, the texts we transformed into abstracted structures and thus reduce their richness. In a sense, the map analogy helps again. Early maps of the New World bear the personal idiosyncrasies of their makers. We can construct ad hoc maps from our personal impressions. Systematic ethnographic reduction requires the systematic analysis of ethnographic texts.

In the following chapters this principle of analysis and concomitant ethnographic reduction is delineated.

6 CULTURAL DOMAINS

Ethnoscience analysis aims to define systematically the meaning of words, or labels—in short, the names of "things" in the context of their use. Defining words (naming units) in context provides the key to understanding the knowledge that underlies the behavior of actor-consultants. Folk theories reflected in folk definitions form charters for human action. If this were not so, inventing theories would have no point.

The ethnographer's primary purpose is to gather a sample of native language (a text) large enough to contain sets of recurrent words. Texts also contain phrases used by consultants as names or descriptions of "things" in their environment; thus the ethnographer looks for words *and* for naming units larger than words. The ethnoscience ethnographic and encyclopedic analyses constitute a series of directions for discovering naming units, especially the relationships between naming units (sentences).

Sets of related words form cultural domains or semantic systems. For example, on Rapa Nui (Easter Island) the word *ika,* fish, defines the cultural domain of fish; among the Navajo *hats'íís,* the human body, defines the cultural domain of all named body parts. In the above examples and in those following, the English words are mere translation labels and should not be considered careful translations.

Translation labels are simply identifiers. In these two cases, the labels for the cultural domains are also words. In ethnoscience ethnographies phrases, rather than words, frequently delimit a domain. "Carol's classes" is a domain, as is "different ways of skipping school," or *yá'át'éehgo iiná,* the good life, in Navajo. An important cultural domain for ethnography is native consultants' knowledge of their own social universes.

Ethnoscience analytical skill consists of the ability to break down the sequential, linear order of texts into the nonlinear, network-like semantic structures that underlie these texts. The process is analogous to the operations human beings perform when they reduce linear speech to nonlinear, multidimensional knowledge in permanent memory. This nonlinear "dictionary," organized into culture domains, aids in the solution of the key problem of ethnography: the accurate translation of native statements (categories) into ethnographic statements, understandable to a reading public in one or several of the world's major languages.

7 BOUNDARIES

The "stage" of a group and/or its actors defines the boundaries of ethnographic systems—for example, the language that reflects the cultural knowledge of the group. Encyclopedic boundaries are formed by social units independent of space (e.g., the language or cultural knowledge of truck drivers). They may also be formed by possible topics of conversation (e.g., the anatomical knowledge of the Navajo). In the encyclopedic approach, boundaries are defined almost exclusively by domain labels. In more traditional ethnography, the speech community (e.g., all speakers of Navajo, English, etc.) also forms a boundary. In an ethnography of truck drivers, the existence of a speech community may be more difficult to establish. Perhaps common experience can serve as a boundary in some cases.

The boundary of an ethnographer's investigation is usually set by the goals of one's study. A microethnography describes a small social unit such as a store or a classroom. Larger units—a school, a factory, or a tribe—often require focusing on less microscopic detail and therefore tend to be more encyclopedic. A study of an ethnoanatomy (the Navajo *hats'íís,* human body) is clearly encyclopedic and has no clear-cut social group, except all speakers of the language to which it refers. The larger the group, the more difficult it becomes to specify the contexts of use. Under such headings as "the human body," "Grand Tour" questions elicit the first level of terms. Through minitours many more related, subordinate terms are gathered. By asking the consultant to group terms in various possible or "acceptable" ways, the ethnographer gathers clues about the consultant's folk systems of classification. The interviews are guided by the need to discover new terms and their position and importance in the total system.

8 CONTRAST SETS

Contrast sets (in one's lexicon) can be defined by comparing and contrasting certain words with other words. Often contrast sets form hierarchies of contrasts; that is, we do not have merely words that contrast with other words but contrast within contrast sets on different levels. These contrast sets or levels form the basis of semantic systems such as folk classifications, including folk taxonomies, folk part/whole relations, causal chains, and others.

The basic technique by which we systematize open-ended interviews is by breaking down the running linear texts of an interview into various folk classifications. The principles of folk classifications are based on well-known structures (e.g., for taxonomies see Conklin 1962, Kay 1971). These provide a framework that allows the ethnographer to place unfamiliar data onto familiar structures. These classifications also allow the ethnographer to check the data for completeness. Data from casual, or Grand Tour queries, may be detailed in some respect while lacking detail in another. The structured method of checking interviews against folk classifications and thus generating new questions contributes to consistent levels of detail in the construction of both ethnographies and encyclopedias.

Stating it in still another way, the interview-analysis-interview cycle (which includes observation) provides the ethnographer with a relatively easy method for finding areas in which data are inadequate or incomplete. In follow-up interviews one can then *systematically* fill in information about the entire social system or the knowledge system one is studying using a step-by-step procedure.

9 WORDS AND NAMING UNITS

The importance of a word or naming unit can be judged only by the ethnographer and consultant together. Such judgment depends on the frequency of use and/or the explanations (assertions) concerning the importance of a concept provided by the consultant. More indirect methods include, for example, the identification of a certain worldview's central (focal) terms. Apparently all cultures have a central thematic focus of some kind. Some may have several. Among the Nuer it is cattle; among the Bedouins it is camels; among the Navajos it is health;

and among the Hopi it is fertility. The most straightforward indentification of foci involves charting the frequency of terms relating to the focal area. Other measures such as saliency, are more difficult to identify (see *hapax logomenon* in Section 8.1).

Through a cycle of interviews and analytic procedures, general cover terms become more detailed. This expansion process can be better understood by viewing analysis as a search for more general words or larger naming units. Naming units stand for sets of objects for which the cover term is a general label.

An actor has a name for most objects that he or she perceives in the environment. Labeling processes proceed at all times because humans usually do not produce a new name for each new object in the universe. New objects are first named by using old, already known labels in new combinations. The new names become labels for their classification; that is, the new is first perceived as something old with *new attributes*. "Horseless carriage," "firewater," and *chidí naat'a'ii'* or "flying automobile" (Navajo for airplane) exemplify this. When an object is named, the name provides a label for a set of similar objects. These sets may contain names for still other sets, and so on. It is these set domains or nested sets that are uncovered in interviews. Concentrating on such hierarchies of naming units gives us one of the most powerful analytical tools for the systematization of interviews.

10 TEMPORAL SEQUENCES

The temporal or sequential organization of words or larger naming units plays a similarly important analytical role. There are two aspects to temporal organization. The first is cases. These are anecdotes or stories, descriptions of unique events. It is often better to maintain the sequential integrity of these stories than to analyze them into underlying semantic structures (taxonomies, folk definitions, etc.). Often it may be appropriate to do both: to use a case as a case *and* to use parts of it to build the ethnographic dictionary.

The second use is often based on unique cases. This is the elicitation of plans. A plan contains a set of directions for performing an action in a customary manner. Perhaps the most notable plans are those which describe daily activities that tend to distinguish several different types of days (e.g., among the Navajo, three types: normal days, ceremonial days and traveling days; see Topper 1972). Plans imply decision making, be it the acceptance of an innovative agricultural technique or the determination of decision points in the flow of activities as human beings get on with their days.

Finally, statistical patterns can be found where data accumulates for analysis. Today we usually see either statistical applications or exclusively ethnographic ones. The two areas neatly complement each other, as we show in Volume 1 (Chapter 5) and Chapter 8 of this volume.

These are the goals of ethnoscience analysis: first, the reduction of ethnocentrism; second, the facilitation of translation (in negative terms, the reduction of semantic accent); and third, the reduction of complexity. The first two are lexicographic in spirit, although they try to break out of the linear confines of traditional, alphabetized lexicography. The third, reduction, is impossible to achieve systematically without the lexicographic base of the first two.

Semantic relations forming lexical/semantic fields are the nonlinear tools of the cognitive ethnographer. We have shown a way of unifying these structures into a coherent theory in Volume 1 (Chapter 2) and following chapters and sections in this volume. With these preliminaries, we are now ready to outline the specific parts of these chapters. No analysis, however simple or sophisticated, can proceed without well-organized data. We consider ethnographic data base management and efficient information retrieval a prerequisite for all subsequent analytical steps.

11 CHAPTER OUTLINE

Volume 2, Part I is divided into eight chapters. In the first we discuss the management of an ethnographic data base. We consider the establishment of an appropriate data retrieval system a vital part of ethnographic analysis. In the second chapter we present the structural methods of "classical" ethnoscience, primarily based on the relations M and T. The third chapter introduces methods that go beyond static structural analysis, primarily the relation Q—that is, verbal action plans. In the fourth chapter we discuss verbal action plans (scripts) and their dependence on decision making. We introduce decision tables, flowcharts, and decision trees. The fifth chapter elaborates and develops techniques of decision modeling. In the sixth chapter we extend our methods to semantic systems based on complex relations as yet rarely used in cognitive ethnographic analysis—for example, causal chains, themes, and values. The seventh chapter demonstrates the applicability of all our methods to the analysis of texts. Finally, the eighth chapter discusses the uses of *hapax logomenon* for data reduction, as well as various statistical techniques that can be applied to ethnographic analysis.

Part II addresses the activities of writing the ethnographic report after analysis is complete. The ninth chapter outlines the necessary steps for preparing to write the report. In the tenth chapter we deal with the problems specific to the actual writing of an ethnographic report.

Part III is an Epilogue. In it we discuss the need for minimum standards for the craft of ethnography. We close this volume with a list of recommended minimum standards covering all topics and techniques discussed in both volumes.

11.1 Data Base Management

Chapter 1 introduces the idea that the efficient organization of an ethnographic data base is part of analysis. This aspect of the ethnographic enterprise has often been neglected in the past, the assumption being that any ethnographer naturally knows how to handle a large body of textual data. Most ethnographers find their first ethnographic data base to be the largest body of textual data (by several orders of magnitude) they have dealt with in their careers. Without easy access to data, attempts at analysis either fail or are based on shallow, haphazard retrievals of information. The ethnographer often has no way of confidently ascertaining what is and is not contained in the data base. If interview transcriptions or journal entries are not easily retrievable the ethnographer may remember some data but have to rely on imperfect recall. Doing a front-to-end search of the entire file is usually out of the question, as leafing through thousands of pages can take days. An efficient data base management system is therefore a prerequisite to a quality ethnography.

11.2 Structural Analysis

The second chapter deals with analysis in a narrower sense. After an ethnographer collects and transcribes interviews and diligently keeps a journal, data (texts) accumulate at an alarming rate. A well-designed information retrieval system helps bolster the ethnographer's confidence. Simultaneously, analysis must begin immediately. In general we favor the elicitation and analysis of unconstrained texts. However, for anyone learning the craft of cognitive/ethnoscience ethnography, understanding and practice with structural analysis methods must precede the application of these techniques and their extension to texts.

In Chapter 2 we therefore concentrate on structural elicitation and its application for learning the use of simple cognitive structures. The tools for elicitation are here simple structural questions. Although it is helpful to keep a tape recorder running during structural elicitation (because often the beginnings of folk definitions emerge here), recording is not absolutely essential. Structural elicitation can often be translated directly into diagrammatical information (most usually tree graphs) that may prove the only record an ethnographer needs. A tremendous amount of systematic, culturally relevant information can be collected, for example, through an inventory of taxonomies alone (see Werner, Manning & Begishe 1983). At the same time, taxonomic information alone reveals only a small part of the ethnographic picture.

Simply put, in Chapter 2 we apply the theoretical foundations laid down in Volume 1, Chapter 2 (especially Section 2.3, the MT schema) to practical structural elicitation. After mastering these skills an ethnographer should be able to move to analysis beyond the simple structures of "classical" ethnoscience.

11.3 Beyond Structural Analysis

In this chapter we concentrate on the elicitation and analysis of texts into verbal action plans. We introduce the relation of serial order Q into ethnographic analysis, and demonstrate the hierarchic nature of plans. Furthermore, plans are interdependent with the part/whole relation, and occasionally with the taxonomic relation.

Usually plans are constructed in "event time," a relative time reckoning in which when an event ends, it is followed by another, regardless of the time required to execute each. That is, the length of the activity arrows in our diagrams is not interpreted. However, we can easily construct plans in absolute or chronological (clock) time if the length of the arrows is made proportional to the duration of the activities they represent (see Volume 1, Figure 3.10).

11.4 Plans and Decisions

The fact that many plans compete for our attention requires that we decide between them. We use decision tables as our eliciting tool. Flow charts and decision trees are derived from decision tables. Decision analysis parallels textual analysis: Both are translations of unrestricted interviews (texts) into formal structures (see Chapter 7). At the same time, decision tables force both ethnographer and consultant to consider every logically possible combination of conditions. Surprisingly, combinations often turn up that neither the ethnographer nor the consultant anticipated.

11.5 Decision Making and Decision Models

Decision modeling is the most recent growth area in cognitive ethnography. It is new and full of rough edges. In the hands of some ethnographers, it has become a powerful predictive tool (e.g., C. Gladwin 1976). Other ethnographers have complained that decision methods are too microscopic and tedious.

Unfortunately, detail and bulk go together. Such are the characteristics of cultural knowledge. The ethnographic situation is analogous to aerial photography: The only safe route to generalization (large-scale map analogy) begins at the microscopic and culminates in the general. In other words, there is no short-cut to generalizations. However, eliciting and analyzing how human beings make decisions in a given cultural setting is a powerful method for understanding their culture.

11.6 Other Semantic Systems

The use of complex relations (see Chapter 6) is not generally accepted in cognitive ethnoscience ethnographies. Their applications have been, almost without exception, experimental and exploratory. Given the importance of causal structure, themes, and values, this is regrettable. It is hoped that more work will soon follow.

Among these structures only the causal (complex) relation seems capable of producing multilevel tree structures. However, some complex relations may represent pervasive cultural themes or cultural schemata.

Values are taxonomically themes. Given the fact that evaluation is probably the most fundamental capacity of all living organisms, the neglect of values in cognitive ethnoscience ethnographies represent a serious deficiency. Until recently themes and values were not amenable to formal analysis. With the discovery of complex relations they are firmly established in the pantheon of lexical/semantic relations—easily derivable from atomic M (modification) and T (taxonomy) (see Section 6.4).

11.7 Analysis of Texts

We favor the analysis of texts. In practice the choice is rarely clear-cut. The efficient ethnographer alternates text elicitation, for the identification of important clues about the culture of the natives, with structural questioning. This helps fill gaps in cultural domains identified by the clues. In ethnographic analysis elicitation of relatively unrestrained texts and relatively constrained structural questioning should alternate.

Letting the consultant(s) talk best ensures that new information keeps accumulating. Structural elicitation makes certain that each area of significance to the project is filled in as completely as possible. Texts alone are rarely complete; they build on previous or assumed knowledge. Thus ancillary structural questions help make an ethnography's coverage exhaustive.

Included in text analysis is the application of the cognitive structures to text first discussed in Volume 1 (Chapter 2). These structures are optimally applied to both native texts and the ethnographer's journal entries. This makes for better comparability and leads to the easy identification of semantic accent and the reduction of discrepancies (see Volume 1, Chapter 1). This is the domain of folk taxonomies, folk part/whole classifications, and other structures that form large lexical/semantic fields. In Case 7.1, plans introduce a new dimension of temporal sequencing also present in the structure of texts. Decision modeling is currently the most sophisticated part of text analysis. The section dealing with this topic closes Chapter 7.

11.8 Ethnoscience and Statistics

The very size of cognitive ethnoscience ethnographic data bases makes them amenable to reduction by various statistical techniques. Ethnographers have started to expand in this area, but more development work is needed.

One approach is to count the frequency of occurrence of every word in a text. The next step is to subtract all words that occur with high frequency in all texts *and* those that occur exactly once. The latter includes, according to a phenomenon called *hapax logomenon*, the vast majority of words in every text. The remaining words provide an excellent indicator of a text's content. This set becomes the focus of more detailed lexical/semantic analysis.

Another approach involves counting recurrent patterns—for example, themes and their negation (see Section 6.3.6) and applying various statistical methods to these counts. Another method involves applying statistical techniques to specially designed structural experiments. The application of either of these approaches remains rare especially in combination with nonstatistical ethnographic work. Most frequently they have been applied independently in cross-cultural or other cultural studies of cognition. A careful reading of many of these reports convinces us that many experimental studies in cognitive ethnography require follow-up ethnographies and many ethographies call for experimental statistical follow-up. In Chapter 8 we explore the complementarity of the structural/ethnographic and statistical/cognitive approaches. We see the greatest potential for the growth of ethnoscience/cognitive ethnography in the interface between these two techniques. In this section we also discuss entailment analysis that bridges statistics and structural elicitation.

11.9 Planning the Ethnographic Report

This chapter is the beginning of Part II: Post-Fieldwork. Whether the ethnographer begins to write while still in the field (a procedure we highly recommend) or after returning from the field, careful preparation improves the final ethnographic report. There are good reasons why writing an ethnography takes so long: the transition from raw ethnographic data to polished prose is difficult. On the other hand, we suspect that ethnographic report writing is further hampered by poor data management techniques as well.

Various methods exist that can make the ethnographer's data management even more efficient. In addition, we deal with several methods for overcoming writer's block. We explain the "scratch list" method. Several outline processors for microcomputers and word processors utilize the same techniques.

The final sections of this chapter deal with "checklists" of topics that every ethnography should include in addition to its central problem orientation.

11.10 Writing the Ethnographic Report

Writing the ethnography is the final task of the ethnographer. Most ethnographies are analytical: They take the culture apart and examine its pieces. Presenting a synthetic picture of a culture is much harder—ethnographic fiction can competently describe the functioning of a cultural system. Computer simulations of the cultural knowledge system framed as a cultural expert system may provide another approach. Both approaches may be viewed as examples of analysis through synthesis.

Other styles are building to a climax toward the end of the paper. Carl F. Voegelin, as editor of the *International Journal of American Linguistics,* pioneered a style that may be well suited to ethnographic presentations: He always combined introduction and conclusion in the first (introductory) section of a paper. By reading this "super-introduction" a reader can more easily judge the usefulness of the rest of the paper's content.

All writing should be for a specified audience. We recommend Spradley's method of imagining writing a letter to a typical representative of the target audience.

All writing should go through multiple drafts. This process demands multiple passes through the text, each pass serving a different function for improving the text. This task can now be accomplished easily with a word processing program on a microcomputer.

A topic very dear to our hearts is proper referencing of the contribution of consultants and informants. We feel strongly that native experts deserve the same professional courtesy in citations (even if we must code their names) as do our professional colleagues.

11.11 Minimum Standards for Ethnography

The art of ethnography can be honed through practice, as can all artistic endeavors. Minimum standards for ethnography address the craft of ethnography. In the two volumes of *Systematic Fieldwork* we have listed many principles that make a difference in the control of ethnocentric bias, of semantic accent, and that facilitate reduction of the complexity of data to practical proportions.

We list a set of 28 standards that should lead to better-crafted ethnographies. We understand that no one could ever apply all 28 standards and actually get an ethnography done. That is not the point. The 28 standards refer to an ideal ethnography. All "real-world" ethnographies are compromises. Through standards we can judge the degree of approximation to the ideal. This applies equally to our own ethnographies and to the evaluation of the ethnographies of our colleagues. Understanding how and why an ethnography departs from the ideal we can utilize them better for the invention of theory or social intervention.

11.12 Summary and Conclusions

Part I represents the culmination of *Systematic Fieldwork.* The chapters preceding it are building up to ethnographic analysis. The two chapters ("Planning the Ethnographic Report" and "Writing the Ethnographic Report") following the eight chapters of analysis, in turn, are utilizing analysis for better communicating ethnographic information to the readers.

In this volume we explore the major features of an ethnography: (1) ethnographic description rich enough to facilitate translation; (2) ethnography as translation—that is, the reduction of ethnocentrism; (3) ethnography as an expert system leading to answers about the culture but including inferred answers that have never been given before; and (4) ethnography is always a sketch. Our descriptions are necessarily reductions of the complexities of reality.

Our approach, though lexicographic/encyclopedic, constructs lexical/semantic fields of linked propositions. We have seen that ethnographic translation is rich in translator's notes. A bilingual encyclopedia provides the ultimate set of translator's notes, including topics not yet anticipated. An ethnography's presentation does not necessarily follow a dictionary or encyclopedic format, but lexicography and encyclopediography are never fully excluded. Finally, ethnography is an exploration of meanings in a language that natives use to interpret their lives.

The most important aspect of any ethnography is the effective management of data, by hand or by computer. In this volume we discuss structural methods, or roughly "classical ethnoscience." Then we go beyond tradition with "Plans and Decision Models." The conversion of texts to lexical/semantic structures and the uses of statistical methods to reduce the lexical/semantic fields to less rich structures closes Part I. In the process we make ethnographic analysis more systematic while simultaneously vulnerable and therefore more explicit and reliable. Finally, preparation and writing the ethnographic report shows how our analyses lead to our final product, an ethnographic report.

In the Epilogue we review the results of both volumes and recommend minimum standards that assure a well-crafted ethnography.

NOTES

1. The term "expert system" comes from the field of artificial intelligence. Subsumed under it are computerized knowledge systems that help in geological exploration, medical diagnosis, the assembly or repair of complex machinery, and so on.

2. In this view every sentence consists of a topic and a comment. This terminology is more general than the terms "subject" and "predicate."

Part I

Data Base Management and Analysis

Chapter 1

Data Base Management

Before we begin with ethnographic analysis it is imperative that our data be organized for quick and appropriate retrieval. Planning for data base management should, of course, begin long before the commencement of the ethnography. As we emphasized in Volume 1, Chapter 5, at the time of proposal writing the ethnographer should have a good notion of how to manage the data. It is possible to get around to organizing one's data *after fieldwork,* but the ethnographer then fails to manage data while *in the field*. He or she will therefore never know for sure what is contained in the ethnographic record and what needs further exploration. This invariably results in an incomplete record.

1.0 INTRODUCTION

The method we advocate in the following pages is based on the experience of many ethnographers. Perhaps the original stimulus for taking ethnographic data base management more seriously than in the past came as a result of a paper by Chambers and Bolton (1980) presented at the Meetings of the American Anthropological Association in Cincinnati. Briefly, the paper exposed the neglect of data base management techniques by ethnographers and by ethnographic training. No minimum standards as yet exist for adequate ethnographic documentation. Estimates of how many pages of field notes an ethnographer brings back from the field range, according to Chambers and Bolton's report, from a few hundred to thousands.

The most shocking part about this survey of ethnographers recently returned from the field is that no one seems to differentiate between "field notes"—or what we call "the journal" in this book—and transcriptions of verbatim statements by natives. The existence of transcriptions is never mentioned, either as part of field notes or as independent documents (Chambers and Bolton 1980). This section therefore proposes a minimal retrieval and information management system for ethnographic fieldwork. The first impetus came from various experiments

Werner has undertaken with information retrieval, especially with the use of edge-punch cards. These beginnings were expanded by Paul Bugos into what we refer to as the Bugos/Werner System of Ethnographic Data Base Management. This system was later augmented by Werner to include computer-asssisted management of ethnographic data.

We proceed from basics to more complex computer-managed data bases. At first we discuss the nature of ethnographic data, clues and cues for the retrieval of desired portions. We finish with a discussion of various techniques for indexing, including the use of computerized indexes. In this endeavor we first cover simple techniques that anyone can implement "by hand." Later we show how efficiency can be increased by using card files, especially edge-punched cards, and ultimately microcomputers.

The methods we discuss are universal. They apply to any general ethnographic work. Ethnographers working on specifically oriented research can and no doubt will include their own elaborations.

1.1 NATURE OF THE ETHNOGRAPHIC RECORD

The ethnographic record consists of four types of data:

(1) The ethnographer's journal. These are texts created by the ethnographer based on his or her perceptions. We have called these TEXT (1) (see Volume 1, Figure 1.7).
(2) The ethnographer's verbatim transcriptions of native texts. These we have called TEXT (2) (see Volume 1, Figure 1.7).
(3) Documents acquired from official sources or natives, such as historical accounts, books, archival materials, and maps.
(4) Materials classified as falling between TEXT (1) and TEXT (2). These contain the results of the ethnographer's analysis and include frequency counts and other statistics compiled by the ethnographer, maps produced by the ethnographer, but perhaps most important, the results of the ethnographer's analysis of both TEXT (1) and especially TEXT (2). This includes folk taxonomies, part/whole trees, other data presented in tree graph form (see Sections 2.1 and 2.4), componential analyses (see Section 2.5), verbal action plans (Section 3.1), decision tables and flow charts (Section 4.1), the analysis of themes (see Section 6.2), and selections of TEXT (1) and especially TEXT (2), which we call cases (see Volume 1, Section 3.2 and Volume 2, Chapter 7).

Almost anything an ethnographer may collect falls into one of these categories. The one possible exception is an actual specimen of, for example, plants, foods, and artifacts of various kinds. However, all of these generic specimens include paperwork—for example, cataloging associated with them that falls into one or more of the four categories of ethnographic data. The most useful distinction may be between (1) specimens that have to be stored physically in some sort of warehouse, refrigerator (e.g., foods, blood samples, etc.), or some other storage place, and (2) general paperwork associated with specific items.

Our major emphasis in this section is on managing paper and information that is most often stored on paper. The management of specimens is sufficiently specialized to fall outside our survey. Nevertheless, the ethnographer whose project includes the collection of specimens must plan for the management of these artifacts. It is his or her responsibility to ensure that specimens are adequately catalogued, documented, and warehoused. This cataloging falls into our type 4 above. Other textual material associated with specimens consist of comments by natives, clearly type 2, and comments, for example observations, made by the ethnographer, clearly type 1. If there are official documents associated with the specimen, these are type 3.

Management of the bulk of these four types of documents is the key problem. Following our advocacy of the separation of TEXT (1) from TEXT (2), some ethnographers may keep these two types of texts in physically separate files. One can similarly imagine a storage and retrieval system in which all four types of documents are kept in separate files.

Regardless of whether one decides to create four separate files or to keep all four types of documents in one master file, the problem confronting every ethnographer is that materials in each of these categories tend to accumulate at rapid rates. This is especially true of transcriptions (TEXT (2)) and almost as true for journal entries (TEXT (1)). These transcriptions form the major bottlenecks of ethnographic fieldwork. If every 45-minute interview results in 20 to 30 double-spaced pages of transcription, fewer than 100 interviews quickly generate thousands of pages.

Therefore, the key problem is to devise a storage and retrieval system that allows the ethnographer easy access to specific types of data as fast as possible. Nothing is more frustrating during (or before) the writing of the final ethnographic report than to know that the relevant datum to a section of the ethnography is there, somewhere, but nobody knows where. In a poorly designed or an unplanned storage and retrieval system, there is often no way to find elusive data short of searching through every slip of paper in the database.

There is no ethnographic project that cannot be enhanced by an efficient storage and retrieval system. There are, however, issues beyond efficiency which argue for the best possible system for data manipulation. If ethnographic methods are to be used for real-life applications—and we think they should—then speeding up the ethnographic process, especially the *lag between the collection of ethnographic data and the writing of the final report,* is imperative. In other words, with efficient data base management it should not take years to write an ethnographic report—for example, a dissertation. Furthermore, the single most important contribution of the microcomputer revolution is the speeding up of storage, retrieval, and analysis of qualitative ethnographic work. The application of computers to quantitative data analysis holds no surprises. In qualitative analysis (ethnography), however, the changes will prove truly revolutionary.

1.2 CLUES AND CUES TO THE RECORD

In order to find anything in a stack of papers, an ethnographer needs *clues* about where to find certain types of information. We define clues as bits of information naturally included in the texts. Most commonly, these are *key words or phrases* embedded in the text. These clues may be highlighted, for example, with a colored marking pen.

We define *cues* as bits of information that are *inserted by the ethnographer into the text*. These cues relate directly to the ethnographer's interest, goals, classifications, ideas about what may be significant about a portion of text, that cannot be gleaned from the key words (clues) embedded in the text itself.

Typically, inserted cues are "titles"—for example, of cases. An anecdote or story embedded in a larger text may not be marked in any special way by the consultant who created the text. It is then up to the ethnographer either to elicit a likely title from a consultant or to invent one. One common source of "titles" (i.e., cues) may be the ethnographer's native research collaborator.

The advantages of a title are obvious. It acts as a shorthand summary for the entire story. It functions as a handy label by which to retrieve it later. Physically, titles and other text annotations are brief "textlets" inserted by the ethnographer as additional clues for retrieval. It is important to consider that these insertions be clearly distinguishable from the original text. A title should also be explicit and descriptive.

Obviously, both embedded key words and inserted titles or short comments that help retrieval can and must be specified (highlighted or inserted) in all texts that an ethnographer collects, no matter what their origin. Thus key words are as useful in the journal as they are in transcriptions. Inserted titles or other cues (words or phrases) are equally appropriate in documents, statistical summaries, tree graphs, and other data falling between journals and transcriptions. The main reason we advocate titles for decision tables, flowcharts (see Sections 4.1 and 4.2) and verbal action plans (see Section 3.1) is that these function as retrieval clues. Similarly, in folk taxonomies and part/whole classifications (see Sections 2.1 and 2.4, respectively) the topmost label of any tree graph is the most convenient label for retrieval.

The most important characteristic of these labels, whether inherent in the text as key words or inserted as titles, is that the labels should be short enough to fit the limitations of a retrieval schema and long enough to convey sufficient information to make efficient and unambiguous searches possible.

1.3 BUGOS/WERNER SYSTEM

As we have mentioned, the first way of dealing with the accumulating records of an ethnography involves storing the four types of documents in four separate files. The second storage and retrieval method is to classify every page of text, no matter what its source, on the basis of key words or inserted titles. Then copies of each page are made corresponding to the number of key words (clues) and inserted cues that appear on that page. Each copy is then placed in its appropriate subject file. In other words, all texts are stored in files with as many subject headings as there are index (clue and cue) categories.

Using the first method, an ethnographer must decide to which of four categories an ethnographic document belongs. At times this may be difficult when texts cross categories. For example, a taxonomic tree structure provided by a native is on the one hand type 2 (or TEXT (2)), but as a result of analysis it becomes intermediate, possibly type 4 (see Section 1.1).

The second method is identical to that used by the Human Relations Area File (HRAF). This indexing is done with finished ethnographies. Each page of any ethnography that is being incorporated into the HRAF files is coded. That is, as many code numbers for categories are written on the margins of each page as apply to that page. This can result in marking ten or more categories per page. If so, ten or more copies are made of that page.

This method of storage and retrieval is appropriate for finished ethnographies rarely exceeding 500 total printed pages. Applied to field data, the method easily leads to the use of reams of paper because of the thousands of pages of field notes. The bulk of raw ethnographic texts (data) already presents a problem; multiple duplication makes the problem worse.

In the Bugos/Werner system, all four types of documents are kept in a master file in chronological order of acquisition, or completion. The documents collected on a certain day, the analyses undertaken, and the transcriptions completed on that day all go into the same master file. At day's end the master file is closed and recorded in the ethnographer's journal entry. In this file only identifying data (cues) clearly separate one document from the next: (The inserted materials include, for example, date(s), location(s), name(s) of consultants and other identifying data).

What we here call "files" may be more easily conceived as "books." Three-ring binders, each holding perhaps 200 pages, are an example. The indexing of clues and cues (see Section 1.4) would then refer to volume number and page number.

This way of handling all of a project's accruing documents is most appropriate in the case of the lone ethnographer. If the ethnography involves a team, the personal journals of each ethnographer must be kept separate because of their confidential nature. The lone ethnographer therefore has the advantage that his or her own personal history is readily available for analysis.

One way to deal with the problem of a multiperson project is to let people analyze data they have collected. They can then use their journals, when necessary, to see how their personal histories may have influenced the collection of ethnographic data. At other times, especially if one person coordinates the final write-up, such restriction may prove impractical. Some form of debriefing (see Volume 1, Section 13.5.3) may be the only way the project writer can determine personal variables associated with the data collection.

In sum, the Bugos/Werner method keeps all four types of records in one continuous file. The entries are filed daily in chronological order as they become available (e.g., when transcriptions or journal entries are completed). This file may be subdivided into volumes and accessed through an index. As we shall see, such a volume of texts may be a *physical file,* (e.g., a three-ring binder) or a *virtual file* stored (for example, on magnetic diskettes or a hard disk).

1.4 INDEXING SYSTEMS

The heart of every information retrieval system is the indexing. In this section we discuss indexing systems that can be created (1) for use "by hand," (2) for use in indexing systems which utilize specialized mechanical aids, and (3) for use with computerized indexing and retrieval systems.

1.4.0 Introduction

Indexing is the extraction of key words (clues) from a given text and the insertion of titles (cues) into the text. Indexing implies also that a list of indexing labels (an alphabetized list of key words and titles—clues and cues) is kept to remind the ethnographer about the categories that his or her system contains. Without such a master list it is impossible to determine the contents of the data base. Obviously, any topic that does not appear in the index is not accessible to retrieval. The only exception to this may be computerized systems in which searches of texts can be performed on key words that may be in the text but that did not make it into the list of indexed items.

1.4.1 Running List

The running list method of indexing was already described in connection with the Human Relation Area File system. The principle here is similar: The first step in analysis is for the ethnographer to decide, upon reading a page of the Bugos/Werner file, what topics are covered on that page.

There is one major difference between the indexing of these topics and the Human Relations Area File system. In the HRAF method the indexing categories are predetermined numerical indexes from Murdoch's *Outline of Cultural Materials* (1960). These headings of ethnographic content may or may not be useful in practice. A numerical index is also a handicap because its use requires at least two "look-ups" (searches)—first to find the numerical value of an index category (e.g., 221 is "Activities of a typical day," 392 is "Kinship Terminology," and 555 is "Mortuary Customs") and then to search for pages in the volumes of field data that contain that index category. To make an ethnographer's indexing system maximally flexible, every ethnographer should design his or her own indexing scheme. It is, if necessary, possible later to translate the key words and titles of the ethnographic indexing scheme into HRAF categories. Because HRAF uses "finished" ethnographies, this translation may be most appropriate *after* completing the final ethnographic report.

To index ethnographic data, each page or group of pages (if the topics overlap pages) is marked in at least two passes. The ethnographer then (1) highlights all key words and phrases, and (2) inserts new titles, key words, or phrases that he or she deems necessary to the project goals. There is no need to repeat key words embedded in text (i.e., by writing them in the margin) provided they are clearly marked with a highlighting pen. Care should be taken that the highlighting pen does not prevent the reproduction of a page. Light-colored highlighting pens are usually safe. As each key word is highlighted it should be entered into the inventory of key words. It is best to keep this inventory in a separate volume of the regular files, perhaps the very first volume.

The *inserted* key words or titles should be written in the margins. A standardized place could be the left margin, near the top of page to which it refers. It is wise to highlight these in a different color. When we use cases (see Volume 1, Sections 3.2 and 7.1) we use the same color to draw a box around that part of the text which represents the entire case. This makes it easy later, upon retrieval, to know where the beginning of the case is and, equally important, where it ends.

If taxonomies and other lexical/semantic structures are used, they should be highlighted in still a third color. In most tree structures the highest term in the graph adequately names the entire structure. It need not be inserted as long as it is clearly highlighted. In other structures the "title" may not be clear and may have to be provided.

The question of what to include usually depends on the goals of the project. We have found, however, one general rule useful: If in doubt about whether a key word in the text, or a title created by the ethnographer applies to a topic, it is safer to include it. In short, we prefer to use the principle "if in doubt, include it." It is always better to have too many index entries than not enough. Any portion of the text left unindexed is not retrievable except by going through all the data consecutively. If the data base is computerized, it is possible to search for new key words, but these must be *in the text*. Such a search may still prove tedious. If the ethnographer was able to afford a hard disk (see below) to store all field data, a search without changing disks might be possible. If the ethnographer's files are on, for example, 100 floppy disks, each disk must be searched individually.

We illustrate the principles of indexing with the example shown in Figure 1.1.

Here *General Assignment Reporter* provides the key word to be highlighted for indexing. CASE 13 also refers to General Assignment Reporter and bears the same inserted title. The title of the case and the mark ending it were inserted in the text by the ethnographer. The highlighting, here in boldface, can be improved with color coding. The key words "General Assignment Reporter" could be in one color, the CASE title in another. Note that the number of the interview (first, sec-

UM: I was a **general assignment reporter**. What I had to do was anything anybody else didn't have to do.

OW: ... tell me about it ...

UM: I got a variety of assignments from my editors, they would tell me...

CASE 13.
GENERAL ASSIGNMENT REPORTER

UM: I would walk in during the day about 2:30 or 3:00 [p.m.] and they'd say "OK, we have a school board meeting which the education reporter cannot cover," [or] we have this strange organization that we hear about and we'd like to check it out," ...let's see ...the county government reporter cannot cover the county board meeting today. Go cover it!

END OF CASE 13

219

Figure 1.1 Sample Page of an Interview

ond, . . . with same consultant) and year do not appear on the page. Presumably this information is given at the beginning of the interview. Repeating this information on each page may be a good practice (compare to Volume 1, Case 12.3).

1.4.2 Card File Index

The master file of the inventory of index items can be kept and organized in an alphabetically arranged card file, as illustrated in Figure 1.2.

Another method of keeping one's index file involves using an address book. A standard address book with fixed pages has the disadvantage that entries are not in exact alphabetical order under each first letter. Since index words (key words and titles) are inserted as they appear in the texts, after many entries under a first letter individual items are difficult to find. If the project is relatively small and there are not too many entries under each initial letter, this system may perform adequately.

A better method is an address book with removable pages. The illustration in Figure 1.3 shows one style of such an address book. The major advantage of these

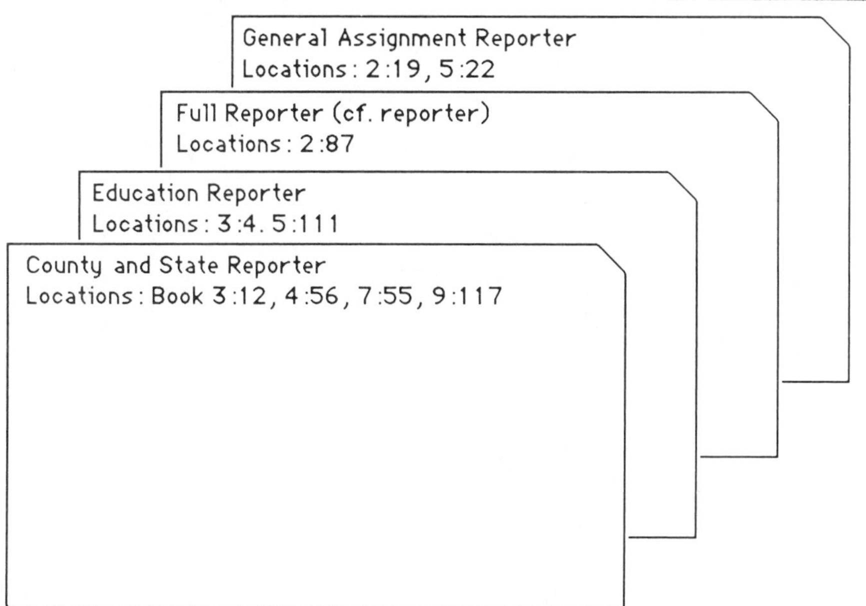

NOTE: Each entry (key word or title) in the index is on a separate card. Each card carries information that tells the ethnographer where to find text on that topic. The reference is by book volume and by page number within each volume. Indexing categories or several consultants may be listed on each card. A more complex referencing system may include additional identifying data (see Volume 1, Chapter 12, Note 3.

Figure 1.2 Alphabetical Card Index File

books is that the index words can be rearranged as they accumulate and kept in exact alphabetical order beyond their first letter. Their disadvantage is that the volume of address slips fills up even a relatively large address book very quickly.

The loose-leaf address book has the advantage that the entries are kept in order. Card files have the disadvantage that after use each card must be inserted in its proper alphabetical place or the card file quickly becomes useless.

The greatest advantage of a card file is that cards can be removed and, for example, arranged by key words in the order in which the ethnographer wants to write about them. Obviously a fixed or loose-leaf address book does not offer this advantage.

1.4.3 Keysort Edge-Punch Cards

Keysort card data retrieval techniques have the advantage that one deck of cards can be accessed through different classifications. Because the relevant information is all encoded physically at the edge of the card, refiling is unnecessary. The cards may remain in random order. How this is accomplished will become clear as we explain the principles of edge-card encoding.

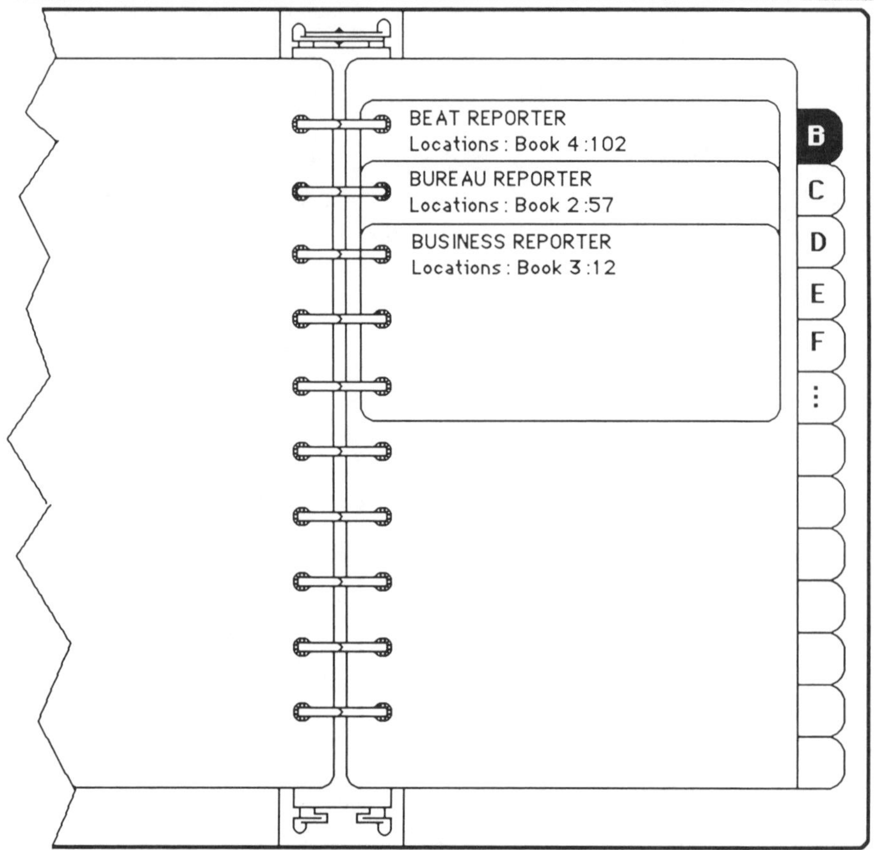

NOTE: The entries under B are in alphabetical and not in chronological order. (Chronological order is implied by the book number: The higher the number, the later the material in it.)

Figure 1.3 Loose-Leaf Address Book for Indexing

Two fundamental types of systems exist for encoding edge-punch cards. The first is a "direct" code, the second is a digital code.

Direct Edge-Punch Encoding

The principle of "direct" encoding is simple. A keysort card consists of holes along the edge of each card. Each hole is numbered and is assigned a special code. If the code is relevant to the content of a card, it is connected with the outside of the card (it is punched out). Thus if a needle is inserted in the hole assigned to a particular topic, all the cards that have been punched drop out. All the irrelevant cards remain on the sorting needle. An example is illustrated in Figure 1.4.

In Figure 1.4, holes 3, 7, and 8 have been punched, implying that the information contained on the card is relevant to Field Relations (3), to Writing (7), and the Glossary (8) of the ethnographic report. This card will drop out of the stack if a sorting needle is inserted in holes 3, 7, and 8. This card could be, for example, a

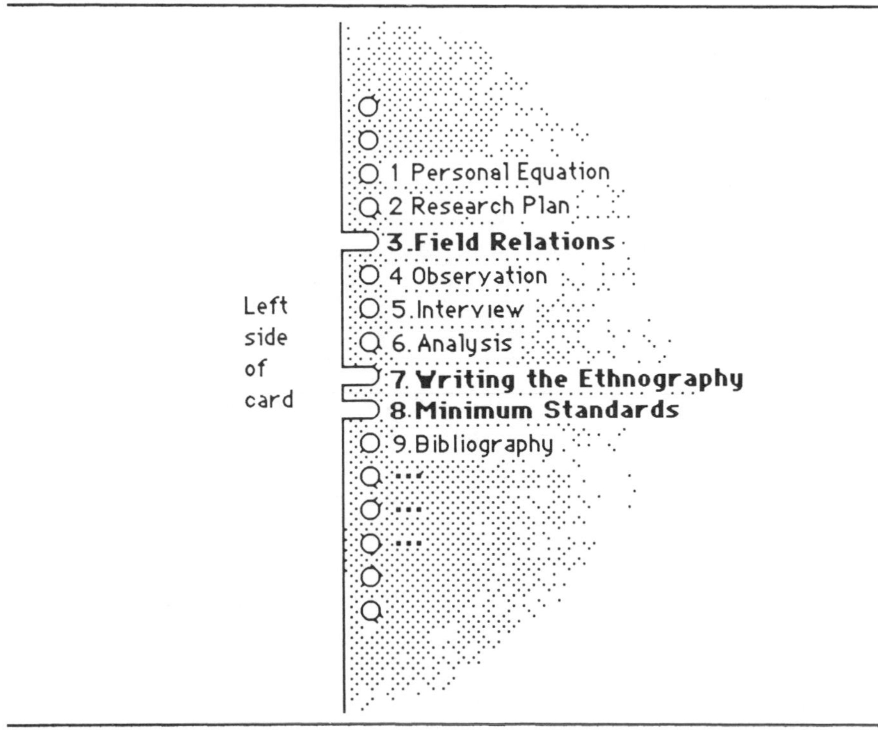

Figure 1.4 Direct Code on Edge-Punch Cards

discussion by Devereaux (1967) about fieldwork and "countertransference"; that is, if the natives decide to assign role X to the anthropologist, he or she may start acting like an X. Observing this fact is important to field relations and should be mentioned in the ethnographic report. The card is also encoded (punched) at 8 because the term "countertransference" needs to be included in the glossary. The card usually contains only information. The assignment of a code is usually kept on a code card. Only the numbering of the holes on the card identifies the code with a particular hole.

The chief advantage of the direct code is that multiple encodings of as many topics as there are holes on the card are possible. Usually the holes run along all four edges of a card. With four to five holes per inch on a 5 × 8 card, the ethnographer can encode 160 to 200 topics, usually adequate coverage except for very large ethnographies.

There are two ways of using keysort cards. Rather than keeping the textual material on sheets of paper, it is typed or written directly onto a card. The edge-punch cards vary in size from 3¹/₄ × 7¹/₂ (82 × 190 mm) to 8 × 10¹/₂ (203 × 267 mm; these can be obtained from McBee Systems, Athens OH 45701). Another supplier (Indecks, Arlington VT 05250) sells only smaller cards (4 × 6, or 92 ×

152 mm to 5 × 8, or 127 × 203 mm). Unfortunately, the cards from McBee Systems are quite expensive.

The second method is to use edge-punch cards for indexing. We discuss each application in turn.

Edge-Punch Cards as Data Cards

Our procedure for this use of edge punch cards is as follows:

First, (leaving enough room on each card for the numerical codes), each card contains ethnographic data. We read through the cards and highlight key words or assign titles to the content of each card. Each new topic receives the next number in sequential order, or in the order in which the topics appear on the cards as we read through them.

Second, in a designated place on the card, each of the codes relevant to that card is entered (in Figure 1.4 these would be the numbers 3, 7, and 8).

Third, after the first pass through all cards, we inspect the categories. If there are fewer categories than holes, there is no problem. If there are more categories than edge holes, we reinspect the list of topics for items that are closely related and could be combined. We also look for items that are exclusive of each other—that is, when either one or the other category occurs but never both. In both cases we reassign numbers until the topics and the number of edge holes coincide. It is best to keep the number of topics smaller than the number of edge holes, just in case further reading of the data (while writing) necessitates more topics.

Fourth, we inspect the cards and convert all old numbers into the new number assignments.

Fifth, we make up an encoding card. The area of this card is covered with the code numbers and the category names assigned to them. Figure 1.5 shows example of an encoding card.

Sixth, with a slightly trimmed eraser at the end of a pencil (to approximate the wedge shape of the punch) and a stamp pad, we mark all categories that are relevant to each card. We have found that it is easier and much faster to punch if one does not have to think about the placement of the holes. The cards stamped with the trimmed eraser can be punched rapidly.

Finally, all marked (stamped) holes are punched.

In many cases, we are now ready to write the final report with amazing speed, always calling only those cards (with the needle sort) that are relevant to the topic at hand. These cards are then arranged in order for writing—for example, on the basis of an outline.

The speed one gains in writing justifies the added time spent encoding and reencoding. In addition, by handling the data several times, the ethnographer becomes familiar with all details. Extra familiarity with the materials also expedites writing.

Edge-Punch Cards for Indexing

If the cards are used only for indexing, a smaller, cheaper card can be used because only *locations* in the master file (volumes and page numbers) appear on

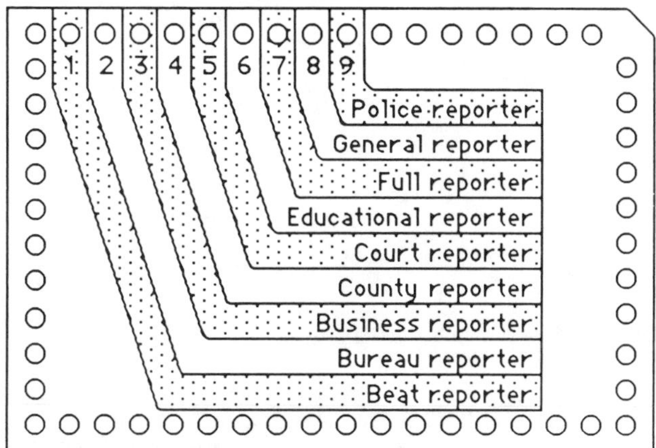

NOTE: Read entries below numbers from top down. The encoding card is usually kept at the front of the deck. It is the key to the assignment of indexing categories to each hole. It is a good idea to mark the encoding card with a special set of punches, just in case the card gets mixed in with the rest of the cards in the deck.

Figure 1.5 Example of an Encoding Card

each card and each card (or set of cards) is dedicated to *one topic*. Every indexing topic—that is, a key word or inserted title—is assigned to a numbered hole. The holes are punched just as in the previous method except that there is now just one punch per card.

To search for a topic the sorting needle is inserted in the appropriate hole. Now only one, or a few cards at most, drops out. The only information contained on these cards is locations where text dealing with the desired topic may be found. These usually give the location by volume and page number. There is no reason why more information (consultant's initials, year of interview, etc.) could not be included as well.

When using edge-punch cards for indexing, digital codes may be used because only one (or just a few) index categories is used on each card.

Digital Edge-Punch Encoding

The principle of this encoding is to use the edge punch as a binary number code. Considering that most people cannot easily remember the decimal conversions of long binary numbers, a mnemonic system is used to remember the binary code more easily. This mnemonic is the assignment of either numbers or letters to holes. For decimal numbering, one needs four holes ($2^4 = 16 > 10$). Several holes, usually the binary 1111, remain unassigned; that is, all numbers from 1 to 10 are encoded by two holes (punches or sortings) or less. For an alphabetic code of 26 characters, five holes ($2^5 = 32 > 26$) are needed. In each case the edge of a card looks like the illustrations shown in Figures 1.6 and 1.7.

In the decimal encoding, numbers are assigned in the order shown in Figure 1.8.

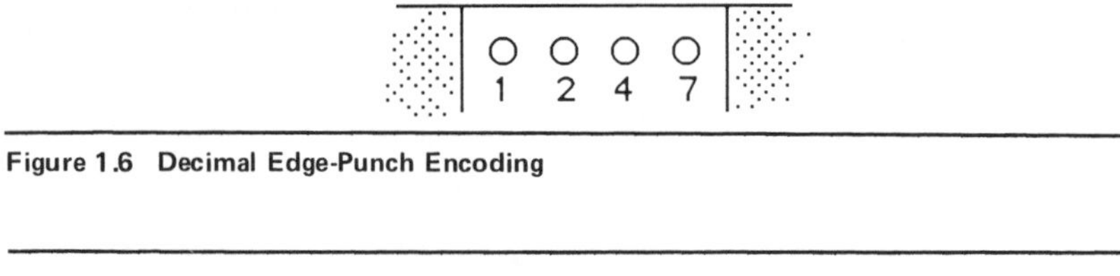

Figure 1.6 Decimal Edge-Punch Encoding

Figure 1.7 Alphabetic Edge-Punch Encoding

Note that the binary numbers are not assigned consistently in the usual manner of powers of two. This is done to reduce the number of necessary sortings to two; that is, a maximum of two insertions of the needle will give the user any number between 1 and 10.

The alphabetic code is assigned analogously. Again, the strict order of binary numbers is not followed in the interest of sorting efficiency. With the exception of Z, any letter of the alphabet can be sorted out with three insertions of the needle (see Figure 1.9).

An example of the use of the decimal code, for example, on bibliography cards is the year of publication (last two digits marked by eight holes). An example of the use of the alphabetic code is the first two letters of an author's or consultant's name (using a total of 10 holes). Sequential sorting of holes 1 (B) through 5 (O), first for the second letter then for the first letter, will arrange all cards in alphabetical order by first and second letter. If there are not too many cards, mistakes in alphabetization beyond the first two letters can easily be corrected manually.

For indexing a possible use of the alphabetic code is to represent a stack of cards by first and second letter. If there are not too many cards, mistakes in alphabetization beyond the first two letters can easily be corrected manually (Figure 1.10).

This method may be used if the index is very large, exceeding the number of holes on the card. The alphabetic code, using five holes, presorts the deck. For each letter of the alphabet all the holes of a card minus five are available for direct coding. However, one code card must be designed *for the direct code of each letter of the alphabet*. This means 26 code cards. Obviously, this method is practical only for a large project with hundreds or thousands of index topics.

Generally, by combining the three methods of encoding very sophisticated coding schemes can be developed. We present an additional example of a specially designed and printed card in Figures 1.10, 1.11, and 1.12. The basic stock is IBM punch cards specially punched with a row of holes around the edge.

We hope that the card illustrated in these figures demonstrates convincingly that many interesting and useful coding schemes can be designed with the help of

0 = no punch	0000
1 = 'one' punch	1000
2 = 'two' punch	0100
3 = 'one' and 'two' punch	1100
4 = 'four' punch	0010
5 = 'one' and 'four' punch	1010
6 = 'two' and 'four' punch	0110
no assignment	1110
7 = 'seven' punch	0001
8 = 'one' and 'seven' punch	1001
9 = 'two' and 'seven' punch	0101
no assignment	1101
no assignment	0011
no assignment	1011
no assignment	0111
no assignment	1111

NOTE: Several unassigned codes require three punches, and therefore three sortings using only two punches per number is simply a matter of economy. Any number from 0 to 9 can be coded by a maximum of two punches.

Figure 1.8 The Assignment of a Decimal Code

edge-punch cards. With a little experimentation we were able to print commercial cards to our own specifications using a spirit duplicator or mimeograph machine.

The disadvantage of both decimal and alphabetic encoding is that each decimal or alphabetic system can accept only one code. Thus categories encoded by decimal number or by letter of the alphabet must be exclusive for each card. Only the direct code gives the user the opportunity to encode multiple topics per card. Of course, one can use each set of four holes independently, but that reduces the available categories per card from a direct code of 160-200 topics to 40-50 on the first level, (four holes per topic) and 400-500 on the second level (10-14 subtopics per topic). In some applications that kind of structuring may be worthwhile. In ethnographic work (as well as in bibliographical work) we have generally found the direct code to be most useful (with the exception of year of publication and name of author or consultant). The larger the cards ($8^1/_2 \times 11$), the more different and sophisticated variations of direct code and digital codes are possible. These approaches may be especially useful if large cards are used with the ethnographic data directly on the cards.

1.4.4 Computerized Encoding Methods

With microcomputers shrinking in size, price, and power requirements almost daily, their use in the field will soon become as natural and commonplace as the use of a tape recorder or camera is today. We and other ethnographers interested in the uses of computers for fieldwork are now devising data management and retrieval systems that maximize accessibility of data for analysis and writing.

Letter		Punch	Code
A	=	no punch	00000
B	=	'B' punch	10000
C	=	'C' punch	01000
D	=	'B' and 'C' punch	11000
E	=	'E' punch	00100
F	=	'B' and 'E' punch	10100
G	=	'C' and 'E' punch	01100
H	=	'B,' 'C,' and 'E' punch	11100
I	=	'I' punch	00010
J	=	'B' and 'I' punch	10010
K	=	'C' and 'I' punch	01010
L	=	'B,' 'C,' and 'I' punch	11010
M	=	'E' and 'I' punch	00110
Mc	=	'B,' 'E,' and 'I' punch	10110
N	=	'C,' 'E,' and 'I' punch	01110
		no assignment	11110
O	=	'O' punch	00001
P	=	'B' and 'O' punch	10001
Q	=	'C' and 'O' punch	01001
R	=	'B,' 'C,' and 'O' punch	11001
S	=	'E' and 'O' punch	00101
T	=	'B,' 'E,' and 'O' punch	10101
U	=	'C,' 'E,' and 'O' punch	01101
		no assignment	11101
V	=	'I' and 'O' punch	00011
W	=	'B,' 'I,' and 'O' punch	10011
X	=	'C,' 'I,' and 'O' punch	01011
		no assignment	11011
Y	=	'E,' 'I,' and 'O' punch	00111
Z	=	'B,' 'E,' 'I,' and 'O' punch	10111
		no assignment	01111
		no assignment	11111

NOTE: Except for the letter z, all others are encoded by no more than three punches. This reduces the number of sortings necessary to retrieve a letter.

Figure 1.9 The Assignment of an Alphabetic Code

Using a Word Processor

All functions that are part of data base management techniques done "by hand" (i.e. with filing cards, address books, or edge-punch cards) can be done more efficiently with a word processor on a mainframe computer or a micro. In the following pages we discuss predominantly the use of micros. The reason is simply that micros are now readily available with powerful text manipulating capabilities. In addition, micros have become portable, allowing the ethnographer to take one or several micros to the ethnographic site. The portability of a micro such as the Osborne 1, Kaypro, Otrona Attache, TRS 80 Model 100 and many others allows them to go places far from the phone lines previously needed to attach a portable terminal to a computer center.

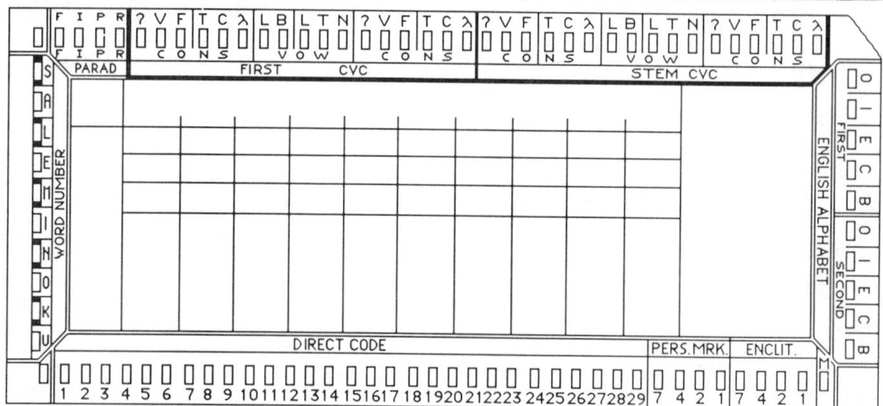

NOTE: PARAD codes the Future (F), Iterative (I), Perfective (P), and Repetitive (R) modes. P and R punched together constitute the Optative (O) mode. The coding of the next set of holes around the top is explained in text. The code applies to the first syllable of the word (First Consonants Vowel Consonant, or CVC set) and the stem syllable. Along the right, the code applies to the first two letters of an English translation equivalent. If the word carries an enclitic (suffix), it is marked on the bottom right. Next to it are the person markers found in Navajo within the word that is a verb. The holes marked 1-29 are reserved for direct coding. A special word number code appears on the left edge of the card.

Figure 1.10 An Edge-Punch Card Designed for Navajo Lexical Items

	ooo	Too	oCo	TCo	ooλ	Toλ	ocλ	TCλ
000		t	c	ch	tl	k	kw	?
?99		t'	c'	ch'	tl'	k'		
oVo	b	d	dz	j	dl	g		
ooF			s	sh	lh	(x)	hw	h
ovF			x	zh	1	gh	w	
							(ghw)	
?Vo	m	n						
?oF	w				y			
					(gh)			

NOTE: The coding here is mnemonic; the consonants are arranged by articulatory position (columns) and mode of articulation (rows). In the columns ooo stands for labials, Too is the symbol for alveolars, oCO for fronted palatals, TCo for midpalatals, ooλ for backed palatals, Toλ for velars, oCλ forlabiovelars, and TCλ for pharingeals. The rows are labeled by ooo for plain stops, ?oo for glottalized stops, oVo for voiced stops, ooF for fricatives, oVF for voiced fricatives, ?Vo for nasals, and ?oF for semi vowels. The coding for vowels is similar.

Figure 1.11 Edge-Punch Coding of Navajo Consonants

There are obvious advantages to having one's own computer ready and available. A comparison in what we had to do only a few years ago demonstrates these advantages.

	ooo	Loo	oTo	LTo	ooN	LoN	oTN	LTN
oo	i	ii	i7	i7i7	8i	8ii	8i7	8i7i7
Lo	e	ee	e7	e7e7	8e	8ee	8e7	8e7e7
oB	o	oo	o7	o7o7	8o	8oo	8o7	8o7o7
LB	a	aa	a7	a7a7	8a	8aa	8a7	8a7a7

NOTE: Starting with the columns, ooo here stands for regular vowels, Loo for long vowels, oTo for high-tone vowels, LTo for length and tone, ooN for nasal vowels, LoN for long nasal vowels, oTN for tone and nasal vowels, and LTN for length, tone, and nasalization. The rows are marked oo for high articulatory position of the tongue and front vowels, Lo for low front vowels, oB for high back vowels, and LB for low back vowels. In this version of Navajo official orthography a 7 following a vowel marks its high tone; an 8 preceding a vowel marks its nasalization.

Figure 1.12 The Coding of Navajo Vowels

Case 1.1 "Good Old Days" of Computing

In 1967-1968 we transcribed interviews with ordinary typewriters. Then one worker repeated the typing by entering the text into a special typewriter that translated letters into punched paper tape. Because telephone lines on the Navajo reservation were not reliable, we shipped the paper tape by mail to the Northwestern University computing center. There the tape was put through a tape reader. The computer made a keyword in context concordance (see below). These were mailed back to the Navajo reservation for text analysis. The whole process required about two weeks. It also required an "advocate" at the Computing Center who saw to it that the tapes were processed expeditiously. This person took care of such trivia as mending the paper tape when it broke.

Transcription is without doubt the major bottleneck in ethnographic research. Repeated typing of the same document slows the transcription process even more (see the section on enhancing transcription later in this chapter).

With a microcomputer with several work stations (several keyboard-TV screen display terminals connected to a central unit), or with several independent but compatible microcomputers, data can be entered directly from cassette to storage medium (usually diskettes). With more than one work station, analysis and entry can proceed almost simultaneously. While one person enters data on one terminal or computer, another person enters analyses on the other. We will further discuss how microcomputers can speed up the entire process.

The word processor has additional advantages. Between transcription and retyping on punched paper tape, we carefully edited each text for mistakes in spelling and formatting (identification of speakers, etc.). Today editing is best done on a computer. Spelling checks are also computerized, at least in English and several Western European languages. Several products allow the construction of a personalized spelling dictionary in any language, including any field language. This means that even in languages used throughout the world, such as English, the spelling dictionary can be adjusted to local dialects.

The spelling checkers are usually only semiautomatic. The editor has ample discretion to override mindless replacement or correction. All spelling program instructions warn that a spelling checker is no panacea for proofreading. For example, if a typist types "last" instead of "least," no current spelling program will find the mistake because "last" is an acceptable English word. A spelling checker tests only for spelling, not for the appropriateness of a correctly spelled word in context.

Word Processor as Indexing Device[1]

It is not strictly correct to call a word processor an indexing device, although many text-processing program packages have indexing capability. But even without this capability a word processor can become a powerful helper for the rapid retrieval of information thanks to the *search function* contained in all minimally adequate editing programs. By depressing a special key or a sequence of control keys, the program calls for the word (phrase) to be found. Another command sequence starts the search. For example, in a software package (program) called Electric Pencil II, depressing the control key (CTRL) and the letter "v" simultaneously produces a computer prompt on the computer's screen: "SEARCH STRING?" The computer will find any string of characters (fragments of words, words, or phrases) that the operator enters on the screen with amazing speed. Usually, as in Electric Pencil, the cursor (which marks where on the screen the action is), comes to rest at the beginning of the line of the first location of the search string. To continue the search in Electric Pencil the operator presses (CTRL) and "c." The cursor immediately jumps to the next line with the next location of the desired string. This continues until there are no more samples of the given word or string in the text. The computer then prints the message "CANNOT LOCATE 'X'", where "X" is the string for which the operator searched.

If the ethnographer knows what key words may be found in a text, and if he or she judiciously inserted "titles" of cases and other commentary in the text, then all of this material is available for search and can be located almost instantly. All an ethnographer needs is a list of significant (for the goals of the project) key words, titles, or phrases that are within the text or that have been inserted by the ethnographer. With such a list, finding any relevant information becomes very easy.

Thanks to the index routines included in many of today's word processing programs, the ethnographer has the option automatically to collect lists of key words and other inserted materials with page references included. For example, in a text formatter called TEXTWRITER, a command "!index" followed by the index entry (in quotes), prompts the computer to collect all indexed items and print them alphabetized, on command, at the end of the text.

In our work we have used the regular lowercase letter strings for embedded key words and phrases and uppercase STRINGS for inserted key words and phrases (titles) (see Figure 1.1). Such an index facilitates a computer search, but because all locations are referenced to the pages of the text, it allows for retrieval of information by hand as well. As we shall see, however, the full potential of computerized searches can be best utilized with a multiscreen or split-screen editor.

For ethnographic work, the size of the maximum document that any system can handle is an important variable to consider when buying a computer, because it circumscribes the size of a search. For example, in the editor we mentioned before (Electric Pencil), documents of more than 20 double-spaced pages become cumbersome. As the document size increases, the performance of the editor deteriorates, slowing to the point where the computer system reacts more slowly than a moderately efficient typist. This usually means that at the beginning of lines, or when inserting text, random letters that the computer cannot keep up with get dropped. This creates an extra editing chore. Some newer editors do not have this problem.

On some newer systems with so-called virtual memory, the size of the document is limited only by the size of the mass storage device. Floppy diskettes, the most popular method of mass storage, can hold from about 50 pages on single-density disk drives of the Osborne 1 computer up to about 500 to 1000 pages on a double-density disk drive and eight-inch floppy diskettes. The difference is significant. In the first case (about 20 pages of text), the ethnographer can search only one interview at a time; with the Osborne 1 and the word processor called WORDSTAR, about two interviews. With a larger system using double-density eight-inch disks, as many as 20 to 40 interviews may be searched at the same time. That is, the 20 to 40 interviews can be set up as one continuous document. Alternatively, the 500 to 1000 pages can be viewed as one volume of field notes, containing interviews, journal entries, analyses of interviews, and references to documents that are stored outside the computer in some physical (nonmagnetic) file. Hard disk or optical storage devices can store an entire ethnographic project. The only limitation on continuous searches may be the software.

Concordances

A concordance is a comprehensive index prepared for a text that lists the words in their immediate context. A concordance is best prepared automatically. These general indexing programs are not yet widely available for microcomputers. When Werner (1982) needed one he had to write his own program (see below, WORDINDEX).

The best time to prepare a concordance of an ethnographic text is *after* the ethnographer has inserted the appropriate cue words, titles, and other identifying materials into the text. The idea of a concordance was made famous by Englishman Alexander Cruden (1701-1770), who spent most of his life collating by hand, the best-known and still standard concordance of the King James Bible (Cruden 1953) [1738]). It is an alphabetical index of key words, omitting only the high-frequency words (such as "a," "an," "at," "in," "the," etc.).

In key word-out-of-context versions (kwoc concordances), the key word is usually listed in the left margin and the context—for example, a Biblical verse or a sentence—is listed to the right of it on the page. In key word-in-context (KWIC concordances), a common method is to list the context (sentence, biblical verse, etc.) on the page and highlighting, for example, by boldface, the key word. The key words are usually alphabetized.

A common form of computerized concordances is the key word centered on a page 14 inches (132-characters) wide, with as many words as will fit to the left and right of it. The sample shown in Figure 1.13 is reduced to a context of 75 characters to make it fit the page of this book. First we present a short text, then its concordance.

Concordances have the tremendous disadvantage for a microcomputer with a slow printer (maximum 30 to 200 characters per second) that the size of the text grows at a tremendous rate, often 20 times the size of the original vocabulary. At that bulk it becomes impractical to use anything but a high-speed printer (one that prints thousands of characters per second).

Concordances have other disadvantages as well. The major one is that the 132-character (or lesser) context is rarely sufficient for ethnographic analysis. We have found that a simple word index is adequate, because very often we had to consult the original text to get the benefit of the full context in which a word was embedded. Because a word index has only as many entries as there are words in the text, it does not proliferate copies of the text as a concordance does. Because many items have to be looked up in the original text anyway, the gain achieved with the printed context of a concordance is negligible.

A word index is simply a program that assigns a number to every word of text. It then prints the text with the numbers. Finally, it alphabetizes all the words of a text and prints out the result. It is called a "word index" because instead of referring to page numbers, the index refers to word numbers. Figures 1.14 and 1.15 illustrate first the numbered text and then the word index. Both were prepared by Werner's WORDINDEX programs (Werner 1982). Figure 1.15 shows the list in alphabetical order.

The concordance and the WORDINDEX shown in Figures 1.14 and 1.15 contain all high-frequency words. These could be eliminated, but with the already relatively slow microcomputers this would add to processing time. Usually running time with microcomputers is no problem. Once the machine is purchased, all processing time is literally free. Even a WORDINDEX program, such as Werner's (1982), can be turned on in the evening and will operate unattended. The WORDINDEX is ready to aid analysis the following morning.

We propose a number of procedures for handling computer-generated concordances or indexes in practice. If all files can be kept on a hard disk, which can store the entire ethnographic record, it may be practical to merge all indexes into a master index that would contain all of the project's index entries. However, given current technology, merging and resorting merged files may not prove practical.

MY EARLY LIFE

Twenty years ago I came among them—the Americans. When I was eight years old, I came among them at a place called Fort Defiance in order to learn the Anglo language. It is a very difficult language. (Adapted from Sapir & Hoijer 1942:435)

CONCORDANCE OF: MY EARLY LIFE

years old, I came among them at	a place called Fort Defiance in order to
learn the Anglo language. It is	a very difficult language.
My early life. Twenty years	**ago** I came among them—the Americans. W
ears ago I came among them—the	**Americans.** When I was eight years old I
ly life. Twenty years ago I came	**among** them—the Americans. When I was e
en I was eight years old, I came	**among** them at a place called Fort Defiance
t Defiance in order to learn the	**Anglo** language. It is a very difficult l
ght years old, I came among them	**at** a place called Fort Defiance in order to
ld, I came among them at a place	**called** Fort Defiance in order to learn t
y Eraly Life. Twenty years ago I	**came** among them—the Americans. When I
s. When I was eight years old, I	**came** among them at a place called Fort D
mong them at a place called Fort	**Defiance** in order to learn the Anglo lan
the Anglo language. It is a very	**difficult** language.
MY	**EARLY** LIFE. Twenty years ago I came
them—the Americans. When I was	**eight** years old, I came among them at a
same among them at a place called	**Fort** Defiance in order to learn the Angl
MY EARLY LIFE' Twenty years ago	**I** came among them—the Americans. When
among them—the Americans. When	**I** was eight years old, I came among them
ans. When I was eight years old,	**I** I came among them at a place called Fo
at a place called Fort Defiance	**in** order to learn the Anglo language. It
to learn the Anglo language. It	**is** a very difficult language.
der to learn the Anglo language.	**It** is a very difficult language.
ance in order to learn the Anglo	**language.** It is a very difficult language
language It is a very difficult	**language.**
called Fort Defiance in order to	**learn** the Anglo language. It is a very d
MY EARLY	**LIFE.** Twenty years ago I came among the
mericans. When I was eight years	**old,** I came among them at a place called
a place called Fort Defiance in	**order** to learn the Anglo language. It is
ears old, I came among them at a	**place** called Fort Defiance in order to l
ty years ago I came among them—	**the** Americans. When I was eight years ol
Fort Defiance in order to learn	**the** Anglo language. It is a very difficu
E. Twenty years ago I came among	**them**—the AMericans. When I was eight y
as eight years old, I came among	**them** at a place called Fort Defiance in
ce called Fort Defiance in order	**to** learn the Anglo language. It is a ver
MY EARLY LIFE'	**Twenty** years ago I came among them—the
earn the Anglo language. It is a	**very** difficult language.
ong them—the Americans. When I	**was** eight years old, I came among them a
came among them—the Americans	**when** I was eight years old, I came among
MY EARLY LIFE' Twenty	**years** ago I came among them—the Americ
the Americans. When I was eight	**years** old, I came among them at a place

NOTE: Note the length of the concordance in comparison to the original text. The context is the 75-character line. Each word in the text creates 75 minus the length of the key word, characters of context in which it is embedded, or about 13 words. Thus a small text of 41 words results in a concordance of about 500 words. With a full 132-character context, the concordance grows to about 800 words, or about 20 times the size of the original text.

Figure 1.13 KWIC Concordance of a Short Text

MY	1	Americans	12	at	23	Anglo	34
EARLY	2	when	13	a	24	language	35
LIFE	3	I	14	place	25	It	36
Twenty	4	was	15	called	26	is	37
years	5	eight	16	Fort	27	a	38
ago	6	years	17	Definance	28	very	39
I	7	old	18	in	29	difficult	40
came	8	I	19	order	30	language	41
among	9	came	20	to	31		42
them	10	among	21	learn	32		43
the	11	them	22	the	33		44

NOTE: All words of a text are numbered from first to last word.

Figure 1.14 First Part of a Wordindex

a	24	Definance	28	language	35	them	22
a	38	difficult	40	language	41	to	31
ago	6	EARLY	2	learn	32	Twenty	4
Americans	12	eight	16	LIFE	3	very	39
among	9	Fort	27	MY	1	was	15
among	21	I	7	old	18	When	13
Anglo	34	I	14	order	30	years	5
at	23	I	19	place	25	years	17
called	26	in	29	the	11		—
came	8	is	37	the	33		—
came	20	it	36	them	10		—

NOTE: The only increase in the length of the indexed document derives from the printing format, whose columnar arrangement requires slightly more space.

Figure 1.15 Alphabetization by WORDINDEX Program

A more appropriate procedure may be to create a separate index for each volume of the combined journal and transcriptions. Then each is arranged so that it is physically located on a single diskette. This way all documentation for a volume of field notes is deposited in one place. This disk therefore contains (1) a magnetic image of several hundred pages of field notes—journal and transcription in chronological order, and (2) a copy of the index or concordance to all of the items in 1. Using a new program that can split the TV screen of the computer console into several windows, index and field notes can be viewed simultaneously. We discuss the uses of multiple screen windows in the next section.

Other Computer Aids to Analysis

Computers can provide a number of additional aids to analysis and fieldwork. In the following pages we will discuss the advantages of multiwindow editing, the possibility of speeding up the transcription of interview tapes, computerized aids to writing, and the use of spread sheets for managing budgets and expenses.

Multiwindow Editing

Editing text with the aid of multiple windows on one television (CRT) screen has been available on large mainframe computers for some time. The availability of this feature for microcomputers is new. The ideal would be a separate program that creates multiple windows in which the user could use his or her own editor, programming language, or spread sheet (see below). Today if the ethnographer wants to use multiple windows, he or she must learn a new editor. This involves a considerable amount of retraining, on the order of several days or weeks, depending on the complexity of a word processor. Furthermore, the user is restricted to editing text only. New multiwindow programs allow a choice of editor, programming language, and other utility programs such as spread sheets, but these are not yet within reach of the average microcomputer user.

The best way to demonstrate the use of multiscreen editing is with an example. We will use the simple example of the text, "My Early Life," from the previous section. The general goal here is to have two or more documents available simultaneously for analysis. In our example we first split the screen into two windows—one upper, one lower. We further split the top window into index on the left and field notes, the combined record of journal and transcriptions, on the right. All of this is stored on one diskette (one book per diskette) and called to the screen on command. The next book is on the next diskette, and so on. Also on the diskette is the index to the book. A multiple window screen might appear as that in Figure 1.16.

Each window on the screen can be operated independently. That is, the text can be scrolled past the window as if it were rolling by on an endless scroll (some programs flip pages instead of scrolling). The three windows of the screen are used as follows: (1) (upper left) To display the index and to show the ethnographer what key words are available in the volume of field notes under scrutiny. There is an implicit assumption that the text has been coded by the ethnographer for examples of difficulties Navajos experience with the English language. The ethnographer might have been able to find the anecdote (case) through the index word "language." (2) (upper right) To display the original text under review. (3) (bottom window) To show the area in which the ethnographer is writing the final ethnographic report. The text of the case has already been moved from the original text (window 2) into the ethnography (window 3).

The advantages of multiscreen editing are obvious. Instead of having to leaf through volumes of text physically, each volume can be perused quickly and efficiently on the screen.

If an ethnographer writes his or her report in the lower window and finds that the topic under discussion calls for a good example, first he or she reviews the key words. The two key words "language" in proximity to each other in the index (upper left window) motivate a search in the upper right window. After successful location of an appropriate case, the relevant text is marked (usually upper left corner and lower right corner) and copied (literally "zapped") directly into the desired location in the ethnographic report. The only thing the ethnographer must do is bring the system up (turn the computer on and select the program to run on it),

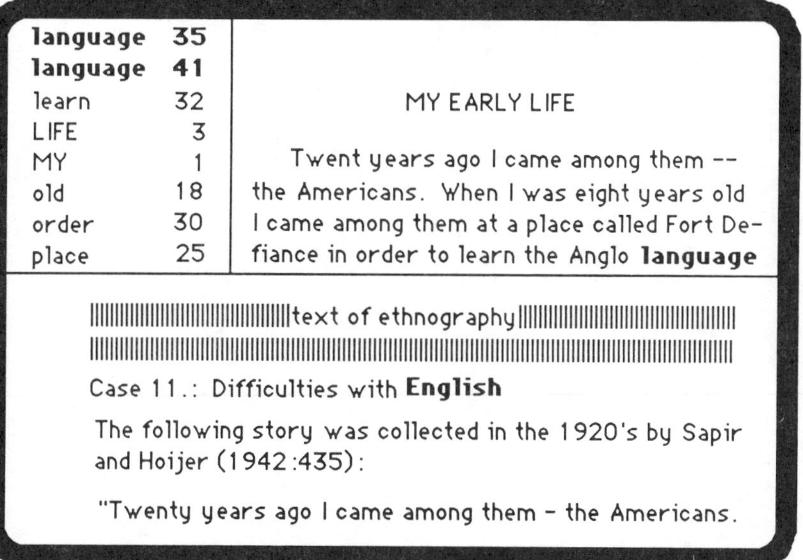

Figure 1.16 Three-Window Computer Screen

set up three windows (in recurring work this too can be automated), decide on a key word, search for it and move the desired text into the final report. No time-consuming searching through slips of paper and retyping was involved.

Computerized searches of this kind now make it possible to look efficiently at large bodies of textual data. This makes Agar's (1979) thematic analysis (see Section 6.3.6) possible: The ethnographer can look easily for many more cases supporting a theme and, just as important, look for the "unless clause" disclaimers that qualify every theme in certain contexts (Agar 1979).

Enhancing Transcription

The largest bottleneck in ethnographic fieldwork is the transcription of tapes. As we have pointed out on several occasions, a simple 45-minute interview results in 20 to 30 pages of double-spaced transcription. Although the bulk of interview data is a serious concern, even more serious is the eight hours it takes to transcribe a 45-minute tape. Microcomputers promise help in this area as well.

Today it is easy to reprogram the keyboard of any computer. An efficiency of 30% to 50% can be gained by switching from the usual QWERTY layout to a Dvorak layout. This design was developed by August Dvorak in the 1930s (Dvorak *et al.* 1936) and consists of a rearrangement of the keys in order of the frequency of occurrence of letters in English texts. The layout is shown in Figure 1.17. Figure 1.18 shows the standard typewriter keyboard for comparison.

Retraining costs are heavy. Katz (1982) estimates that it takes about 40 hours to retrain on a Dvorak keyboard. Interestingly, Katz found that switching from the Dvorak keyboard back to the traditional QWERTY arrangement was easier than

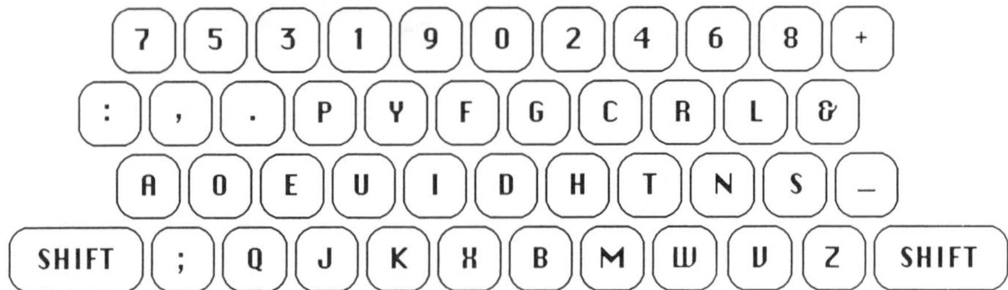

NOTE: The typist's fingers rest on the second row from the bottom. The letters there have the highest frequency of occurrence in English texts. Adapted from Katz (1982).

Figure 1.17 August Dvorak's Keyboard Layout

NOTE: The percentages of letter frequencies for English are given on the right. Adapted from Katz (1982).

Figure 1.18 Standard Typewriter Keyboard

he thought. He was able to rearrange the keys on his typewriter/terminal with a program called SMARTKEY. This software makes it very easy for anyone to reprogram the keyboard of any computer that uses the CP/M operating system. Similar programs are available for other systems. This has the tremendous advantage for anthropologists that the letter frequency of any text in any native language can be accommodated and the keyboard accordingly redesigned. Transcription speed may thus be increased in any language.

A 30% to 50% increase in typing speed is not negligible. It allows for either 30% to 50% more interviews or for 30% to 50% more time for analysis and writing.

Reprogramming a traditional keyboard is just the beginning. Even more efficient keyboards are conceivable that can utilize the multistrike capability of systems such as STENOTYPE, used by court recorders. Unfortunately, court recorders often read their transcription into a tape recorder. The recording is then conventionally transcribed. This is no improvement. However, if the stenotype transcription becomes machine readable and can be edited by a spelling checker program, still further increases in transcription speed may be possible.

There are other possibilities. Grossman's (1976) QUICKHAND alphabet based on the shorthand system (essentially English without vowels) could be adapted to typewriters. Dictionary programs could then insert vowels and decipher abbreviations automatically.

Simple speech recognition devices with limited vocabularies are available today. At least for English and some world languages, more sophisticated machines with unlimited vocabularies seem to be just around the corner. In the case of exotic language, with few speakers, the wait for efficient and accurate speech recognition devices may prove considerably longer.

It is safe to predict that the future's greatest advances of computer-aided ethnography will be increases in speed, efficiency, and accuracy of dealing with qualitative textual data.

More Computerized Aids

Almost everyone who has tried typing and editing on a computer has given up on typing with typewriters. Typing directly into a machine eliminates a tremendous amount of unnecessary retyping by eliminating the clerk-typist. A document or text has only to be typed into a machine once and will remain there virtually forever.[2] Certainly any number of drafts can be obtained by editing the original: deleting the unnecessary, adding the necessary, and improving the organization by moving parts of the text into better locations. Text editing with a microcomputer for many ethnographers has become a way of life.

Equally important are spelling checkers. Although no substitute for careful proofreading for the sense of a passage, these programs avoid the most frequent spelling errors, especially those that are difficult to detect because they look plausible. At least one of these programs enables the writer to check overused phrases, frequently repeated words, and other "grammatical" information in one's writing. It is safe to predict that these programs too, as time goes on, will become more sophisticated. The trend to watch goes beyond the improvement of one's own writing. Some future technology will prove useful for content analysis of the ethnographer's interviews as well.

The extension of these programs to other languages, even exotic ones, will also become possible. Today many computerized dictionary systems allow the user to build his or her own dictionary which could ultimately be in any language.

Experts in the microcomputer field claim that the first spread sheet program (called VISI CALC) was responsible for the sale of 15,000 Apple II computers. Today there is a whole family of these programs. They are ideal for any numerical data that can be arranged in tabular form. Budgets, expense accounts, tabulation of questionnaire response statistics, and many other applications can be effectively handled by spread sheet programs (also CALC programs). As long as an ethnographer takes a computer to the field, a CALC program may be excellent for managing time, money, consultants, inventory, photographs, tapes, and correspondence.

Today many computers are purchased with standard sets of software. For example, the Osborne 1 portable computer comes equipped with WORDSTAR for word processing and text formatting, with MAILMERGE for merging form letters (e.g., questionnaires) with names, with SUPER CALC for spread sheet calculations, and with two BASICs (one interpreter basic, easy to use but slow running; the other compiler basic, hard to use but faster). The trend linking hardware with software will no doubt continue. One thing an ethnographer of the future will need is additional software that is directly applicable to ethnographic analysis. Chief among these will be automatic indexing programs.

1.5 SUMMARY AND CONCLUSIONS

The most important aspect of ethnographic fieldwork is an effective data management system. Every ethnographer should collect data of high quality, but no matter how good the data are, if the appropriate materials cannot be found easily they are useless. Data management is also important for data quality control in the field. If the ethnographer cannot quickly ascertain what he or she has already collected, the ethnographic record will remain incomplete.

Ethnographic data are most commonly texts. We have discussed (1) texts created by the ethnographer (TEXT (1)) and (2) text created by consultants (TEXT (2)). To this we add (3) documents and (4) materials that are intermediate between TEXT (1) and TEXT (2), usually the results of analysis (e.g., taxonomies, plans, decision tables). Occasionally ethnographers collect specimens (e.g., objects of material culture) that require specialized cataloging.

It is conceivable that an ethnographer could maintain four simultaneous files, one for each type of data. With an efficient access and retrieval system, we think a single chronologically ordered file (books of three binders, for example) will prove more effective.

The key to data management is indexing. We call "clues" words or phrases contained in the texts we have collected. These are also called "key words." "Cues" are words or phrases (e.g., titles of cases) that the ethnographer inserts into texts. Together clues and cues are the indexing categories. We keep a running list of these, alphabetically arranged, in an address book or in a card file. Each index entry "points" to locations in the text files where specific information may be found.

There are a number of mechanical methods for keeping ethnographic records. Keysort cards are one; the use of microcomputers is another. Direct coding, where each hole on a keysort card is assigned a topic, is best suited for handling cards that contain the textual data themselves. Digital codes (numerical, alphabetical, or specially designed) are best used for index cards or combinations of index and data cards—for which only the ingenuity of the ethnographer sets limits.

Computerized methods start with the use of a word processor. Once the data are typed into a machine (preferably directly from tape to diskette) it can be edited and otherwise manipulated. Any key words or inserted clues can be located almost instantly with various search commands. Perhaps the most useful computer programs index texts automatically. These techniques range from (1) collecting and alphabetically sorting tagged items in a text, to (2) concordances, key words in some contexts (usually sentence, or 132 character), or (3) word indexes where each word in a text is numbered and the numbered words are then sorted alphabetically. In some editing systems data, index, and the ethnographic report itself can be seen simultaneously in three (or more) windows on the display screen. Blocks of texts (e.g., cases) can be moved easily from one window to another. This further reduces the need for retyping.

Computers can aid ethnographic work in still other ways. Transcription speed can be increased up to 50% with a Dvorak keyboard, based on English letter frequencies. New programs allow the redefinition of typewriter keys to match letter frequency in any language.

There are numerous programs that simulate textual or card files on a microcomputer. Spread sheet programs allow for efficient management of budgets, schedules, and other data than can be arranged in tabular form. These programs can also be used for simple statistical calculations (e.g., chi-squares).

Microcomputers are becoming cheaper and more portable. The time is near when taking a micro into the field will be as natural as taking a tape recorder or a camera. The major impact of microcomputers in ethnography will be the improvement of the quality and accessibility of textual (qualitative) data for ethnographic analysis.

NOTES

1. A word processor often comes in two parts: an editor for deleting, inserting, and moving text, and a formatter that arranges text in paragraphs, offsets titles and determines line spacing, characters per inch, page size, and so on. It is usually the text formatter that contains an indexing capability.

2. This may be news for anyone who has inadvertently lost computer files. Many of the newer text editors make accidental loss of data very unlikely.

Chapter 2

Structural Analysis

The methods of structural analysis form the core of classical ethnoscience. Central to these methods is the MT schema (see Volume 1, Section 2.3.2). Consequently, this section of analysis concentrates on elicitation and analysis of folk taxonomies (in the narrow sense) and the relation of modification or attribution. Ancillary to these are the cross-culturally problematic part/whole (PW) relation and the serial order relation (Q).

2.0 INTRODUCTION

All techniques presented in this section are either alternate forms of the MT schema (e.g., componential analysis, including Lounsbury's extensions) or are techniques for extending the scope of taxonomies (e.g., tree drawing) or eliciting cosmologies (e.g., texts) or attributes (e.g., slip sorting or word associations).

2.1 TAXONOMIES

By asking such questions as "What kinds of X are there?" or "Is X a kind of Y?" or "What kind of thing is X?" a cultural domain can be explored systematically. As soon as the ethnographer identifies at least two taxonomic levels, he or she can ask for more examples.

In one of our interviews (in a text, after transcription), a university student whom we will call Carol mentioned a class that she found boring. We can immediately view this assertion as part of a hierarchy (see Figure 2.1). Carol agreed that "A boring class is a kind of class." She volunteered other kinds of classes immediately by naming "easy classes," "hard classes," and "micks." The members of one level of a hierarchy of terms (in Carol's case, boring classes, easy classes, hard classes, and micks) form what is called a "contrast set."

A contrast set is linked to a general or superordinate term by the taxonomic sentence "X is a (kind of) Y" (=T). In the next example (Figure 2.2), the super-

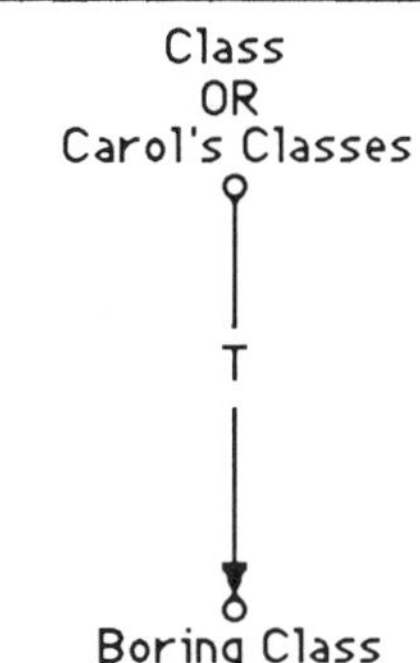

Figure 2.1 Taxonomy of Carol's Classes I

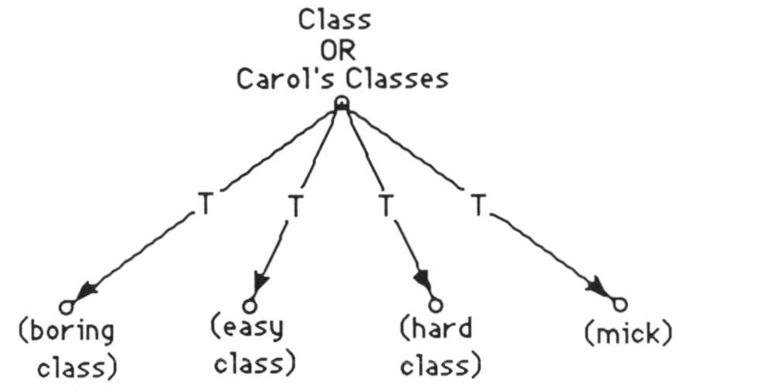

Figure 2.2 Taxonomy of Carol's Classes II

ordinate term is "class." The words, phrases, or best "naming units" (X and Y) are labels attached to the "nodes" (o); the arrow represents the taxonomic relation (is a kind of) and is labeled T. The direction of the arrow is set by convention: It points from the general to the specific term. The direction of the arrow also implies asymmetry; that is, if (X) T (Y), then not (Y) T (X), for example, " A mick is a class," but not "A class is a mick."

If elicited through interviewing consultants this structure is called a *folk taxonomy*. One of the aims of systematized interview analysis is to discover a contrast set and to expand it. In our case, in further interviews Carol had a lot more to say about the quality of the classes she attended at the university: That was the expansion. The expansion goes on until no more information is forthcoming. This reaching of "diminishing returns" provides the commonsense equivalent for "exhaustiveness."

Taxonomies are not restricted to classes or to school life. They pervade every aspect of human life. In "A Taxonomic View of the Traditional Navajo Universe," Werner, Manning, and Begishe (1983) found numerous classifications relating to all aspects of Navajo life, from the classification of all physical objects to the classification of good and bad behavior (following the Navajo pattern of good and bad thought). A similar effort on Rapa Nui (Easter Island) by Gomez and Werner (in preparation) shows the different classifications prevalent in the life of the small Easter Island community. Folk taxonomies of less ambitious scope have been gathered in virtually all major (and many obscure) languages of the world. The best source for the study of folk classifications including folk taxonomies is Conklin's bibliography published by the Anthropology Department at Yale University (1972).

One word of caution: In the ethnographic literature the term "folk taxonomy" is often applied indiscriminately to any folk classification or to any tree structure. We consistently use "folk classification" as the generic term. *Folk taxonomy is exclusively the relation that links naming units by "X is a kind of Y."*

2.2 FOLK DEFINITIONS

Systematic expansion of contrast sets is one fundamental technique for assuring that one's interviews cover a field as uniformly as possible. After the initial classifications, or folk taxonomies, are gathered, a second technique is applied: the elicitation of folk definitions. In their simplest form, folk definitions are answers to questions of the form "What does X mean?" Most investigators in ethnoscience and linguistics were surprised (e.g., Casagrande & Hale 1967) at how readily consultants in many parts of the world fall into the habit of making folk definitions. Human beings do not realize how often in everyday dealings, especially with children, we are called upon to describe words using other words.

A folk definition is thus a definition composed by a consultant during an interview. A *composite folk definition* is a definition derived from a number of folk definitions by different consultants. A composite folk definition can also be extracted from texts (see Chapter 7).

Ethnoscience analysis can be viewed as a set of techniques for making folk definitions more systematic. The systematization involves finding the entire contrast set and obtaining complete definitions of each member of the set as far as is possible.

In many areas (domains) of a culture, there are other ways of obtaining information about the meaning of words. For example, if one seeks botanical knowledge, it is often useful to inspect specimens of plants with the consultant. In a situation with live models, the consultant can be asked to describe the object in hand. This method has the advantage of immediacy. The question can be interpreted as a tour, a kind of a walk, touching on each salient part of the plant from flower to root. Having the actual physical object in hand affords the advantage that the morphology of the object, its physical features, imposes an order on the interview. Any imposition of order is a step toward systematization. The analyst's task, as in most ethnoscience, is to translate the linear order of answers to questions into systematically related sets of terms. The relationships are rarely linear and can best be represented as a tree graph (e.g., a taxonomic tree) or as a grid or network of interconnections forming a lexical/semantic field (see Volume 1, Section 2.3.2).

Folk definitions have also proven useful when dealing with abstract objects that cannot be held in hand for definition (although this situation is more difficult and will require special attention). English examples are "sincerity," "love," "virtue." In the definition of such terms the consultant is not held to a particular order by any constraint other than the structure of associations in his or her mind. Such associations can be amazingly fickle and may vary from one interview to the next because of the verbal (and nonverbal) context in which they are mentioned; however, the variation between consultants or variations between the folk definitions obtained from the same consultant at different times are not beyond systematization. Each interview contains parts that are shared with previous folk definitions, as well as parts that are unique. Clear contradictions between definitions rarely occur. What seems to make them rare is that unambiguous contradiction is usually difficult to detect. At present we do not know why this is so (however, see Section 3.3 in Volume 1).

Generally, any two interviews A and B, compared sentence by sentence, offer the picture shown in Figure 2.3. More usually the unique parts of each folk definition are additive. This is not restricted to consultants. For example, we treated the articles (definitions) on the spleen in Stedman's (1966) and Dorland's (1965) medical dictionaries as if they originated with different consultants. The results were the same; both dictionary entries contained shared information. The unique parts consisted of a more thorough description of the location of the spleen in Stedman's dictionary, whereas Dorland's work described the color and texture of the tissue in considerably more detail. Obviously, as in the case of

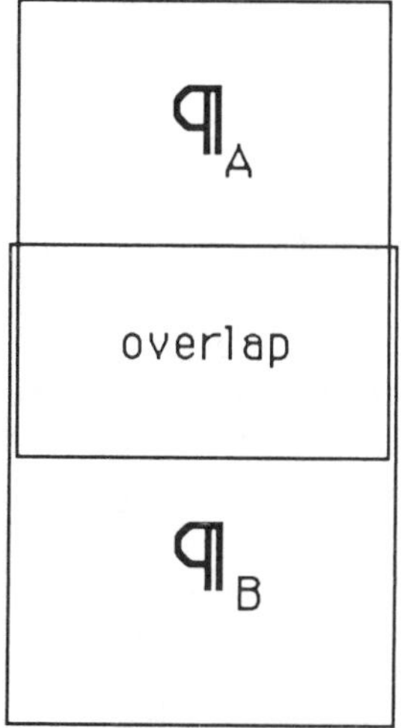

Figure 2.3 Overlap in Folk Definitions

consultants, combining the two (or more) sets of information is the best policy. It is also clear that if one combines many folk definitions in this manner, the distinction between a dictionary (containing minimal information) and an encyclopedia (containing maximally available information) disappears or becomes a gradual blending of one into the other as the length of the articles (definitions) increases.

2.2.1 Systematization of Folk Definitions

The method for the systematization of folk definitions is very simple and straightforward. The first steps include

(1) isolating a contrast set to define,
(2) gathering folk definitions for each member of the set, and
(3) tabulating the answers by listing the attributes (preferably in short sentence form) as mentioned in each folk definition.

There should be a paragraph of text associated with each node of a contrast set.

In the illustration of the systematization of folk definitions (Figure 2.4), the arrow labeled "T" stand for the taxonomic relation. As part of the analysis, each sentence of the consultant's text should occupy a different line inside the paragraph of folk definition. If the consultant uses complex sentences, it is advisable to reduce these to a constituent set of simple sentences out of which each complex sentence was constructed. This reduction of a complex sentence to a set of simple sentences is based on current linguistic theory. For ethnographic purposes it is best to rely on the intuition of a native speaker. After reduction, a separate line should be used for each simple sentence. For example, if someone defines a chrysanthemum as a "large, brightly colored, spherical flower," we analyze it as shown in Figure 2.5.

It is immediately apparent from the analysis that "A chrysanthemum is a kind of flower; that is, there is a folk taxonomy in which "flower" is the cover term for all flowers and "chrysanthemum" is one of the flowers (a member of the contrast set of flowers). The sentences we have listed under "chrysanthemum" give various kinds of information. The first one refers to the relative size of the flower, the second to its coloring, the third to its geometrical shape.

The second step in the systematization of the folk definition is achieved by insisting that all definitions on one level of a folk taxonomy (a contrast set) should have the *same amount of detail,* if possible. Gaps in detail indicate boundaries of specialization or some (usually unknown) variation in context. For example, while defining flowers, we may elicit "A dandelion is a small yellow spring flower considered a weed by many Americans." The analysis is shown in Figure 2.6.

By comparing the two definitions, some of the holes in the pattern are immediately obvious. (The short lines in Figure 2.7 symbolize the holes.)

Both folk definitions mention the size of the flower. We have a match there. Both mention color, but "brightly colored" is less specific than "yellow." We have

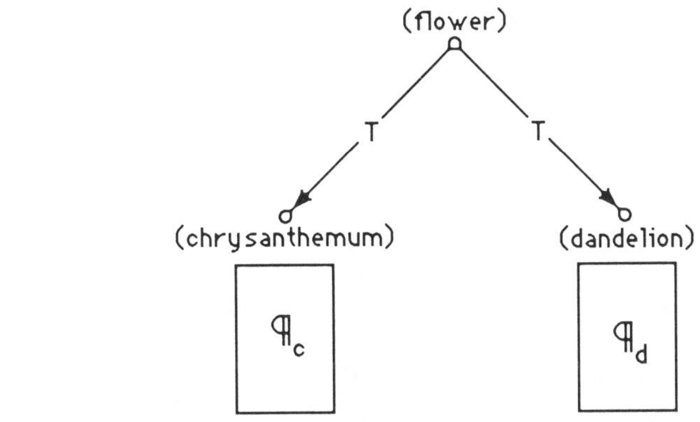

Figure 2.4 Flower Taxonomy with Folk Definitions

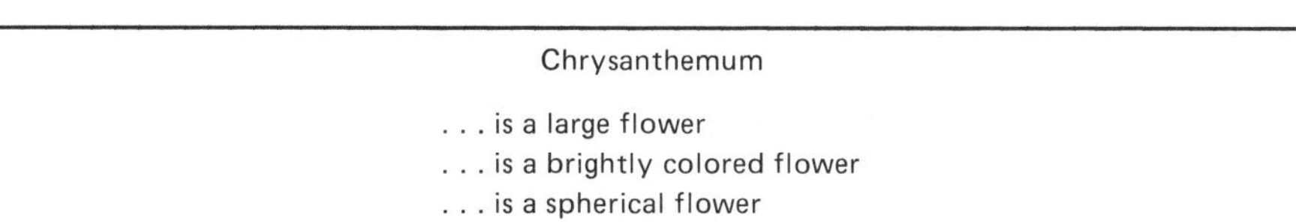

Figure 2.5 Folk Definition of "Chrysanthemum"

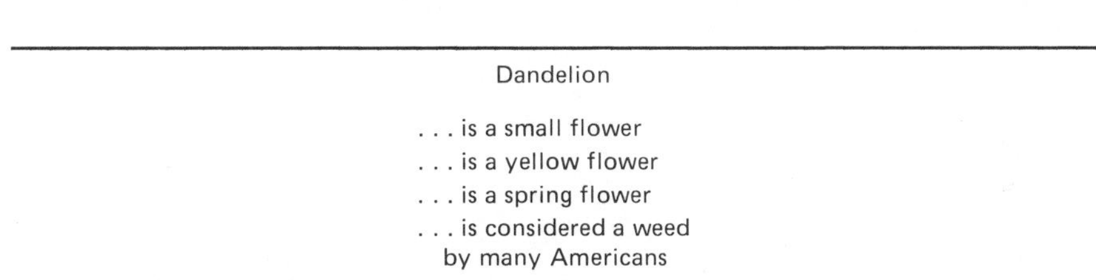

Figure 2.6 Folk Definition of "Dandelion"

to ask more detailed questions about the color of chrysanthemums. We will discover that although dandelions are always yellow, chrysanthemums come in a wide variety of colors that may need more careful description. In the folk definition of chrysanthemums, the shape of the flower is mentioned; for dandelions it is not. Again, further questions should be asked about dandelions and its flower shape. Similarly, a dandelion is characterized as a spring flower; no such characterization is made about chrysanthemums. The ultimate object is to supply the same amount and the same type of information for each flower. In a dictionary format of an ethnography, this leads to uniformity of coverage.

The *order of elicitation* in obtaining such uniform data is a significant clue to the consultant's knowledge of the subject (see Sanday 1968). Intimate details of special interest are usually mentioned first. The order of elicitation can provide clues as to the social group to which the consultant belongs, and other information. For example, a gardener may know more about chrysanthemums than about

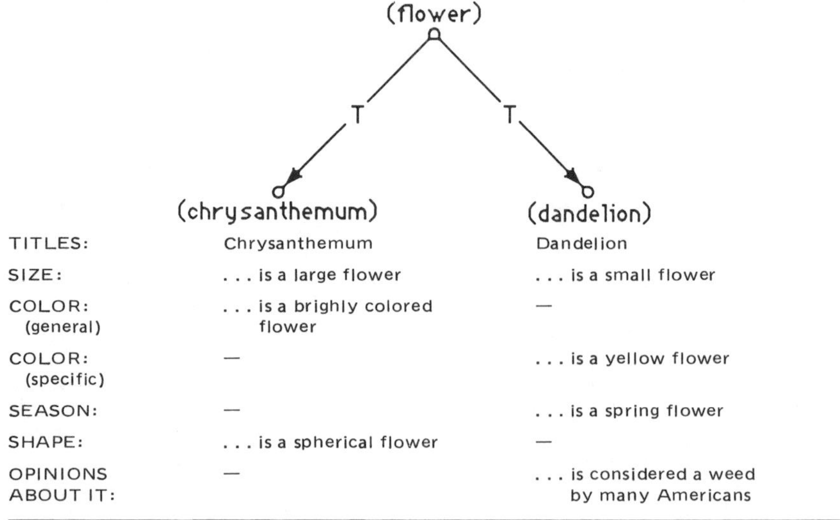

TITLES:	Chrysanthemum	Dandelion
SIZE:	. . . is a large flower	. . . is a small flower
COLOR: (general)	. . . is a brighly colored flower	—
COLOR: (specific)	—	. . . is a yellow flower
SEASON:	—	. . . is a spring flower
SHAPE:	. . . is a spherical flower	—
OPINIONS ABOUT IT:	—	. . . is considered a weed by many Americans

Figure 2.7 Comparison of Folk Definitions

dandelions; a specialist on weeds or wild flowers, more about dandelions. Experts can give more information (more encyclopedic folk definitions) on areas within their expertise.

Many of the clues linking cultural knowledge to a subgroup (e.g., specialists) need still to be discovered and placed into the theoretical framework of ethnoscience.

2.2.2 Serial Order in Folk Definitions

It is important to keep track of when and what information was obtained. For example, it is significant that although dandelions are spring flowers, the florist industry has made chrysanthemums available during any time of the year. It is equally significant for chrysanthemums that the flower is large and spherical. Similarly, the weedlike character of dandelions (which drives lawn fanciers to despair) is, in American culture, equally significant. In other words, the order of mentioning, at least the first set of attributes, gives one an important clue to the most salient features of a term (usually restricted by the interests of a given consultant). The gradual elicitation of equal amounts of the same kind of information is especially useful for an outsider in the culture of the consultants. Insiders are expected to know the less salient features, and in many instances these are important in certain contexts. (We subscribe to the view that any part of cultural knowledge may be salient in some—perhaps rare—context.)

The outsider who seeks information does not know offhand which parts of the information he or she is collecting are salient and which are not; therefore, one should elicit as many features as possible. The order of elicitation gives clues to

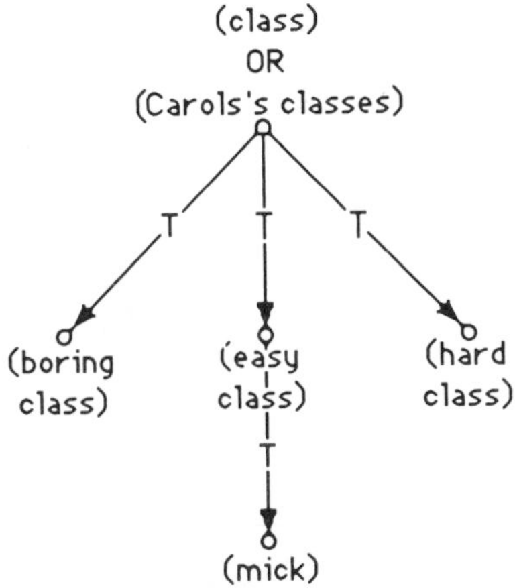

Figure 2.8 Taxonomy of Carol's Classes III

the ethnographer about what came first and hence what was more readily available to the consultant's recall.

The specific features mentioned by a consultant also depend on the consultant's perception of how much the ethnographer (or any hearer) knows about the topic of conversation. It is not unusual to find speakers who have unrealistic expectations of a hearer's (interviewer's) knowledge. The best example of how varied such perception must be is demonstrated by the unsystematic nature of entries in most commercial dictionaries. Traditional lexicographers apparently never attempt to make definitional style uniform—that is, to assure the user that each similar term (of the same or a related contrast set) has roughly the same amount and same kind of information. (In all fairness to lexicographers, a check for consistency in definitions with several tens of thousands of entries is difficult.)

The technique described above helps the ethnographer to structure subsequent interviews, thus allowing him or her to make certain that the terms of a culture are described in equal detail as well as in detail of comparable variety. Such work on more detail includes the redefinition of the levels of a taxonomy. In the case of Carol, our college consultant, further interviews disclosed that a "mick" was a kind of easy class, so the taxonomy had to be restructured as shown in Figure 2.8. In other words, the elicitation of folk taxonomies and of folk definitions feed into each other: Folk definitions often affect the structure of previously obtained taxonomies.

Further questioning via folk definitions showed, for example, that "boring class," "easy class," and "hard class" should not be part of the same contrast set. Carol said that some easy classes as well as hard classes may be boring or interesting. Thus we have here a cross-classification (see Figures 2.9 and 2.10).

Evens et al. (1980) call such cross-classifying, independent taxonomies "orthogonal taxonomies" (see also Wallace and Atkins 1960). That is, each such

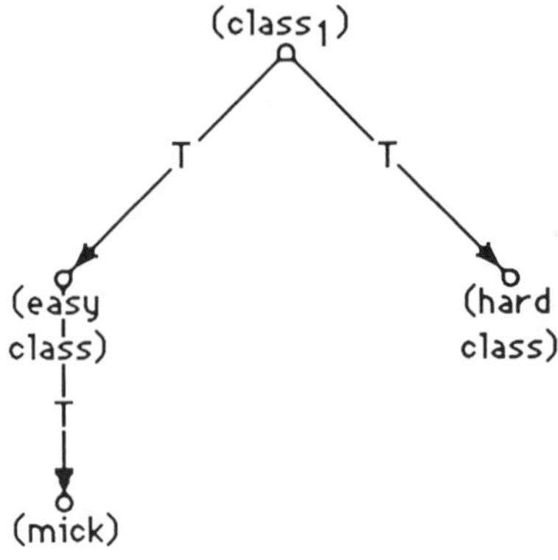

Figure 2.9 Taxonomy of Carol's Classes IVa

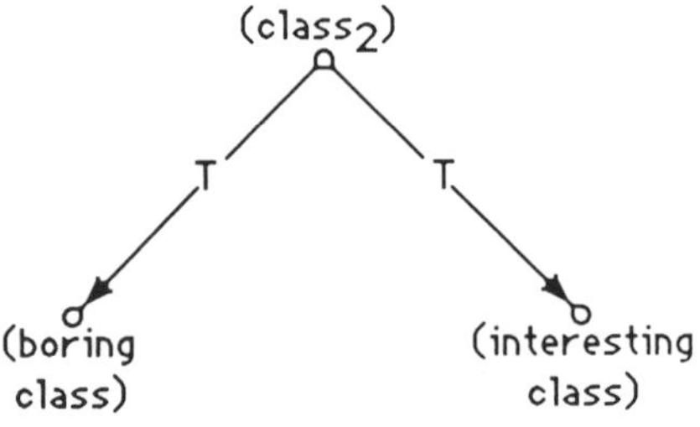

Figure 2.10 Taxonomy of Carol's Classes IVb

taxonomy is an independent classification, as if in another dimension. The classifications of people as enemies-friends, babies through old age, by nationality, kinship allegiance, occupation, and so on are common examples of orthogonal taxonomies with the same superordinate node. Each is an alternative way in which to classify the same set of objects. Each is an alternate, independent contrast set. Focusing one's attention on one set, the competing classifications seem to recede in importance. It is difficult for most humans to keep more than one orthogonal contrast set in focal awareness at one time.

We have mentioned several factors that affect the elicitation of taxonomies. One is the social group(s) to which the consultant belongs. Others are context, assumptions about the knowledge of the hearer, limitations of human awareness, and certainly other factors. As our example of Carol's classes demonstrates, it is therefore unrealistic to expect to elicit a valid taxonomy on the first try.

2.3 WORD ASSOCIATIONS

For a variety of reasons it is sometimes difficult for a consultant to make up folk definitions. It is possible in these cases to use another form of elicitation, a variant of the word association tests used by psychologists. In ethnoscience, word association is *not* used as a psychological test. In psychology, the consultant is presented with a stimulus word (the word to be defined from the ethnographer's viewpoint) and the consultant responds with the first word(s) that come(s) to mind. The response should be as quick and as automatic as possible. Casagrande and Hale (1967) discovered that such word associations and folk definitions have much in common. The pairs that occur in word associations and the pairs of words into which one can analyze folk definitions display similar relationships.

2.3.1 Semantic Relations of Casagrande and Hale

In addition to the lexical/semantic relation of taxonomy, Casagrande and Hale (1967) discuss 12 other types of relations that reflect lexical/semantic principles of organization. They found these relations in their work with about 800 folk definitions in Papago (an American Indian language of southern Arizona). All of these relations can be used in the systematization and analysis of folk definitions in any languge.

Casagrande and Hale (1967) define a definition as a statement of a lexical/semantic relation between the concept being defined and one or more other concepts presumed to be known to the hearer (or reader) and having properties considered relevant to the term being defined. These properties are discussed using a set of presumably mutually exclusive types of lexical/semantic relations.

Twelve Relations of Casagrande and Hale

Each type of relation is defined and exemplified below. The presentation follows the order of frequency of occurrence in the Papago folk definitions.

(1) Attributive. X is defined with respect to one or more distinctive or characteristic attributes Y. Such attributes can be stimulus properties such as color, size, shape, or texture. Or they can be extrinsic, expressing some evaluative notion, such as pretty or dangerous. (*Example:* "Apples are edible, red fruits.")

In addition, attributive relations can also emphasize some distinctive marker of the object under consideration. (*Example:* "Lobsters have claws.")

Habitat, behavior, or action are also attributes used to define objects. (*Example:* "Bees make honey and live in hives.")

Finally, age, sex, line of descent, and generation are additional features, usually associated with kin terms or status terms that can be used in definitions. (*Example:* "A mother is the woman who gives birth to the child.")

(2) Contingency. X is defined with relation to a usual or necessary antecedent or concomitant Y. There are two possibilities: Either X can be defined in relation to some condition or event Y which X usually follows, or X is defined with reference to some condition or event Y which is its usual or necessary concomitant. (*Examples:* "A rainbow is what comes after rain." "If it rains, it thunders." "If you are hungry, you eat.")

(3) Function. X is defined as the means of effecting Y. This definition follows from the sentence type, "We perform Y with (the aid of) X" or "Y is performed with (the aid of) X." (*Example:* "The ear is that through which we hear when something is said.")

(4) Spatial. X is oriented spatially with respect to Y. (*Example:* "Fingers are digits on the end of the hand.")

(5) Operational. X is defined with respect to an action Y of which it is a characteristic goal or recipient. (*Example:* "Brushes are used to paint with.")

(6) Comparison. X is defined in terms of its similarity to and/or contrast with Y. *(Example:* "A coyote is an animal like a dog.")

(7) Exemplification. X is defined by citing an example of an appropriate cooccurrent Y. Relationships of this type are the inverse of the relationships of attribution. In exemplification, the attribute itself is being defined rather than the possessor of the attribute. X may be an adjective being defined by citing a noun. (*Example:* "Red is the color of an apple.") X may also be a noun that is being defined by citing a characteristic possession of it. (*Example:* "Antlers are what deer have.")

(8) Class Inclusion. X is defined with respect to its membership in a hierarchical class Y. Characteristic definitions of this sort follow the formula "X is a Y." (*Example:* "A filly is a horse.")

(9) Synonymy. X is defined as being equivalent to Y. Complete synonymy of terms is a debatable issue. The equivalence of X and Y in this type of definition is often only approximate, but the meaning of each term is very close to the meaning of the other. (*Example:* "A car is an automobile.")

(10) Antonomy. X is defined as the negation of Y which is considered its opposite. *(Example:* "Short is not tall.")

(11) Provenience. X is defined with respect to its source Y. (*Example:* "Milk comes from cows.")

(12) Circularity. X is defined as X. In definitions of this type, the concept being defined and the concept to which it is related are represented by the same morpheme (word). Thus circular definitions give very little or no information about meaning. (*Example:* "The truth is simply the truth.")

Although Casagrande and Hale's (1967) relations have been used in the analysis of folk definitions, all applications have been difficult. There are several reasons for this: (1) The relations are not exclusive of each other. (2) The functions of these relations may be assumed by "titles" for sections of a composite folk definition (see Figure 2.7). (3) This set of relations can be reduced to a much smaller set than that indicated by Casagrande and Hale.

A reduced set of relations is proposed, for example, by Werner and Topper (1976): the MTQ schema, which is explained in Section 2.3 of Volume 1. Their reduced set is identical to fundamental or atomic definitions. An atomic definition is the simplest possible definition; it consists of two words (or naming units), the one to be defined and the other a generalized attribute. Thus "Grass is green" is an atomic definition relating "grass" to "green" attributively. Similarly, "Grass is a plant" is also an atomic definition relating "grass" to "plant" taxonomically or as class inclusion in the Casagrande and Hale (1967) set.

2.3.2 Word Association Chains

Folk definitions constructed from word associations utilize this similarity between atomic definitions and word associations; however, the consultant is asked not only to mention just the *first* word that comes to mind but also to keep mentioning as many additional words as possible. This limit is usually reached with a chain of about 5 ± 2 words. The method works as shown in Figure 2.11.

Often, as in Figure 2.11, the "tail" of the chain, "Abe" and "Bicentennial," can be disregarded. The word associations of the consultant have trailed off into irrelevant or less relevant directions that do not contribute directly to the folk definition. The first two responses are useful; however, usefulness is determined not by the interviewer but by the responding consultant himself or herself.

After the chain is obtained, we continue the elicitation by asking the consultant to explain why he or she selected a particular term. The resulting dialogue determines the relevance of an association to the definition. The justification of a certain word by the consultant usually sheds additional light on the definition.

For the chain in Figure 2.11, we obtained the following text: "A sincere person is a good person. It is only good persons that are capable of sincerity. I would imagine that sincerity is a form of honesty." From this response we deduce the folk definition by the word association technique as shown in Figure 2.12 (if necessary after more discussion with the consultant).

In other words, the word association technique is primarily a method for reducing the consultant's anxieties about having to define a term and thus exposing his or her knowledge (or lack of it) to public view and possibly criticism. The more intuitive nature of word associations compared to regular folk definitions makes

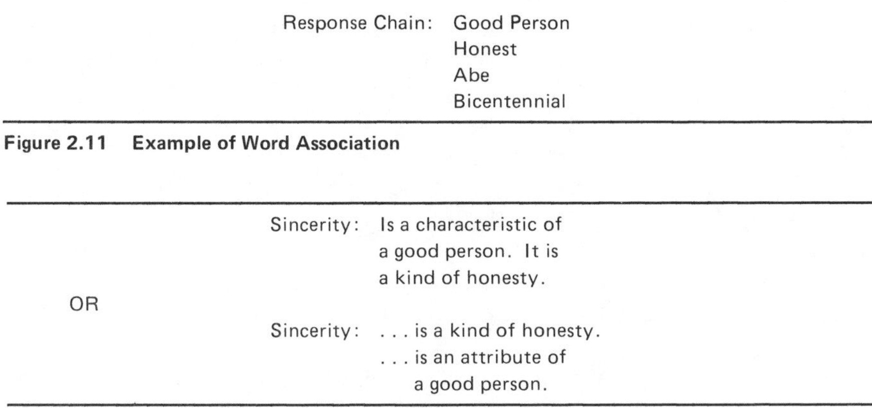

Figure 2.11 Example of Word Association

Figure 2.12 Folk Definition from Word Association

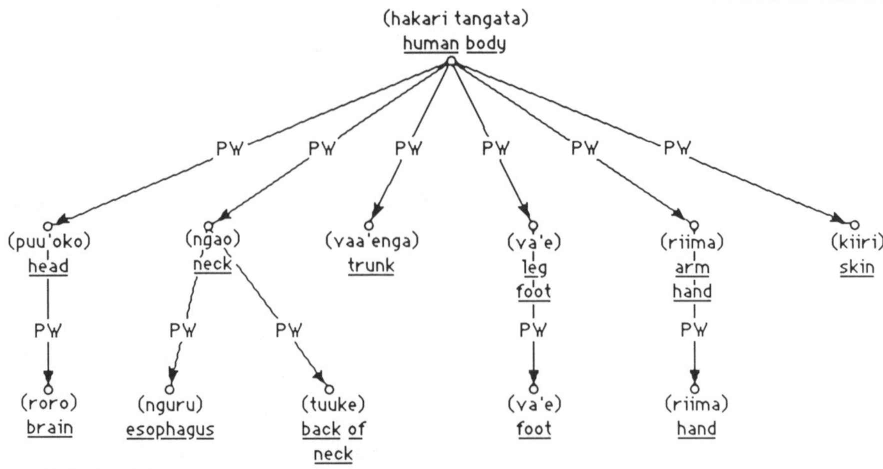

Figure 2.13 Body Parts on Rapa Nui (Easter Island): A Partial Set

responding easier. The results, as far as we can tell, remain the same; therefore, folk definitions by word association chains are useful, especially when working with children who are often not yet articulate enough to form and produce ordinary folk definitions with ease.

2.4 PART/WHOLE RELATION

In many areas of human cultural knowledge it is important to understand how parts constitute some whole. Interestingly, Casagrande and Hale (1967) were surprised when their sample failed to yield this relation, which they called "constituency." However, some of the examples we list under Attribution ("Lobsters have claws"), Exemplification ("Antlers are what deer have"), and possibly Spatial ("Fingers are digits on the end of the hand") can be interpreted as paraphrases of the part/whole relation. In some languages the preferred form of talking about parts may not be the PW relation but one of its paraphrasers—for example, its inverse. (For some items "A has B" is the inverse of "B is a part of A"). The most typical examples of this relation are body parts. In every human language there are several levels of parts and subparts that compose the entire human body. For example, Figure 2.13 shows a classification of body parts by the inhabitants of Rapa Nui (Easter Island). Translation labels are in quotes. (Note that the arrows are now labeled PW.)

The items on the various levels of this part/whole classification are linked by the sentence, *"Te X he pareehe o te Y."* Translated: "The X is a part/piece/portion of the Y."

We symbolize the linking part/whole sentence by an arrow labeled PW. The part/whole relationship applies to anatomical terms, tools, houses, the landscape, and many other phenomena of everyday life. We have found that while the sentences standing for the part/whole relation in English are elicited with relative ease from adults, in other languages and in the case of children (Litowitz & Novy 1984) elicitation becomes more difficult. Part of this difficulty is due to the complexity and multiple ambiguity of the part/whole relation (Iris *et al.* 1984).

The prepositions used by various peoples of the world to link parts to wholes also sometimes make recognizing a part/whole relation difficult. The prepositions "at" and "with" seem to be quite common. It seems that every language gives a slightly different meaning to its part/whole relation—for example, in English, "The hand has a thumb" to "The thumb is a part of the hand"; in Hopi, "The thumb is at the hand"; in Navajo, "The thumb occupies some of the same space as the hand"; and in Rapa Nui, "The thumb is a piece/portion of the hand." It is therefore uncertain whether the part/whole relation is the "same" in all cultures. In any case, its status as a universal is less certain than that of the taxonomic relation. Universal relations allow us to see strange categories (taxons) in familiar structures (Topper 1972:48). Note "X has a Y" as a possible inverse to the part/whole relation in English. Similar inverses are possible in other languages.

There is at least one theoretical orientation, all descended from Łešnievsky's meroetic (part/whole) logic (see Tarski 1937, or Luschei 1962), which claims universality and the fundamental position of the part/whole relation. Werner and co-workers (e.g., Werner & Topper 1976) were able to derive the part/whole relation from the atomic relation of modification (M). So far we have been unable to derive T from PW (for details see Volume 1, Section 2.3.2).

The depth of a classification (part/whole mixed with taxonomic in Figure 2.14) is a rough indication of the depth of a consultant's knowledge on a given topic. The depth of the Rapa Nui part/whole classification in Figure 2.13 is attested by following the "branch" in the tree structure through the subordinate node *"puu'oko"* (head) to the terminal nodes.

The example in Figure 2.14 also shows how in some systems the part/whole and the taxonomic classifications alternate; that is, whereas the teeth are part of the inside of the mouth, the different kinds of teeth are variants or types of (kind of) teeth.

2.4.1 Serial Ordering of Part/Whole Relations

The part/whole relation and a culturally determined strict ordering of the parts does not seem to be uncommon. In the Rapa Nui example (Figure 2.13) the order of the head, neck, trunk, legs and feet, arms and hands, and the skin is (to the best of our knowledge) arbitrarily or loosely from top to bottom. The Rapa Nui consultants were noncommital about a strict order, and we used the "usual" order from head to toe.

In Navajo, however, the order of the body parts is strictly prescribed. The anatomical parts are mentioned in prayers in every Navajo ceremony; but since the direction of growth is from the earth toward the sky, the proper or sacred *(diyin)*

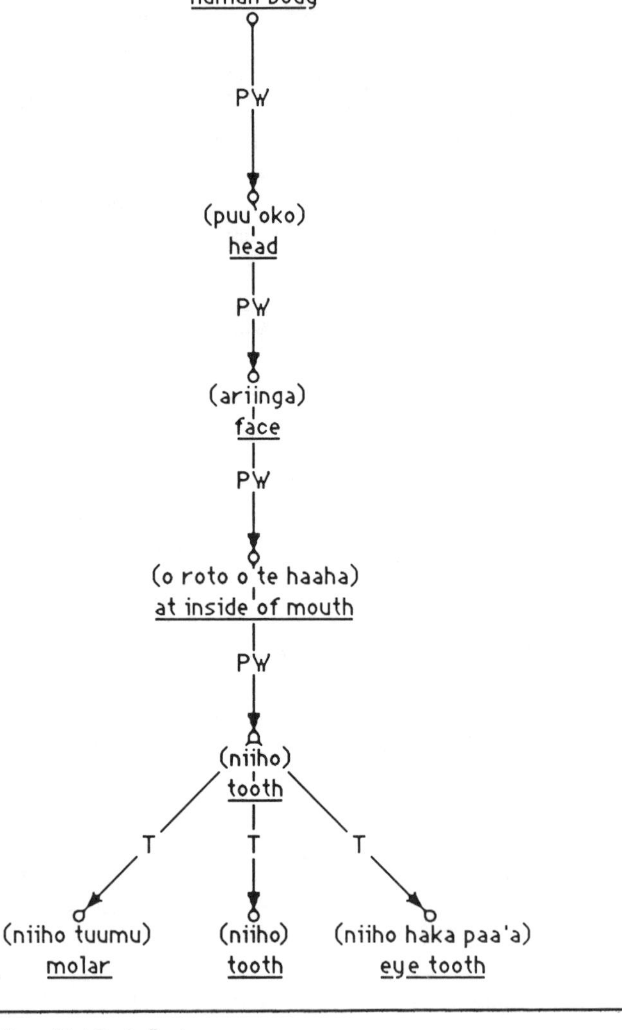

2.14 Subsystem of Rapa Nui Body Parts

order of presentation or description of the body is from the feet to the head. This is diagrammed in Figure 2.15.

Other ordering of parts may be dictated, for example, by the order in which a tool or a piece of machinery is assembled. Technical manuals often describe repairs by specifying the best order in which to take a piece of equipment apart. This seems to imply that the part/whole relation and the relation of ordering are often intimately associated. This is indeed the case and far exceeds the examples cited

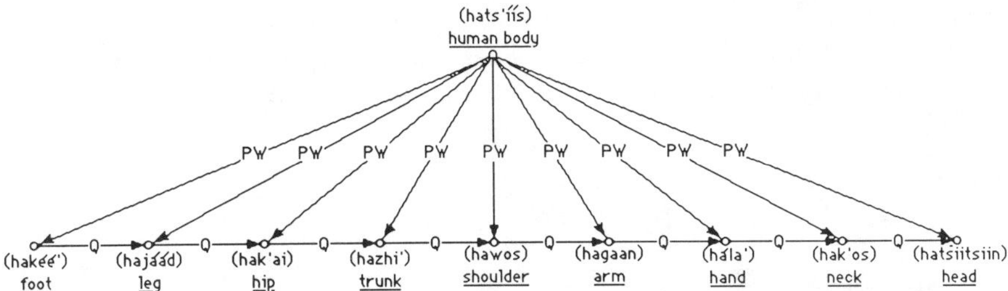

NOTE: The arrows from left to right are marked Q, implying the ordering or queueing relation of the parts of the body in Navajo.

Figure 2.15 Linear Ordering of Navajo Body Parts

above. We will discuss the interrelation of order and part/whole in the section on plans (3.1).

In English and other languages, there is a special "abstract" way of talking about parts: "X is an aspect of Y." The exact relationship between part/whole and "aspect of" is at present not completely understood. We suspect that many other relations of spatial organization, such as the part/whole relation, have applications to abstract concepts in many, if not all languages. Our chief example comes from an analysis of the concept of "thought" in English (Werner & Begishe 1968) based on dictionary definitions (as if they were consultant's folk definitions). See Figure 2.16.

In this instance, the arrow of the part/whole relation can be replaced by the aspect relation; that is, "thought (acts) are an aspect of thought" seems to us to sound better than "thought (acts) are a part of thought." In Navajo, for example,

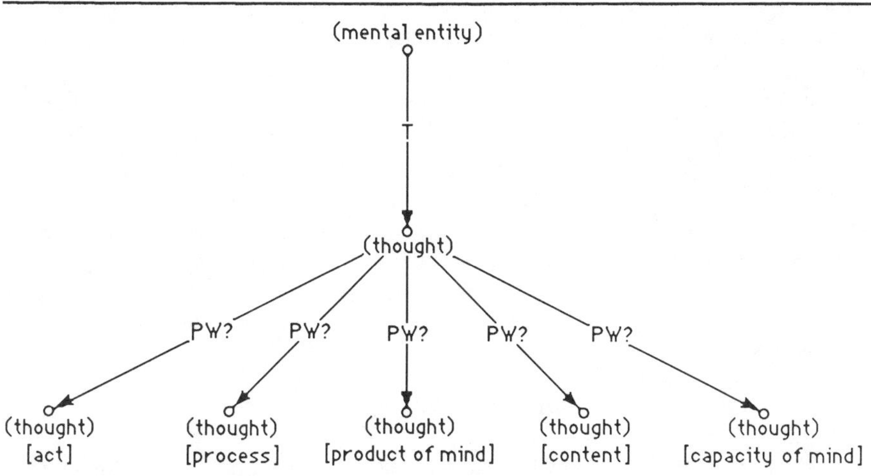

Figure 2.16 Aspects of Thought

application of concrete "classificatory verb stems" to abstract concepts abound. The "roundish object" category may be used for stories and tales, while the mixed objects category may be applied to the internal parts of the body or to thoughts (see Garrison 1974).

2.5 ANCILLARY TECHNIQUES

Although the techniques described in this section are termed "ancillary," their importance in the analysis of interviews or in an ethnoscience ethnography is far greater than their position at the end of this section on structural analysis implies. Part of the reason for this is that ethnoscience theory has not made significant inroads with the evaluative/affective dimension of human cultural knowledge. We do not know how to include evaluative statements into an ethnoscience ethnography in any other form but intuitively as informal comment rather than as theoretically motivated statements (however, see Sections 6.2. and 6.3 and Colby 1975). Our theoretical models do not tell us how such evaluations and "pure" unevaluated cultural knowledge (what we tend to describe in ethnoscience) are connected. At the same time, we are more than casually aware of the fact that there are indeed few, if any, aspects of human cultural knowledge that are not also evaluated in one way or another. It is because of this lack of theoretical consistency with the rest of ethnoscience theory that the techniques best suited to the elicitation of evaluative statements are listed last (see also Section 6.2 and following).

2.5.1 Context-Sensitive Elicitation

It is conceivable that a taxonomy of values can be constructed from elicited data by following the techniques listed below, although we believe values are not only hierarchically taxonomic. In addition, values or evaluations are context sensitive; for example, in some cultures a man should marry his mother's brother's daughter, but there are contingency plans for cases in which the mother has no brother or the brother no daughter. In other words, values are arranged (by the relation Q of order?) by priority or preference. For example, "Do A; if A is impossible, do B; or else C." This looks to us like an ideal situation for the application of decision tables (see Chapter 4). Madelyn Iris (n.d.) used these in a study of how contexts determine how one Navajo would address another given the complexities of Navajo clan kinship reckoning, sexual attraction, and the values the speaker attaches to the quality or nature of the ensuing relationship to each other and to their social milieu.

Case 2.1 Context and Kinship Terminology

A young Navajo woman, married, with one small child, recently drove up to her mother's sheep camp and met a young man from another part of the reservation. She had never seen this man before but found him very personable and attractive. The attraction was mutual and in order to protect themselves from gossip while they maintained a platonic relationship they decided to find out if they were both of the same [mother's] clan. The young man quickly stated that this being the case they should call each other "brother" and "sister." The woman's daughter is being instructed to call the young man "mother's brother" (Iris, n.d.).

The use of a specific set of kin terms served to define the relationship established by the young man and woman. It placed them in a perspective or "context" that, in spite of their mutual attraction, could be viewed by other Navajos as proper.

2.5.2 Slip-Sorting Techniques

These techniques are perhaps the most valuable ones for eliciting value judgments, though they are not restricted to that exclusively. Cultural items the consultant is expected to evaluate, sort, and so on are each listed on a separate card, sheet, or slip of paper. The consultant is then asked to sort the cards in a number of ways that come to mind. For example, cards with the names of classmates can be sorted in at least the following ways: by evaluation on a good-bad student continuum, by evaluation of who is liked or disliked, or by friendship cliques.

After sorting, consultants are asked to explain their choices. This procedure supplies additional information about the reasons for a particular evaluation. After such a discussion, it is sometimes possible to shuffle all cards and ask for a sorting in some other way by specifying a different context. For example, Mim Dixon (personal communication) elicited different sortings of food terms when she asked students to sort them in preparation for a long hike or for going out on the town for gourmet dining. The entire sorting procedure may thus be repeated several times. Such alternative sortings are analogous to the orthogonal taxonomies mentioned in Section 2.2.2 (especially Figures 2.9 and 2.10).

The following example of an actual interview session with slip sorting is used to illustrate how a consultant's responses to the technique, plus the interview questions that follow, provide a list of contrast sets, taxonomic relations, and folk definitions (adapted from Werner, Schoepfle, *et al.* 1976).

Case 2.2 Different Kinds of Students

The consultant was a high school student discussing different kinds of students encountered in his school. (E: Ethnographer, S: Student).

E: When you go through classes throughout the day, I guess you encounter different groups of students. Rather than my asking you what kinds of students there are, could I have you take any class you have throughout the day—it doesn't matter what class—and just list the people in that class, one name to a card, and then group these cards any way you want?

S: Like how?

E: Any way you want.

S: OK. [both pause here] Right now?

E: Sure, take your time . . . and when you have the names on these cards, put the cards in different stacks, any way you want to, according to any rule you feel like. [Both pause]

S: OK. [The student writes names of other students on the cards and places them in different stacks.]

E: OK, I see five different piles of cards here; how are they different?

S: By their ability in class.

E: Uh-huh.

S: Well, [first pile] Darlene, Doris, and Brian . . . they understand it pretty good . . . they can get it through their head and keep it there. And [second pile] Geraldine, Jennifer, Betty, and Phil, they're all about the same. . . . I guess they understand it too and keep it in their head, but they disagree about some things they have to do.

E: Uh-huh.

S: Then [third pile] Kim and Gerry . . . they just take the notes down. I guess they memorize it.

E: They take notes down . . . and memorize it, you say?

S: So they'll remember it, I guess.

E: I see, and the next group?

S: Kathy and Beverly, Bobby and Phyllis [fourth pile] . . . ummm . . . they just fool around in that class. . . . They get it a few times . . . not really all the time. And Gloria and Betty [fifth pile] . . . they just don't care, I guess.

E: Don't care?

S: They don't learn anything in there.

E: When you mention the first group and the second group . . . you say, they could keep it in their head, but the second group disagrees with what they have to do . . .

S: Yeah.

E: I'm not clear . . .

S: Well, they can get it, they can remember, they don't really forget . . .

E: Don't care as long as they get a good grade. . . .

S: Yeah, just so they learn it; something like that.

E: And in the second group, they can keep it in their head, but they disagree on what they have to do . . .

S: Yeah, they say they like what they're being taught, or don't like what they're being taught.

E: When you say they don't agree with what's being taught, what are some of the ways in which they don't agree, like . . . what do they say?

S: How the teacher teaches it, what kind of assignments he gives . . . I think that's it.

E: OK, in the third group, they take down notes and memorize . . .

S: Well, I don't know if they memorize it, but they just take notes. I don't know if they learn anything or not.

E: Do they disagree with what's being taught? Do they ever disagree with the teacher?

S: Not really.

E: I see, and how do they differ, say, from those that don't care as long as they get a good grade?

S: I don't know. [laughs]

E: OK, the next group fools around and gets it a few times?

S: Yeah, well, they listen once in a while . . .

E: Uh-huh.

S: . . . to some stories that are, you know, . . . some interesting stuff that they're being taught.

E: Uh-huh. How are they different, say, from those that disagree?

S: Well, they just never really listen . . . to what's being taught.

E: Never listen . . .

S: Yeah, just talking to each other all the time . . . they listen every once in a while.

E: Uh-huh, and the fifth group . . . they don't care, and they learn nothing?

S: Yeah, . . . they hardly come to class, and when the tests come, they just start saying stuff like they don't know what it's all about. The teacher tries telling them that they weren't here a certain time, when they were taught, but they don't . . . well . . . they just put anything on the test.

Going through the interview we get the following definitions and classifications:

Pile 1: Students who can get it through their head
they understand it
they can keep it in their heads

Pile 2: Students who can get it through their head
they understand it
they can keep it in their heads
they disagree about some things they have to do

Note that the titles were adjusted so that both piles are labeled the same way. At this point, Pile 2 looks like a subpile of 1. Piles 3, 4, and 5 are labeled as follows:

Pile 3: Students who take down notes and memorize them
(thus they remember it)
Pile 4: Students who fool around in class
they get it a few times, not really all the time
Pile 5: Students who don't care
they don't learn anything

At this point the ethnographer decided to probe further to see if there is more structure to the classification. The new attributes are listed as the consultant mentioned them for each group.

Pile 1
they can get it
they can remember
they don't really forget
they don't really care what it is as long as they get a good grade
they just learn it
Pile 2
they say they like what they're being taught
they say they don't like what they're being taught
Pile 3
they take notes
they (may?) memorize [see previous response]
they may learn something
they don't disagree with what is being taught
Pile 4
they listen every once in a while to some stories,
interesting stuff that they are being taught
they rarely listen
they just talk to each other all the time
Pile 5
they hardly come to class
when tests come, they say they don't know what it's all about
they just put anything on a test

By combining all attributes it is clear that there are two groups of good students who can "get it through their heads": "Students who will learn just anything" for a good grade and students who dislike some subjects and say so, thus the slip sorting, combined with the further probing results in the taxonomy shown in Figure 2.17 according to classroom performance.

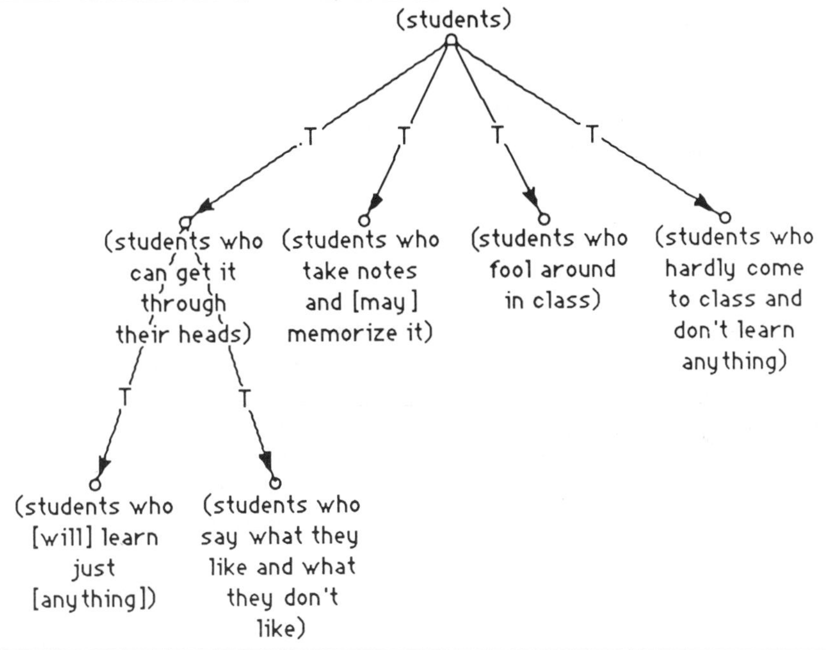

Figure 2.17 Kinds of Students from the Slip Sorting

Obviously, at this point the two lists of attributes are collated. If further interviews with the consultant are possible, one could attempt to obtain the same type and same amount of information for each group of students. For example, one would want to know if the good students (Piles 1 and 2) ever take notes; or, since the last group (Pile 5) hardly ever comes to class, if the other groups (Piles 1, 2, 3, 4) hardly ever miss class, and so on.

The order in which this student-consultant listed his peers implies that he belongs to the group of Pile 1 and evaluates the group in Pile 5 negatively or most negatively. Further questions along this line might reveal the student's attitudes toward her peers more explicitly.

The technique of analysis applied in this example to an interview—in this instance with the aid of card sorting—we have termed "white card analysis" (see Section 9.1). That is, the taxonomic tree classification in Figure 2.17 and the attribute lists for each taxon of the taxonomy are first recorded on white 5 × 8 (127 × 203 mm) file cards, one for each consultant. Only later do we try to combine white cards into composite definitions derived from several consultants. We do this on a yellow card. This technique of analysis is described in detail in Section 9.1.

An alternative to the simple slip-sorting technique is the triad test (see Section 8.5). Here, each set of slips is separated into every possible combination of three. The consultant chooses any two cards out of the three that are most similar or, alternatively, the one card that is least like the other two. He or she is then asked to explain this choice. In addition to value judgments, the consultant also responds to similarities and differences in attributes. Thus this technique can be used to validate folk definitions or word associational definitions (see Sections 2.2 and 2.3). It has been used successfully in combination with multidimensional scaling. Unfortunately, at present there exist no studies exploring the correlation of texts or folk definitions with the graphs of multidimensional scaling.

2.5.3 Tree Drawing

Consultants can be taught the principles of taxonomic or part/whole tree diagrams quickly. The best teaching method involves drawing a previously elicited taxonomy. With a little encouragement, consultants will start drawing tree structures on their own. These drawings, though rarely as analytically clean as one would hope, give the ethnographer important clues to the semantic fields and the interconnections between words or naming units. In other words, while the ethnographer must clearly separate, for example, a taxonomic tree from a part/whole tree, consultants do not readily accept the same rigorous methodological constraints. Therefore the ethnographer's task is to inspect a consultant's tree structures and to determine, usually in a special interview, the exact meanings of the lines the consultant has drawn between certain lexical items. Very often obscure relationships between terms are implied by a consultant's connecting lines. In dealing with Navajo psychological/ethical terminology, we discovered that the consultant's line connecting two terms was often our first clue to an important relationship between these terms (Werner and Begishe 1968). For example, in the Navajo suicide terminology, Marilyn Morgan (1973) discovered that the lines drawn by consultants implied a plan and a causal chain of events. But ascertaining the exact nature of that underlying relation was not always easy and often required lenghty additional interviews.

Tree drawing, in addition, is one of the principal techniques for eliciting *upward* in taxonomies or part/whole tree structures. There are no easily formulated questions in any language that make elicitation upward through a taxonomy as easy as the almost automatic procedures so effective when working downward from a general term to the specifics under it. Questions such as "What is a plant a kind of?" (in search of a term such as "living things") are met by most consultants with disbelief or lack of understanding of what is wanted. By tree drawing it can be shown how such a classification extends downward and, by analogy, how it may also extend upward to more general terms. After some thought many consultants are able to produce superordinate nodes without too much difficulty.

2.5.4 Belief Systems/Abstract Terms

The ultimate method for eliciting upward or, more accurately, for eliciting some of the most general concepts of a culture is through the elicitation of texts dealing with the consultants' system of belief. In Navajo culture, as in many nonliterate cultures, the body of mythology, especially the mythology dealing with cosmology, contains some of the most valuable clues about the most general and salient terms (words, naming units) of that culture. For the interested reader we recommend especially Werner, Manning, and Begishe (1983), "A Taxonomic View of the Traditional Navajo Universe."

H. Russel Bernard (personal communication) introduced in his study of modern Greek belief systems an innovative field technique. From preliminary texts he obtained a small set of key terms that consultants recognized as crucial to the belief systems of modern Greeks. He printed each term at the top of a 5 × 8 card and then asked a group of consultants to define each term (folk definition). Next, he requested each consultant to underline what he or she considered key terms of the Greek worldview within the transcribed definitions. Each underlined term was then placed on a new set of cards. These were then added to the stack of unprocessed cards. The project was completed months later when Bernard reached diminishing returns.

2.5.5 Componential Analysis

In a componential analysis the basic assumption is that the terms to be analyzed form a legitimate semantic domain and that the data to be analyzed can be adequately described by decomposing complex meanings into a minimal set of atoms of meaning or semantic components (also called semantic features). The aim is to discover the makeup of the meanings of words or names in the object language and state these meanings as minimally adequate *bundles of semantic features* in a meta-language (the ethnographer's language of description) as parsimoniously as possible (for details see Tyler 1969). Componential analysis therefore provides a method for defining the meaning of terms according to minimal criteria employed by the users.

Componential analyses have been applied most often to systems of kinship terms. Kinship systems seem to be universal cultural knowledge systems. The boundaries between kin terms and nonkin terms (domain boundary) are relatively easy to locate. The set of kin terms is generally small (rarely more than 50 terms) and the domain is highly lexicalized; that is, many (most) possible combinations of components (attributes) have a word or phrase attached to them (Weinreich 1963). Other domains of cultural knowledge rarely possess all of these characteristics that together make a set of words or phrases amenable to componential analysis.

Componential Procedures

A componential analysis begins by constructing what has been called a "paradigm." Each paradigm has "dimensions"; each dimension has contrasting components. In the analysis of kinship, typical dimensions are sex, relative age, generational distance, and collateral distance. The features or components of each dimension form the set of values a component can assume in each dimension (Lounsbury 1964). Thus for the dimension of sex, the features are either "male" or "female," often indicated as either (+male) or (-male)—that is, "female." For the dimension generational distance, the features are in the form of degrees, indicated by +1 or +2 for ascending generations and -1 or -2 for descending generations. Each word (name) of the domain (e.g., kin term) can be defined by listing the components associated with it; that is, one and only one component for each dimension. For instance, a componential definition of the English kin term "mother" is (+female, +1 generation, +0 degrees collaterally)—that is, she is female, one generation above "ego" and in a direct line with "ego," the user of the term "mother."

Wallace and Atkins (1960) specify five steps to follow when doing a componential analysis:

(1) The ethnographer records the complete domain or set (or a defined subset) of words or names that belong together. In a kinship system, these are either terms of reference or terms of address. When recording the terms, boundary setting is usually accomplished by a taxonomic question. In kinship studies in English, the question "Is X a relative (of yours)?" will exclude all nonrelatives.

(2) The ethnographer then applies to the words or names obtained through step 1 the traditional kin-type notations—for example, Fa (father), FaBr (father's brother), DaHuBr (daugher's husand's brother). This set of descriptive terms has been called an "etic" grid. Componential analysis is difficult in domains that do not have an easily identifiable etic grid. The "eticness" of this grid is debatable; for example, FaBrSo (father's brother's son) and "cousin" are both naming units in English, hence they are "emic." On the emic/etic controversy, we refer the reader to Fisher and Werner (1978).

(3) The ethnographer must sort the kin terms into groups of kin-types. There should be a sorting (often a sorting of slips with a kin term on each slip) by each dimension. For example, a sorting on the dimension of sex will result in two piles, one for each sex.

(4) The ethnographer defines each term by using a symbolic notation; the value of each dimension receives a symbol. Values of a dimension must be recognizable as a set. It is a good idea to identify each dimension as a set of values; for example, Dimension D(sex) = (+male, -male); D(generation) = (. . .+2,+1,0,-1,-2,. . .), and so on.

(5) The ethnographer states the semantic relationships among the terms and the structural principles linking the terminological system.

Case 2.3 Componential Analysis: Yankee Kin Terms

The following example of a componential analysis was done by Wallace and Atkins (1960) following the five steps outlined above. One boundary setting criterion used in their study was the question "Is X a blood relative?" Five terms—"uncle," "aunt," "cousin," nephew," and "niece"—are used in their extended sense; that is, the term "cousin" included, for example, all "second cousins once removed," and so on. All aunts in the sense of "great aunt" and nephews in the sense of "grand-nephew" were included under "aunt" and "nephew" respectively.

In the first step a list of recorded kin terms (consanguineal or blood relative only) is given as well as the traditional kin-type notation (step two) (see Figure 2.18).

Step three proceeds by noting certain principles of grouping. All terms (except cousin) specify sex, collateral distance (lineal or nonlineal descent), generational distance, and number of links, ascending or descending.

Given these specifics, only three dimensions are required for defining all "Yankee" terms. The first dimension, designated arbitrarily "a," is sex. It has two values:

a(1) = male
a(2) = female

The second dimension, designated "b," indicates generation (vertical distance). We show only two generations in each direction from "ego's" generation. This dimension has therefore five values:

b(1) = two generations above ego
b(2) = one generation above ego
b(3) = ego's own generation
b(4) = one generation below ego
b(5) = two generations below ego

The dimension of lineality or collaterality (horizontal distance) is indicated by "c." The values are:

c(1) = lineal relationship
c(2) = colineal relationship
c(3) = ablineal relationship

Goodenough (1956), who introduced these terms for the dimension of collaterality, defines them in the following manner:

lineals = persons who are ancestors or descendants of ego
colineals = nonlineals whose ancestors include or are included in all the ancestors of ego
ablineals = consanguineal relatives who are neither lineals nor colineals

(Colineal and ablineal relatives are sometimes called collaterals.)

Grandfather:	FaFa, MoFa	Uncle:	FaBr, MoBr, FaFaBr, MoFaBr, etc.
Grandmother:	FaMo, MoMo		
Father:	Fa	Aunt:	FaSi, MoSi, FaFaSi, MoFaSi, etc.
Mother:	Mo		
Brother:	Br	Cousin:	FaBrSo, FaBrDa, MoBrSo, MoSiSo, MoSiDa, FaFaBrS, FaMoBrSo, MoFaSiDa, etc.
Sister:	Si		
Son:	So		
Daughter:	Da	Nephew:	BrSo, SiSo, BrSoSo, SiSoSo, etc.
Grandson:	SoSo, DaSo	Niece:	BrDa, SiDa, BrDaDa, SiDaDa, etc.
Granddaughter:	SoDa, DaDa		

Figure 2.18 Abbreviations for Kinship Terms

Figure 2.19 a two-dimensional componential diagram in matrix form. It is graphed by using the dimensions and the specific values of each dimension. The intersections of the dimensions create componential definitions. Each definition can contain only one value from each dimension.

It is now possible to read off the "componential" definition for each term from Figure 2.19. We indicate the neutralization of a set of values by listing all that apply. If all values of a dimension are listed, then the dimension is neutralized, or irrelevant to the definition. The comma between components implies that the bundles of components form sets (Figure 2.20).

Multiple values given for a dimension imply the neutralization of contrast for that dimension; for example, for "cousin," a(1,2) implies that sex of a cousin is either male or female; generation is either same as ego's, descending one or two steps, or ascending one or two steps. Only the ablineality of cousins is unique.

The value of a componential paradigm is that it is very easy to "read," especially if it shows a kin term system very different from our own. This is because many dimensions are cultural universals, at least in the sense that there exists a universal pool of dimensions from which every kinship terminological system selects a subset. In addition, a componential paradigm has no overlapping terms, nor does any one term include another. Each term is discriminated from the next by at least one feature or component (or one value of a dimension).

Before accepting a componential analysis, several unresolved analytical problems must be considered (Wallace & Atkins 1960):

(1) The problem of homonyms and metaphors
(2) The problem of denotation versus connotation
(3) The problem of complementarity, paradigms, and spaces
(4) The problem of noncommutative relational concepts
(5) The problem of psychological reality
(6) The indeterminacy of semantic analysis

	c_1		c_2		c_3
	a_1	a_2	a_1	a_2	
b_1	grandfather	grandmother	uncle	aunt	cousin
b_2	father	mother			
b_3	ego		brother	sister	
b_4	son	daughter	nephew	niece	
b_5	grandson	granddaughter			

Figure 2.19 Matrix of English Kinship Terms

Grandfather:	a(1), b(1), c(1)
Grandmother:	a(2), b(1), c(1)
Father:	a(1), b(2), c(1)
Mother:	a(2), b(2), c(1)
Brother:	a(1), b(3), c(2)
Sister:	a(2), b(3), c(2)
Son:	a(1), b(4), c(1)
Daughter:	a(2), b(4), c(1)
Grandson:	a(1), b(5), c(1)
Granddaughter:	a(2), b(5), c(1)
Uncle:	a(1), b(1,2), c(2) (in ascending generation steps irrelevant, i.e., neutralized)
Aunt:	a(1), b(1,2), c(2) (in ascending generation steps irrelevant, i.e., neutralized)
Nephew:	a(1), b4,5), c(2) (in descending generation steps irrelevant, i.e., neutralized)
Niece:	a(2), b(4,5), c(2) (in descending generation steps irrelevant, i.e., neutralized)
Cousin:	a(1,2), b(1,2,3,4,5), c(3) (sex and generation neutralized)

Figure 2.20 Componential Definitions

To these we add our own concerns:

(7) The problem of the universality of components as the building blocks of all meanings in all cultures (see Volume 1, Section 2.3)
(8) The relationship of paradigms to taxonomies

There is a large specialized literature concerning componential analysis and its problems. Here we discuss only items 6, 7 and 8 because these link componential analysis to our ethnoscience goals and theories.

(1) The indeterminacy of componential solutions has been exaggerated. The "Yankee" terminological system is typical. The indeterminacy assumption is based on the fact that more than one componential solution exists. Anthropologists have overlooked the fact that all variant solutions (there must be six or more by now) differ only because of different measures of "collaterality." The dimensions of sex and generational direction and distance never vary. If we consider the controversial nature of these multiple solutions as an epistemological window (see Volume 1, Section 1.2), then we must try to resolve the discrepancy. It is easily demonstrable that variations in measuring collateral distance coincide with different assumptions about residence. Or, if our culture residence patterns vary, then whom we consider a close or distant relative will also vary. This is the root of the so-called indeterminacy of the Yankee kinship system.

(2) The universality of components is difficult to ascertain; hence a componential analysis is usually language specific. More precisely, most components seem to be language specific and do not apply to all languages, or language-universal components are difficult to discover (see Volume 1, Section 2.3.1)

(3) Components and attributes are formally identical. Thus a componential analysis is the *analysis of one level of a taxonomy*. This fact is often obscured because analysts exclude collective terms. For example, the above paradigm excludes terms such as "parents" for "mother" and "father."

Thus Figure 2.19 may be redrawn as shown in Figure 2.21.

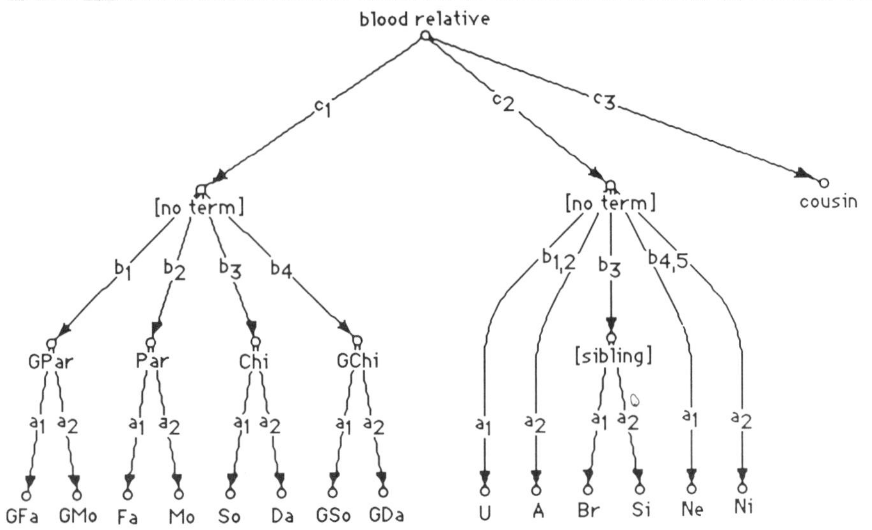

Figure 2.21 Tree Graph of Figure 2.19

It is easy to see that Figure 2.21 is a taxonomy ("X is a kind of Y") with some unlabeled or covert nodes.[1] If we view the components as modifiers, we can redraw this figure as an MT diagram (see Volume 1, Section 2.3.2).

We thus establish the theoretical unity of componential analysis as a special case of the MT schema: The number of attributes is kept to a minimum. In most cases in Figure 2.22 just one attribute is used to modify the taxon above it and thus creates a subordinate term.

Componential analysis as a method for understanding the structure of one taxonomic level needs amplification. First, a single level can be defined, because of the transitivity of the taxonomic relation, as any *subtree of a taxonomy.* Thus Figures 2.21 and 2.22 show the attribute structure of the subtree labeled "blood relatives." The multilevel taxonomy of this subtree was obscured by ignoring the intermediate labels (e.g., "parent," "child," "sibling").

A componential analysis establishes *minimal criteria* for separating one term in a set from all other terms in the same set. These minimal criteria, however, no longer apply if we enlarge the original set. Any such enlargement requires the introduction of new dimensions and corresponding values; thus the minimal definitions expand as we expand the relevant vocabulary.

There is no guarantee that human beings use *minimally adequate* definitions in speech and everyday interaction. The outsider to a culture surely needs *maximally adequate* definitions in order to understand the natives in a variety of contexts. In ethnoscience ethnographies and encyclopedias, we always seek "maximally adequate definitions. Componential analysis is most useful when the domain of words is highly structured (dense), as in the area of kinship. There are few areas of

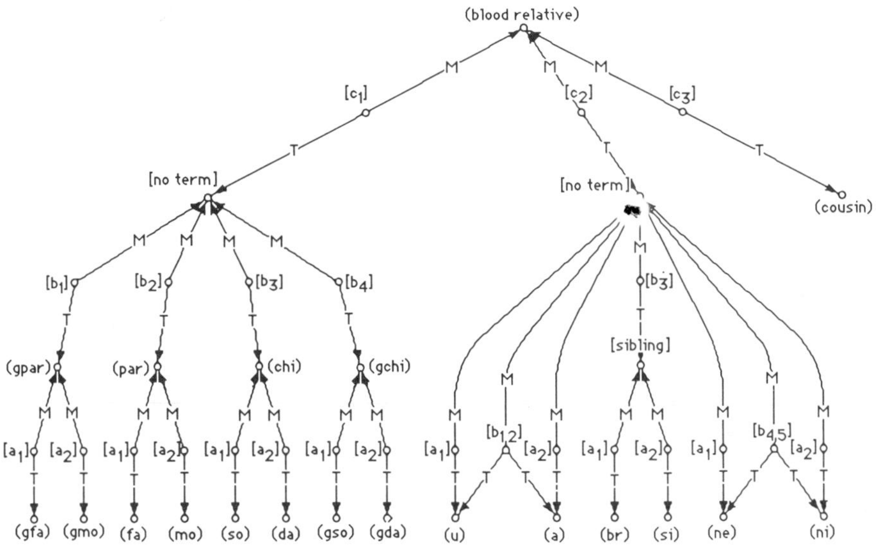

Figure 2.22 MT Graph of Figure 2.21

human vocabulary that meet this criterion. Nevertheless, componential analysis is a useful technique for analysts who want to identify semantic structural density in areas outside of kinship. The assumption is that semantic structural density implies *cultural saliency*.

The natives themselves operate with maximally adequate definitions proportional to their expertise in some field of cultural knowledge. In most real-life situations, obstacles to perception (noise in the system) may require the use of some subset of a maximally adequate definition. For example, in the dark after a news bulletin about an escaped lion, a loud roar alone will suffice to send most people running for the safety of their homes. Only an anthropologist might stop to consider whether the lion's roar is part of a set of salient features of a minimally adequate definition. (He or she also may not survive such reflection.)

2.5.6 Extensions of Componential Analysis

Lounsbury (e.g., 1964, 1969) devised additional operations related to componential analysis which link its application to cultural analysis (e.g., Lounsbury 1965). These procedures make, first, the initial stages of componential analysis more explicit by employing a more systematic notational system. Second, "reduction rules" (and "expansion rules") explain complex meanings by deriving (expanding) them from a set of core kinship terms. The rules (which work in both directions—expansion or reduction), establish terminological equivalences between classes of kin. These equivalences can be used to understand the social organization—especially the workings of kinship—better. In the Trobriand case,

Sex	Lineality	Collateralty	Affinality
m ⟶ male	+ ⟶ parent link	0 ⟶ sibling link	= ⟶ marriage link
f ⟶ female	– ⟶ child link		
a ⟶ either male or female, or sex of relative does not matter			

NOTE: "⟶" in this context means "stands for."

Figure 2.23 Basics of Notational System

Lounsbury (1965) shows how these rules can help in a general understanding of a culture.

We first illustrate the application of the more systematic notation, especially the notational system of Romney and D'Andrade (1964). Second, we explain the reduction/expansion rules of Lounsbury and illustrate how to formulate them. However, the method is specialized and its application sufficiently restricted that we can only hint at its possibilities without exploring them in detail. We refer the interested reader to the literature.

Basic Notational System

We use English kin terms for illustration and assume that we have elicited a list of core kin terms that cannot be defined by other kin terms. Next we define *all* terms of the domain by using the core concepts alone. At this stage an adequate notational system must clearly identify the core terms and show how combinations of these terms uniquely define all others.

There are many such notational systems. Easiest to apply is the system used by Wallace and Atkins (1960) (see Figure 2.21). Romney and D'Andrade (1964) and Fenton (1974), building on Romney and D'Andrade's work, simplified it by reducing the number of primitives. This elegant notational system is based on the dimensions of sex, lineality, collaterality, and marriage (affinality) reduced to bare essentials (see Figure 2.23).

Through this notation the Yankee kinship term "grandfather" can be written as

Grandfather: a+m+m (any ego's father's father)
Grandfather: a+f+m (any ego's mother's father)

Since the two terms in this system are identical,

Grandfather: a+a+m (any ego's parent's father)

Fenton (1974) expanded the notation by adding several new symbols to include kinship categories used in the Navajo system. These are not needed in the Yankee system but appear in many other kinship systems of the world (see Figure 2.24).

In Figure 2.25 we transcribe the terms for blood relatives (consanguineals) in the Yankee kinship system.

e → elder within same generation

y → younger within same generation

b → represents person of one (unspecified sex only

. . . → represents "in the context of"

d → represents persons of a particular sex, not necessarily different from b

NOTE: Adapted from Fenton (1974:62).

Figure 2.24 Extensions of Notational System

	Ranges		Ranges
Grandfather	a+m+m a+f+m	Uncle	a+m0m a+f0m a+m+m0m a+f+m0m a+m0f=m a+f0f=m etc.
Grandmother	a+m+f a+f+f		
Father	a+m		
Mother	a+f	Aunt	a+m0f a+f-f a+m+m0f a+f+m0f a+m0m=f a+f0m=f etc.
Brother	a0m		
Sister	a0f		
Grandson	a-m-m a-f-f		
		Nephew	a0m m a0f-m a0m-m-m a0f-m-m f=m0m-m f=f0m-m etc.
Granddaughter	a-m-f a-f-f		
Cousin	a+m0m-m a+m0m-f a+f0m-m a+f0m-f a+m0f-f a+f0f-m a+f0f-f a+m+m0m-m a+m+f0m-m etc.	Niece	a0m-f a0f-f a0m-m-f a0f-m-f f=m0m-m m-f0m-m etc.

NOTE: Adapted from Romney and D'Andrade (1969:372-373).

Figure 2.25 Retranscription of Yankee Kin Terms

To demonstrate that the notational system is applicable to any kinship system in the world, we present a set of Navajo terms. It is based on consanguineal terms from Aberle (1961), transcribed by Fenton (1974:63-64) (Figure 2.26). Lounsbury uses a similar notational convention; however, we find his system more difficult

hama7 sa7ni7	a+f+f	ha7di7	a0f
	a+f+a0f		a+bob-f^{e}
			a+m0f-m-f^{e}
hana7li7	a+m+a		a+m+f0m-f^{e}
	a+m+a0a		
	a+m+m0f-a	halhnaa'aash	m+b0c-m
	a+b0b-a-m-a		
		hacheii	a+f+m
hama7	a+f		a+f+a0m
	a+f0f		a+f+m0m-m
hama7ya7zhi7	a+f0f	hatso7i7	a-f-a
	m0f-f		a0a-f-a
	m+m0b-f-f		a+f0m-f-a
			a+m0f-f-f-a
hada'i7	a+f0m		
	a+f+a0a-m	hak'a'i7	a+f^{y}0f^{e}
			a+f+a0a-f
habi7zhi7	a+m0a		
	a+m+b0b-a	hazhe7'e7	a+m
	a+m+m0f-a		a+m0m
	a+m0f-m-m-a		
		hada'	m0f-a
haya7a7zh	f-m		m+b0b-f-a
	f0f-m		m+m0f-f-a
	f+b0b-f-m		m+m0f-m-f-a
haye'	m-m	hach'e7'e7	f-f
	m0m-m		f0f-f
	m+b0b-m-m		m+b0b-m-m
hanaai7	a0m^{e}	hatsi'	m-f
	a+b0b-m^{e}		m0m-f
	a+m0f-m-m^{e}		m+b0b-m-f
	a+m0f-f-m-m^{e}		
	a+m+f0m-f^{e}	hatsili7	a0m^{y}
		hadeezhi7	a0f^{y}
		hazeedi7	a+b0c-a

NOTE: Read b0b as "siblings of same sex," b0c as "siblings of opposite sex." We use the Navajo possessive prefix "ha-" for emphatically human possession (i.e., *his* or *her*). The 7 denotes high tone of the preceding vowel, the "lh" denotes the barred or voiceless "L."

Figure 2.26 Navajo Consanguineal Kin Terms

than Romney and D'Andrade's (1964). The reader may refer to Lounsbury (1964, 1969) for comparison.

Equivalence Rules: Reduction and Expansion

Lounsbury proposed three kinds of equivalence rules: skewing rules, merging rules, and half-sibling rules. All of these can be found cross-culturally, but unlike our lexical/semantic relations (of modification (attribution), taxonomy, and sequence (the MTQ schema)), they are not found together universally. That is, any kinship system may use any number of these rules from none to all three.

The intention of these equivalence rules is simple. According to Lounsbury they work "in reducing the seeming complexity and voluminousness of detail . . . to a few fairly simply stated underlying principles. [We show] the former to be merely the automatic consequences of the latter" (1969:217). These equivalence rules are rules for reduction and expansion. They are complementary: If they are applied in one direction, they expand the sense of core kinship terms; if applied in the other, they reduce that sense.

> Written as reduction rules, [these rules] operate always on more remote kin types (secondary terms) to "reduce" them to the genealogically closer kin types to which they are terminologically equivalent. . . .
>
> Written as expansion rules, on the other hand, they operate always on genealogically closer kin types to "expand" these, i.e., to derive from them more distant kin types which are their terminological equivalents [Lounsbury, 1969:217].

These rules therefore define equivalence classes. They postulate the terminological (and often behavioral) equivalence of the kin types on the left of the rule (rewrite) arrow with the kin types on the right. Because these rules can be viewed as a mapping of one set of kin types onto another, they have also been called *transformations*. Sometimes the rules have corrollaries, usually applications to reciprocal kin types (e.g., f0m and m0f).

Skewing Rules

A skewing rule "expresses the formal equivalence . . . between two kin types of different generations" (Lounsbury, 1969:217). In symbolic notation the following formula characterizes a skewing rule.

$$\text{f0m} \ldots \rightarrow \text{f} - \text{m} \ldots$$

Stated in natural language, it is "Let any woman's brother, as linking relative, be regarded as equivalent to that woman's son, as linking relative" (Lounsbury 1969:208).

A corollary states the reciprocal rule:

$$\text{m0f} \ldots \rightarrow \text{m} + \text{f} \ldots$$

Again in English, "Any male linking relative's sister will be equivalent to that male linking relative's mother" (Lounsbury 1969:208).

Merging Rules

A merging rule "expresses the formal equivalence . . . between siblings of the same sex" (Lounsbury, 1969:218).

$$mOm \ldots \rightarrow m \ldots$$

and

$$fOf \ldots \rightarrow f \ldots$$

In English, "Let any person's sibling of the same sex, as the linking relative, be equivalent to that person himself directly linked" (Lounsbury, 1969:208). In this case no corollary rule is applicable.

Half-Sibling Rules

The half-sibling rule "expresses the formal equivalence between half siblings and full siblings" (Lounsbury, 1969:218). This rule has greater cross-cultural applicability than the skewing rule. The formulas look as follows:

$$a + m - s \rightarrow aOm$$
$$a + m - d \rightarrow aOf$$
$$a + f - s \rightarrow aOm$$
and
$$a + f - d \rightarrow aOf$$

In plain English, "Let any child of one's parents be regarded as one's sibling" (Lounsbury 1969:218).

With these formulas it is easy to represent any exotic kinship systems that appear in the ethnographic literature. Lounsbury investigated the well-known matrilineal/patrilineal mirror image systems, called the Crow and the Omaha system of kinship. In the 1960s and 1970s Lounsbury's elegant set of rules was applied to many analyses of kinship terminologies. The popularity of the approach has waned in recent years, primarily because the method does not seem applicable to cultural domains outside kinship. Viewing core kin terms as equivalent to distant relatives seems akin to metaphoric extension. Some day, perhaps, expansion rules may be revived if someone finds a way of applying them to metaphors.

2.6 SUMMARY AND CONCLUSIONS

Structural analysis is the first step in ethnoscience ethnographies. The beginning ethnographer will find the structures of taxonomy (T) and modification (M) familiar patterns that help to organize the exotic content of another culture. Taxonomy and modification are thus meta-ethnographic structures that form the basis for all cognitive analysis. This does not necessarily mean that in a given culture taxonomies are necessarily the most important structures. They are only the most basic structures that expedite the discovery of the culturally important schemas (e.g., complex relation; see Volume 1, Section 2.3.2, and themes; see Section 6.3).

We interpret taxonomies, narrowly calling them "taxonomies" only if the linkages conform to the frame "A is a kind of B." Apparently every human language has an easily elicitable taxonomic frame (question). Our view of folk classification can be represented as shown in Figure 2.27.

Folk definitons round out folk taxonomies. Each taxon (node label) should receive its own encyclopedic folk definitions. Iteration from taxonomic elicitation to folk definitions and back is the only way to ensure that our taxonomies approximate the knowledge of the natives.

Folk definitions can be made more systematic by eliciting the same content categories for each member of a taxonomic contrast set. For example, all comparable animals should contain (unless culturally inappropriate) the same type of information (e.g., same titles—see Figure 2.7). Only compelling reasons supported by several consultants should lead an ethnographer to abandon this principle. One problem may be "orthogonal taxonomies"—alternative classification or alternative subtrees, semantically independent from each other, under the same superordinate taxon.

Eliciting folk definitions is very simple in one sense because it makes sense to ask what certain words or phrases mean. This method is more sophisticated than componential analysis because it permits the elicitation of complex attributes. Complex attributes, or encyclopedic information, are crucial for an adequate ethnographic analysis. For example, the complex plan for making bleu cheese forms part of the definition of "bleu cheese." In everyday life we never know which aspect of encyclopedic knowledge will become salient in unexpected situations (contexts).

The serial order of elicitation, what is elicited when (on first, second, or third try), also reflects on saliency in context. For example, we classify foods differently depending on whether we are preparing for a long backpacking weekend or a tour of gourmet restaurants in the city (Mim Dixon, personal communication).

Word association, saliency, context, and order of items in folk definitions are all closely related. Word association chains are useful for constructing folk definitions—for example, with children who have not yet learned explicit word defining behavior. This latter ability may also vary across cultures.

Casagrande and Hale (1967) discovered 12 (13) types of atomic definitions to analyze folk definitions further. Unfortunately, their atomic definitions are not as easily applicable as we first thought. Furthermore, the ones that are not atomic (e.g., Attribution = Modification and Constituency = Taxonomy) can be shown to be complex relations derivable from the MTQ schema[2] (see Volume 1, Section 2.3.2).

The part/whole relation is one of these derived complex relations (see Volume 1, Sections 2.3.2 and 2.4), though some logicians (e.g., see Tarski 1937, or Luschei 1962) claim part/whole (PW) to be more fundamental than taxonomy (T). We know of no convincing representation of T using PW, whereas PW is easily constructed from M and T (see Volume 1, Section 2.3.2).

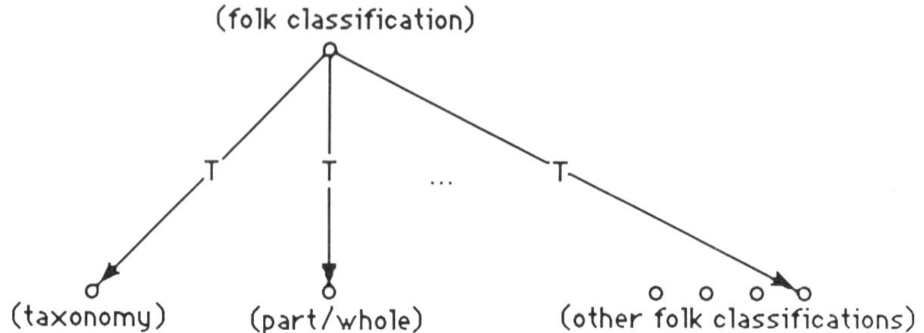

NOTE: This figure underlines our notion of folk classification in the broad sense and folk taxonomy in the narrow sense. We carefully avoid "folk taxonomy" as a generic term for all folk classifications of tree structures.

Figure 2.27 Folk Classification Taxonomy

The PW relation may be ordered—for example, in plans (see Section 3.1). It also has an "abstract" version, which may be paraphrased in English as "A is an aspect of B." Several ancillary techniques make elicitation context sensitive through interviewing for cases. Other folk classifications and folk definitions can be elicited by letting a consultant talk while slip sorting previously elicited terminology. Tree drawing and the elicitation of cosmologies seem to be the only safe techniques that allow for extending taxonomies upward.

Finally, componential analysis is a very useful technique for minimally distinguishing one naming unit from another. The method works best with densely lexicalized domains such as kinship terminologies.

Outside of kinship studies, "titles" in systematized folk definitions (see Figure 2.7) are the analogues to componential dimensions. These titles seem more appropriate for illuminating the cultural ramifications of terminological systems than narrow componential analyses.

Lounsbury's elegant extension of componential analysis brings to light aspects of kinship systems difficult to discover using any other method. That all kinship systems generalize onto different sets of kinsmen the meanings of core kin terms is a striking insight. But the utility of "transformational kinship analysis" (expansion and reduction rules) outside of kinship has yet to be demonstrated.

Folk taxonomies and folk definitions therefore remain the main line of attack in ethnoscience ethnographies. The second line are the techniques discussed in the following chapters.

NOTES

1. Because of the transitivity of the taxonomic relation, covert nodes can always be eliminated.
2. The "contingency" relation is the logical relation of implication.

Chapter 3

Beyond Structural Analysis

The preceding pages covered the aspects of traditional ethnoscience. In this section we go beyond simple lexical/semantic fields and relations (the MT schema; see Volume 1, Section 2.3.2) to plans (the MTQ schema; see Sections 3.1 and 4.1, this volume) and decisions. Decision criteria are attributes. If conditions are met (the correct attributes are present), a particular plan may be performed.

3.0 INTRODUCTION

Plans introduce the notion of sequence or temporal order and therefore time. This makes ethnographies dynamic—that is, it converts them from atemporal structures to structures that include time. This is usually "psychological time," though we do introduce a method for projecting psychological time onto astronomical (absolute) time (see Section 3.1.5).

The hierarchical structure of plans provides an ideal vehicle for the representation of action-oriented cultural schemata.[1] Two characteristics of plans are involved. First, no largest plan exists (a still larger plan can always be constructed). There is no limit to the information that can be packed into a plan. Second, any large plan subsumes tremendous amounts of cultural knowledge under a relatively simple label.

Sequences of activities require decisions—most simply, whether or not to undertake an activity; Chapter 4 will be devoted to decisions. The conditions for performing an activity should be seen as attributes that must be matched before an activity can commence. Thus decisions can be seen as tools for specifying contexts in which particular plans can be enacted.

In the following sections we explore plans.

3.1 PLANS

In all learning and in all activities, ordering events or actions through time plays an important part. There are virtually hundreds of psychological experiments dealing with serial learning. In the ethnographic description of a group, series of limited activities form important aspects of daily life. "Grand Tour" questions of time often involve the day as the unit of exploration. Obviously, larger units, such as the week, month, year, or lifetime (life histories), are equally feasible. Ultimately, feasibility is dictated by the intended uses of the research. For many applications the day is by far the most readily accessible unit. Relative to the length of the ethnographer's stay in the field, days are highly recurrent. They occur with a high enough frequency during a 12- to 18-month field trip to allow for recording of variation and (possibly) change over time. An 18-month stay in the field is not unusual for many ethnographic projects. Optimally, that permits about 550 days of living with the group under study. At that rate of repetition it is likely that the ethnographer will begin to see some significant patterns, at least on the recurrent daily scale.

Grand Tour questions about time (e.g., the day) are usually followed at some later time by minitour questions about subactivities occurring *during* a day. In other words, named activities form hierarchies that can be broken down into increasingly smaller units just as the part/whole relations mentioned earlier. That is, subactivities are always parts of larger activity sequences.

The verbal descriptions of actions are called *plans* or, more accurately, *verbal action plans*. Directions on a can of STP Gas Treatment, on a can of photographic developer, or in a recipe for cooking a stew are all verbal action plans. In ethnoscience ethnographies we are concerned with the systematization of plans. This entails determining what features are shared by all directions for activities and considering the question of how the description of plans can be made more consistent.

The first step in understanding verbal action plans involves determining the relations between the units used in them. An action sequence consists of some activity A followed by some other activity B: B is followed in turn by C, and so on. The basic linking relation between activities A, B, and C is the sequencing relation "is followed by" or simply "and then" (symbolized by Q for Queueing or seQuence, (see Volume 1, Section 2.3.2). There is no problem finding equivalents in other languages, no matter how exotic. In other words, sequential organization of human activities is a cultural universal.

3.1.1 Diagramming Verbal Action Plans

There are two practical methods for diagramming verbal action plans. The first is more suggestive and easier to follow. (The advantages and disadvantages of each graphing method will be discussed later.) A graph of nodes and arrows connecting the nodes is interpreted as follows: The *nodes* are the relation of sequencing or ordering symbolized by the letter Q and expressed in English by "is followed by" or "and then" (see Volume 1, Section 2.3.2). The arrows are labeled with the names of activities, most usually by predicates or verb phrases (verbs describing actions with their prepositional phrases, verbs with direct objects and prepositional phrases, or simply predicates). Figure 3.1 shows a simple example of a

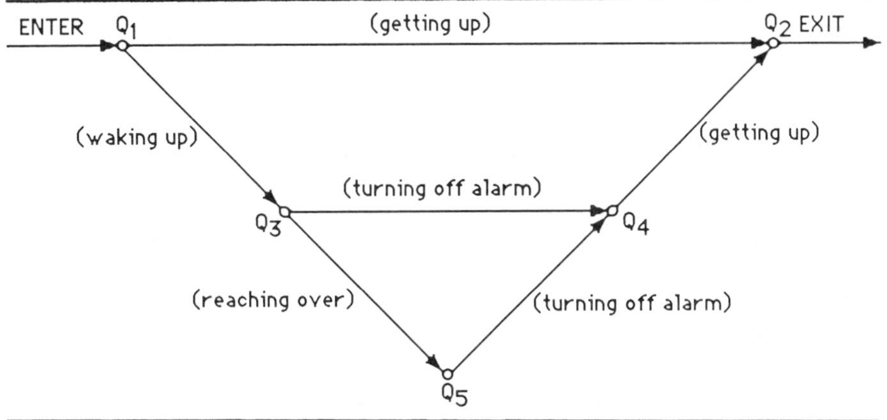

Figure 3.1 Verbal Action Plan: GETTING UP

descriptive fragment from the beginning of the daily activities of someone in our culture.

Several aspects of the graph in Figure 3.1 are notable: (1) The figure shows a definite starting point (ENTER) and a definite endpoint (EXIT). (2) The figure also shows the hierarchy of segments in contrast with Shank and Ableson (1977). For example, the plan "Getting Up" is the name of the entire plan but also of one of the subplans. Similarly, the subplan "Turning Off Alarm" is also the name of one of its own subplans. This fact shows the referential ambiguity of verbs. (3) Any path through the graph including the shortest (Q1-Q2) and the longest (Q1-Q3-Q5-Q4-Q2) is a *possible description of the activity* depicted by the verbal action plan. In everyday life a narrator (teacher) may describe some parts of a plan in great detail while describing others by mentioning only their higher labels. The alternation of detail and label depends only on the narrator's (teacher's) assumptions about the knowledge a hearer (learner) may already have.

3.1.2 Eliciting Verbal Action Plans

Figure 3.1 represents three levels of detail in the description of this verbal action plan. The highest level, "Getting Up," can be viewed as the first response to a Grand Tour question. The ethnographer continues by asking the first-level minitour question: "What do you do when you get up?" The answer is on the second level: "I wake up (waking up), (and then) I turn off the alarm (turning off alarm), and (then) I get up (getting up)." On the next lower level, still finer detail is obtained by questions about "waking up" and "getting up." We have eliminated such detail for the sake of simplicity. However, in the book *Working*, Studs Terkel (1972) describes the waking up "plan" of a steelworker: "When I wake up in the morning, I first open one eye, then the other eye and then I say 'Aw fuck!'"[2] This example shows that plans are easily elaborated. The question, "What do you do when you turn off the alarm?" is answered by "I reach over and (then) turn it off by pressing the button" (i.e., turning off alarm (by pressing button)).

An interesting feature of plans graphed in this manner is that *every possible path through the graph represents a plausible answer* to "What do you do first thing in the morning?"; that is, (1) "I get up," and (2) "I wake up, turn off the alarm, and get up," or (3) "I wake up, reach over, turn off the alarm (by pressing button) and get up," are all answers depicted by Figure 3.1. With more detail elicited for "waking up" and "getting up," further possible paths become available, and these too can then be added to the graph.

The large number of alternative responses to a question about a verbal action plan also explains why it is always difficult to elicit a plan from a consultant. A human being who responds to a question about a particular plan always takes into account a best guess of the questioner's knowledge about all things related to the question. It is on the basis of such guessed knowledge that a consultant then picks one particular, often very limited, path of some degree of detail through the full plan graph. At other times the information seeker may ask a limited question—for example, "How do you turn this darn alarm off?"

Consultants who have worked with us on plans from Grand Tour questions through many minitour questions of greater and greater detail are often surprised, even annoyed, after the third pass. They usually say, "You've asked me that three times already." In other words, it appears that the consultant sees "in his or her mind's eye" the entire plan as a whole from the very beginning of the questioning. Such a plan has a cover label (e.g., "getting up") that literally stands for the entire sequence, including *all* complex detail. This title of a plan, or the most general label for a plan, stands for the *entire* plan. To a consultant, asking for more detail implies more questions about the *same* plan that he or she already perceives as a whole with all its detail after the initial question. Each pass evokes the same plan in the consultant's mind, thus creating the impression that the researcher is asking for the same information, not just for more detail. Only with very willing (or docile) consultants were we able to get one more level of detail (a fourth), and even they refused to cooperate beyond the fourth try.

There is still another reason for consultants' refusing to break down plans further. An extremely detailed description of activities is very cumbersome in all human languages. That is, there seems to exist a level of optimal description (the last, or lowest level in "turning off the alarm"; see Figure 3.1). Giving more detail, asking what a human being does as he or she actually depresses the button on the alarm, becomes extremely tedious. One can easily imagine such a tedious plan in our example: "I get a firm grip on the alarm clock with the palm of my left hand, which I press against the crystal. I then curve my index finger around the clock and feel for the button on the back. I position my finger carefully in order to hit the button straight, perpendiculary to the back of the clock. I flex the muscles of my finger and depress the button, release my grip on the clock and withdraw my hand." Needless to say, there are few (specialized) situations in any culture, even for a very naive ethnographer, in which such fine detail is warranted; however, the ethnographer should never take too much for granted in the description of any activity. Graphing of plans reveals cultural differences very vividly. The following case illustrates:

Case 3.1 Navajo Weaving and Planting

Simple activities that translate into English as "weaving" or "planting" require very detailed descriptions because both activities are very different in Navajo culture than in Anglo culture. The Navajo loom is upright and has no shuttle. The colored wool is threaded by hand between the vertical warp.

Traditional Navajo planting starts in the center of the field spiraling clockwise (sunwise) outward to the edges, planting with a digging stick every three to four feet. Another important prerequisite of planting is the performance of appropriate planting prayers and songs. Planting may therefore be viewed as having two plans: a secular one of placing seeds into the ground, and a sacred one of performing the appropriate ceremonies that guarantee a good harvest.

3.1.3 Atomic Plans of Action

This lowest optimal level of description of verbal action plans applies to the description of every verbal action plan. In our simple example, this level was reached at the point of turning off the alarm on the lowest level of the graph. In the waking up sequence, the actual moment of leaving the bed constitutes the simplest, or *atomic* plan of action. In short, the objective of plan elicitation is to reduce all activities to sequences of atomic plans. As we have shown, below the level of atomic plans the explanations quickly become very cumbersome and voluminous.

Interestingly, atomic plans represent the barest semantic content of verbs, a description that is generally analogous to definitions found in good dictionaries. This level of atomic plans seems also the least culture bound. It represents a grouping or chunking of elemental, often universal notions. Such chunking tends to become more culturally unique as analysis ascends to more global, molar plans. The higher, more molar levels seem to follow and to elaborate the basic idea of an atomic plan in culturally specified ways.

For example, Euro-American weaving involves a warp, a weft, a shuttle, and generally a wooden horizontal loom. The definition of weaving (American Heritage Dictionary 1969:1452) reads, "to make [cloth] by interlacing the threads of the weft and the warp on a loom." This is clearly an atomic definition. It covers both the American and the Navajo case. The respective plans for weaving in the two cultures quickly deviate as we move to more molar levels of description (see Case 3.1).

The planting example is similar. Planting means "to place or set [seeds] in the ground to grow" (American Heritage Dictionary 1969:1003). This atomic plan applies again to both cultures, Navajo and American. And again, they begin to

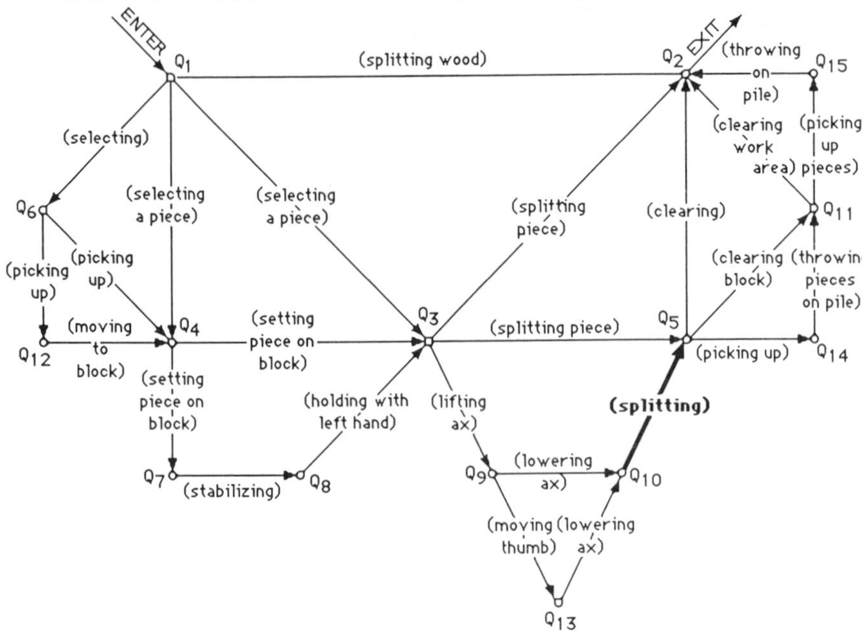

NOTE: The atomic plan "splitting" is marked by a boldface arrow. Adapted from Werner (1966).

Figure 3.2 Plan: SPLITTING WOOD IN CENTRAL EUROPE

diverge sharply as soon as we consider more molar descriptions. We illustrate this point further in the following case and plan:

Case 3.2 Plan: Splitting Wood in Central Europe

> In the following complex plan of splitting wood, the lowest (atomic) level of "split" corresponds closely to the dictionary definition (Webster's New Collegiate Dictionary, 1953, slightly edited): "To divide lengthwise, and/or with the grain, and/or with the layers." We assume that many languages of the world distinguish between dividing with the grain versus across the grain. This is what we mean by the more probable universality of atomic plans. This also implies that it may be easier to find translation equivalents for atomic plans than for molar plans such as "splitting wood in central Europe" or "planting among the Navajo." The important point to remember is *not to mistake the translation of the atomic plan for that of a molar plan.*

There is a second way to graph verbal plans. This method of representation has the advantage that it shows the similarity of plans to some of the semantic structures (i.e., part/whole) that we have discussed before; but it has the disadvantage that it does not show as clearly the integrity or wholeness of plans, though it does show more adequately how one plan always follows another (at the same level of explicitness). This highlights the Miller, Galanter, and Pribam (1960) statement that human beings are never planless, except perhaps when they sleep.

The basis for the second style of representation for plans is the part/whole relationship; a subplan is represented as part of a dominating plan. The first two levels of the splitting wood plan can therefore be represented as shown in Figure 3.3. (For the sake of clarity, we first graph the part/whole relation exclusively. This is followed by a second graph in which the part/whole relation is supplemented with all necessary relations Q of queueing or sequencing.)

Figure 3.4 is the same diagram with all the Queueing (sequencing) relations Q inserted. The complexity of this method of graphing increases rapidly with the addition of nodes. Compare this with the explanatory elegance of Figure 3.2.

The familiar part/whole relation in this graph is a bonus; it is familiar to us from other contexts. It also demonstrates the unity of the theoretical model more clearly by tying plans more intimately to the lexical/semantic relations of M (modification) and T (taxonomy) discussed in previous sections (see Volume 1, Section 2.3.2).

Along more theoretical lines, Figure 3.4 also contains taxonomic relations: The most general level of the taxonomy contains the atomic plan.[3] As one ascends (in either one of the two types of graphs representing plans) through the graph, the atomic plans become increasingly specific and complex through the addition of more and more attributes. These more inclusive activities are therefore *subordinate* taxons to the most general taxon, or the atomic plan. Werner and Topper (1976) discuss these counterintuitive points in detail in their theoretical paper (see also Volume 1, Section 2.3.2).

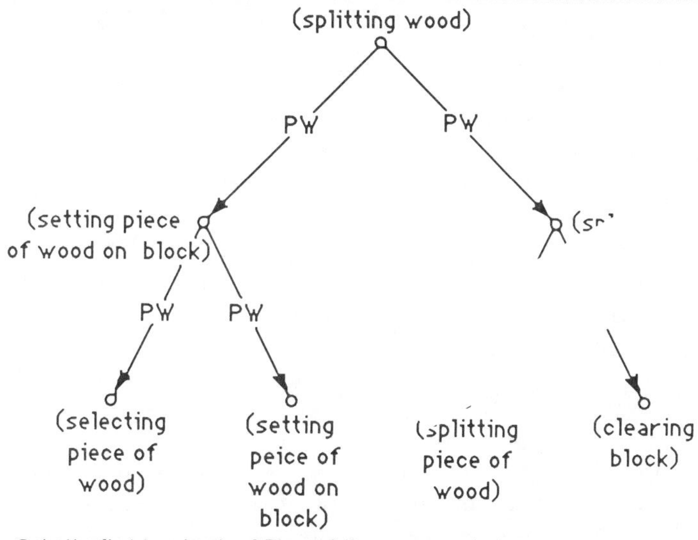

NOTE: Only the first two levels of Figure 3.2 are represented.

Figure 3.3 Part/Whole Representation of SPLITTING WOOD

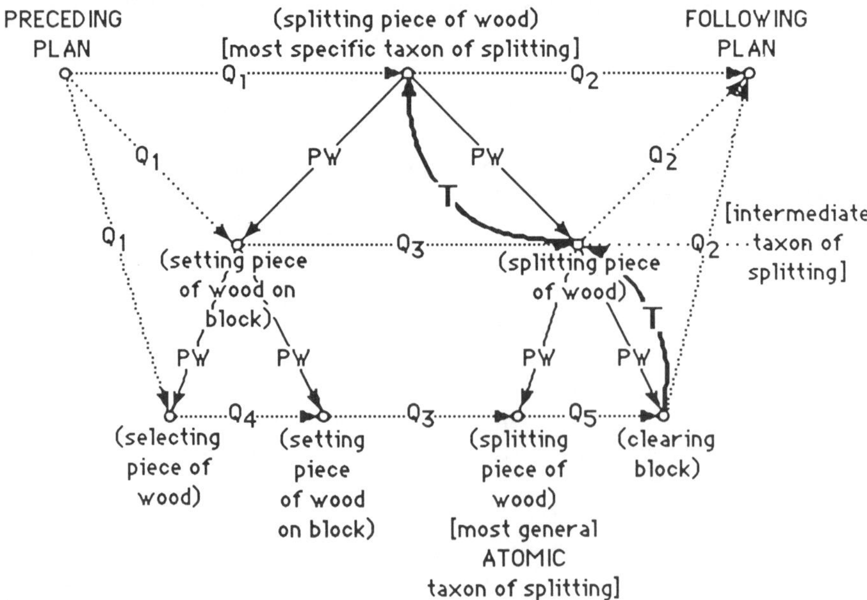

NOTE: This is the inverse representation of splitting (a Block of) Wood. The numbering of Q nodes in original plan (Figure 3.2) with arrows is labeled Q in this graph (in addition to those labeled PW and T) and the nodes labeled by the activities. The atomic relation is at the top of the taxonomy of activities. As the plans get more molar, the attributes increase and the labels become more specific as one moves up in the graph (see Volume 1, Section 2.3.2).

Figure 3.4 Part/Whole Graph with Q Relations

For practical purposes it is best to follow the first graphing convention. This method immediately implies a representation of verbal action plans as list structures. A list representation is easier to type or typeset than either of the graphing conventions. It resembles the part/whole representation of verbal action plans because each indentation can be interpreted as a level in a part/whole representation such as Figure 3.3. Figure 3.5 is a list representation of splitting wood.

Each indentation shows a different level of description. It is as difficult to see in this representation as it is in Figure 3.4 what sequence of label is an appropriate description of the action plan. This is in sharp contrast to Figure 3.2. In other words, no representation shows every possible verbal description of a plan as *any* possible path through the graph as well as Figure 3.2. Therefore, in most applications, in spite of problems of typing or typesetting, the form of representation in Figure 3.2 is preferable. This is a clear anthropological example in which the choice of the symbol system enhances a solution (Polya 1957).

Our final example is a Navajo version of our getting up plan. The plan "One Gets Up" was elicited by Werner and Begishe in Oljeto, Utah, from Mr. Bob Bitini, an older traditional Navajo. There are two reasons for presenting this illustration. First, it is an actual ethnographic example. It demonstrates the utility of

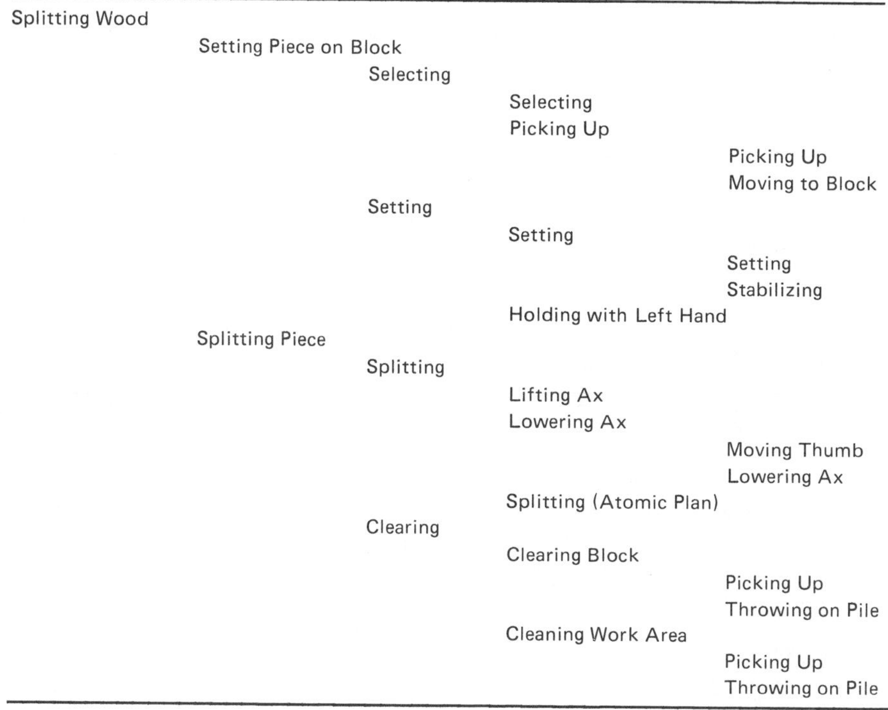

Figure 3.5 List Representation of Plan from Figure 3.2

plans for the representation of activities in any culture. We hope the example also demonstrates how different getting up can be in another culture. Second, we illustrate a final representation of a plan. It combines our graph representation (as in Figure 3.2) with a list representation, as in Figure 3.5. It is labeled Figure 3.6.

The following list shown in Figure 3.7 explains Figure 3.6.

3.1.4 Plans and Groups

Most human activities require the presence of others. If groups of individuals can be related across several activities (consequently to each other), then the result is a plan in which mutual social activities are projected onto the plan through time. That is, a verbal action plan listing at each step the participants in the actions shows the movement of social networks (groups) through time.

A traditional sociogram (answers to the questions, "Who works with whom?" "Who likes whom?" or "Who interacts with (talks to) whom most often?") is a set of verbal action plans in which the time dimension is collapsed or eliminated. The result is a "projection" of the movement of a group through time onto "social space"; that is, whereas a sociogram can tell us who interacts with whom, it does not tell us anything about the order of these interactions or what proportion of the day is devoted to interactions between the members of a given group.

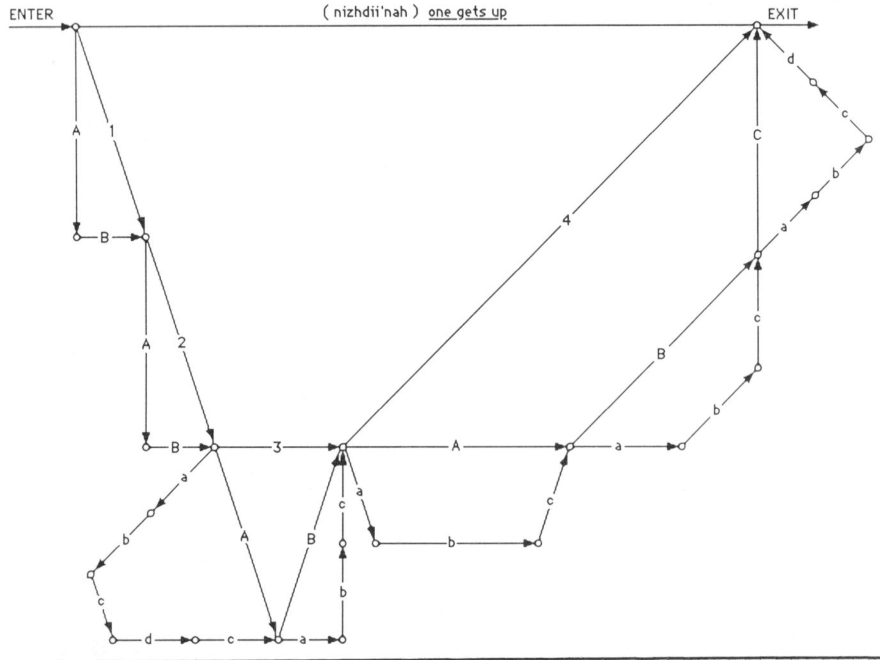

Figure 3.6 Example of Graph and List Representation

Plans, on the other hand, allow us to assess the relative importance of certain groups in the life of a consultant. We assume that the more time an actor spends within a group of others, the greater significance this group assumes for him. Although this measure of group importance may not always be uniformly valid, it follows from a series of hypotheses about group behavior first formulated by George Hohmans (1950).

Schoepfle (1977) has used plans successfully as a method for eliciting clique structure in a school setting. He asked students for the plans of their daily activities. Subsequently he also asked each student to list with whom he or she performed particular plans.

The illustration in figure 3.8 provides a simplified example of a verbal action plan including the social network of the actor/consultant. It is important to realize that the plan is *Jane's plan*. The other actors move in and out of her plans. This type of plan becomes more like a case if it describes unique events (e.g., What happened at school *yesterday*). Sometimes it is possible to elicit generalized plans if the population that interacts with the consultant is the same over a period of time. Work groups in an office may provide a good example.

The same verbal action plan is presented in a list (list of lists) representation in Figure 3.9.

A plan like this is specific to a certain actor/consultant (in this case, Jane). Other actors may select or remember different activities, often with different

1. ch'ééedzídzí' *one wakes up*
    - A. jikighal *one opens eyes*
    - B. k'ad daats'í hoos'iid dziniiziih
      one thinks perhaps it is about time [to get up]
2. nízhdii'nah *one gets up*
    - A. beeldléí nahgoo kojiil'iih *one puts aside the blanket*
    - B. hakee' [t'áádoo be'astl'óní] biih níjít'is *one puts on shoes [untied]*
3. ch'íjíghááh *one walks outside*
    - A. ch'íjíghááh *one walks outside*
        - a. ch'íjíghááh *one walks outside*
        - b. nahgóó tázhdíghaah *one goes outside to defecate or urinate*
        - c. so' [deiyíkáhgíí] jinííl'iih *one looks at [setting] stars*
        - d. k'adláah [bíighahnih] jiniziih *one thinks [it is that time]*
        - e. aadéé' ya'ánííjídááh *one starts back inside*
    - B. yah'aníijídááh *one comes back in*
        - a. [hooghan góne'] yah'aníijídááh *one gets back inside [into hogan/house]*
        - b. [hatsésk'ehji'] názhnídaah *one sits down [on one's bed]*
        - c. hakee' háázdiidlééh *one takes off one's shoes*
4. ééhní jídááh *one puts on clothes*
    - A. kééhnídzíí' is *one puts on shoes*
        - a. yistléh biih nídzít' is *one puts on socks*
        - b. hakee' biih nídzít' is *one puts on shoes*
        - c. hakee' be' jitl'óóh *one ties one's shoelaces*
    - B. tl'aazh'éé' biih nídzít' is *one puts on pants*
        - a. tl'aazh'éé' nízhdii'ááh *one gets the pants*
        - b. tl'aazh'éé' biih níjít' is *one puts on pants*
        - c. tl'aazh'éé' bilh dah'ajinil *one buttons the pants*
    - C. deji'éé' biih níjídááh *one puts on shirt*
        - a. deji'éé' nízhdiiltsos *one picks up the shirt*
        - b. deji'éé' biih jighááh *one puts on shirt*
        - c. deji'éé' bil dah'ajinil *one buttons the shirt*
        - d. deji'éé' hats'iit'ah abíjiilchi' *one tucks in the shirt*

NOTE: It is important to understand that traditional Navajos get up before sunrise. During the summer this is usually before 4:00 a.m. Adapted from Werner (1966).

Figure 3.7 List for Figure 3.6

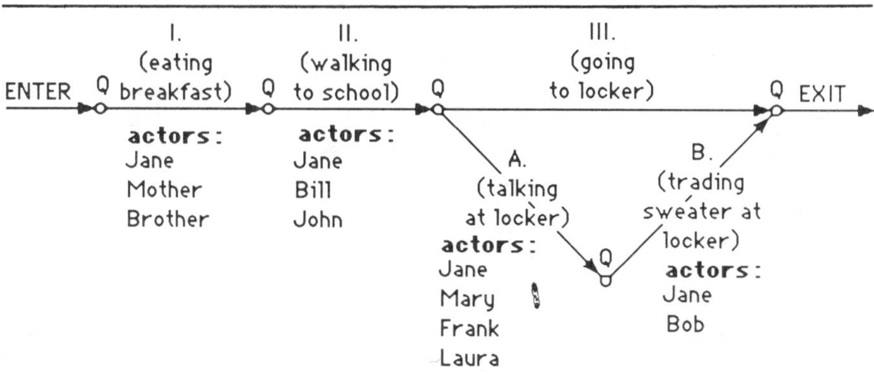

Figure 3.8 Plan and Social Network

I. Jane eats breakfast with Mother and brother.
II. Jane walks to school with John and Bill.
III. Jane goes to her locker.
  A. Jane talks with Mary, Frank, and Laura at locker.
  B. Jane trades sweaters with Bob at locker.

Figure 3.9 List Representation of Figure 3.8

actors. By providing each branch of a plan with a list of participants, Schoepfle was able to read directly off the graphs who associated most with whom or who selected whom for interaction in particular settings. Thus instead of asking for a sociogram, Schoepfle was able to determine sociograms from the graphs. At best, this method allows for a comparison of elicited sociograms with sociograms derived from plans. Note that Bernard and Killworth (1973; see also Killworth & Bernard 1974) discovered discrepancies between reports of liking and frequency of observed interaction. Unfortunately, they had no access to temporal structure of interaction or to the quality (emotional tone) of interaction that may affect reports on interaction.

How to reconcile discrepancies in the plans and the perception of membership in the activities described by verbal action plans is at present left to the discretion of the ethnographer. Readers interested in group dynamics are referred to the vast literature on the topic in social psychology. Experimentation with the correlation of plans to sociograms is urgently needed.

In our plans we note the emergence of a clique when, in a social group of non-substitutable individuals, the actor executes more than one feature of a plan with recurring others. Students in a particular classroom are not necessarily a clique, but those who seek each other out to participate in various repeated activities are usually members of a clique.

The organization of a clique is significant. It shows that a sequence of individuals may be substitutable in a particular activity. In the above example, the actor might trade sweaters with someone else in the event of Bob's absence. If the participation of one individual is impossible, then the actor chooses an alternative individual, always in some order.

There is an alternate representation applicable to multiperson plans. The method is complex and requires the elicitation of a considerable amount of detail. The idea is simple. The analogy for the employment of this representation comes from music. The most explicit known documents that coordinate multiperson plans are musical scores of orchestras. Each instrument is assigned one transcription, one line of notes that progresses from left to right. The score is transcribed in the same units of time. This creates a synchronization or coincidence of activities vertically. This convention prescribes when one instrument should stop and another begin. Perhaps more important, the vertical synchrony also represents harmony. The sound of one instrument (activities) complements or enhances the sound of all others playing (acting) at the same time. This is similar to any human activity in which several actors must act in concert. The metaphor "concert" is multiply apt.

The ethnographic task of collecting multiperson plans (scores) is complex but it can be done, especially if there is some theoretical motivation for the task. Note, for example, that in the musical analogy the complexity of the score can easily be extended to orchestras of several hundred players (actors).

The elicitation of such complex multiperson plans must proceed with a careful combination of conversation (interview) and observation of the activities in question in naturalistic settings. The major difference between the representation outlined above for multiperson plans and the representation of Figure 3.8 is that in the former each person appearing in the plan is assigned his or her own plan (Figure 3.8), just like Jane's plan, perhaps each representing one band of plans and subplans across a page from left to right. The vertical alignment of activities represents synchrony.

3.1.5 Plans and Time

Multiperson plans have introduced time and synchrony as important aspects of plans. All plans implicitly contain time. We could call it task time and distinguish it from astronomical (calendric) time. Task time means that a plan represents progression through time using time units of a nonuniform length: a task taking a long time to complete receives a line in the graph of the same length as a task noticeably shorter. It is understood that one task commences only after the task preceding it is completed.

The above paragraph implies that a superimposition of task time and astronomical time is possible: We make the length of the appropriate arrow proportional to the absolute time it takes to accomplish the activity. The graph in Figure 3.10 applies this notion to the multiperson graph in Figure 3.8.

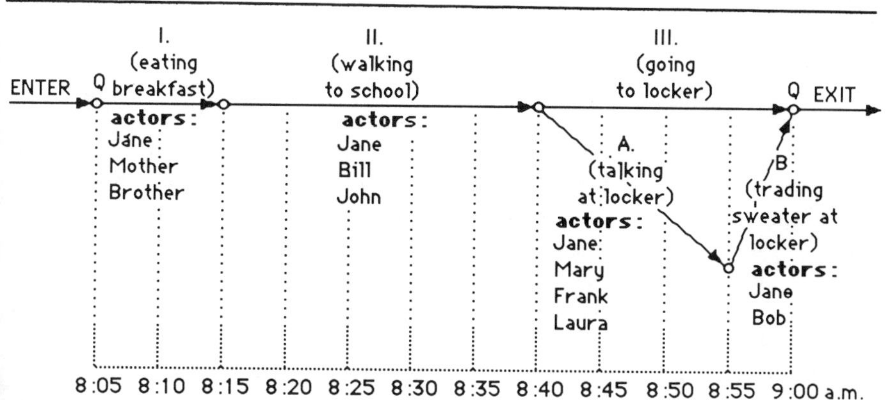

Figure 3.10 Plan, Time, and Social Network

Obviously the same method of combining task time and absolute astronomical time can be used with single-person plans.[4] The method we sketched in these paragraphs may become very useful in certain applications or theoretical problems.

3.1.6 Summary and Conclusions

Plans and their diagrams so far have not been used extensively in anthropology. The work of Roberts (1956) was seminal. The main sources are still Werner (1966), Martin Topper's dissertation (1972), and several articles by Topper (e.g., Topper *et al.* 1974), Werner, Schoepfle, *et al.* (1976), and Werner and Topper (1976). Parts of Schoepfle's dissertation (1977) can be cast into a plan framework. More recently Christina Gladwin (personal communication) has applied plans to her work in agricultural ethnography. In artificial intelligence the work of Schank and Abelson (1977) follows similar ideas, though failing to recognize the hierarchical nature of plans.

Plans or, more precisely, verbal action plans can be diagrammed in at least two ways: in our standard manner in which nodes are labeled by verbs or verb phrases, and the arrows are labeled as the relation Q ("____ and then ____"). This follows the example of Bierman (1964). The inverse Bierman model is more revealing. Here the nodes are the relation of queueing and the arrows are labeled by verbs or verb phrases. This representation shows the hierarchy of plans and the ambiguity of verb (verb phrase) usage. It also marks clearly the beginning and the end of each plan. This method of diagramming is excellent for showing why most plans when first elicited are incomplete: Any path through the graph is a possible way of talking about the activity depicted by the graph. The amount of detail given in eliciting verbal action plans depends on the speaker's assumptions about the hearer's knowledge of the activity.

Atomic plans are least culture specific; molar plans are most culture specific. Atomic plans can be further described in ordinary language only with difficulty. There seems to be in every language a discrete level of verbs at which description by labeling is easy, but all attempts to include more detail make further description cumbersome.

A counterintuitive insight into the nature of plans is that atomic plans are taxonomically the most general and least culture-bound aspects of language. As we ascend to more molar labels the verbal action plans become more and more (culture) specific. Thus the higher a term in a plan, the lower it is in its taxonomy. Atomic plans with the fewest attributes are the most general taxons. More in-depth study of plans will allow for the study of groups over time. For the first time we may see social networks as functions of activities with others through time.

As far as we know no one has used the combination of plans and astronomical time except in a few experimental graphs prepared in classes. We see a great potential for their application, both to non-Western concepts of time and to a more objective study of activities. Equally promising but underutilized are plans for the study of social networks.

NOTES

1. We also mention cultural schemata under complex relations (see Volume 1, Sections 2.3.2 and Chapter 6 in this volume). For more on cultural schemata, see Casson (1983).

2. Obviously, the steelworker's comment expresses his attitude toward work and should not necessarily be taken seriously as a "true" plan.

3. Note that atomic plans that appear "on the bottom" of a plan are the most general taxons. All higher-level plans are further down in the taxonomy. For details see Werner and Topper (1976).

4. We are grateful to Alison Holmes, who brought this possibility of combining task time and absolute astronomical time to our attention.

Chapter 4

Plans and Decisions

All three of our methods for the graph or list representation of plans (including the addition of social group structure) are still oversimplifications. At many points in a plan the actor(s) must make decisions, choosing between two or more alternatives. In this section we discuss how to link alternative plans.

4.0 INTRODUCTION

There are three devices for the representation of decisions: (1) decision tables, (2) flowcharts, and (3) decision trees. Of these, the decision table is easiest to construct: It is elegant and thorough. It brings to the attention of the ethnographer and the consultant combinations of conditions and actions considered explicitly in the text. We demonstrate that all three representations of decisions are isomorphic. In other words, one can be unambiguously converted into another. However, decision tables have a tremendous advantage: In addition to representing decisions they are also a powerful heuristic elicitation device. For this reason we discuss decision tables first.

4.1 DECISION TABLES

A decision table is a device for putting conditions and actions into a schema that makes the decision process explicit. In addition, the major power of a decision table as an eliciting tool stems from the fact that it forces the ethnographer to consider *all possible combinations* of conditions. It also forces the consideration of all decisions, not just those explicitly stated in texts obtained from consultants (e.g., Jaffrey's 1975 paragraph, Case 4.1).

In a decision table we find the following: (1) All possible combinations of conditions are stated. (2) We try to find outcomes for each of these combinations. (3)

All outcomes that are suggested by these combinations can be described, even those not mentioned explicitly by the consultants in the texts of the first round of elicitation. The ethnographer must, however, be careful that implied conditions and actions found through a decision table are confirmed and not fabricated by the ethnographer.

Decision tables were invented by systems and industrial engineers. They were originally used for determining, for example, the flow of paper in an organization or the steps involved in purchasing raw materials for a factory. Since then these tables have been used in a variety of applications in which it becomes important to understand how tasks get done. This is fundamentally an ethnographic task. Nevertheless, the use of decision tables in ethnography is still very new.

Decision have four components (Pollack 1963, 1971; McDaniel 1970; Gildersleeve 1970). These are shown in Figure 4.1.

It is a good idea to name (or number) each decision table (see Figure 4.10). This makes reference to them easier and keeps track of each table as well. In an ethnography with several dozen decision tables, it is easier to organize and sequence them if each table bears a distinct name. We will follow this convention consistently. Furthermore, as we demonstrate in Chapter 5, a decision table is often the formal representation of a case. The name of a decision table is therefore analogous to the *title* of a case.

The CONDITION STUB in the upper left corner contains all the conditions an actor must consider in his or her environment or context. These usually take the form of questions (for example, "Is the beer ready?" "Do we have large posts?" "Has mother returned from the store?"). These conditions are sometimes called "attributes" (see Volume 1, Section 2.3.2) because they are identical to attributes that have to be checked before a particular word becomes appropriate for use in a discourse.

The CONDITION ENTRY in the upper right part of the table contains the rules by which each condition is evaluated. If the condition applies, a Y for "yes" is placed in a rule. If it does not apply, an N for "no" is so placed. The "rules" are the columns of the condition and action entry stubs.

Such yes/no tables are called "pure." In mixed-entry tables the answer to a condition may be "yes," "no," and "does not apply" or any other nonbinary

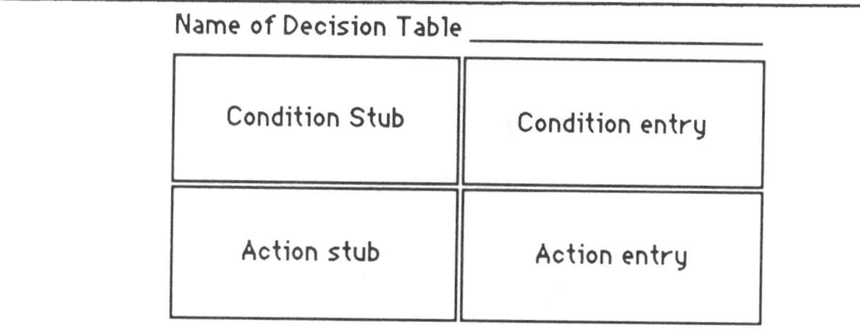

Figure 4.1 Four Parts of a Decision Table

entry. For example, outcomes of a decision may depend on the grading of the responses to a decision. There may be one outcome that applies when a condition is strongly positive and different ones when it is positive, neutral, negative, or strongly negative. For instance, in an election one may send money and ring doorbells if one feels strongly about a candidate, send money if one feels positive about him, do nothing if one feels neutral or negative, or send money and ring doorbells for the opposition if one feels strongly negative about the candidate. In this situation we may use + + + (zero) - and - as the symbol in the rules instead of simple Y and N. However, in the following examples we use only pure binary decision tables. All mixed-condition tables can be reduced to pure ones.

The ACTION STUB contains a list of the possible outcomes or actions.

Finally, the ACTION ENTRIES contain check marks, usually X, if a given column of (Y or N) answers to conditions applies to an outcome.

In a pure decision table the combinatorial possibilities are, because of the two possible (Y and N) answers to each decision, 2^n, where n represents the number of conditions. Thus if we accept a size limit on decision tables that can be easily accommodated by 8 1/2 × 11 (216 × 279 mm) letter-size paper, then about five conditions, or $2^5 = 32$, is the limit of what can be squeezed onto a single page. It is a good policy to break up very large decision tables into manageable units. Often a natural temporal succession of decision suggests a segmentation into subtables.

Earlier we presented a plan of a male consultant that shows how he gets up in the morning. We repeat the plan in Figure 4.2.

Let us assume that this is the weekday pattern of persons described in our ethnography. Subsequently we find that they do something else on weekends. They do not wake up to an alarm but sleep until they wake up naturally. The second, weekend plan, consists therefore of only two activities (Figure 4.3).

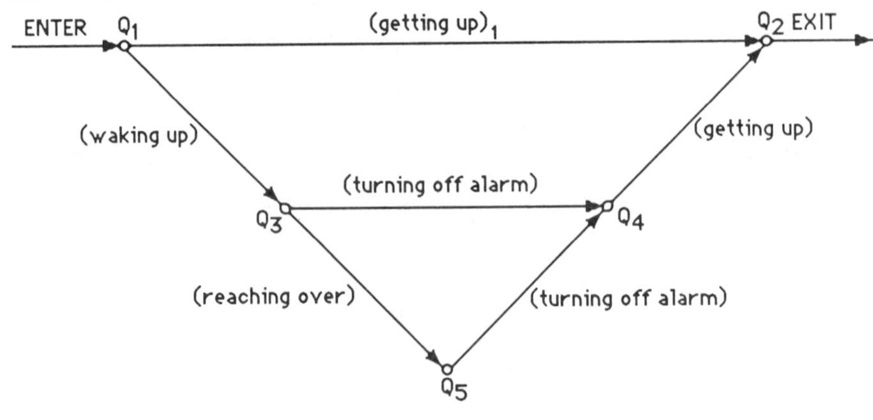

NOTE: This is a repetition of Figure 3.1.

Figure 4.2 Plan GETTING UP Renamed GETTING UP (1)

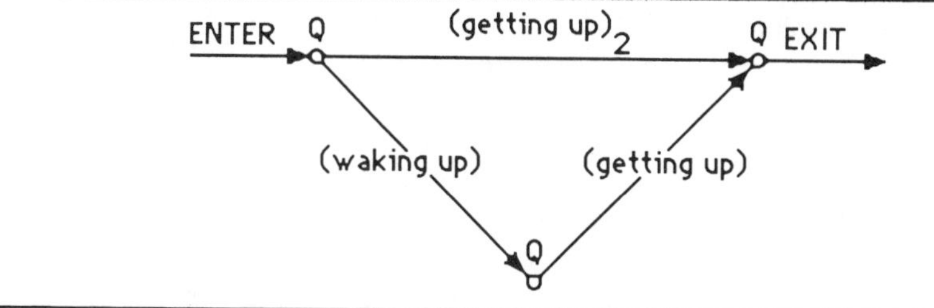

Figure 4.3 Weekend Plan or GETTING UP (2)

Name of Decision Table:

Getting Up	1	2	3	4
1. Is today a weekend? (Today is a weekend)	Y	Y	N	N
2. Did the alarm ring? (The alarm rang)	Y	N	Y	N
1. Getting Up$_2$ Plan	X			
2. Sleep		X		
3. Getting Up$_1$ Plan			X	
4. (when awake) do Weekend Plan				X

Figure 4.4 Decision Table: GETTING UP

An example of a decision table linking Getting Up (1) with Getting Up (2) is given below. There are two conditions; therefore, there are $2^2 = 4$ possible combinations of conditions. The decision table in our example can be represented as follows. First, we name the table. Since the table in Figure 4.4 is about decisions concerning getting up in the morning, we call it GETTING UP.

We have not specified the plan our consultants follow when they oversleep. Our next step in the interviewing procedure is therefore to interview them about what they do in such a circumstance, a possibility we did not consider previously. In the process we may find that sometimes the alarm does go off and the consultant still does not wake up. This possible outcome necessitates the introduction of another condition, perhaps with exactly the same outcome as the oversleep plan, but we cannot be sure without further interviewing.

The simplest possible decision table has only one condition and therefore only $2^1 = 2$ possible outcomes. In the plan for splitting wood, the decision table shown in Figure 4.5 calls up an alternate plan.

Following Topper (1972), we use the convention of symbolizing decision points by square nodes within the graph of a plan. In order to show the decision points in a plan or a series of plans, we place a number referring to a decision table inside each square node (see upper left corner of decision table in Figure 4.5).

In Figures 4.6-4.9 we first show the plan for splitting wood as it was presented in Case 3.2 (that is, Plan A). Then we show the alternative plan when two hands

Name of Decision Table: D1. Large Piece of Wood	1	2
1. Is the piece of wood large and heavy?	Y	N
1. Do Plan B (below)	X	
2. Do Plan A (original Plan below)		X

Figure 4.5 Decision Table D1: LARGE PIECE OF WOOD

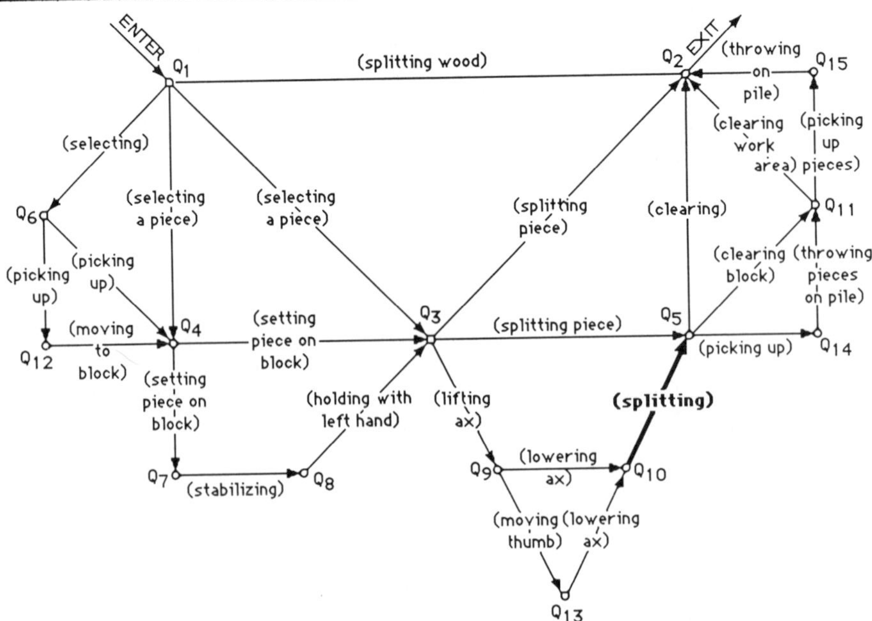

NOTE: The atomic plan is marked by boldface. From Werner (1966) and Figure 3.2, slightly modified.

Figure 4.6 Plan A for SPLITTING WOOD IN CENTRAL EUROPE

are used. The two splitting wood plans can then be represented as shown in Figure 4.6.

The alternate plan between nodes Q3 and Q4 is illustrated in Figure 4.7.

The two plans, depending on the size of the piece of wood can now be combined (see Figure 4.8). In this case the situation is relatively simple because both plans that follow from the decision table are splitting wood plans. In other instances it may be necessary to refer to entirely different sequences of activities which may follow. For example, splitting wood may be followed by "making fire" or "drinking beer." In such cases the decision table representation is modified (see Figure 4.9).

The decision table in Figure 4.9 must contain the conditions that select alternatives 2, 3, and 4 over 1 and vice versa. The plans for splitting wood 1, alternative

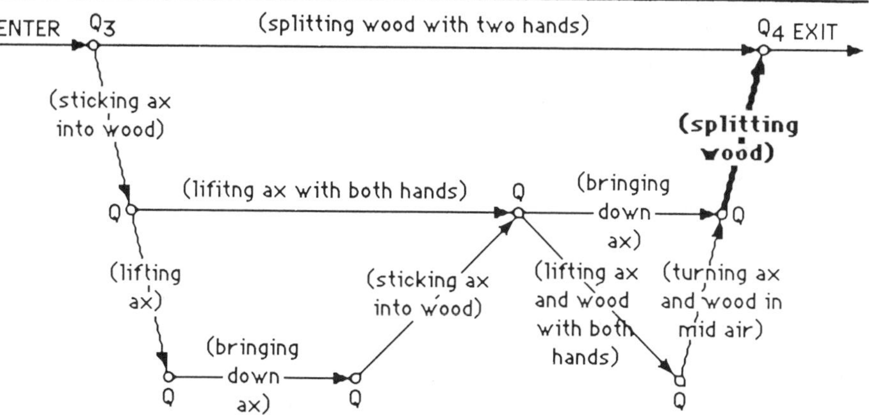

NOTE: Compare numbering of Q nodes with original plan. Atomic plan Splitting Wood appears in boldface.

Figure 4.7 SPLITTING WOOD: Plan B

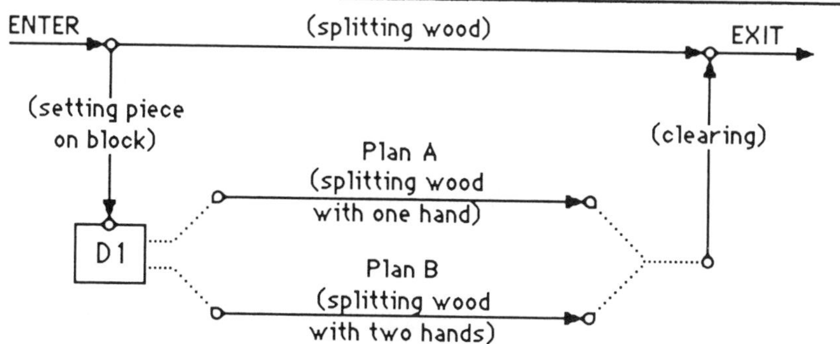

NOTE: Compare numbering of Q nodes with original plan. D1 refers to the decision table in Figure 4.5.

Figure 4.8 Combined Plan A and B: SPLITTING WOOD

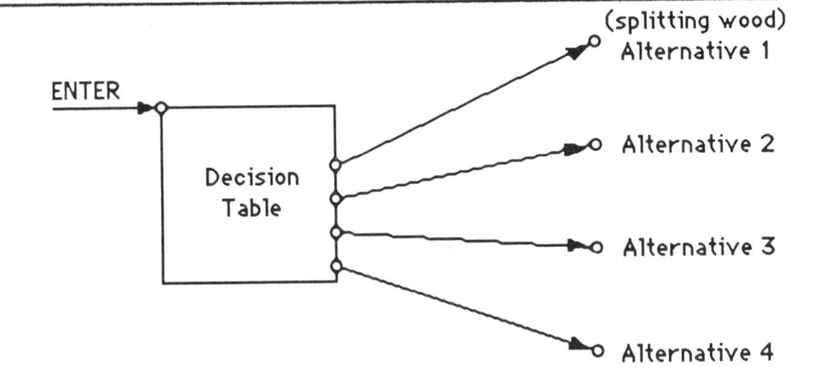

Figure 4.9 Alternative Plans from a Decision Table

2, alternative 3, and alternative 4 can then be listed separately and should be referred to by decision table numbers and the page number (of the hypothetical report) on which the appropriate decision table appears.

In order to explore the power of decision tables more fully, we give an extended example. We will follow through from a text (a long paragraph). Although this text was selected from a book, it bears all the characteristics of an ethnographic interview.

4.2 DECISION MODELS

We take the following example through all the steps of analysis and hope to show in the process how the details of decision modeling work. The case comes from a cookbook by Madhur Jaffrey (1975), *An Invitation to Indian Cooking*. The introduction of this book includes an essay on how the author became interested in Indian cooking and in writing about Indian cuisine. This is followed by an overview of how to select and use important ingredients that are part of many dishes. At one point Jaffrey discusses how to select, buy, and prepare spices for cooking. She pays special attention in this section to how to accomplish this in an ordinary supermarket.

Case 4.1 Buying and Preparing Spices

"There is a slight problem with supermarket spices which you might as well be aware of. Those spices which do not 'move'—i.e., sell fast—tend to stay on the shelves and get stale. A few lose their aroma, others fade in the light, some get oily and rancid. Therefore try to buy only whole spice and grind them yourself in small quantities. The grinding can be done in a coffee grinder, or, if the spices are slightly roasted first, some can be crushed between waxed paper with a rolling pin. The electric blender will grind spices, if you do them in sufficiently large quantities. If all else fails, you could use mortar and pestle, though that tends to crush spices rather than grind them.

> Whole spices retain their flavor for very long periods. Make sure you store them in jars with tightly screwed lids, well away from dampness and sunlight. Ground cumin and coriander are fine if bought from Indian spice dealers in small quantities" (Jaffrey 1975).

This paragraph is similar to parts of an interview that an ethnographer may want to translate into a decision model. In the following pages we take this paragraph through all the steps of analysis.

4.2.1 Conditions and Actions

The first step is to number each sentence, then to look carefully at each sentence and analyze its content into conditions that must be met for an action to take place. An action is thus the consequence of meeting certain conditions. These analytical steps are far from obvious. There is frequently more than one interpretation of the text. Misjudgment or misinterpretation of passages is common. It often takes several rounds of analysis before the resulting decision table (or flowchart) looks right or appears to be intuitively correct. In between it may often be necessary to ask more questions of one's consultant(s). The final product should be accepted only after thorough critique by natives.

Jaffrey's paragraph can be analyzed as follows: We break the paragraph into sentences and look within each for conditions and resulting actions. We also comment on our interpretations.

(1) "There is a slight problem with supermarket spices . . ." ACTION 1: Buy spices in supermarket. *Comment:* There is an implicit assumption that buying spices in a supermarket is perhaps not the best, but for most Americans it is certainly the most convenient way to buy spices. All conjectures, like this one, should be checked with the consultants.

(2) "Those spices which do not 'move'—i.e., sell fast—tend to stay on the shelves."

(3) "[Spices in supermarkets] tend to get stale."[1] *Comment:* This is a condition because Jaffrey implies that it is an important check before proceeding with a purchase. CONDITION 1: [Are spices in supermarket stale?]

(4) "A few lose their aroma, others fade in the light, some get oily and rancid." *Comment:* This looks like a list of things to look for in determining whether the spices are stale or not. It is conceivable that these criteria could be used for another decision model for determining if the spices are stale. We exclude this part of the decision model for the sake of brevity. That is, we assume that the user of the model is capable of establishing the freshness of the spices. In a cross-cultural context such competence should not be assumed without further testing.

(5) ACTION 1: ". . . buy only whole spices and grind them yourself in small quantities." *Comment:* Here Jaffrey tells the reader what to do. This sentence describes one outcome based on the conditions, the first of which appeared in sentence 3. This sentence also anticipates condition 7.

(6) ACTION 2: "The grinding can be done in a coffee grinder . . ." *Comment:* This is another action. However, the condition is implied. The sentence can be restated, "If you have a coffee grinder, then you can use it to grind spice." This sentence makes the condition explicit. CONDITION 2: [Do you have a coffee grinder?]

(7) ACTION 3: ". . . if the spices are slightly roasted first, some can be crushed between waxed paper with a rolling pin." *Comment:* This action looks more like a condition. However, it is a very local condition. Paraphrased, the sentence reads, with the condition made explicit, "If you have a rolling pin, you can grind spices, after slightly roasting them, between waxed paper with a rolling pin." Thus the condition becomes clear. CONDITION 3: [Do you have a rolling pin?] (waxed paper implied).

(8) ACTION 4: "The electric blender will grind spices . . ." *Comment*: The implication is again that "you have an electric blender." CONDITION 4: [Do you have an electric blender?]

(9) CONDITION 5: ". . . if you do [the spices] in sufficiently large quantities." *Comment:* This seems to be a major condition. The choice of the blender versus the other methods depends on the quantity of spice.

(10) ACTION 5: "If all else fails, you could use a mortar and pestle, though that tends to crush spices rather than grind them." *Comment:* There seem to be several interpretations possible. We assume that if a cook has neither electric blender (for large quantities) nor a coffee grinder or a rolling pin (and waxed paper), then the last resort is the mortar and pestle, because there are problems assoiated with its use. The condition of owning a mortar and pestle is implied. CONDITION 6: [Do you have a mortar and pestle?]

(11) "Whole spices retain their flavor for very long periods." *Comment:* Jaffrey jumps around. In this and the next sentence she assumes that the cook has bought whole spices in the supermarket. The action of buying is implied. The above sentence simply states why buying whole spice is a good policy. That is an important condition for the purchase. CONDITION 7: [Is spice whole?] ACTION 6: [Buy spices whole.]

(12) "Make sure you store [whole spices] in jars with tightly screwed lids, well away from dampness and sunlight." In the following analysis we will ignore this action for the sake of simplicity. *Comment:* This sentences is a direct consequence of buying the whole spice. It gives advice (presents a plan) for storing the spice.

(13) "Ground cumin and coriander are fine if bought from Indian spice dealers in small quantities." *Comment:* This sentence returns to the buying of spice. It contains both a condition, the assumption that the cook does need cumin and coriander, and an action (i.e., what to do if there is such a need). CONDITION 8: [Do you need] cumin and coriander? ACTION 7: "Buy from Indian spice dealer in small quantities."

We can now summarize the CONDITIONS and ACTIONS in abbreviated form in the following table:

CONDITIONS
(1) Are spices stale?
(2) Do you have coffee grinder?
(3) Do you have a rolling pin?
(4) Do you have a blender?
(5) Do you have a sufficiently large quantity of spice?
(6) Do you have mortar and pestle?
(7) Is spice whole?
(8) Do you need cumin and coriander?

ACTIONS
(1) Buy spices in supermarket.
(2) Buy and grind spices yourself.
(3) Grind in coffee grinder.
(4) Roast slightly, grind with rolling pin between waxed paper.
(5) Grind in electric blender.
(6) Use mortar and pestle.
(7) Buy spices whole.
(8) Buy from Indian spice dealer in small quantities.

We will soon see that if all the conditions are answered either affirmatively or in the negative, there are 2^8 or 256 combinatorial possibilities. It is a rule of thumb that a decision table (the first structures we will use for this analysis) should not exceed the size of one $8^1/_2$ × 11 inch (216 × 279 mm) page. In any case, it is appropriate and advantageous to look for a way to split up large decision tables in some principled manner.

In our example the split is reasonably clear. Conditions 1, 7, and 8 belong to the conditions for initiating the "Buy spices" or "Do not buy spices" plans at the supermarket, or cumin and coriander at the Indian store. The rest of the conditions—2, 3, 4, 5, and 6—deal with what to do once the whole spices are purchased. Following this sequence of events, first at the stores and second at home preparing the spices, we apply to our problem two consecutive decision tables.

There are further problems. Conditions 1, 7, and 8 are incomplete. Jaffrey's basic assumption in her paragraph is the need for spices in Indian cooking. Therefore the most basic condition (we will call it 0) is, "Do you need other spices?" The word "other" refers to spices other than cumin and coriander.

There are more assumptions that must be made but are not mentioned in Jaffrey's paragraph. All of these need to be checked with Jaffrey or another appropriate consultant. For example, there is a basic assumption that most people in American culture go regularly to supermarkets. Therefore buying in a supermarket is easier than buying in an Indian store, which may be available only in larger cities. A further assumption is that once we have made the trek to an Indian store, spices other than cumin and coriander may be available there. Finally, even at the Indian store spices may be sold whole or ground and may get stale anyway, particularly if for some reason they are not moving. We assume the validity of these assumptions. In actual ethnographic work every one of them would have to be validated.

As a result we now have four conditions for our first decision table: (1) Do you need spices (condition 0)? (2) Do you need cumin and coriander (condition 8)? (3) Is the spice stale (condition 1)? (4) Is the spice whole (condition 7)?

The associated actions appear to be (1) Buy and grind spices yourself (action

2), and (2) Buy spices from Indian store (action 8). With these preliminaries we can attempt to construct the first decision table. Given four conditions we anticipate $2^4 = 16$ rule combinations (Figure 4.10).

The rule of inserting the Y and the N is simple. In the first row (condition 1), insert 2^{n-1}, Y and the same number of N. In our example this is $2^3 = 8$, therefore eight Y and eight N. In the second row insert first 2^{n-2} Y and the same number of N; then repeat $2^1 = 2$ times. In our example write 2^{4-2} or $2^2 = 4$, or four Y and four N, repeat 2^1 times, and so on. Stated more simply, in each row use only half the number of the Y and N in the row above it and repeat until the row is filled. Continue until in the last row just one Y and one N alternate ($2^0 = 1$). Sometimes combinations of Y and N lead to new actions that must be elicited—that is, when the original text does not explicitly state all possible outcomes. This happens quite frequently.

The ethnographer next checks each column of Y and N and marks the appropriate actions. This can be done directly with a consultant. After an initial text, a preliminary decision table is constructed with conditions and possible actions (outcomes). Each rule column (from 1 to 16) is then checked with the consultant and the X is marked whenever an outcome is appropriate. New outcomes are elicited as needed.

In rules 1 and 2 (Figure 4.10) everything is fine: If the spice is stale, do not buy. In rule 3 we run into trouble: If the cook needs cumin and coriander, these are purchased at the Indian store. While there we can also buy other spices. However, if the spice is whole, it must be ground at home. The two actions are in sequence: first buying, then an implied trip home, and finally the grinding of the spices at home. To be safe, in an ethnographic setting we should check this with our consultants.

The best solution, therefore, is to separate the first two conditions in Figure 4.10 from the last two. The first two imply a decision to buy spice at the supermarket or the Indian store; the last two, what to do with the spices once they are bought. Now we can draw the two resulting decision tables (see Figure 4.11).

In Figure 4.11 if the cook needs spices *and* cumin and coriander, a trip to the Indian store is inevitable. Our assumption is that all spice needs can be met at the Indian store (this assumption must be checked with consultants). If only spices other than cumin and coriander are needed, it is simpler to buy these at the local supermarket. If, however, the cook needs only cumin and coriander, the choice is the Indian store. Finally, if there is no need for spice of any kind, no action is necessary.

With these preliminaries we are now ready to look at the second half of our decision table concerning the buying of spices (Figure 4.12).

There is another assumption to be made: If the spice is neither stale nor whole, it is all right to buy it and use it because it is in small quantities. (This assumption, like all others, must be checked with consultants).

It is apparent from looking at Figures 4.11 and 4.12 that more than one combination of conditions may yield the same action outcome. The next step therefore is to test if such duplication represents redundancies that can lead to simplification.

Name of Decision Table (first attempt):

D1 Buying spices	1	2	3	4	5	6	7	8	9	10	11	12	13	14	15	16
1 Need spices?	Y	Y	Y	Y	Y	Y	Y	Y	N	N	N	N	N	N	N	N
Need cumin and coriander?	Y	Y	Y	Y	N	N	N	N	Y	Y	Y	Y	N	N	N	N
3. Are spices stake?	Y	Y	N	N	Y	Y	N	N	Y	Y	N	N	Y	Y	N	N
4. Are spices whole?	Y	N	Y	N	Y	N	Y	N	Y	N	Y	N	Y	N	Y	N
1. Buys and grind yourself				X	...											
2. Buy in Indian store			X		...											
3. Do not buy	X	X			...											
4. ...					...											

Figure 4.10 Decision Table: First Attempt

Name of Table :

D2 Buying spices	1	2	3	4
1. Need spices?	Y	Y	N	N
2. Need cumin and coriander?	Y	N	Y	N
1. Buy in Indian store	X		X	
2. Buy in supermarket		X		
3. Do nothing				X

Figure 4.11 Decision Table: BUYING SPICES I

Name of Table :

D3 Buying spices II	1	2	3	4
1. Is spice stale?	Y	Y	N	N
2. Is spice whole?	Y	N	Y	N
1. Do not buy	X	X		
2. Buy and grind yourself			X	
3. Use as is				X

Figure 4.12 Decision Table: BUYING SPICES II

4.2.2 Elimination of Redundancy

We present three rules for the elimination of redundancy: REDUCTION RULE 1 and two auxiliary reduction rules (Gildersleeve 1970). Ultimately only

REDUCTION RULE 1 is needed. The two auxiliary rules show how sometimes further simplification is possible through manipulation of the columns of Y. The reduction rule is simple. If two decision rules (two columns) are *identical except for one row* consisting of a "Y" and an "N," then the condition that applies to that row is irrelevant to the outcome. Put another way, if there is a condition that can be positive (Y) or negative (N) for the same action or outcome, then that condition does not matter: No matter which way it is, the outcome remains the same.

In Figure 4.13 Rules 1 and 2 have the same outcome (Action 1). The same outcome is guaranteed no matter what the state (Y or N) of condition 3 is. Therefore condition 3 contributes nothing to the outcome (action 1). The two rules can therefore be collapsed into a combined rule 1/2. In this manner almost any decision table (except perhaps the simplest ones) can be simplified.

Two auxiliary rules are variations on the same theme. They apply in situations in which further manipulation of columns may sometimes lead to further reductions. It is obvious that these rules can apply only if the first reduction rule has already been applied previously (Figure 4.14).

In this four-condition decision table the three decision rules (columns 1, 2 and 3) seem to be the maximum achievable simplification. This state could have been

Name of Table:

Reduction Rule 1	1	2		1/2
1. Condition Number 1	Y	Y	reduces to	Y
2. Condition Number 2	Y	Y		Y
3. Condition Number 3	N	Y		–
4. Condition Number 4	N	N		N
1. Action Number 1	X	X		X

NOTE: For reduction both columns must be identical except for one row. The outcomes (Action Number 1) must also be identical.

Figure 4.13 Reduction Rule I

Name of Table:

Auxiliary Reduction Rule 2	1	2	3		1.1	1.2	2	3		1.1/3	1.2/2
1. Condition Number 1	Y	Y	Y	expands to	Y	Y	Y	Y	reduces to	Y	Y
2. Condition Number 2	Y	Y	N		Y	Y	Y	N		-	Y
3. Condition Number 3	–	N	Y		Y	N	N	Y		Y	N
4. Condition Number 4	N	Y	N		N	N	Y	N		N	-
1. Action Number 1	X	X	X		X	X	X	X		X	X

Figure 4.14 Auxiliary Reduction Rule I

Name of Table :

Auxiliary Reduction Rule 2	1	2	3		1.1	1.2	2	3		1.1/2	1.2	3		1.1/2/3	1.2
1. Condition Number 1	Y	Y	N		Y	Y	Y	N		Y	Y	N		–	Y
2. Condition Number 2	N	Y	–	expands to	N	N	Y	–	reduces to	-	N	-	reduces to	–	N
3. Condition Number 3	–	Y	Y		Y	N	Y	Y		Y	N	Y		Y	N
1. Action Number 1	X	X	X		X	X	X	X		X	X	X		X	X

Figure 4.15 Auxiliary Reduction Rule II

Name of Table:

Reduction of Buying Spices I	1	2		1/2
1. Need spices?	Y	N	reduces to	-
2. Need cumin and coriander?	Y	Y		Y
1. Buy in Indian store	X	X		X

Figure 4.16 Reduction of BUYING SPICES I

Name of Table:

Reduction of Buying Spices II	1	2		1/2
1. Is spice stale?	Y	Y	reduces to	Y
2. Is spice whole?	Y	N		-
1. Do not buy	X	X		X

Figure 4.17 Reduction of BUYING SPICES II

reached by a gradual reduction of neighboring columns with the same action (outcome). However, further reduction is possible if column 1 (Rule 1) is first expanded again. Then columns 1.1 and 3, and 1.2 and 2 may be further reduced following the main reduction Rule 1 (Figure 4.13).

This rule is completely analogous to the second auxiliary reduction rule. In this case column 1 (Rule 1) is expanded, which then makes two reductions possible. The two auxiliary rules demonstrate how the ethnographer can further reduce redundancy. The basic principle in these further reductions is the main reduction rule (Figure 4.13).

With these basic tools we are now ready to look at the second half of our decision model concerning the home preparation of spices.

4.2.3 Reduction of BUYING SPICES I and II

First we apply the reduction rule to all decision rules (columns) that share action 1 of BUYING SPICES I: Buy in Indian store. The reduction of BUYING SPICES II proceeds analogously.

Conditions 1 in BUYING SPICES I and 2 in BUYING SPICES II have turned out to be irrelevant to the buying of spice in the Indian store and not buying at all, respectively. The only relevant condition for executing these actions is whether the cook needs cumin and coriander or whether the spice is stale.

We have reduced the redundancy as much as possible in these two decision tables. We can now incorporate the changes and draft two new versions of the decision tables named BUYING SPICES I and II. These tables appear in Figure 4.17.

We have renumbered the decision rules since there is no reason to maintain the old numbering.

Decisions for BUYING SPICES are shown here as a sequence of two decision tables. The lines connecting decision table BUYING SPICES I with II imply that when conditions 1 and 2 of BUYING SPICES I are met, BUYING SPICES II applies regardless of whether the spices are bought at the supermarket or the Indian store.

4.2.4 Reduction of GRIND SPICE YOURSELF

We now apply the same procedures to the second half of this decision model. We assume that the purchase of the spices has proceeded according to the paragraph outlined by Jaffrey (1975), translating into the decision tables BUYING SPICES I and II. The cook has bought the necessary spices, returned home, and is ready to commence with the decision table named GRIND SPICE YOURSELF (Figure 4.19).

The use of a mortar and pestle is a default plan; that is, it applies when all else fails. The cook has no blender, no coffee grinder, and no rolling pin with wax paper. There is an underlying assumption on the part of Jaffrey that people who have no blenders, no coffee grinders, and no rolling pins with wax paper, or who

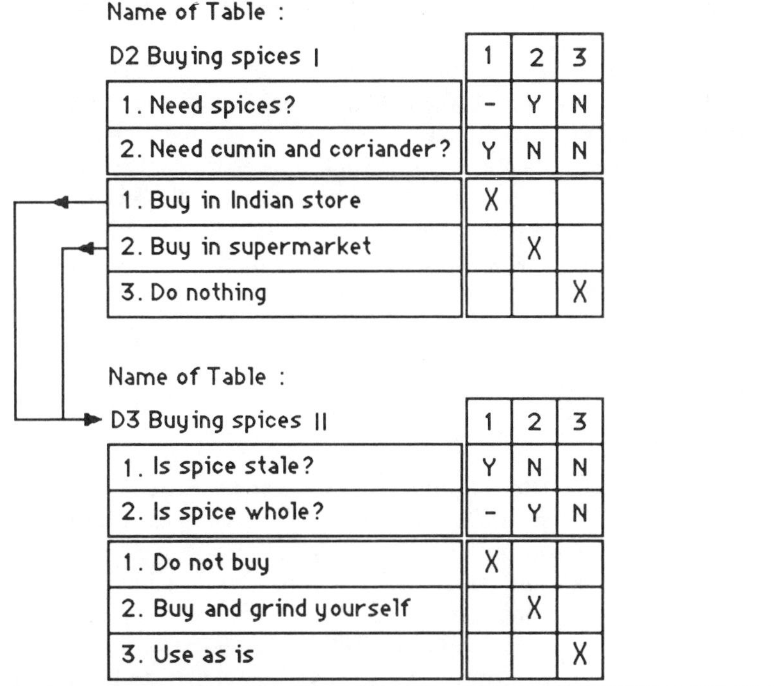

Name of Table :

D2 Buying spices I	1	2	3
1. Need spices?	-	Y	N
2. Need cumin and coriander?	Y	N	N
1. Buy in Indian store	X		
2. Buy in supermarket		X	
3. Do nothing			X

Name of Table :

D3 Buying spices II	1	2	3
1. Is spice stale?	Y	N	N
2. Is spice whole?	-	Y	N
1. Do not buy	X		
2. Buy and grind yourself		X	
3. Use as is			X

Figure 4.18 Reduced BUYING SPICES I and II

Name of Table: Grind Spice Yourself	1	2	3	4	5	6	7	8	9	10	11	12	13	14	15	16
1. Do you have a coffee grinder? (condition 2)	Y	Y	Y	Y	Y	Y	Y	Y	N	N	N	N	N	N	N	N
2. Do you have a rolling pin? (condition 3)	Y	Y	Y	Y	N	N	N	N	Y	Y	Y	Y	N	N	N	N
3. Do you have an electric blender (condition 4)	Y	Y	N	N	Y	Y	N	N	Y	Y	N	N	Y	Y	N	N
4. Do you have large quantity? (consition 5)	Y	N	Y	N	Y	N	Y	N	Y	N	Y	N	Y	N	Y	N
5. Do you have mortar and pestle? (condition 6)	(if all else fails option)															
1. Grind spices in blender in large quantity (action 4)	X				X				X				X			
2. Grind spices in coffeee grinder in small quantity (action 2)		X	X	X		X	X	X								
3. Grind spices slightly roasted in small quantity with rolling pin between wax paper										X	X	X				
4. Use mortar and pestle (action 5)														X	X	X

Figure 4.19 Decision Table: GRIND SPICE YOURSELF

were unsuccessful with all of these methods, do own a mortar and pestle and would resort to its use. Here we accept this assumption, though any ethnographer would normally check this notion with consultants.

The condition for the use of the mortar and pestle because it is the default value are the "N" (Rule 16) for the availability of the first three devices. Therefore this condition is implicitly incorporated through the use of the first four conditions. By eliminating the mortar and pestle condition we have reduced the possible combinations from $2^5 = 32$ rules to a more manageable $2^4 = 16$ rules.

We now proceed to apply the reduction rules to the table (Figure 4.20), then advance to the reduction of the second condition of this decision table (Figure 4.21). We continue with the reduction of actions 3 and 4 in Figures 4.22 and 4.23. The reduced decision table of Figure 4.19 appears in Figure 4.24.

With these preliminaries we can now redraw the decision model as a sequence of three decision tables (see Figure 4.25).

4.3 FLOWCHARTS

The two decision tables forming the decision sequence of our model entitled BUYING SPICES and GRIND SPICE YOURSELF can easily be converted into a flowchart. The main advantage of a decision table is that it makes the presentation of simultaneous decisions possible. Because it forces the ethnographer to consider all possible combinations of decisions, it is superior to flowcharts *as an eliciting tool* as well. However, flowcharts are easier to read because one has to follow only the progression of lines (arrows) and decisions (diamonds) to arrive at appropriate outcomes.

Name of Table :

Grind Spice Yourself: reduction of action 1	1	5	9	13		1/5	9/13		1/5/9/13
1. Do you have a coffee grinder? (condition 2)	Y	Y	N	N	reduces to	Y	N	reduces to	-
2. Do you have a rolling pin? (condition 3)	Y	N	Y	N		-	-		-
3. Do you have an electric blender (condition 4)	Y	Y	Y	Y		Y	Y		Y
4. Do you have large quantity? (consition 5)	Y	Y	Y	Y		Y	Y		Y
1. Grind spices in blender in large quantity (action 4)	X	X	X	X		X	X		X

Figure 4.20 Reduction of GRIND SPICE YOURSELF I

Name of Table:

Grind Spice Yourself: reduction of action 2	2	3	4	6	7	8		2	3/4	7/8	6		2	3/4/7/8	6		2/6	3/4/7/8
1. Do you have a coffee grinder? (condition 2)	Y	Y	Y	Y	Y	Y		Y	Y	Y	Y		Y	Y	Y		Y	Y
2. Do you have a rolling pin? (condition 3)	Y	Y	Y	N	N	N	red. to	Y	Y	N	N	red. to	Y	-	N	red. to	-	-
3. Do you have an electric blender (condition 4)	Y	N	N	Y	N	N		Y	N	N	Y		Y	N	Y		Y	N
4. Do you have large quantity? (consition 5)	N	Y	N	N	Y	N		N	-	-	N		N	-	N		N	-
2. Grind spices in coffee grinder in small quantity	X	X	X	X	X	X		X	X	X	X		X	X	X		X	X

Figure 4.21 Reduction of GRIND SPICE YOURSELF II

Name of Table:

Grind Spice Yourself: reduction of action 3

	10	11	12		10	11/12
1. Do you have a coffee grinder? (condition 2)	N	N	N		N	
2. Do you have a rolling pin? (condition 3)	Y	Y	Y	reduces to	Y	Y
3. Do you have an electric blender (condition 4)	Y	N	N		Y	N
4. Do you have large quantity? (consition 5)	N	Y	N		N	-
3. Grind spices slightly roasted in small quantity with rolling pin between wax paper	X	X	X		X	X

Figure 4.22 Reduction of GRIND SPICE YOURSELF III

Name of Table:

Grind Spice Yourself: reduction of action 4

	14	15	16		14	15/16
1. Do you have a coffee grinder? (condition 2)	N	N	N		N	N
2. Do you have a rolling pin? (condition 3)	N	N	N	reduces to	N	N
3. Do you have an electric blender (condition 4)	Y	N	N		N	N
4. Do you have large quantity? (consition 5)	N	Y	N		N	-
4. Use mortar and pestle	X	X	X		X	X

Figure 4.23 Reduction of GRIND SPICE YOURSELF IV

The distinction between decision tables and flowcharts is ultimately only a surface difference, although one that can make a difference in readability. The two structures are completely isomorphic. By this we mean that any flowchart can be converted unambiguously into a decision table and vice versa.

To convert a decision table to a flowchart is simple. The rows and columns of the condition entry of a decision table are permuted (interchanged) until the pattern for the flowchart emerges. That is, first the most complete row (condition) is moved to the top of the chart. Then all Y are moved to the left and all N to the right. The remaining rows are then moved one at a time so that the next split affects only the "Y" or the "N" side in the row above it. The procedure can be illustrated best by an example. One at a time we convert the three decision tables in Figure 4.25 into a single flowchart (Figure 4.26).

It is clear that the first condition divides the results into action 1 and actions 2 and 3. We represent this more graphically in Figure 4.27. The flowchart is now easy to construct. The first decision diamond concerns the need for cumin and coriander. The Y branch directs the reader to the Indian store. The N branch leads to the need for other spices. Here the Y branch recommends buying at the super-

Name of Table:

Grind Spice Yourself (reduced)	1	2	3	4	5	6	7
1. Do you have a coffee grinder?	-	Y	N	N	Y	N	N
2. Do you have a rolling pin?	-	-		N	-	Y	N
3. Do you have an electric blender	Y	Y	Y	N	N	N	N
4. Do you have large quantity?	Y	N	N	N	-	-	-
1. Grind spices in blender in large quantity	X						
2. Grind spices in coffeee grinder in small quantity		X			X		
3. Grind spices slightly roasted in small quantity with rolling pin between wax paper			X			X	
4. Use mortar and pestle				X			X

Figure 4.24 Reduced GRIND SPICE YOURSELF

market. The N branch leads to no action if there is no need. We present the resulting flowchart in Figure 4.28.

We now continue with the conversion of the second decision table to a flowchart. The conditions in BUYING SPICES II are already properly arranged. We now continue with the conversion of the third decision table to a flowchart.

Converting BUYING SPICES I and II was relatively trivial. The conversion of the table GRIND SPICE YOURSELF is more complex. Before conversion we repeat Figure 4.25 (see Figure 4.30).

The next step is to reorder the rows and columns to facilitate conversion to a flowchart. Row three (decision 3) needs to be moved into first place. The Y and N are already ordered with all the Y on the left and all the N on the right. Row 3 unambiguously subdivides all rules (the entire rule set) into the Y set and the N set. The next row to be moved into second position is number 4. This rule set makes no difference for the N set above it, while it unambiguously subdivides the Y set into one Y branch and three N branches. The first condition (row) now becomes the third. It divides the N set of the preceding row 4 (now in row 2) and the N set of row 3 (now in row 1) into a Y and an N branch. Finally, row 2 is last. It divides the N two rows above it. With these preliminaries we now redraw Figure 4.30 (see Figure 4.31).

The flowchart clearly emerges from the pattern of the Y and N. Figure 4.32 makes it more graphic.

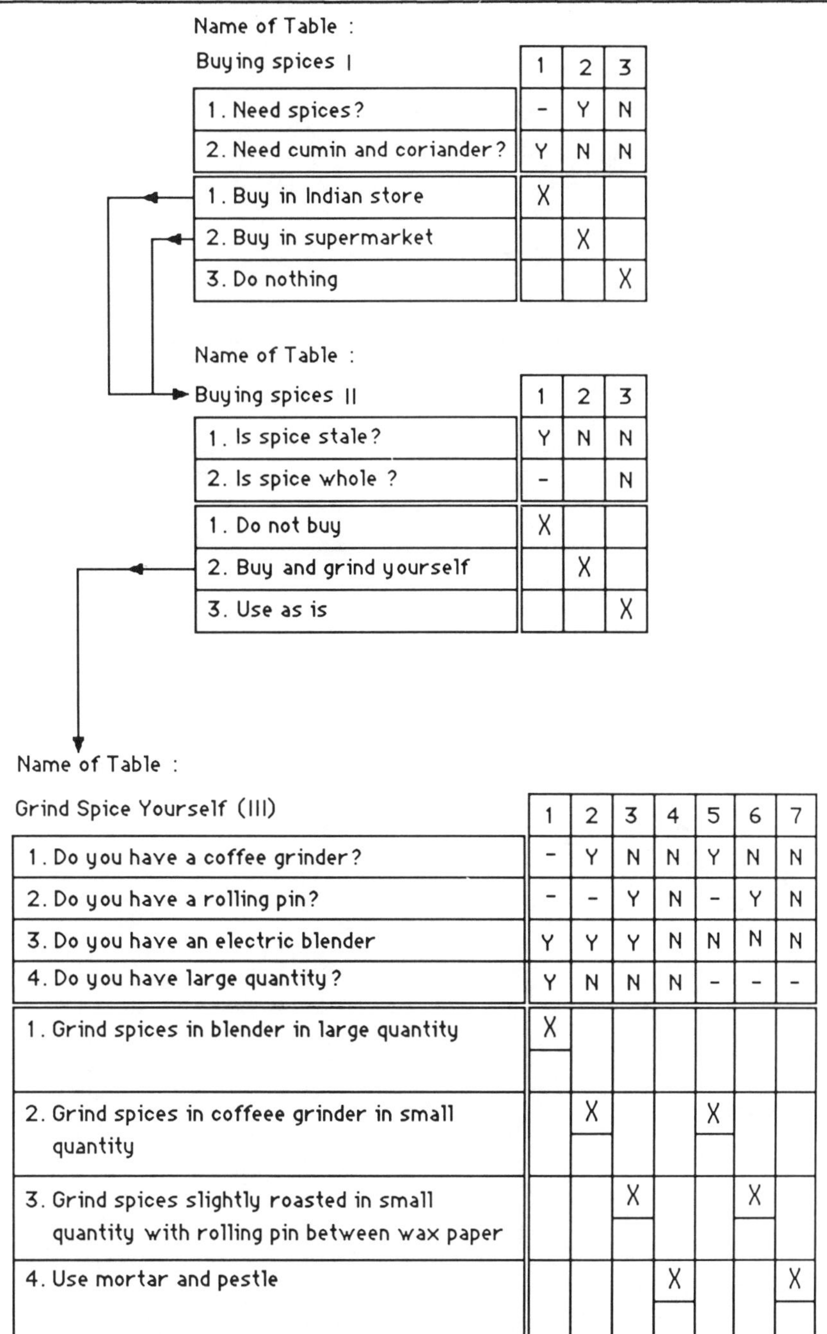

Name of Table :

Buying spices I

	1	2	3
1. Need spices?	-	Y	N
2. Need cumin and coriander?	Y	N	N
1. Buy in Indian store	X		
2. Buy in supermarket		X	
3. Do nothing			X

Name of Table :

Buying spices II

	1	2	3
1. Is spice stale?	Y	N	N
2. Is spice whole ?	-		N
1. Do not buy	X		
2. Buy and grind yourself		X	
3. Use as is			X

Name of Table :

Grind Spice Yourself (III)

	1	2	3	4	5	6	7
1. Do you have a coffee grinder?	-	Y	N	N	Y	N	N
2. Do you have a rolling pin?	-	-	Y	N	-	Y	N
3. Do you have an electric blender	Y	Y	Y	N	N	N	N
4. Do you have large quantity?	Y	N	N	N	-	-	-
1. Grind spices in blender in large quantity	X						
2. Grind spices in coffeee grinder in small quantity		X			X		
3. Grind spices slightly roasted in small quantity with rolling pin between wax paper			X			X	
4. Use mortar and pestle				X			X

Figure 4.25 BUYING SPICES and GRIND SPICE YOURSELF

Name of Table :

Buying spices I	1	2	3
2. Need cumin and coriander?	Y	N	N
1. Need spices?	-	Y	N
1. Do not buy	X		
2. Buy and grind yourself		X	
3. Use as is			X

Figure 4.26 Reordering of BUYING SPICES I

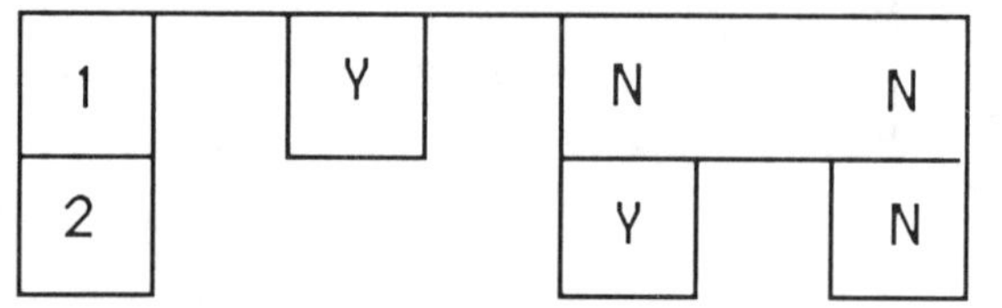

Figure 4.27 Conversion of Decision Table 1

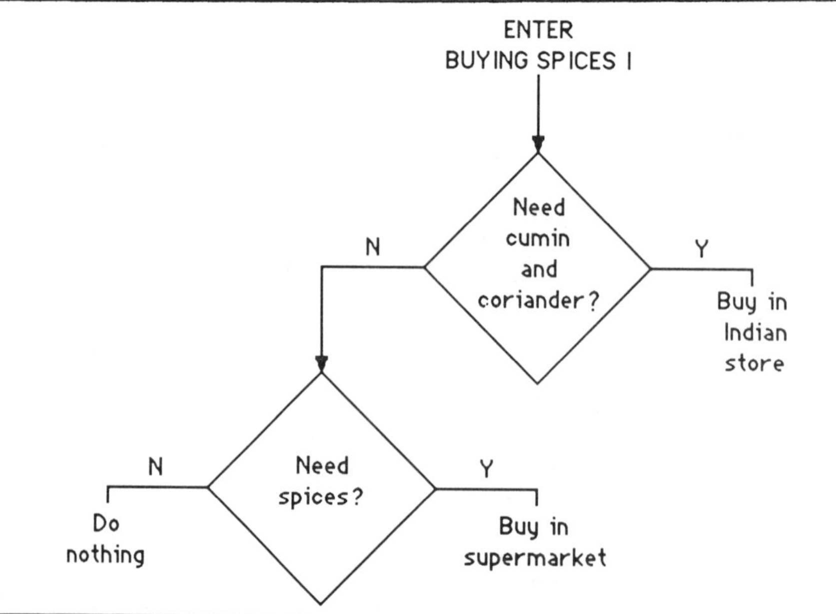

Figure 4.28 Flowchart: BUYING SPICES I

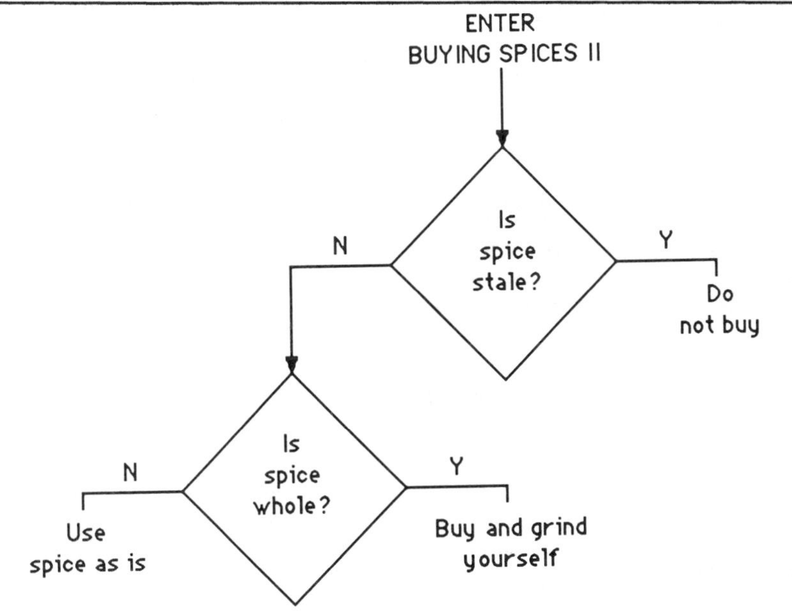

Figure 4.29 Flowchart: BUYING SPICES II

Name of Table:

Grind Spice Yourself (reduced)	1	2	3	4	5	6	7
1. Do you have a coffee grinder?	–	Y	N	N		N	N
2. Do you have a rolling pin?	–	–	Y	N	–	Y	N
3. Do you have an electric blender	Y	Y	Y	N	N	N	N
4. Do you have large quantity?	Y	N	N	N	–	–	–
1. Grind spices in blender in large quantity	X						
2. Grind spices in coffeee grinder in small quantity		X			X		
3. Grind spices slightly roasted in small quantity with rolling pin between wax paper			X			X	
4. Use mortar and pestle				X			X

Figure 4.30 Decision Table III of Figure 4.25

Name of Table:

Grind Spice Yourself III

	1	2	3	4	5	6	7
3. Do you have an electric blender	Y	Y	Y	N	N	N	N
4. Do you have large quantity?	Y	N	N	N	-	-	-
1. Do you have a coffee grinder?	-	Y	N	N	Y	N	N
2. Do you have a rolling pin?	-	-	Y	N	-	Y	N
1. Grind spices in blender in large quantity	X						
2. Grind spices in coffeee grinder in small quantity		X			X		
3. Grind spices slightly roasted in small quantity with rolling pin between wax paper			X			X	
4. Use mortar and pestle				X			X

Figure 4.31 Reordering of Figure 4.30

1	Y	Y	Y	Y	N	N	N
2	Y	N	N	N	-	-	-
3		Y	N	N	Y	N	N
4			Y	N		Y	N

Figure 4.32 Conversion to Flowchart

The conversion into a flowchart is now easy. It is illustrated in the lower part of the flowchart in Figure 4.33,which merges BUYING SPICES and GRIND SPICE YOURSELF into one master flowchart.

In order to amplify the conversion of decision tables to flowcharts, we consider a special case.[2] It is best illustrated with a hypothetical example. The decision table in Figure 4.34 can be converted to a flowchart.

Condition 1 is clearly subdivided into the Y set and the N set. Everything under the Y set of this row follows precedent. However, on the right side, the N set is unusual. Here we have to take condition 3 first, which subdivides the N set of condition 1, *and then* condition 2, which subdivides the N set of condition 3. In

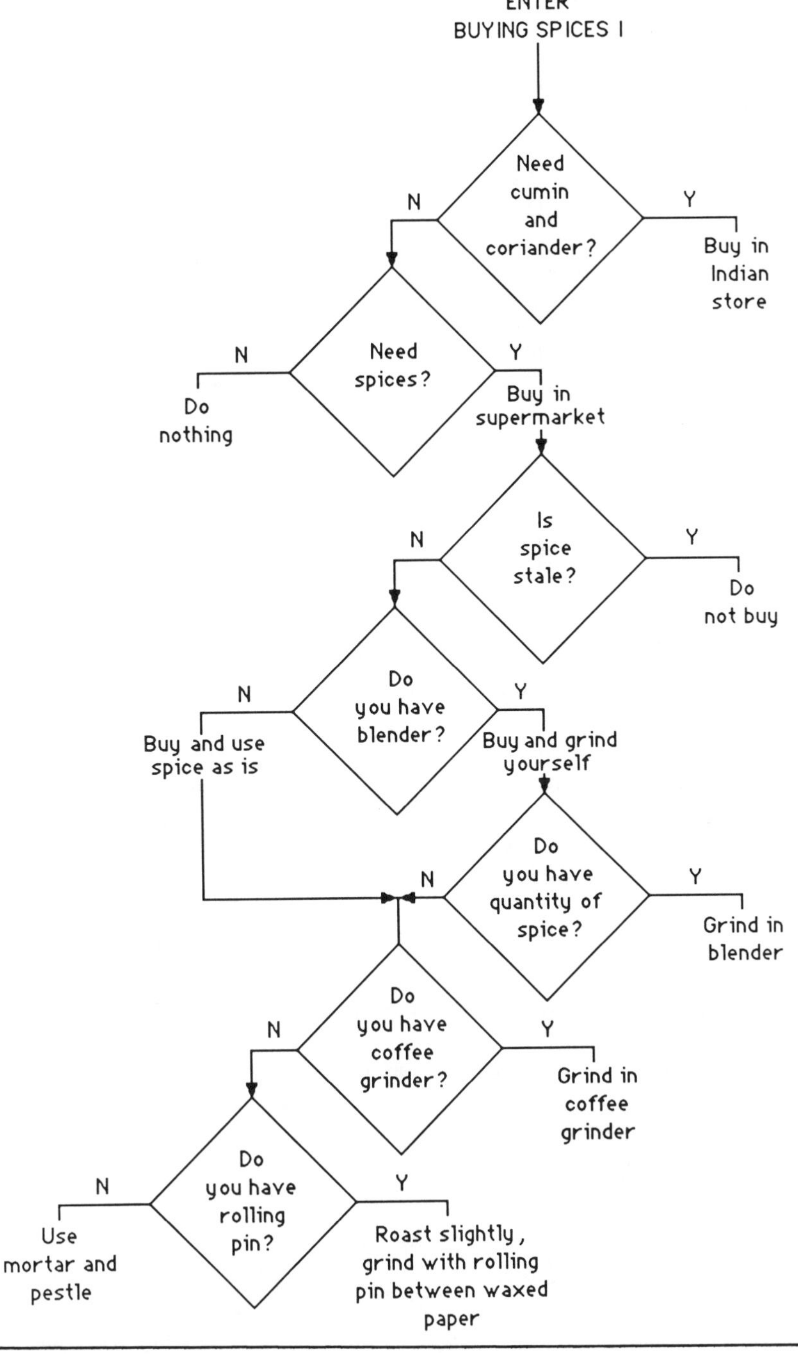

Figure 4.33 Flowchart of Jaffrey's (1975) Text

Name of Table:

Special case of flowchart reduction

C1	Y		Y		Y		N		N		N
C2	Y		Y		Y		-		Y		N
C3	Y		N		-		Y		N		N
A1	X								X		
A2			X								
A3					X		X				
A4											X

NOTE: The style of presentation is a combination of the earlier style and the style of Figure 4.32

Figure 4.34 Special Case of a Flowchart Reduction

other words, while the left branch follows the sequence condition 1, then 2, then 3, the right branch follows the sequence Condition 1, then 3, then 2.

The general rule is as follows: If a condition completely partitions a decision table's rule set, then in the two branches immediately below it, the order of the following conditions may be reversed in different branches of the graph.

For the sake of clarity we follow the general principle with the flowchart of the decision table in Figure 4.34.

The reduction rules and the rules for converting a decision table to a flowchart in most cases are sufficient to reduce any decision table to its simplest form and to convert this version to a flowchart. The rules are automatic—that is, they represent an algorithm. Therefore, any decision table is isomorphic with a flowchart. For dealing with subtleties and exceptional cases, the reader should consult the specialized literature.

4.4 DECISION TREES

Decision trees are the final form for the representation of decisions that we discuss. This graphing method is also isomorphic with decision tables and flowcharts. Although a decision tree adds no new information, it is usually easier to type and may therefore be used in typescripts. Figures 4.35, as well as 4.28 and 4.29, show the identity of the two representations.

A little rearrangement and treatment of the conditions as attributes makes clear that a decision tree is an abbreviated version of the representation of a decision model in the MTQ schema of lexical/semantic relations. (For details see Volume 1, Section 2.3.2). The resulting decision tree in the MTQ schema appears in Figure 4.36.

This completes our presentation of the formal aspects of decision tables, flowcharts, and decision trees. These models apply to decisions made by a single actor—the creator of the paragraph of text that is converted to a decision table and related forms. The next section deals with the representation of multiperson decisions.

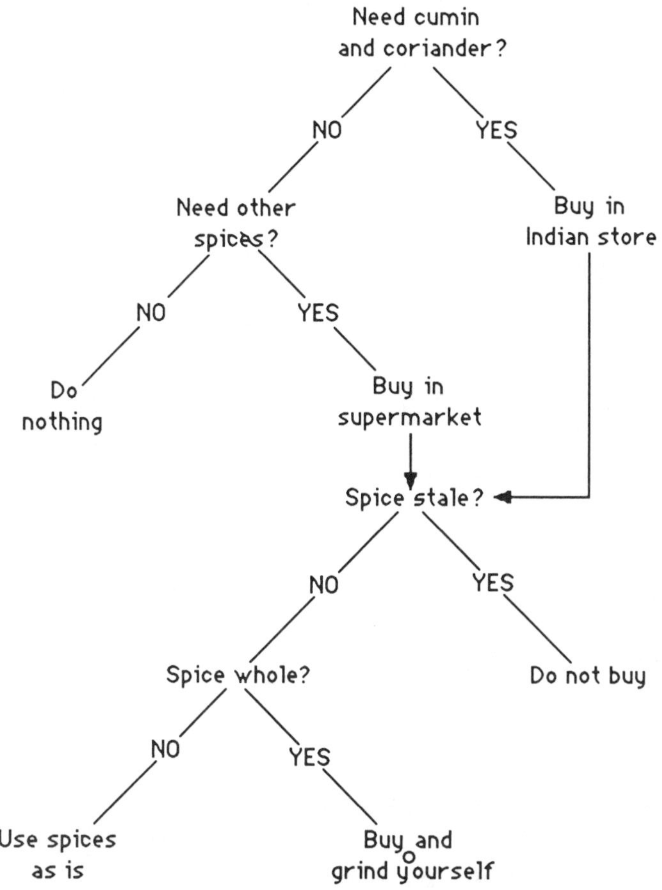

Figure 4.35 Decision Tree: BUYING SPICES I and II

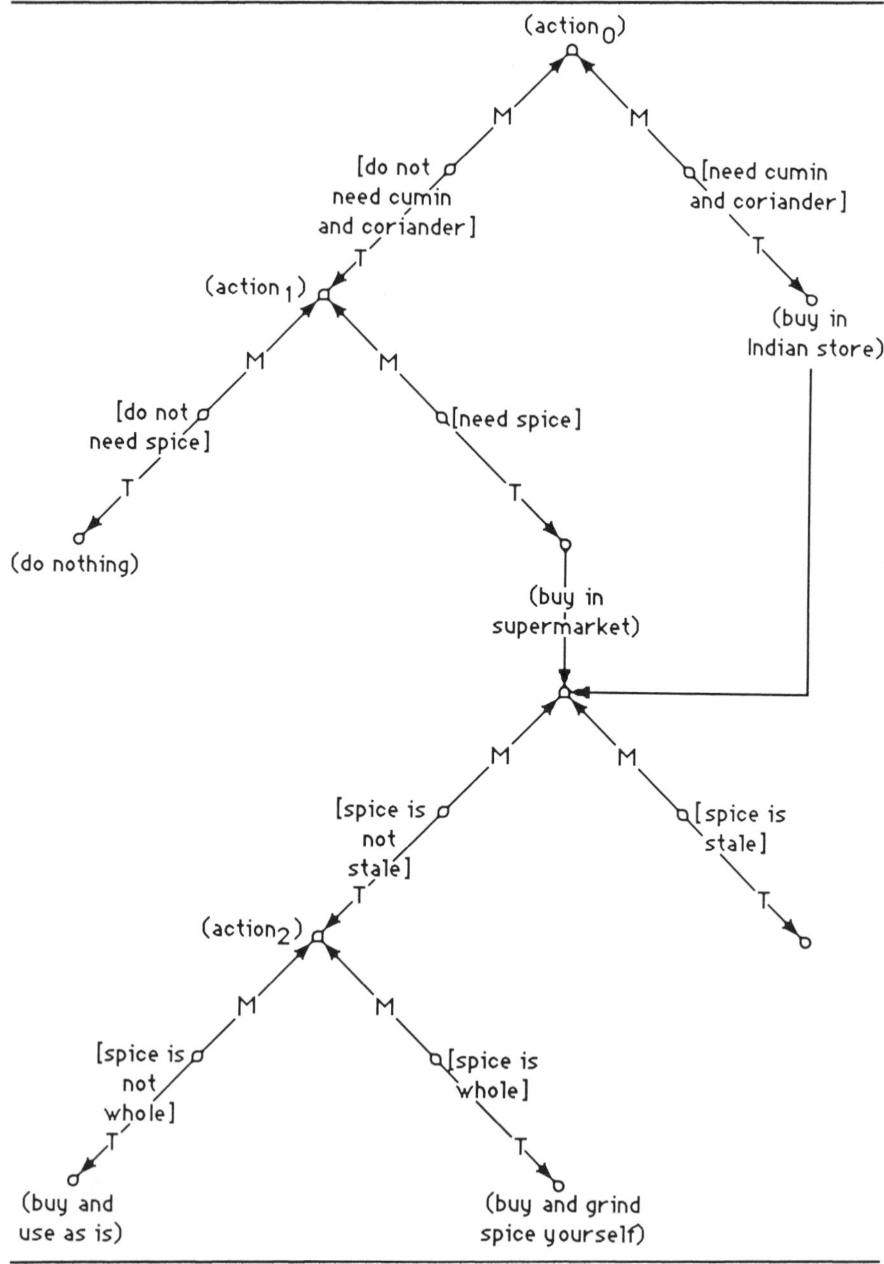

Figure 4.36 Decision Tree in MTQ Schema

4.5 MULTIPERSON DECISIONS

All the methods and procedures in the preceding sections dealt with a text elicited from a single consultant and its conversion to a decision table, a flowchart, or a decision tree. In this section we touch briefly on the uses of these (isomorphic) devices for the description of multiperson decisions.

Christine Gladwin has achieved particularly striking predictive results by constructing composite flowcharts based on interviews and on direct observations of a sample of consultants (Gladwin 1976). Her work also combines decision modeling with statistical information.

The following section presents a single case from which we draw generalizations. We describe how Gladwin (1976) arrived at the first flowchart of this section (Figure 4.37). This description consists of several steps. At each step we generalize the methodology. The final part of this section is a "backtranslation" of the flowchart in Figure 4.37 into a decision table (Figure 4.38). Because this example is lengthy we do not follow our usual procedure of labeling this example as a case.

The flowchart in Figure 4.37 is based on intensive ethnographic fieldwork with a sample of individuals. For the successful design of this type of a multiperson decision model, Gladwin recommends a sample of 25 to 30 consultants. This could be a random sample—in Gladwin's example, about one-third of the farmers in a village. In the following pages we present in sequence each step in this procedure.

(1) Select a random sample of 25-30 individuals for intensive work (out of a population of about 100). It may take several months of work to arrive at a reliable decision model. It is therefore important to select consultants who are willing to participate in intensive interview sessions over several months. The flowchart of this section and other flowcharts, descriptions, and so on not shown here were based on three months of intensive interviewing and observation (Gladwin 1976).

(2) Make certain that consultants understand the need for prolonged interviewing and observation (for example, in the farmer's fields). The combination of observation and interviewing is very important. This type of work cannot be done reliably in the isolation of a white room setting. The best way to visualize the interaction between observation and conversation is through the homing-in model (see Volume 1, Section 1.3.7). Observation and conversation follow each other in regular iterations. Each iteration comes closer to the native's point of view.

Many decisions are semiautomatic, out of immediate awareness, and are therefore difficult to elicit away from the "grass hut" setting. The observation and interviewing cycle aids in uncovering implicit processes that have become second nature to consultants. These processes are rarely made explicit in ordinary interaction. Of course, in every community there are eloquent individuals who can verbalize better than others. The best combination for ethnographic discovery is a well-documented observation/interview cycle *and* articulate consultants.

(3) Organize work around regular iterations of observing activities and controlled interviewing. This observation and conversation leads to the statement of hypotheses. These specify decision criteria, which can be submitted to the sample population for testing.

(4) Formulate decision criteria as hypotheses to be tested. In order to test the decision criteria, two conditions must be met. First, the decision criteria must be

formulated in a language that the consultants can easily understand. This means that they must be formulated in the native language and in an idiom that the consultants use themselves for talking about their activities. Second, to take full advantage of the formalization of decisions, the ethnographer must construct decision tables or flowcharts.

(5) Design a decision table or a flowchart based on decision criteria formulated in the language specific to the consultants. The early formalization has the disadvantage of commitment to a rigid pattern, but this rigidity also contains a tremendous advantage. An early formulation correct in all detail is rare. Commitment to formal models such as decision tables and flowcharts provides the ethnographer with a rigid structure for the data. This rigidity makes testing easier. The formal model is much *more vulnerable to disconfirmation* than less formal (e.g., entirely verbal) procedures. Discrepancies with the "reality" of the consultants' actions become glaringly apparent and therefore readily amenable to correction.

(6) Submit decision tables or flowcharts for comments by the sample of decision makers who provided the original data. The first test is descriptive adequacy. By this we mean answers to the following questions: "Does the decision model describe all activities adequately?" and "Does the model describe all activities exhaustively?" A decision model is "generative" in the sense that one can "read off" the charts and tables the activities resulting from decisions. Descriptive adequacy demands a detailed description of every activity that may result and the assurance that no potentially possible course of action is excluded.

(7) Test descriptive adequacy of the model by generating an exhaustive sample of possible activities. Test the adequacy of the description of each activity so generated. On a higher theoretical level, decision models make predictive claims. These claims must also be tested first with the sample of decision makers who were responsible for providing the observational and conversational data from which the decision tables and flowcharts were constructed.

(8) Test the predictions of the decision model with the sample population. At this stage the model may be translated into the language of the users of the report, the client who commissioned the study, or the scholarly community. It is important to keep in mind that this is a translation and not the real decision model. *The original decision model is always in the language of the consultants.* Translations may be in the language of anthropologists, economists, medical personnel, or policy planners—whoever might be the ultimate "consumer" of the ethnographic report.

(9) Translate the decision model into scholarly language, so that professionals may inspect the logical consistency of the model. At this stage the model can be tested with a population other than the people from whom the original decision criteria were elicited. That is, it is now useful to draw a random sample—in Christina Gladwin's case, from the population of all the other farmers of the village who did not participate in the construction of the model. The original model, in the native language and utilizing local native usage of this language, is now presented to a (preferably) random sample of this population.

(10) Test model, adequacy, and predictions with a random sample of consultants who did not participate in the construction of the model. After testing and possibly fine-tuning the final model, fit may be translated in improved form for its use by professionals.

The result of these procedures may be a flowchart or a decision table. Figures 4.37 and 4.38 show both. The flowchart is adapted from Gladwin (1976). This is the decision model as it was presented to the scholarly community, in this case agricultural economists.

The flowchart and the decision table summarize a tremendous amount of work—first, the decisions derived from the original sample of 25 and, second, the final test with a random sample of an additional 34 farmers. Third, the flowchart specifies the nature of the decision to three different soil types or planting types

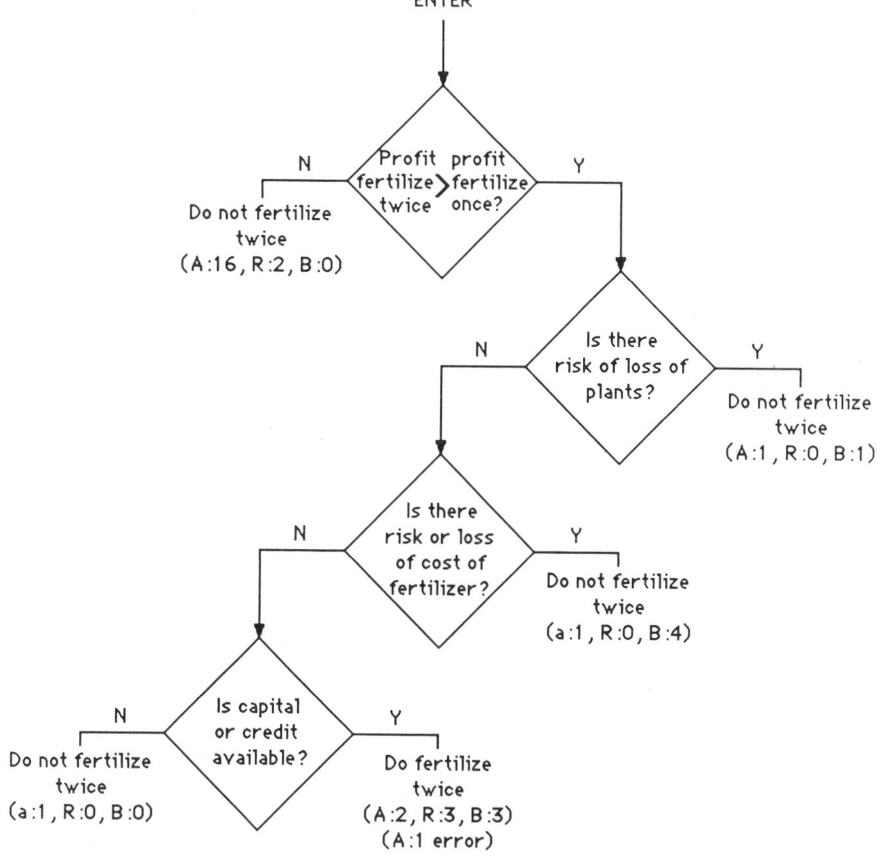

NOTE: The symbols are as follows: A = arena, sandy soil; R = irrigated fields; B = barro or loamy soils. Numbers indicate the number of farmers who used a particular decision sequence. Adapted from Gladwin (1976).

Figure 4.37 Testing Flowchart with Sample Population

(A: *arena,* sandy soil; R: irrigated fields; and B: *barro,* or loamy soils). Fourth, the flowchart demonstrates the tremendous degree of accuracy attainable using these methods. There was only one error in the random sample test on 34 farmers. The flowchart in Figure 4.37 illustrates.

The decision table, as we have shown, does not have the advantage of easier comprehension of the sequential nature of decisions. However, it does capture better the simultaneity of considering in a decision several factors at the same time. An added bonus is the more adequate presentation of numerical data. The numbers assume the same role that the X did in the Action Entry quadrant of decision tables (Figure 4.10). This method of marking action outcomes can be elevated to a general principle of multiperson decision tables:

If a decision table is a composite of many individual decisions then the X in the Action Entry quadrant can be replaced by the frequency of that particular outcome. The decision table in Figure 4.38 illustrates.

4.6 SUMMARY AND CONCLUSIONS

Decision tables, flowcharts, and decision trees are isomorphic representations of decisions: how to choose between alternative plans. However, decision tables

Name of Table:

When to Fertilize Twice		1	2	3	4	5	
1. Profit fertilize twice > profit fertilize once?		Y	Y	Y	Y	Y	
2. Is there risk of loss of plants?		-	Y	N	N	N	
3. Is there risk of loss of cost of fertilizer?		-	-	Y	N	N	
4. Is capital or credit available ?		-	-	-	Y	N	
1. Do not fertilize twice	Soil A	16	1	1		1	
	Soil R	2	0	0		0	
	Soil B	0	1	4		0	
2. Do fertilize twice	Soil A				2*		
	Soil R				3		
	Soil B				3		
TOTALS		18	2	5	8	1	34

* 1 error

NOTE: Adapted from Gladwin (1976).

Figure 4.38 Testing Decision Table with Sample Population

are easiest to use for the elicitation of decision data (conditions and actions). Decision trees and flowcharts are easier to read, but the simultaneity of decisions that a decision table is able to capture is lost.

The rules (algorithm) for constructing a decision table and of reducing redundancy are simple. Complexity is introduced when the number of conditions and actions becomes large—larger than will fit on an $8^1/_2 \times 11$ (216×279 mm) sheet of paper. Rearranging rows and columns for converting decision table to flowcharts can also introduce errors.

Decision tables and flowcharts can be used to describe the decision processes of groups of people—for example, farmers of a village and their planting decisions. Although the formal complexity rarely increases, the elicitation process, even for relatively simple sequences of decisions, can become elaborate.

NOTES

1. Brackets imply statements added or reconstructed as a result of analysis.
2. We are grateful for this example to Gregory Starrett. Other similar examples could be listed. We leave these cases to the ingenuity of the ethnographer. Our examples cover most major solutions.

Chapter 5

Decision Making and Decision Models

Decision models take us well beyond "classical" ethnoscience. In this section we explore the implications of the advance.

5.0 INTRODUCTION

Ethnoscience or cognitive ethnography can efficiently uncover the overall structure and context of cultural knowledge. This context involves, as was originally defined by Goodenough (1956), the shared meta-knowledge individuals must have in order to adapt to the social and nonsocial environment in which they live. Social scientists in general have had difficulty obtaining this kind of background information. Anthropologists, while often able to collect this information through years of steeping themselves in the cultural life of the natives, were either unable to make this meta-knowledge quickly available or unable to place it in a form that can be evaluated by other social scientists.

We propose that ethnoscience ethnography constitutes an ideal approach for obtaining such knowledge precisely because it can be done more quickly than a style of ethnography relying on unspecified participant observation alone. Its results can be evaluated not only by scientific peers but also by natives—the human subjects of the ethnography. Ethnoscience's scientifically healthy vulnerability to criticism is made possible because of its explicitness. That is, both its elements and the relationships between these elements are formal, simple, definable, and can be stated in terms that natives can easily understand. With folk definition[1] as the basic unit of meaning and analysis, elegance is enhanced because the elements are interconnected by the simple lexical/semantic relations of modification (M), taxonomy (T), sequence (Q), and other, more complex derived relations (see Chapter 6). Thus definition and general modification (attribution) provide the elemental building blocks of all complex lexical/semantic structures.

Knowledge can be elicited "from the top down" through systematic interview of knowledgeable consultants. By combining open-ended interview and follow-up questions, we can begin with the most general and abstract terms people use when referring to their experience and work our way down through the lexical/semantic structure. This process is well described as the "craft" of interviewing. It can be done almost automatically simply by asking a native informant to define what he or she has just mentioned in a taxonomy, a folk definition, or a plan (plans can be viewed as parts of folk definitions; all of these are texts).

There are limitations to this approach if we restrict ourselves to the elicitation of folk definitions, taxonomies, sequences, and logical if-then relationships. These limitations are most acute when we examine what people tell us about behavior, as well as behavior that involves considerable uncertainty. At this point the ethnographers find themselves under increasing pressure to supplement pure cognitive ethnography with the more indefinite art of general ethnography, and thus to expand systematic interviewing with participant and other types of observation. This involves moving out of "white rooms" into "grass huts" and even into "grassy fields" (see Volume 1, Figure 6.5 and Case 10.1). We may ignore much of what is important in life if we ignore some activities simply because consultants are unable to state *directly* what rule or pattern applies to what they do.

Some of these limitations are inherent in the ethnographer as a human being. Certain events occur in a community that cannot be anticipated (much less predicted) and surprise the ethnographer, even though he or she feels relatively comfortable. Other limitations are based simply on the fact that ethnoscience ethnography concentrates primarily on that aspect of knowledge which is verbalizable, or that can be deduced from verbal statements, as opposed to that which is based on patterns out of awareness and must be inferred through experimentation, clinical analysis, or mathematical modeling. For these reasons we find that some of an individual actor's behavior can become automatic, out of awareness, and therefore difficult or perhaps impossible to elicit. In addition, behavior may depend on too many environmental considerations for the consultant to itemize them immediately all out of context. The situation gets more complex if we move from individuals to groups. The complexity further increases with the size of the group (see Volume 1, Figures 2.4 and 5.6 and Section 1.3.5).

These limitations based on the nature of verbalizable knowledge warrant more discussion. First, for behavior out of awareness, at one time or another all of us have found it difficult to describe some motor function, such as whittling or shaving, in detail. Similarly, an observer finds it difficult to see when or how a baker knows when the dough has risen properly and is of proper consistency to begin baking. Many highly skilled activities, performed with Zen-like (postattentive) control, fall into this category.

Both actor and observer must learn a skill by acting out portions of the behavior while observing and conversing. In these situations an actor notes things he or she has never noticed before and reports them to the interviewer. An observer can ask an actor what led to a specific behavioral event and what it meant and then make further inferences, checking with the actor regularly.

The solution to these limitations is clear. The ethnographer must shift his or her attention methodically between participation or intensive observation and conversation: asking the consultant what is happening. This iteration is like a homing-in process (see Volume 1, Section 1.3.7) in which the researcher begins to understand the knowledge associated with an activity through observation, even experimentation, and then asking about the observed event or experimental outcome, observing and experimenting some more, asking about the outcomes, and so on until time, patience, or money runs out.

Quinn (1976) illustrates the problem in her study of formal dispute settlement among the Mfantse. She observed actors and events that transpired during actual incidents of dispute settlement and asked actors about what they had to consider for each individual decision. This is analogous to making definitions and generalization from cases (see Volume 1, Section 3.2). In a few situations an ethnographer can be present as a case happens. This arrangement is often ideal for observation/conversation and their iteration. Many other parts of native life are not so easily accessible. The different accounts of multiple participants (see discussion of the Rashomon Effect in Volume 1, Section 3.2.2) can help solve some of these problems (see Volume 1, Section 1.2).

Christina Gladwin (1976) found that Mexican farmers made vague generalizations about why they refused to adopt a method of crop fertilization recommended to them by agricultural extension agents. Moreover, they rejected the innovation despite the fact that its superiority (better crop yield) was demonstrated in special plots (H. Gladwin and Murtaugh, 1980). When conducting ethnographic research on behavior under uncertainty, ethnographers must hypothesize (sometimes in considerable detail) what the actors are doing, what makes them decide to do it, and then confirm (or, better yet, test) the hypotheses through more observations and more conversant actions (interviews).

In many of these cases, several salient characteristics of behavior emerge. First, the actors do not always recall the factors that make them act as they do, though they may understand their actions well enough to explain them when actual instances are brought to their attention. Thus Quinn found that the Mfantse know quite well what sort of kinship and network conditions influence them in deciding who is liable in a dispute and how much reparation they must pay. They simply did not look at the subject the way the ethnographer did. The same holds true for the farmers with whom Gladwin worked. Obviously, the reverse is also true: Our consultants teach us new ways of viewing their activities.

Second, the actors may not know exactly what environmental conditions influence their decisions but may base their decisions on some indirect *indicator* of that condition. These indicators are referred to as *heuristics* in this section and will be discussed in greater detail below.

In another study, Quinn (1978) found that the Mfantse fish sellers do not know whether favorable or unfavorable market conditions will greet them when they start selling their fish; they work under considerable uncertainty. As a result, the Mfantse merchants do not calculate demand for fish in markets but instead look for large numbers of canoes along the coast, which implies a large catch and indirectly a saturated market. Under these conditions merchants often decide to smoke their fish to prevent spoilage and wait a few days before selling after the number of canoes decreases. These heuristics (the canoes) are the indicators of environmental conditions that actors take into account to infer uncertain or unknown conditions.

Both Quinn and Gladwin recommend that the ethnographer must immerse himself or herself in a context—that is, become observers and conversationalists in "grass huts" (see Volume 1, Section 6.5 and Figure 6.5)—if they want to achieve a better understanding of activities that extend beyond a superficial description. We agree, and add that this observation must be monitored using ethnoscience techniques, based on ethnoscience ethnography that goes on before, during, and after "grass hut" observation. In other words, observation can be done just as elegantly and methodically as ethnoscience ethnography and can and should precede it. Conversational participation while observing is even better.

5.1 DECISION MAKING

Through the study of decision making and the modeling of these decisions behavior can be better understood. In order to do this we discuss the following points:

(1) decision making in general and modeling of decisions in particular;
(2) how to construct a decision model by means of decision tables, flowcharts, and decision trees (see Chapter 4);
(3) how one constructs a decision model in the field under ethnographic conditions; and
(4) what is the psychological reality of these models (i.e., do they reflect people's knowledge of what is going on, or simply predict what people are going to do?)

Our assumption about all behavior is based on the premise that *all purposive behavior must be preceded by a decision to initiate that behavior* (see Chapter 4). We are restricted in our topic of discussion only because it is clear that some behaviors—for example, behavior that is out of control—is not purposive.[2] We must exclude behaviors initiated by reflex or that are due to surgical brain stimulation.The domain of purposive behavior is thus large. It includes various psychotic, schizophrenic, and neurotic behaviors. Furthermore, we make no a priori judgment about the rationality or irrationality of purposive behavior.

If behavior is purposive and initiated by a decision, it follows that in some way the actor knows what he or she is doing: the actor is *in control*. The initiating decisions are based on the actor's observations of the environment and the effect of his or her behavior on it. The actor can base subsequent decisions on what was perceived. Thus he or she is capable of introspection about what is perceived and what is decided based on perception.

Cognitive psychologists such as Miller, Galanter, and Pribram (1960) and, more specifically, Powers (1973) have formulated models for describing how behavior and perception are related. Powers in particular maintains that behavior *is* the control of perception and is intended by the individual actors to bring what they observe in line with what they assume they should be perceiving. That is, *behavior establishes a congruence with actors' folk theories*.

Each behavioral/perceptual act can be described as a TOTE unit. The acronym TOTE stands for "Test-Operate-Test-Exit (Miller, Galanter & Pribram 1960).

(1) In the initial *test* state the individual, in a behavioral perceptual act, determines whether or not the environment is as it should be or is as one normally perceives it. If it is not, then *error* is perceived, which must be corrected or better eliminated (next step).
(2) To *operate*, the individual executes a behavioral/perceptual act that intends to bring the perception of a situation into congruence with what should be or what customarily is the case. The behavior eliminates error.
(3) In the final test state the individual, in a perceptual act, determines whether or not the error was fully eliminated and whether his or her perceptions of the environment are congruent with expectation (folk theory).
(4) To *exit*, if the error is corrected and the actor's perception of the environment meets expectations, attention shifts to something else.

A TOTE unit can be seen to occur in each behavioral event, or frame. By behavioral frame we mean a single coherent unit or event of purposive behavior for which some outcome can be anticipated. Frames of verbal or motor acts are thus composed of some perception of the situation, the perceived or described act itself, and some test to make sure that the act achieved whatever it should have achieved and, finally, an exit to the next activity.

Behavior frames that proceed in sequence are usually combined to form *plans*. Plans are also hierarchical (see Volume 1, Section 2.3.2 and Chapter 4 in this volume). Each behavior frame (action or plan) is usually composed of smaller plans that stand in a sequentially ordered part/whole relationship to the more inclusive one. On the verbal level, the smallest plans are atomic plans. Below this level, description of plans becomes cumbersome. For example, walking is an atomic plan. Further description of the plan of walking may take several pages (Werner 1966 and Section 3.1.3, this volume).

Because crucial features of the environment must be accounted for, another important logical relationship must be included: taxonomy. Not only do individuals base action on what they perceive; they also make choices among a range of possible actions. The literature on decision making abounds with examples in which sequences of behavior proceed smoothly until an individual must choose what to do next. This decision is made on the basis of what is perceived in the environment. These environmental perceptions can be tested or elicited as sets of attributes. We demonstrate in Volume 1 (Section 2.3.2) that *attributes and taxonomies* are intimately connected. We also show that conditions for the performance of plans are attributes as well (see Volume 1, Section 2.3.2).

5.2 DECISION MODELS IN THE FIELD

Most of the texts we use for our examples of decision modeling were written in a form from which we could infer relationships between conditions and outcomes. Many cases in which decision modeling is applied involve management of production and marketing (Gildersleeve 1970). For those with even a rudimentary familiarity with computer programming, the contents of Chapter 4 should be reasonably familiar (Pollack 1963, 1971, 1974; Lombardi 1963).

In many other situations throughout the world where industrial management has not been accepted, information in digested form is not immediately available, the ethnographer must provide the bridge between what he or she has collected in interview and observation and what is required for a decision model. There is no single formal body of steps to which one can resort in designing a decision model. Fortunately, several ethnographers have discussed stages through which they have gone to generate these models. We have found it difficult to distill a single approach because adjustments must be made depending on specific ethnographic goals. We nevertheless make comparisons and discuss the merits of each approach.

In the following discussion, we compare the process we recommend with those used by anthropologists such as C. Gladwin (1976, n.d.), H. Gladwin and Murtaugh (1980), Topper (1972), Schoepfle *et al.* (1979, 1982), Young (1980), and Young and Garro (1982). They reflect differences not only in type of ethnographic fieldwork but also in degrees of cultural difference between the ethnographer and consultant, and degrees of involvement by a native research staff. The influence of these differences is brought up throughout our discussion.

To begin, we review and compare research on the following distinct stages through which all ethnographers who design models proceed:

(1) determining the domain of cultural knowledge in which the decision model is embedded;
(2) determining what constraints impose (within that given domain) upon a decision model;
(3) generating intuitive rules, in the terminology of the ethnographer, about behavior and the conditions upon which the behavior is based;
(4) validating the intuitive rules by rephrasing them in terminology the natives would use; and
(5) validating the overall model.

5.2.1 Knowledge and Decision Model

Establishing a domain of knowledge that can be enhanced by decision modeling is no different than establishing cultural domains in general. They can be obtained through Grand Tour questions (see Volume 1, Sections 10.1 and 10.2). This implies that the domain of the decision study is marked by an appropriate term or phrase used by consultants. Thus a decision model can be obtained for sequential activities (plans) ranging from microethnographic examples such as the subplans of a routine day (Topper 1972, 1974) to those that occur during social drinking (McNeley 1979). On the other hand, they can include domains as far-reaching as political strategies among Navajos for mitigating anticipated environmental damage (Schoepfle *et al.* 1979), conservation strategies for yearly cycles of livestock transhumance among Navajos (Schoepfle *et al.* 1982), and the adoption of agricultural innovations by Mexican peasant farmers (C. Gladwin, 1976, n.d.; H. Gladwin and Murtaugh 1980).

5.2.2 Elimination by Aspect: Judgments

Because of the specificity of the behavior to which models are often directed, there is a need to eliminate various subtopics within a domain which the model does not address. For example, in studies of decision making of people purchasing automobiles, Gladwin and Murtaugh (1980) report that people rapidly eliminate large categories of automobiles *before* beginning to compare cars with the desired comfort features, design, and cost. Thus they quickly eliminate pickup trucks, vans, and four-wheel drive vehicles when they make a decision to buy a small car with high fuel economy. Similarly, Schoepfle *et al.* (1979) discovered that individual Navajos do not begin to consider the negotiations for the mitigation of adverse environmental impacts resulting from strip mining until they had determined whether or not their social status within a community still allowed them access to traditional grazing land. Without such access (common especially among younger Navajos) their ties to land are weakened.

Christina Gladwin (1976, 1980) refers to this stage as "elimination by aspects." She borrows the term from the works of Tversky (1972). This cognitive psychologist (and others) has emphasized that people do not always base their decisions on statistically valid judgments of probability. Instead, they normally make systematic errors in judging probabilities (Tversky & Kahneman 1974). Whenever people base their decisions on these judgments, the results differ from statistical generalizations scientists make about human behavior. These "folk-probablistic" judgments are based on the following principles:

(1) Errors of representation: People assume the likelihood of some event or process because it has attributes expected in popular conception. For example, Tversky and Kahneman (1974) found that people judge an individual who is "shy and withdrawn, invariably helpful, but with little interest in people, or in the world of reality . . . a meek and tidy soul" more likely to be a librarian than a farmer or airline pilot because the attributes fit more closely to the folk theory about librarians.

(2) Errors of emphasizing sample proportion over sample size: People assume, for example, that any sample of men will average six feet tall because the average for the whole population is known to be six feet; or that the likelihood of a

coin toss of heads is 50% for both large and small samples, whereas both the population mean and the 50% probability are likely only for large samples.

(3) Errors of predictability toward representativeness: People will predict as more likely what they hope will happen, or what they feel should happen. For example, if people have heard that certain students are smart, then they will expect high performance from those students (the Pygmalion effect; see Rosenthal 1968).

(4) Errors of availability: People will judge the probability that an event will occur according to how easily the event (or similar kind of event) can be recalled or brought to mind. For example, the "good old days" are based on the easier recall of pleasant memories.

These assumptions may be in error statistically, but they are what people use for making judgments and are therefore important imputs to decision modeling. Tversky and Kahneman (1974) call these commonsense assumptions *heuristics*, or nonstatistical assumptions about what happens in the real world.

When discussing "elimination by aspects," we may freely interchange their term "aspect" with our own term *attribute* (see Volume 1, Section 2.3). People normally eliminate large or important decisions by considering crucial attributes of classes of objects first. Gladwin and Murtaugh (1980) refer to this stage as "preattentive" and emphasize that these decisions, though purposive, are not always conscious.

We acknowledge a need for including preattentive decision making but accompany our agreement with warnings. All of these pertain to our concern regarding the inevitable multiple ambiguity of activities performed out of awareness. Gladwin and Murtaugh, for example, note that some behavior is learned in such a way that if the actor thinks about it while performing it, it will go wrong. Examples are frequent and obvious: Typing becomes extremely difficult when concentrating on hitting each key or on the order in which the keys are hit. Similar cases include playing the piano and many other skills for which one must obtain what is colloquially referred to as "muscle memory." Philosophers (e.g., Polanyi 1969) refer to this as the tacit dimension of knowledge.

5.2.3 Elimination by Aspect: Constraints and Contexts

A related class of decisions apparently requires no choices be made, or else the impacts of these decisions change little from day to day. For such activities people may consider the outcomes so obvious that they need not reflect upon them unless a traumatic event forces reconsideration. For example, people in industrial societies regularly get out of bed at certain times in the morning, eat breakfast, get dressed, and commute to work, all without paying much attention to the decisions they make. Their living environment makes such consideration either trivial (if they are relatively content) or excruciatingly futile (if they are not). Other activities, such as the traditional Navajo habit of running early in the morning, are of religious importance. If various associated subactivities were not followed in prescribed order, considerable harm to friends and relatives could result (Begishe 1982). The possible choices are no choices at all. They are often made on a high level of abstraction. For example, an entire Navajo family may convert to Christianity and traditional beliefs and practices become automatically obsolete.

There are many examples in which people are not aware of what they are doing while doing it. In other situations they may consider the need to follow a sequence of activities so obvious that considering choices seems pointless. All of these cases are preattentive, but with one important caveat: *they are preattentive with respect to the activities within a certain domain that is the object of study*. We should not assume that they are in some way a permanent part of the subconscious and therefore inaccessible to interview. An individual may talk freely about these situations in other contexts. This skillful articulateness seems to vary tremendously among individuals.

These limits to inarticulateness need to be emphasized because a researcher, hampered by a lack of time and funding, might ignore certain behaviors as nonconscious (and therefore not accessible to interview), whereas the actor may simply have considered the subject irrelevant. The contexts the ethnographer created through his or her questions did not include (or exclude) explicit references to the situations.

Case 5.1 Navajo Ecological Zones

An example illustrates how this problem may enter the conduct of the research. Schoepfle and his Navajo research collaborators were reviewing interview information about different ecological zones traditional Navajos use while moving their herds of livestock from desert lowlands to wooded highlands. It appeared that while some families use intermediate zones in nearby mountains for irrigated farming, others do not. None of the families volunteered information about the reasons for this variation. The answer emerged when Kenneth Nabahe asked the families about the effects of the imposed stock reduction, which had occurred almost forty years before.

The reductions of stock decreased the family food supply enough so that some children had to leave home to go to school. With these children gone, there was not enough manpower left to cultivate and maintain the corn plots. All available manpower had to be mobilized to herd livestock from desert lowland to mountain-top pasturing (Schoepfle *et al.* 1982).

Elimination of choices by aspect or attribute, though not necessarily something an actor may think about every day, is nevertheless something that can be discussed in an appropriate context of ethnoscience ethnography. This is particularly true when it is known that other related subjects contain at least partial information on why something is or is not eliminated. Unfortunately, the discovery of these domains or contexts depends, as in Case 5.1, on luck. Of course, luck can be enhanced by systematic exploration of related areas.

Gladwin and Murtaugh (1980) carefully separate the eliminated conditions at this stage from choices that may be made in the models themselves, because elimination by aspect is a more sweeping, general decision. It is analogous to conventional understanding of environmental constraints because these limit, and thus decrease the number of, options available to the individual. Most environmentally imposed choices are more severe: No choices can be made at all.

For example, we may compare the choice of whether or not to get out of bed in the morning depending on whether or not it is the weekend. This consideration does not pose a constraint because the options available to a person are not necessarily increased or decreased; a person may still get out of bed early or late, regardless of whether or not it is the weekend. Considering whether or not a person wants to risk losing a job is another issue. If it is a job he or she does not want to lose, the person will get out of bed early on weekdays. The fact that an individual does not want to lose his or her job means that the late rising option is no longer available on weekdays. Weekends can be said to be simply correlated to the choice because it is the job that poses the causal constraint on the decision.

5.2.4 Development of Decision Rules

Christina and Hugh Gladwin maintain that so-called hard-core decision making starts after eliminating choices by aspect—that is, after an actor has eliminated all environmental constraints and therefore all aspects (attributes connected to choices that might conceivably be made) that the individual either cannot or will not consider. Unfortunately, this is also the area for which ethnographers provide direct information only with difficulty. The researcher must now mediate between choices based on observation and specific elicited questions. Thus ethnographers' choices do not involve mediation. Rather than abstractly stating how the ethnographer may achieve this mediation, we provide illustrations of how it is actually done by cognitive ethnographers.

Case 5.2 Social Cost of Navajo Relocation

Schoepfle et al. (1979) had successfully elicited texts from Navajos in which they found words and phrases that made explicit social costs that the speakers anticipated as a result of proposed coal strip mining. Folk definitions of these costs were constructed by linking decision conditions (attributes) taken from the texts with the words and phrases. Taxonomies were constructed based on these definitions. However, these taxonomies did not provide a *rank ordering of costs*. It was difficult to see which costs were linked to other costs.

The relative standing of a cost was identified by determining indirectly what circumstances *counteract* these costs. After these effects were identified, the ethnographers asked their Navajo consultants about mitigating circumstances that should be considered first in order that other choices might become worthwhile.

Since Navajos made many comments about what they felt would mitigate development but had not placed their comments in an order of priorities, Schoepfle examined the interview material and discussed the mitigating factors with colleagues Begishe and Morgan, both of whom are bilingual Navajos. They intuitively proposed a decision model in English that made explicit the most crucial elements of the mitigating influences. A list of these appears below, representing a *strategy* Navajos use to negotiate with governmental, administrative, and corporate organizations compensation for the adverse effects of energy development:

(1) Assurance that land be set aside elsewhere near the reservation upon which the relocatees may settle.
(2) Assurance that the relocatees be relocated in extended family groups rather than nuclear family households, so that reciprocal relationships among family and neighbors remain easy to maintain.
(3) Assurance that relocation be close to where they currently live, and preferably on land they already hold.
(4) Assurance of relocation a safe distance from the mine, in order to ensure their own safety.
(5) Assurance that land be reclaimed through replanting of grass and leveling of soil piles around the strip mine.
(6) Assurance that the grazing permits not be invalidated or bought from the present holders, so that once the land is reclaimed it could be reoccupied.
(7) Assurances of preservation of sacred prayer sites and burial sites of their ancestors or else guarantees that burial sites will be moved.
(8) Assurance that the Bureau of Indian Affairs (a division of the U.S. Department of the Interior) or the Navajo Tribal government not require that livestock be reduced, or that should it be necessary to order a reduction in numbers, that livestock be penned at feedlots and kept there at mining company expense (Schoepfle *et al.* 1979, 1982).

Begishe and Morgan then reexamined the Navajo texts and, following this reanalysis, proposed a new model. The differences are significant (see below; compare also Chapter 8, especially Figure 8.5).

Quinn (1976) had attempted to elicit, through ethnoscience ethnography, the means by which local Mfantse elders managed to resolve disputes brought to their attention in court. Her consultants (elders) were able to provide her with general categories, such as kinds of disputes and dispute settlement solutions. But they were unable to give her rules or steps that consistently connected kinds of disputes with kinds of settlements.

Case 5.3 Mfantse Dispute Settlement

"At first, attending to their frequent mention of 'murdering' cases, 'disgrace' cases, 'false allegation' cases and other classes of cases, I assumed that these broad categories would hold the key to the way pacification fees were determined. But the categories in which the cases fell proved inconsistent with the

> pacification fees set. If I inquired why *usua* was charged in one case of false allegation, but not in another similar case of the same sort, I was inevitably told 'each case has its own pacification.'
>
> "I tried to collect lists of all relevant contingencies, but they were endless, and each time another contingency was introduced to explain why two seemingly identical cases were treated differently, Kwesi Kakraba (a chief informant) would explain patiently, 'Each case has its own pacification' " (Quinn 1976: 7).

Quinn's solution was to observe these courts in process and thus record cases of actual decisions under "grass hut" conditions. Then she interviewed the judges about each case to see what factors they took into account in rendering a decision. She then generalized from a number of these cases to see what kinds of judgments followed from the judges' considerations of these factors.

Gladwin (n.d.) encountered a slightly different situation. She needed to find out why peasant farmers refused to adopt the use of a fertilizer suggested by the Mexican government. Their refusal mystified the agricultural extension experts because the fertilizer's contribution to producing greater crop yields had been clearly demonstrated in special experimental plots (Gladwin and Murtaugh 1980).

Case 5.4 Adaptation of Fertilizer by Mexican Farmers

> Christina Gladwin at first proposed rules for the farmers' decisions based on risk. That is, she proposed that the farmers refused to adopt the fertilizing technique because they feared damage to their crops. She based her proposal on how often she heard the farmers reply that "if it doesn't rain, the plants dry up; if it rains too much the plants 'burn' from the water" ("burn" in this context, means that the plants turn yellow from water-related root damage). To test her proposal she obtained information on the kinds of crops planted in different fields and whether or not the farmers fertilized the plants in the different fields differently. From this question she intended to generate (or perhaps elicit) a taxonomy with contrast sets showing whether or not the individual farmer adopted the recommended fertilizing technique. She found that farmers fertilized regardless of the crop.
>
> Next she changed her approach by going out into the fields while the farmers were planting and observing what they did. Her learning occurred not in two or three interviews but in the three months of the planting season while she walked with farmers through corn fields asking questions about drought, water, insect damage and about different appearances of corn, and so on. "In short, I had to acquire knowledge of the farming system by direct observation before I could make sense out of elicited decision criteria. With that knowledge, I then acquired the farmer's plans or cognitive strategies to grow corn in the village, since 'any complete description of behavior should be adequate to serve as a set of instructions, i.e. it should have the characteristics of the plan that could guide the action described' (Miller, Galanter and Pribram 1960: 16)" (Gladwin n.d.:13).

> Thus Gladwin had to resort to interview and observation in order to be able to formulate questions that the farmer could understand. She then constructed the rules for her decision model by first proposing an overall *plan,* or sequence, of planting activities.

How plans became the framework becomes clear when Gladwin describes the choices farmers had to make at each step of activity in the plan. Observation as well as interview became important. She found that the farmers considered not just the risk to the crops in their decisions to use fertilizer but also profitability. For example, they worried not only about whether or not crop damage would result but also whether or not the expenditure for the commercial fertilizer would be justifiable in terms of probable monetary return.

Gladwin's description highlights a pattern found in ethnographies by Topper (1972) on the Navajo Day and by Schoepfle *et al.* (1982): that a decision model can be formulated

(1) as plans, or sequences of activities (see Section 3.1);
(2) as a series of subplans, or plans that are part of various larger plans;
(3) as a series of alternative subplans occurring at various choice points;
(4) as the choice points at which the alternative subplans were identified and highlighted; and
(5) as the social and physical environmental features that indicate which alternative subplan should or could be chosen.

Young (1980) highlights still another variant in his research on medical decision making among Tarascan Indians in Mexico. The ethnographic team first went through an open-ended interview in which they elicited lists of disease types. Then they determined, for each disease type, whether the consultants sought Western or traditional medical services. To determine how the Tarascans decided, the ethnographers used a contrastive question frame, or a "paired comparison."

Case 5.5 Comparisons for Tarascan Medical Decisions

> If you or another person in your household were ill, when—for what reasons—would you (consult) (use) ____________ instead of (consulting) (using) ____________? (Young 1980:109).

They found, however, that asking why the villagers resort to one or another medical system for specific illnesses often resulted in trivial answers such as "I went to the medical practitioner because the healer wasn't there" (Garro, personal communication). They therefore proposed a classification of illnesses and then elicited attributes for them. These attributes referred to specific conditions in the environment that might influence a decision one way or another. The ethnographers next composed stories referring to hypothetical situations (comparable to what we call cases or hypothetical cases; see Case 7.6) that described individuals

Situation	Approximate English Translation of Description
1) Serious; Money available Remedy known	Let's say that there ia person who has a very grave illness. This family has a fair amount of money, because they have draft animals and just sold one. They have had this illness in the family before and they now know of the remedy that cured the illness before. What do you think they are going to do?
2) Serious; No money available Remedy known	Let's say that there is a person who has a very grave illness. In this family, money is scarce. Sure, they're eating, but there is nothing left over. They have had this illness in the family before and they now know of the remedy that cured the illness before. What do you think they are going to do?

NOTE: Adapted from Young (1980).

Figure 5.1 Tarascan Elicitation Frame

encountering these environmental effects. The final step presented these stories as interview elicitation frames (see Figure 5.1).

By systematically adding and subtracting attributes from these stories, Young and Garro (and their co-workers) built a decision model for showing those circumstances in which consultants seek out Western rather than traditional practitioners.

5.2.5 Translation into Native Model

On the surface, the translation of the proposed ethnographer's model into one the natives can understand simply takes what the ethnographer has done and rephrases it in the categories of the natives. Simple retranslation can become the first test of the validity of the model because what human beings are doing is determined by whether important elements of the model correspond to topics talked about by the consultants. Obviously, the closer the fit, the easier to test the model's validity.

It is for these reasons that we have placed such importance on the process of systematic translation and interpretation throughout this handbook. To illustrate, we can compare the decision process proposed by Schoepfle (mentioned in Case 5.2) to that proposed by Begishe and Morgan, which is included in Figure 5.2. The original model was phrased in Navajo; here we provide a relatively free translation into English.

This model differs from Schoepfle's because Begishe and Morgan had the advantage of being able to speak and read Navajo and could therefore understand the *context* of the interview excerpts. In other words, they were able to look not only for crucial attributes for the terms already elicited but also to anticipate *attributes (conditions) not yet elicited* which supplied information confirming those mitigating circumstances most important to the Navajo consultants.

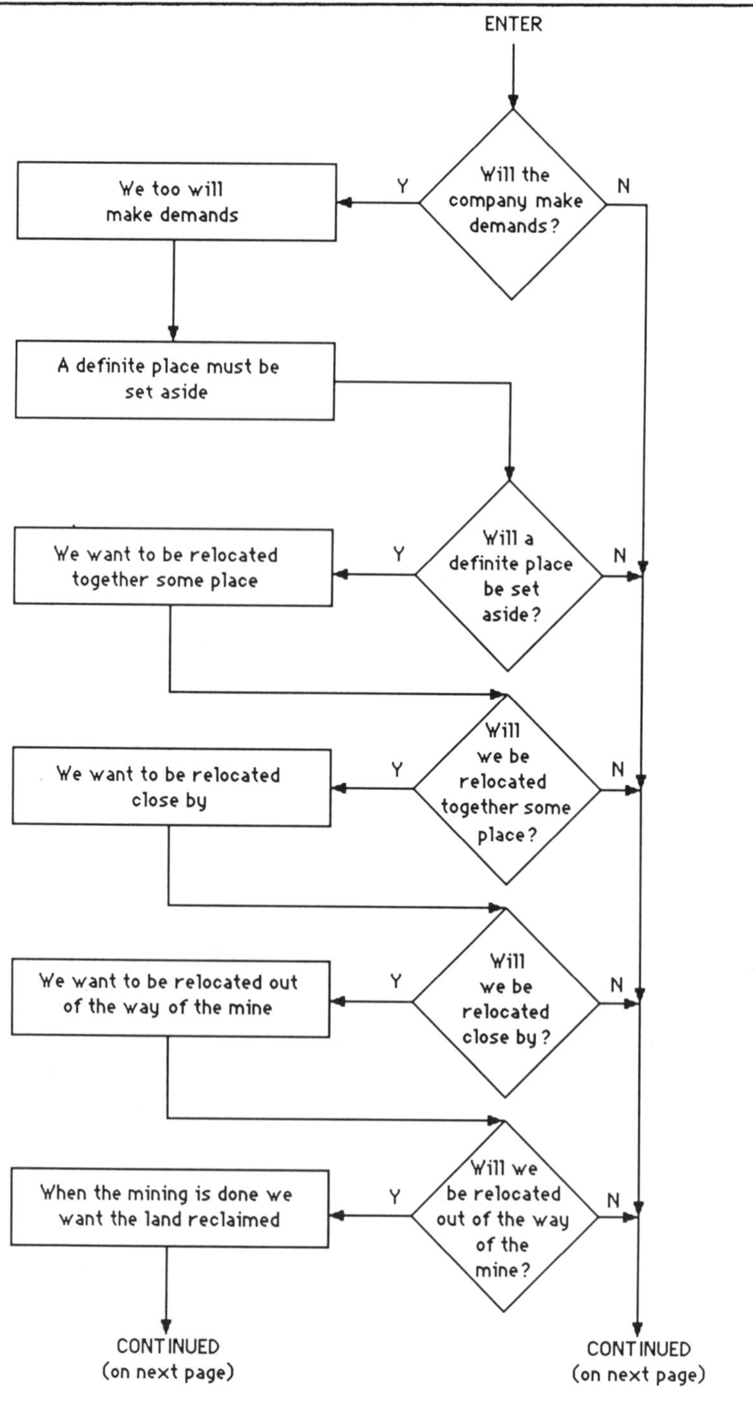
ENTER
Will the company make demands?
Y
N
We too will make demands
A definite place must be set aside
Will a definite place be set aside?
Y
N
We want to be relocated together some place
Will we be relocated together some place?
Y
N
We want to be relocated close by
Will we be relocated close by?
Y
N
We want to be relocated out of the way of the mine
Will we be relocated out of the way of the mine?
Y
N
When the mining is done we want the land reclaimed
CONTINUED (on next page)
CONTINUED (on next page)

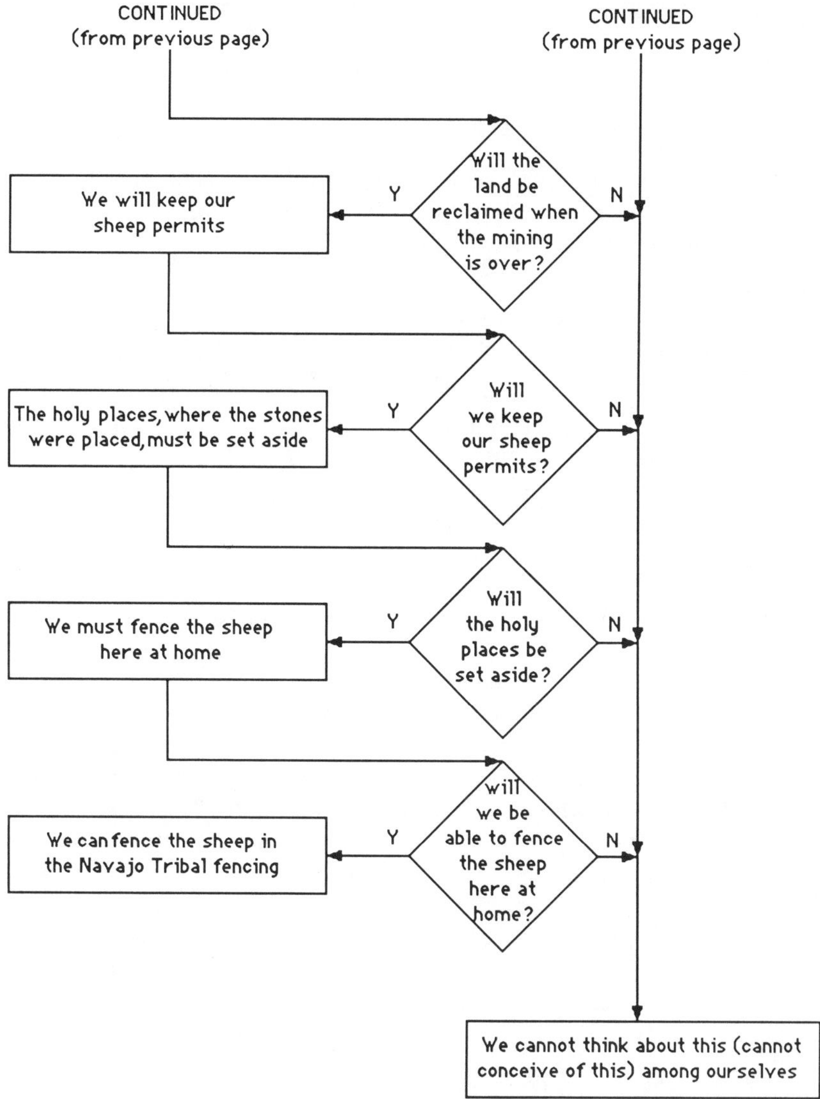

NOTE: The results of several interviews are summarized in this graph by Kenneth Y. Begishe and Rose Morgan, two Navajo researchers. The original is in Navajo.

Figure 5.2 Hierarchical Ordering of Mitigating Conditions as Seen by Navajos Facing Relocation

Clearly, life is easier if the ethnographer can work from simple taxonomies, sequences, and definitions that have already been elicited. However, as with any ethnography, major syntheses go on in the mind of the ethnographer. The analytical ethnoscience structures, the recorded and transcribed interview texts, and the journal entries are all checks on the ethnographer's memory and on possible ethnocentric distortions. This is as true of decision modeling as it is of general ethnography.

5.2.6 Validation of Decision Model

The power and applicability of the decision model depends on how strong a statement may be made for its validity. Following Lazarsfeld (1967), there appear to be four major techniques for validating the models:

(1) consultant approval,
(2) testing the logical consistency of the model,
(3) simple statistical testing of the model's predictability, and
(4) statistical testing of mathematical models that stand for the decision model itself.

Most authors mentioned in this chapter have used a combination of these techniques. In the following sections, rather than compare the relative strength of each of these validation procedures, we have chosen to emphasize how they complement each other.

Consultant Approval

This approach involves presenting the decision model in the form of a decision table, flowchart, or decision tree, first to the consultants with whom one has worked and then to another group of consultants with whom one has not worked. The objective is to see whether the model accurately depicts what consultants know about the subject. The first group allows the ethnographer to test whether the model can be explained to consultants who are relatively familiar with the ethnographer's approach and who can comment on it in detail. The second group, unfamiliar with the ethnographer's style, then comments on whether or not the model makes sense in general.

Schoepfle *et al.* (1979) utilized this approach for obtaining Navajo approval for their model of Navajo demands for mitigating measures to ease relocation. They first presented the model in the community where they had been working and then, once a number of adjustments and corrections had been made, to people outside the community.

Case 5.6 Social Cost of Navajo Relocation

In these situations, it is not clear what is being validated. For example, when the Navajo consultants said they liked the model, they also added that

1) they were impressed with the fact that the Navajo language could be written and arranged in such a diagrammatic (and presumably systematic) way;
2) through the presentation, they saw considerable potential in such modeling for effecting rational community level planning;

3) they were grateful to the ethnographers for taking the trouble to listen to what they had to say.

The following quote illustrates this (English translation of Navajo original).

> "Me too. I like this—that is, the way this research has been presented. You see, when things are researched in depth, then it is clear that the kinds of people you describe do emerge. There are indeed those who want change; those who say 'no' and the group that says 'wait a minute; easy!', whose members are here at this meeting tonight. Also, you can see the group which is simply in the middle. When it is researched in this manner we better understand the wishes of these groups and can understand better the plans of the [proposed coal] mine and of other groups. In this way I believe and hope that things will change for the better. Right now, we do not understand one another, and that is the reason for the present [factionalism and confusing conditions]" (Schoepfle *et al.* 1979:84).

Such comments are gratifying to hear. They demonstrate ethnoscience ethnography's potential as a planning tool. Nevertheless, a number of questions remain unanswered. First, do the consultants like the model because they like the ethnographers (or in other circumstances dislike the model because they dislike them)? Second, are the consultants so unfamiliar with looking at themselves in the way indicated by the model that they offer support (or, in other circumstances, withdraw support) based on a superficial view of the work (i.e. the "I never thought of it that way!" reaction)? Third, the natives are often happy to see *anything* that makes even a half-hearted attempt to represent their viewpoint because they perceive that ethnographers in many parts of the world have often misrepresented the interests of native peoples.

Thus the consultants may approve the model, but for reasons different from what the ethnographer would like. The insurance that factors such as those mentioned above are not part of validation depends on the personal integrity and ethics of the ethnographer. This makes validation a risky undertaking.

We recommend, therefore, that informant approval, though necessary, is not sufficient. Still, it is a prerequisite for other validating techniques. For example, if a model predicts people's behavior and simultaneously represents the way they talk and think, then the resulting model has more explanatory power than one whose validity depends on statistical predictability alone.

Logical Consistency

The logical consistency of an ethnographic description is a key criterion of cognitive anthropology. In the past it had far greater popularity than informant approval. The use of logical consistency as a criterion of validity has been perhaps most energetically pursued by French structuralists, but it is equally important to any formal analysis, including cognitive anthropology.

Aspects of logical consistency—for example, parsimony and elegance—form part of any scientific model. Vulnerability to criticism and disconfirmation are included in this package. The use of formal devices—here decision tables and their derivative structures—makes decision models inherently vulnerable. That is, an explicit decision model can be shown to be demonstrably wrong or it can be restated with greater parsimony and elegance.

In the Schoepfle *et al.* (1979) model, logical consistency from the native's point of view was added to the text. Native logical consistency was the main criterion for proposing the final model in the language of the consultants (see Figure 5.1). They used quotes from their interviews to support the prioritized list of processes mitigating the environmental and social costs of surface coal mining. The Navajos were asking for these. The native language model presents the logical consistency of the Navajo argument. In this sense approval by natives at its best also tests for logical consistency from the native point of view.

Statistical Predictability

Once we can establish that the consultants consider the model realistic and that both consultant and ethnographer are satisfied that it makes logical sense, the model must answer the question of whether or not it adequately distinguishes between what people say they do and what they can be observed to do. Two different questions emerge:

(1) Is it possible to present each decision, one at a time, to a consultant, and then to see if he or she follows or does not follow the outcome that the model predicts?
(2) Is it possible for an ethnographer to observe whether the consultant actually does what the model predicts?

Christina Gladwin (1976) treated both of these problems. When she first proposed her model on the basis of risk alone, she observed that (1) some individuals said they simply did not agree with what the model predicted, and (2) some individuals said they would do what the model predicted *ordinarily,* but added that they themselves did not actually do so. Gladwin concluded that the model was incomplete. She assumed that individuals in the second case were prefacing their comments with an implicit "all things being equal." The fact that all things were not equal led her to apply systematic observations combined with in-depth interviewing.

Once she obtained an improved model and phrased it in terms of native categories, she was able to set up a testing procedure based on the following steps:

(1) She obtained a sample of 30 people whom she had not interviewed or observed before. These were people from the community where she was working.
(2) She then separated individuals within the sample according to decision criteria (conditions; see Figures 4.37 and 4.38).
(3) Next she asked each individual whether or not they made the particular choice which the model predicted.
(4) Finally, she determined whether or not the number of exceptions was statistically significant or could be explained in some other manner.

For example, determining whether considerations of profitability influence the acceptance of fertilizing techniques, Gladwin first identified groups of farmers who said "no" to the question "would fertilizer work?" and weeded their fields before the rainy season. She then hypothesized (above) that these farmers did not consider fertilizing at planting worth the extra effort.

Case 5.7 Social Cost of Navajo Relocation Revisited

Schoepfle *et al.* (1979) did not test their ranking of various mitigating circumstances. Instead, they checked whether or not individuals agreed with the process. They hypothesized that before an individual decides to favor coal mining, vehemently resist it, or demands environmental impact mitigations, he or she first considers his or her status.

The ethnographers assumed that the Navajos first consider whether or not they

(1) had graduated from high school;
(2) had a well-paying job;
(3) were making plans for their children's future education and inheritance;
(4) had any livestock (i.e., had sheep earmarked for them by their parents);
(5) were to inherit their parents' grazing permit;[3]
(6) felt obligated to assume responsibility for the care of their parents.

If the answer to each of these questions was no, then it was to the consultant's advantage not to object to the mine or to demand mitigations. Instead, they planned to accept a job with the mines, move off the reservation, or relocate nearby on the reservation if land was available.

The ethnographers then presented this hypothesized model (see Case 5.2) to a group of 10 Navajos with whom they had been working. This led to an agreement between consultants and ethnographers. Next, the model was tested by 48 other Navajos with whom interviews had been conducted and whom the model fit. Finally, 75 additional Navajos were interviewed. The model was confirmed.

Statistical Testing

For some applied research the validation of a decision model with the population identified with the ethnography is adequate. For example, in the field of social environmental impact assessment, the insights made available through ethnographic inquiry often cannot be easily duplicated through quantitative methods alone (Finsterbusch 1977). However, if various political or adminstrative entities within a population agree with the research results, they approve it and use it for their own purposes (Tonigan 1982; Jorgensen 1981). We call this (half seriously) "political validation." The issue here is the representativeness of ethnographic data. That is, we must determine whether or not our ethnographic findings describe adequately what people think in other, related populations. For example, are the findings of one Tarascan community applicable to all Tarascans? To determine whether or not they are, two general approaches have been followed: comparing communities that differ along important dimensions (such as modernity versus traditionalism, access to health care facilities versus no access, rural versus urban), and comparing the demographic variables of the ethnographer's community to the general population.

It is beyond the scope of this section to assume the superiority of one approach over the other. Cook and Campbell (1979) maintain that the second approach confers stronger validity on a study. However, they too recognize that realities in the field often make the first comparison more appropriate.

Stastistical testing of decision models employs a wide variety of techniques from simple statistics to complex multivariate techniques and entailment analysis. These topics are briefly treated in our section on statistical ethnoscience (Chapter 8). For greater detail the reader should refer to the specialized literature.

5.3 SUMMARY AND CONCLUSIONS

Traditional ethnoscience is formal with easily definable relations between units (MTQ) and complex relations derived from these. Most important, ethnoscience results can be easily presented to consultants for comments. The basis of traditional ethnoscience is folk definitions in "white rooms" or "grass huts." There are limitations to this approach when, as in decision modeling, we investigate behavior subject to uncertainty. Here we reach the limits of verbalizable knowledge or knowledge inferrable from verbal statements. We need to expand our tool kit to include observation (with or without participation), experiment, clinical analysis, and mathematical modeling. Nevertheless, all of these extensions of traditional ethnoscience must contain *conversation* with the natives in "white rooms," "grass huts," and even "grassy fields."

All behavior, even under uncertainty, is preceded by purposive decisions that initiate it. Behavior can be seen as the control of our perception to bring it into congruence with our folk theories about the world around us. In ethnography the ethnographer forms a bridge from elicited texts to decision models. He or she determines the cultural domain of the study, explores environmental constraints, generates the abstracted intuitive rules and validates the rules as well as the model.

Decisions occur in two stages. Although judgments of folk probability (Tversky & Kahneman 1974) are often mathematically in error, they still provide the basis for human decision making. Equally important is "elimination by aspect," which is severely constrained by environmental factors. These are often so obvious to the actors that they find it difficult to talk about them. Yet we have found that in other, usually related contexts they can be made explicit. Finding the proper context in which to talk about these contraints on decisions requires some luck, but luck can be greatly enhanced by systematic ethnography.

The development of decision rules must be followed by translation of the model into language the native consultants can understand. This leads to validation. The first step is to find consultant approval. Unfortunately, consultants rarely respond to the adequacy of the model alone. The fact that they are taken seriously and are sought out for counsel may color their validations.

Logical consistency rests in the nature of formal models: They can be tested, refuted, and restated. Approval by native consultants must address the logical consistency of the model from the native point of view.

Statistical predictability takes the decision model beyond the population that helped create it. Statistical testing incorporates other techniques (from simple statistics to multivariate analyses) to validate the results. Statistical predictably can be equated with Campbell and Fisk's (1959) notion of *replication by same or similar techniques*. Statistical testing equates with their notion of *validation by unrelated or expanded techniques*.

NOTES

1. Folk definitions in the broadest sense are texts elicited in "white rooms" and "grass huts" (see Volume 1, Section 6.5).

2. The best example of out-of-control behavior is skiing down a slope out of control—that is, while things are happening too fast and too unpredictably (for one's skill level) for control. Behavior that is out of control is often dangerous.

3. A grazing permit is a federal government document allowing the Navajo to graze their livestock on land to which they have traditionally had access.

Chapter 6

Other Semantic Systems

Beyond taxonomies, part/whole structures, and plans, the field of lexical/semantic relations that form large, complex fields seems to narrow (see Volume 1, Section 2.3).

6.0 INTRODUCTION

The two notable exceptions to the above are the "requires" relationship, as the work of Hirschman demonstrates (see Section 6.1), and causal trees, as shown in the work of Ahern and Colby (see Section 6.2). Unfortunately, causal trees often seem shallow, though this may result from the relative neglect of this relation by ethnographers.

Values seem to form fields because they can be viewed as high-level, inclusive criteria (attributes) that influence or color many activities and attributes at lower levels. The pervasiveness of values confers on them the status of themes.

In evolutionary terms, evaluative judgments of organisms originate with the single cell. Perhaps the intractability of investigating evaluative statements has pushed them into the background of cognitive anthropology and ethnoscience. This is a serious deficiency. Several years ago Ladd (1957) pointed out that values are stated in language and therefore are ideal for ethnoscience investigations. Our brief presentation here is intended merely as a beginning.

The final section of this chapter summarizes the remaining semantic systems. It is a catchall section to cover briefly anything left out so far.

6.1 THE "REQUIRES" RELATION[1]

The "required for" (RQ) relation follows the canonical form of complex relations (see Volume 1, Section 2.3), where the name of the relation is "required" and the preposition is "for." Like the complex part/whole and causal relations, the RQ relation can produce large lexical/semantic fields.

The RQ relation is characterized by the frame, "A is required for B" (RQ) or its inverse, "B requires A" ($\overline{RQ}$) and the question frame, "What is required for X? What do you require for X?" or "What do you need for X?" This question frame can be reapplied to each elicited answer. Given long RQ chains of elicitation, the structure eventually leads to value-laden theoretical realms of the lexical/semantic field. These provide important insights into the culture under study.

The middle level answers to the RQ frame are often useful for identifying criteria for decision modeling. The RQ relation can be exemplified by the old saying, "For want of a nail, the battle was lost." This statement—and its inverse—can be diagrammed as shown in Figure 6.1. Following our convention, the arrows originate at the predicate and point to the subject of the sentence: Nails are REQUIRED FOR (RQ) successful battle." Note the inverse ($\overline{RQ}$) of the canonical complex relation RQ in "Successful battle REQUIRES ($\overline{RQ}$) nails." The ($\overline{RQ}$) form may be easier to elicit (in English?) than RQ. In the graphs we mark RQ or $\overline{RQ}$ unambiguously. In the text we use RQ generically for both RQ and $\overline{RQ}$.

It is possible to expand this structure by reconstructing (or eliciting, if this were actual ethnographic material) middle levels. A possible expansion could be the diagram in Figure 6.2. This example highlights an important feature of the RQ (and $\overline{RQ}$ relationship: It is transitive (e.g., If (A)$\overline{\mathrm{RQ}}$(B) and (B)$\overline{\mathrm{RQ}}$(C), then (A) $\overline{\mathrm{RQ}}$ (C)). Any labeled node therefore "requires" all subsequent labeled nodes. Thus all of the following statements can be read off Figure 6.2. Note that these sentences manifest the $\overline{\mathrm{RQ}}$ relation:

Successful battle requires a cavalry in good order.

Successful battle requires new shoes for horses.

Successful battle requires nails.

A cavalry in good order requires new shoes for horses.

A cavalry in good order requires nails.

New shoes for horses require nails.

The transitivity of the $\overline{\mathrm{RQ}}$ (and *RQ*) relation enhances ease of elicitation. Different consultants may reveal different levels of the same structure, but the data

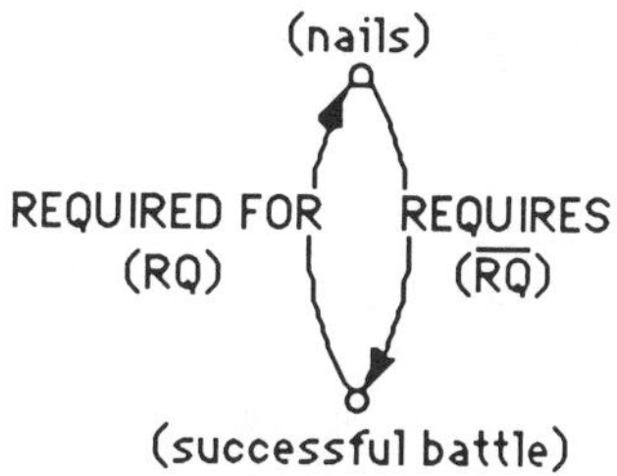

Figure 6.1 Example of "Required for" (RQ) and "Requires" ($\overline{RQ}$) Relation

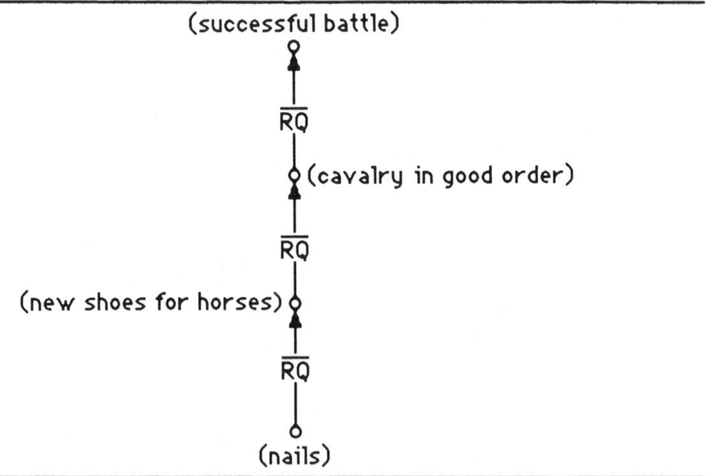

Figure 6.2 Mid-Level Expansion of Figure 6.1

elicited from one consultant can therefore be easily integrated with data from another.

A more realistic ethnographic example of RQ structure was elicited by Hirschman in an interview with a Navajo grandmother speaking about irrigation farming on the Navajo Indian reservation (Figure 6.3) Note that a subtree of part/whole relation is integrated into the structure.

In several cases the terminal nodes of this RQ tree structure could have led to further questions. For example, "What do you need to pull weeds?" might provide information on tools, manpower requirements, time allocations, and so on. It seems that no RQ structure is exhausted until very abstract and general levels are reached. Thus one might eventually elicit answers along the lines of "correct observance of taboos," or "God's will," or "chance," or even "good luck" (see Figure 6.12 for a comparison). Depending on ethnographic or theoretical goals, an ethnographer may want to pursue elicitation to this level or may prefer to stop before the answers become too abstract.

RQ data are easily used to construct a preliminary decision model. Each of the nodes identified in the intermediate RQ tree is necessary to bring about the result or state described by the top node. Thus the absence of one or more requirements renders impossible the production of a result. In the example of Figure 6.3 the consultant did not plant alfalfa during the 1985 season because she could not afford to hire a tractor.

Each node on the second level (from the top) of the RQ tree translates into a condition that can be used in a decision table. A simplified decision table "Growing Alfalfa" might appear as shown in Figure 6.4. In the decision table in this figure only the "yes" answers to all of the conditions yield the outcome (action) "grow alfalfa"; the presence of one or more no's yields the "Do not grow alfalfa" outcome.

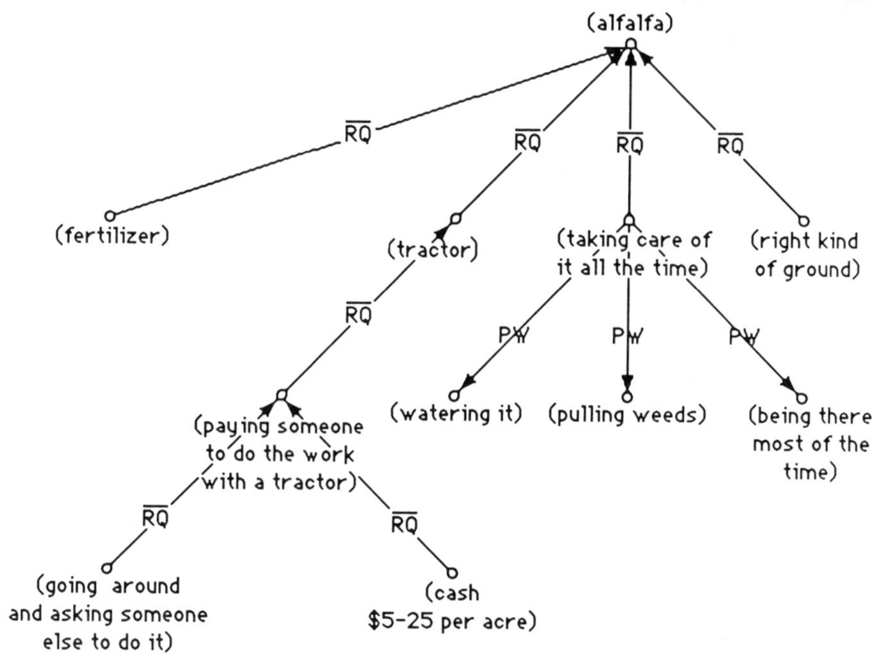

Figure 6.3 GROWING ALFALFA

Growing Alfalfa	1	2 - 32
Fertilizer available?	Y	All other combinations
Person with tractor available?	Y	
Cash available?	Y	
Right kind of ground?	Y	
Enough time for care of crop?	Y	
Grow alfalfa	X	
Do not grow alfalfa		X X X ...

Figure 6.4 Decision Table: GROWING ALFALFA

Considering the simplicity of the decision table, it seems pointless to translate an RQ structure into decision table format. However, that format provides a much more thorough and systematic way of verifying data, especially if some of the combinations of yes's and no's suggest alternatives not encountered before.

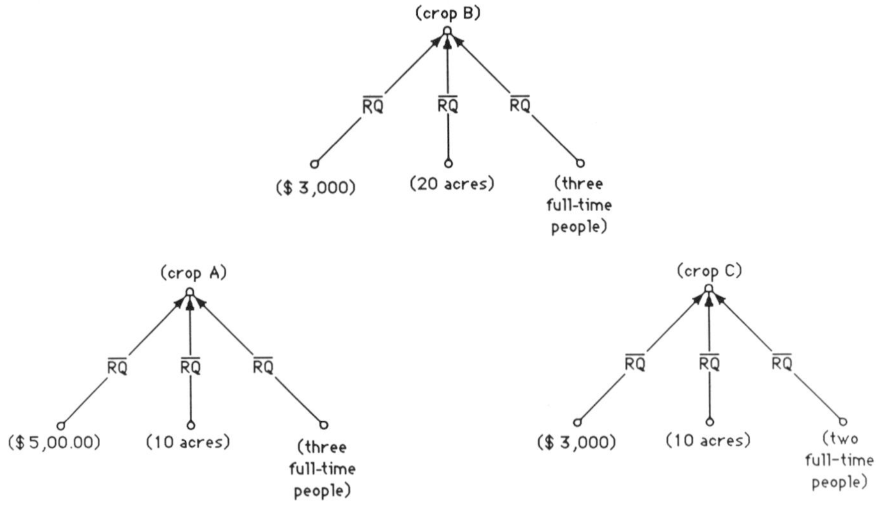

Figure 6.5 Comparison of Three Crops

It is, of course, possible to *combine RQ structures* for alternative decision to construct a more sophisticated decision table. In the hypothetical example illustrated in Figure 6.5, the requirements of three crops are compared. Each crop requires varying degrees of money, land and labor. By determining actual values for each requirement it becomes possible to construct a decision table for crop selection. For the sake of simplicity let us assume that everyone has access to at least $3,000, 10 acres, and two people. If they do not, the outcome would have to be "do nothing" or "explore other alternatives." Once the decision table has been set up, the ethnographer must return to the consultants to fill it in. In this example we assume that he or she discovered that the crops are ranked from A to C (A > B > C). The decision table in Figure 6.6 results. Reduction and appropriate reordering of the decision table yields Figures 6.7 and 6.8.

Not all decision criteria can be reduced to the presence or absence of requirements. However, the establishment of a preliminary decision model based on requirements can provide a point of departure for more comprehensive elicitation and modeling.

Some RQ structures require the introduction of alternatives, related by an "or" (or D = Disjunction) relationship (see Volume 1, Section 2.3). At times a consultant might say something along the lines of, "In order to do this I need either A or B, but not necessarily both." This can be represented graphically (see Figure 6.9). The elicitation of alternative requirements (provided by the same or different consultants) provides more detail for the development of decision tables.

RQ relation is equally suited for eliciting real as well as hypothetical situations. The same consultant who decided not to grow alfalfa supplied another RQ structure dealing with the expansion of her grazing land. At the time of elicitation this project was not approved but was under consideration (Figure 6.10).

Crop Selection	1	2	3	4	5	6	7	8
$ 5000.00 ?	Y	Y	Y	Y	N	N	N	N
20 acres ?	Y	Y	N	N	Y	Y	N	N
Three people ?	Y	N	Y	N	Y	N	Y	N
Grow A	X		X					
Grow B					X			
Grow C		X		X		X	X	X

Figure 6.6 Decision Table Based on Figure 6.5

Crop Selection	1	2	3	4
Three people ?	Y	Y	Y	N
$ 5000.00 ?	Y	N	N	-
20 acres ?	-	Y	N	-
Grow A	X			
Grow B		X		
Grow C			X	X

Figure 6.7 Reduced Decision Table of Figure 6.6

The RQ tree in Figure 6.10 affords a number of possible avenues for further exploration. The information included under "asking for another 15 acres" might eventually be restructured as a verbal action plan showing how to navigate through a bureaucracy.

The appearance of the label "getting help from the Co-op" proved particularly revealing. It indicated a misunderstanding between local perceptions and the Co-op. The self-proclaimed purpose of the Co-op was agricultural development, which contradicts the expectation that the Co-op was an inexpensive way of getting grazing land leveled.

It is possible to move to lower levels of the RQ structure just as one can move upward. We discovered this by a serendipitous mistake of interpretation. Instead of the question "What do you need for [growing] melons?" the Navajo translator

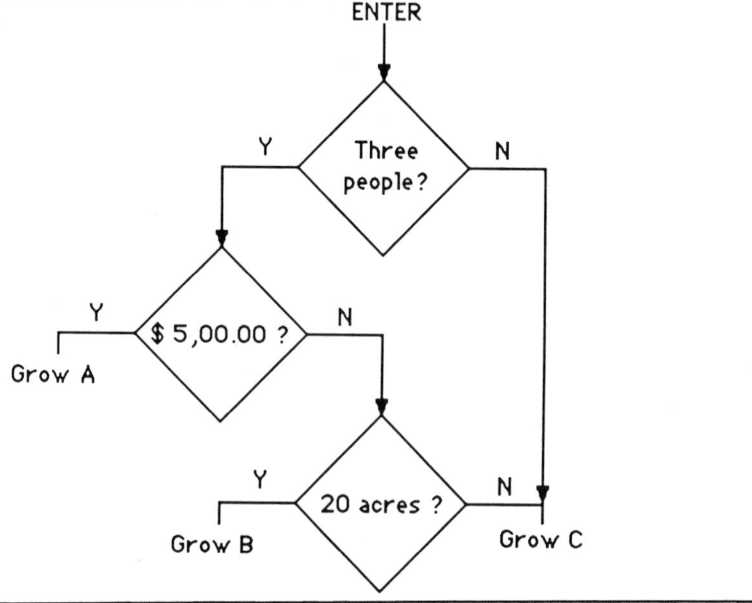

Figure 6.8 Flowchart of Crop Selection

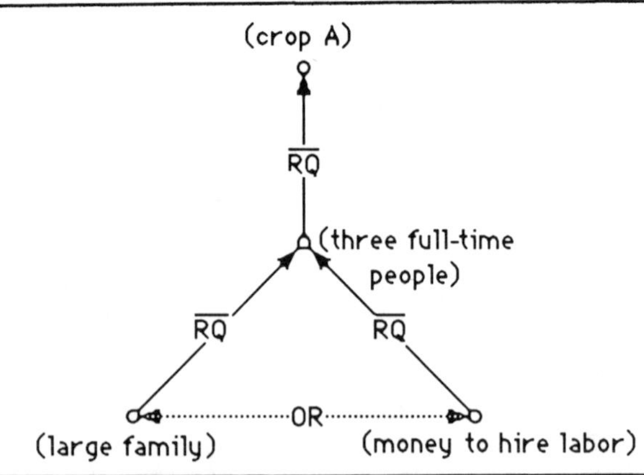

Figure 6.9 Alternative Requirements

rendered "What do you need melons for?" This resulted in no information being elicited on the requirements for growing melons. However, a picture emerged that showed the economic interdependence of an area of the Navajo Indian reservation still dominated by subsistence farming, exchange, and barter (Figure 6.11). In this example the information could have been organized by the causal relationship, which sometimes can be interpreted as an inverse of both RQ relations: "Successful battle because of nails," or "Nails caused a successful battle."

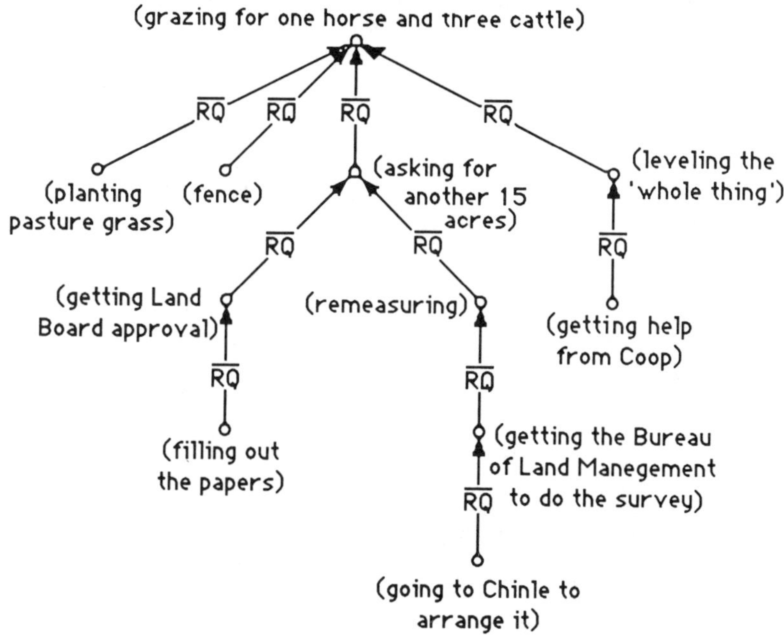

Figure 6.10 Expansion of Grazing

Systematic use of the "requires" structure in ethnographic interviewing and analysis can provide a shortcut to an important variety of information in any cultural domain. RQ data can often be further elaborated as verbal action plans, decision tables, or causal structures (see Section 6.2).

The major strength of the RQ relation lies in its utility as a point of intersection between other kinds of lexical/semantic relations. It is equally capable of supplying insights into theoretical constructs, value structures, and the details of everyday living.

6.2 CAUSAL CHAINS

To the best of our knowledge, the first ethnographer to propose that causal chains offer important insights into the workings of a culture was B. N. Colby (1975). His view can be summarized by the causal diagram Shown in Figure 6.12, which was adapted from a research proposal.

One of Colby's aims was to semiautomate the procedure for eliciting causes. The consultant sat at a computer terminal. A computer queried him about the possible causes for the bailiff's visit. The complex causal tree structure that was elicited eventually reduced all causes in Mayan life (the culture of the consultant) to five ultimate causes. The major surprise was that the supernaturally oriented Mayans naturally recognized chance as a causal agent.

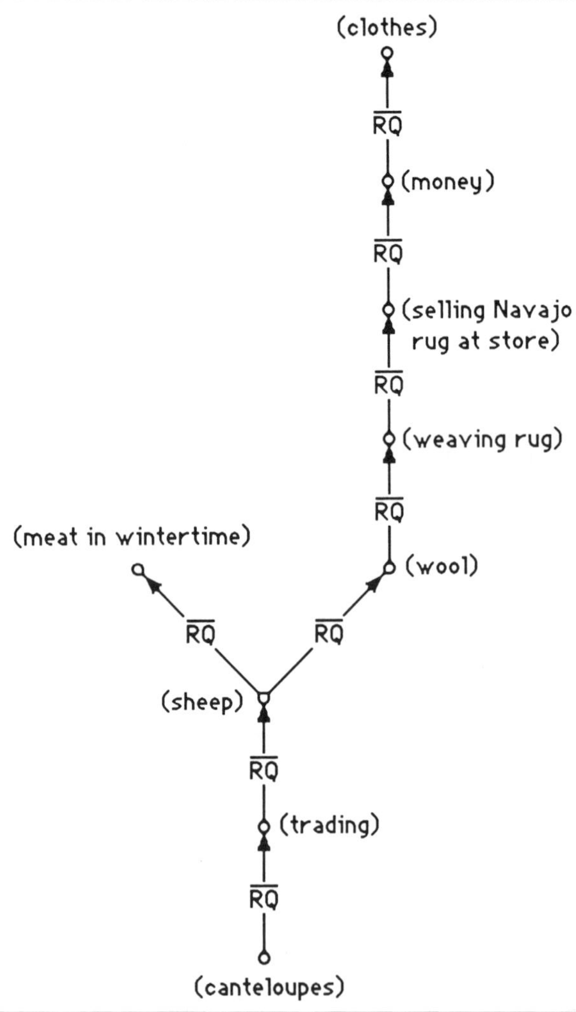

Figure 6.11 MAKING A LIVING

Within our circle of collaborators, Julie Ahern (1979) was the first to use causal tree diagrams as the major organizational principle of her ethnographic report. Theoretically, very little is known about how human beings talk about causes. We know that cause is a complex relation of the familiar canonical form "A is the cause of B" or its inverse, "B because of A" (Volume 1, Section 2.3). Colby's (1975) and Ahern's (1979) work implies that causes, like taxonomy, part/whole, and plans, may form extensive lexical/semantic fields. We present Ahern's causal tree structure in the following case.

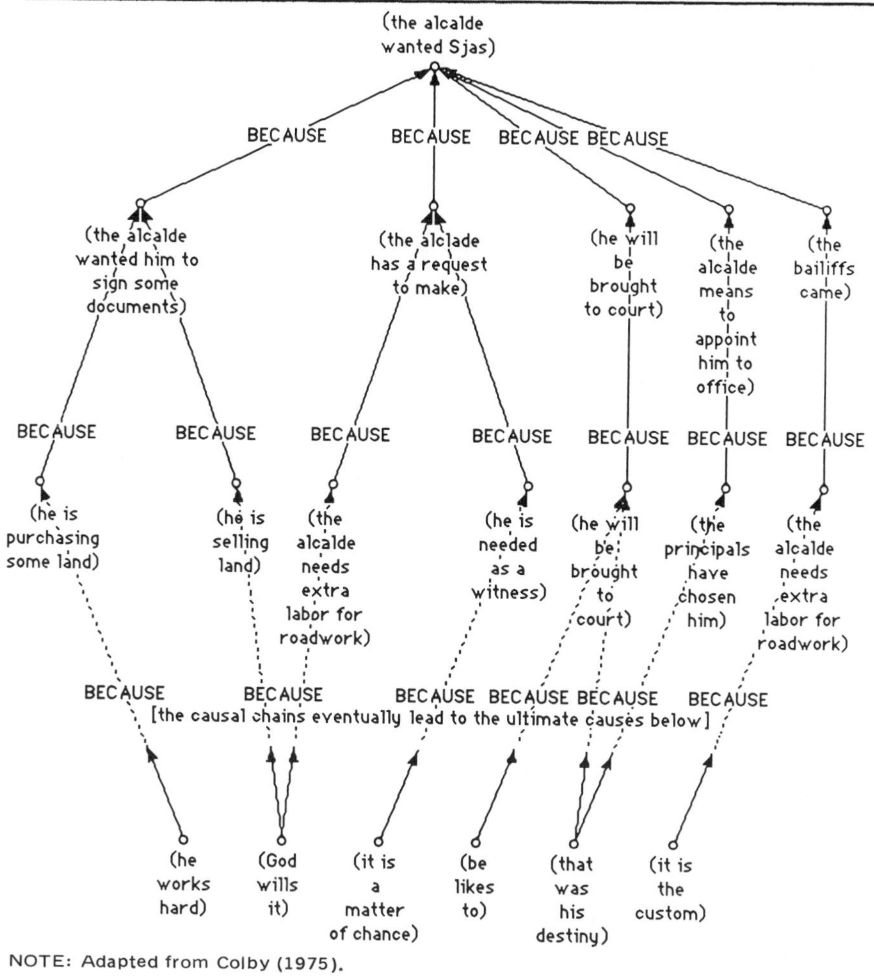

Figure 6.12 Causal Tree of Aspect of Mayan Culture

Case 6.1 Why Navajos Dislike Lava Flow State Park

Julie Ahern's task during the summer of 1978 was to investigate why the Navajo Indian population of the Tower Rock community (adjacent to Lava Flow State Park) has a strained relationship with the park. Her tree diagrams, originally presented on a single page (see Figure 6.13), showed the results of her research (based on interviews) visually and succinctly. We will present her results with comments one level at a time.

The park used to be private land (about one square mile). The owner, before selling it to the State of New Mexico and the City of Gallo, Arizona, let the Navajo

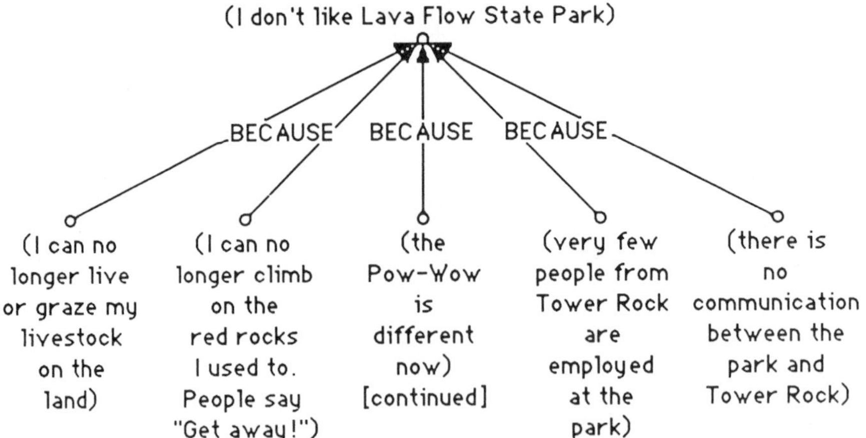

NOTE: The causal relation arrow is marked BECAUSE. The direction of the arrow is always from subject to predicate. Alternately, the lowest level can be read as the cause of the higher level.

Figure 6.13 First Level of Causes

population use it. After the park was established, the area was fenced and declared off limits to Navajos and their livestock. The town of Gallo has a yearly Indian ceremonial. Since the establishment of the park it has been permanently relocated to newly built facilities there.

"Illegal" stands are erected by transient merchants outside the park on the one-mile road strip between the park and the village. But no one claims jurisdiction and no one cleans up the mess the stands leave behind. Limiting the number of food stands and booths inside the park has caused the "illegal" booths outside the park. The Pow-Wow no longer functions as a meeting place for Indians. It has become "professionalized" (formal). Booths and performances are reserved for recognized "professionals" and are by invitation only.

Rodeos and parades are important events for most Indians. The difficulty of getting from one to the other (about five miles apart) is perceived as "inconvenient" (Figure 6.16).

With richer data than what Ahern was able to collect in a few weeks it may be possible to weigh the various branches and estimate which causes are more salient than others. Even without "weighing," the causal tree (in tree form or in list form) provides a powerful and succinct way of showing the explicit reasons for a particular attitude.

Attitudinal and evaluative questions for ethnoscience ethnographies are taken up in the next section. Both causal structures and expressions of attitudes and evaluations at present are underutilized in ethnoscience.

It is clear from Case 6.1 that causal trees show promise for applied anthropology. The director of Lava Flow State Park was surprised at the depth of resent-

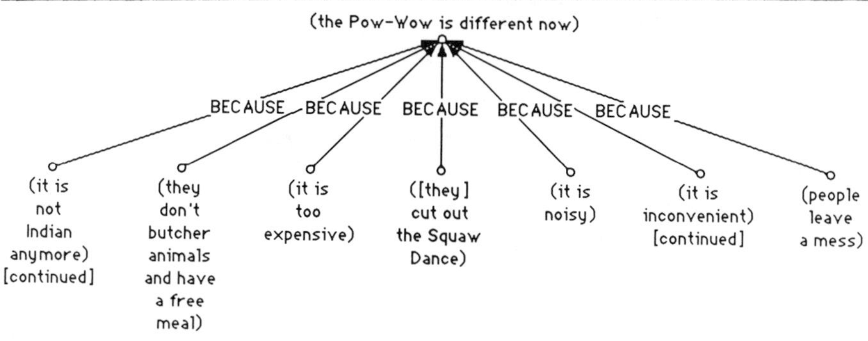

Figure 6.14 Second Level of Causes

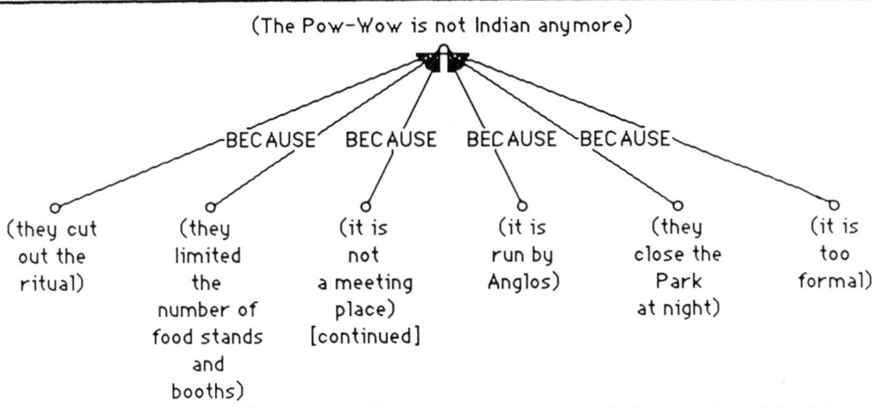

Figure 6.15 First Part of Third Level of Causes

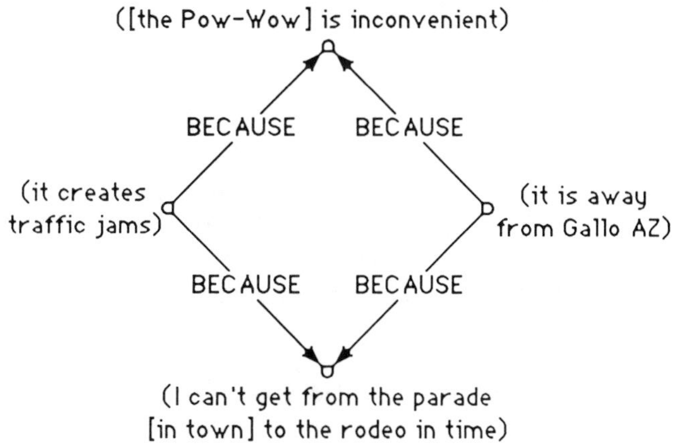

NOTE: This figure has an interlocking causal structure.

Figure 6.16 Second Part of Third and Fourth Levels

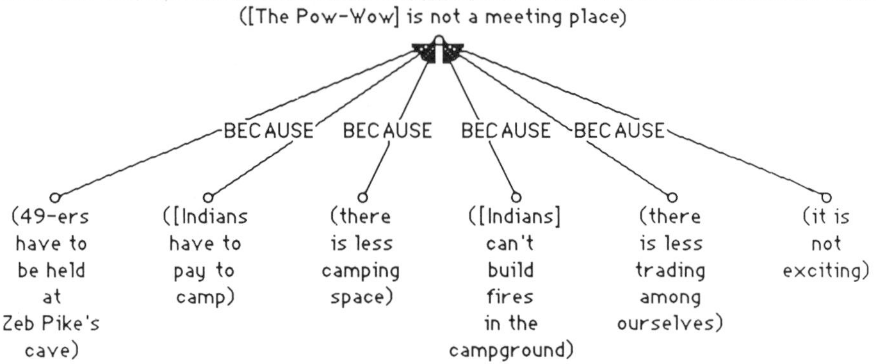

Figure 6.17 Fourth Level of Causes

ment shown by the surrounding Indian community. He too could have arranged to discover the causes of Indian discontent by their importance to the park, separating those that depend on policies that could be changed easily from those where change would require major policy shifts. Easy changes can be implemented immediately. More complex changes usually require multilateral negotiations (in our case, involving at least administration, the governing board of the park, and the Indian community).

6.3 VALUES AND EVALUATIONS[2]

The study of values should be ethnoscience par excellence. Values are embedded in language, and therefore the same theoretical machinery that is applicable to vocabularies in general is appropriate here.

6.3.0 Introduction

Some anthropologists and almost all philosophers agree that values and/or systems of values (value orientations, morality systems, or ethical systems) can be studied only through language. "Ideologies can be investigated only through the explicit discourse of an informant" (Ladd 1957: 13), and "it would seem that the most promising way to discover what a person thought would be to ask him and that solely to observe his behavior might be totally misleading. . . . Ethical opinions, as a species of belief or at least analogous to them, can most profitably be investigated by means of obtaining statements from the informant" (p. 14).

Before going further, it will be useful to review briefly what we mean by values or value systems.

6.3.1 Values

Figure 6.18 summarizes our position. It is based on the work of Talcott Parsons and Edward Schils (1951) as paraphrased by Max Black (1961) with some elaborations of our own.

Actions are fundamental to the study of values. Actions, in turn, require choices—there are always alternative things that one can do. We studied conditions for selecting certain activities over others through decision modeling (see Chapters 4 and 5). Verbal action plans and decision tables can be easily incorporated into a semantic field theory. Semantic fields can be envisioned as a network of semantic or lexical relations. To incorporate values and value orientations into semantic fields is a much more difficult task.

While a human being performs an activity, he or she thinks; that is, one engages one's knowledge and feels or takes some affective position to what one does. If we define values, following R. Kluckhohn (1962: 289), as "not 'desires' but rather as the desirable," we can paraphrase *values as that which we ought to want*. The affective feeling associated with some activity becomes, then, the difference between our "raw wants" and our "refined oughts": If the "oughts" outstrip the "wants," we tend to feel coerced. If the "wants" dominate the "oughts," we derive some satisfaction from the activity. The balance between "oughts" and "wants" is obviously modifiable by learning and may change gradually throughout one's lifetime. Conversion experiences seem to imply that the balance of "wants" and "oughts" may also change, sometimes abruptly.

Action is
- (1) something you do to try to get something done
- (2) impossible without knowing, thinking, and having feelings (about it) at the same time

Choices are
- (1) an integral part of human life
- (2) concerned with
  - (a) what you want (what is best for you)
  - (b) what you ought to do (what others say is the right thing to do, or what they expect you to do)

Values are what you ought to want
Thought is knowledge (cognition)
Feeling is wants minus oughts (affect)

Elicitable entities are
- (1) actions (plans)
- (2) choices (decisions)
- (3) values (requirements)
  - (a) wants
  - (b) oughts
- (4) knowledge
- (5) feelings

NOTE: Adapted from Parsonian theory via Max Black (1961) with elaborations.

Figure 6.18 Definitional Frame of Values

Thus we will use the term "value" in the sense that it is "not only what we want but also feel that it is right and proper to want for ourselves and others" (Kluckhohn 1962: 289). Evaluation, then, is the comparison of what we do with what we ought to be doing.

It would be wrong to consider values a recent wrinkle in the evolution of the human mind. Nothing could be further from the truth. The great difficulty we experience in the study of values derives from the fact that they are the most fundamental partition of our understandings of the world around us. "An amoeba placed on a plate of water with a drop of sulfuric acid placed nearby will pull away from the acid (I think). If it could speak the amoeba, without knowing anything about sulfuric acid, could say, 'This environment has poor quality'" (Pirsig 1974: 244-245). Following the argument of Von Foerster (1970; see also Volume 1, Section 1.3, especially Figure 1.5) the nerve endings on the surface of our bodies (in all organisms) can only report the presence of stimuli. It is a fundamental property of the *processing* of preceptions that we can evaluate a situation with "No! I don't like it!" and pull back literally or figuratively.

The ability to evaluate our perceptions and to act upon their evaluation is an ancient and very basic quality of all animate beings. This quality makes values commonplace. "And yet it is precisely because they are commonplace that they are interesting and important" (Kluckhohn 1962: 295). For these reasons values and value systems should have a central position in ethnoscience ethnography.

6.3.2 Two Approaches to the Study of Values

Ethnoscience theories and models of artificial intelligence have a lot in common. It is in the spirit of this perceived similarity that Michael Arbib (1972) saw anthropologists as preferring *lexical/semantic structure over lexical/semantic processes*. However, even Arbib sees process more in terms of algorithms than as the evaluation of outcomes. Although it is true that in ethnoscience ethnography only Colby (e.g., 1975) has made progress in the consideration of values, experimenters in artificial intelligence have not done much better. Our own thoughts are predicated on the assumption that there are two fundamentally different approaches to the study and theoretical modeling of values:

(1) The description of ethical systems. This approach involves the development of theory and methodology for the elicitation, analysis, and presentation of ethical systems embedded in a general theory of cultural knowledge. This is essentially a *third-person* approach. By this we mean that it is encyclopedic: It describes the ethical system of a culture as if the system belonged to an omniscient idealized (third) person in that culture. The system of values and evaluations is described but does not contribute directly to the creation of action except as *discourse about action*. But since action is never actually performed but only "talked about," so to speak, there appears to be no room for a feedback system that controls action, or, more accurately, that controls perception through action (Powers 1973).

(2) *The modeling of ethical systems.* This approach involves the development of a theory that can take descriptive statements of an ethical system and convert then into a *self-regulating, ethnically behaving model* of action with full consideration of ethical consequences. In other words, this is a *first-person* approach because it simulates activity as if performed by a sentient human being. We contend later in this chapter that in this approach the theory of control systems with negative feedback will play a significant role.

6.3.3 Description of Ethical Systems

In our own theoretical framework we strive for comparability and for the incorporation of values and evaluations into a general semantic field theory of cultural knowledge systems. We believe that the MTQ schema (see Volume 1, Section 2.3 and Werner and Topper 1976) containing the lexical/semantic relations of attribution (M), taxonomy (T) and sequence (Q) is theoretically sufficient if combined with modal logic (see below). However, considerable work remains to be done (see Volume 1, Section 2.3).

Various methodological approaches apply. We have mentioned decision table logic (see Chapter 4), which works with attributes or conditions, some of which are very mundane. A condition for making bread is often simply "Am I hungry?" The logic does not transfer well to values or "oughts" (but see Section 6.1). The problem is that although conditions may be present or absent, the absence of a value is more difficult to interpret, or attempts at interpretation may be irrelevant. That is, we behave or do not behave within the context of a value (see "unless" clauses for themes in Section 6.3.6).

Causes and values are closely related. A value is what ought to happen; a cause in human affairs may be seen as the compromise between social oughts and individual wants that underlie action. Colby (1975) developed a field technique for elicitation (implemented by the QUESTOR computerized eliciting program). His idea is disarmingly simple. Colby takes a statement about an everyday event and reduces this event through step-by-step questioning to its ultimate causes. The diagram in Figure 6.19 illustrates (see also Figure 6.12).

In Colby's schema the question moving up in the diagram is a "Why?" The question moving downward in the diagram is "How?" Figure 6.19's diagram was elicited in response to such simple questions.

John's motivations for wishing success for his article in this example looks overly calculating. However, we claim that this is an artifact of the eliciting situation. The causal questions must be augmented by at least some "oughts" and "wants." We suspect a different causal value structure can be elicited with each of the following questions:

(1) Why did John want to ride home on his bicycle?
(2) Why ought John (want to) ride . . .?
(3) Why must John . . . ?

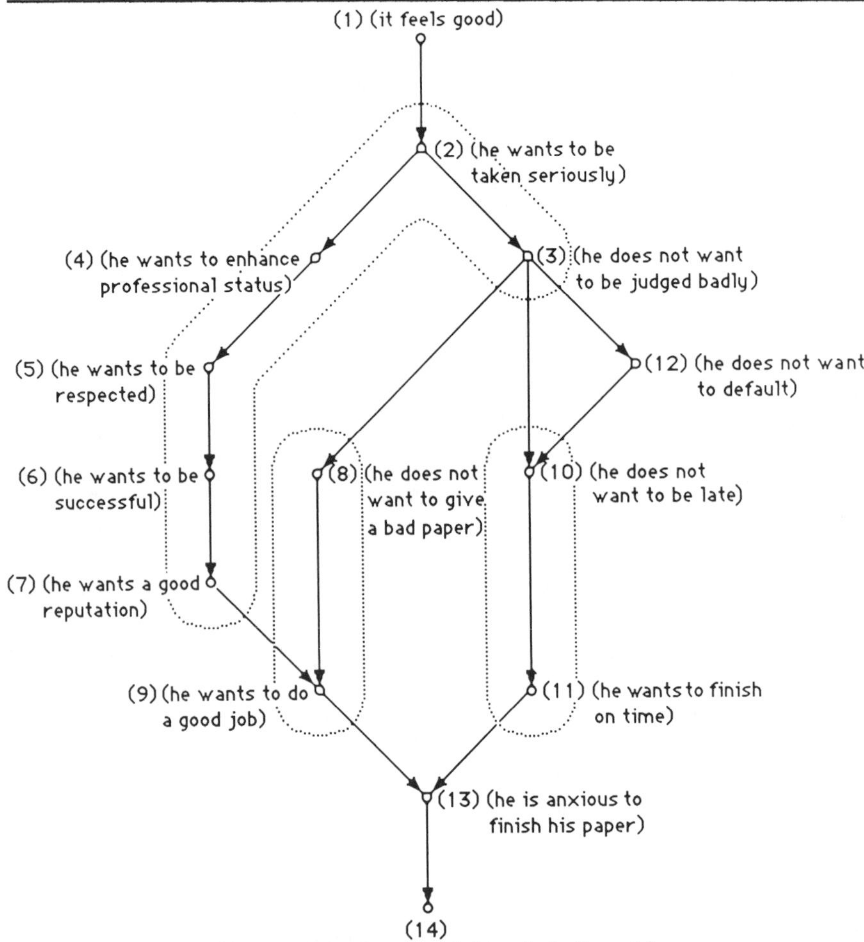

NOTE: The arrows labeled B stand for "X because Y" where X is the term at the head of the arrow and Y the term at its tail. For example, "(He wants to be taken seriously) BECAUSE (it feels good"). The dotted ovals represent "supernodes" combining terms that appear on the "same" level (see Figure 6.20).

Figure 6.19 The Elicitation of Causes and Values Following Colby (1975)

(4) Why should John . . . ?
(5) Why would John . . . ?

Further experimentation is necessary.

Colby's elicitation procedure displays other interesting features. The causes of Figure 6.19 are not all on different levels. It is possible in some cases to reverse their order (X BECAUSE Y and Y BECAUSE X) and thus collapse nodes to create the "super"-nodes pictured and enclosed by dotted lines. In this way the diagram can be simplified (Figure 6.20).

The cause of John's riding was his anxiety. The anxiety has three possible

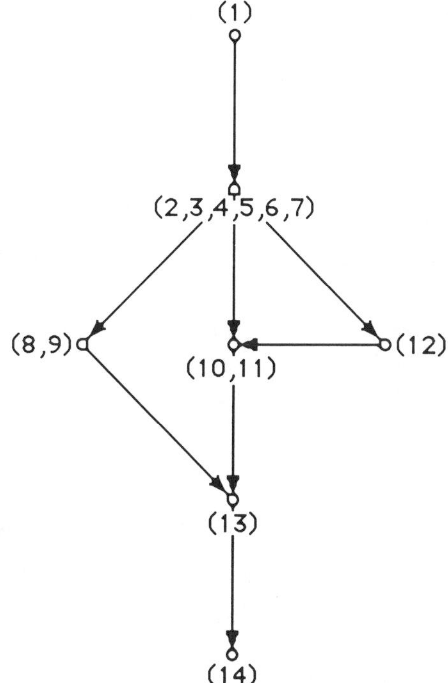

NOTE: Simplification is accomplished by looking for instances of symmetry (i.e., "X BECAUSE X"). We assume that all such symmetries are on one level of the diagram. Numbers correspond to the propositions in Figure 6.19.

Figure 6.20 Simplification of Figure 6.19

causes: (1) He wanted to do a good job (node labeled 3, 8 from (6.19); (2) he wanted to finish on time (4,9); or (3) he did not want to default (11). All three have a single cause, essentially paraphrasable as "success" (5,6,7,10,12,13). Ultimately John wanted "success" because it "feels good" to be successful. Thus causal chains may be shorter than Colby's (1975) work implies. Further experimentation with elicitation techniques will be necessary to determine exactly how elicited sentences can be translated with some assurance into lexical/semantic relations and associated fields.

Modal logic as an extension of symbolic logic is another promising avenue of investigation. We are particularly impressed by Snyder's system (1973). By applying an analogue to quantified symbolic logic, Snyder is able to reduce cancelation rules (or proofs) for theorems to the cancellation proofs of quantified symbolic logic. This is based on the formal similarity of the quantifiers ALL and SOME to modal operators such as "necessity" and "possibility," the operators of so-called alletic logic. By a set of rules that place constraints of greater and greater stringency upon the quantificational analogue, Snyder derives deontic logic or the logic "oughts" with the operators "obligatory" and "permissible." That is, of course, the logic of values. Snyder's system is capable of deriving the theorems of several other logics such as temporal logic "always" and "sometimes" and the logic of "knowledge" and "belief." Interestingly, in natural (at least Indo-European) language there exists an extensive set of terms that fit the quantificational analogue framework. Figure 6.21 lists some of these. Analogues to these exist almost certainly in non-Indo-European languages as well.

6.3.4 Hierarchies of "Wants" and "Oughts"

Some items on the list in Figure 6.21 are more relevant to the study of values than others. In any case, we perceive a rich possibility for investigation here, especially in more exotic languages, where such work is almost entirely nonexistent.

So far very little has been done with hierarchies of values. In the following we will restrict ourselves entirely to "wants" and, through investigation of "oughts," may follow similar arguments.[3]

"Wants" are necessarily preferences, even though the alternatives with which they are compared are null: We prefer to survive, we prefer to eat, we prefer to eat apples, we prefer to eat Winesaps. The development of such a progression implies the existence of simple preference hierarchies. Problems arise, however, when other preferences are involved. We may prefer Winesaps, but do we prefer Winesaps in Peoria to Jonathans in San Francisco? In such a case we must evaluate the preferences by comparison to a reference value.

The process of evaluation becomes the process of choosing which combination of preferences we value more. The following illustrations may be conceptually trivial, but the analytical points are not. It is easier to make the points with simple variables.

Let us assume that we can either eat Winesaps in Peoria or we can eat Jonathans in San Francisco. If we value Jonathans at 0, Winesaps at 1, Peoria at 0, and San Francisco at 1, there is no choice (1,1). But if we switch preference levels on, say,

Analogue to ALL	Analogue to SOME
necessarily	possibly
obligatorily	permissibly
always	sometimes
everywhere	somewhere
every way	some way
must	may
must	can
can, will	could
will	would
shall	should
will	may
certainly	probably
definitely	possibly
permanently	tentatively

Figure 6.21 Possible Candidates for Logics Based on Snyder's (1973) Quantificational Analogue

apples, with presence of apples valued at 1, we get a clear choice (1,2). It is preferable to eat apples in San Francisco than in Peoria.

Two points are obvious. The first is that it is preferable to lower our standards for apples rather than to lower our standards for cities; this demonstrates that preferences between categories of preferences are (high-order) preferences that must be dealt with. The second point is that preferences generate preferences. We have generated the more complex preference: It is better to eat any kind of apple in cities we like than in cities we don't like.

It follows that other sets of preferences in combination with these sets will generate additional preference statements. Suppose we take the parallel statement(s): It is preferable to eat oranges (bananas, mangoes, etc.) . . . In combination with the one generated above, these will eventually generate by taxonomic generalization: It is preferable to eat fruit . . . If, then, we take statements that are parallel on this level of generality, such as this one, It is preferable to eat meat (cheese, bread, etc.) . . ., in combinations with the statement generated above, we will generate taxonomically: It is preferable to eat any food in cities we like than in cities we don't like. This establishes location as a higher preference category (value) than food. Note that our comparison category (food) has reached the same level of generality as our preference category location.

Now suppose we have a similarly derived statement: It is preferable to live in any location in cities we like than in cities we don't like. Can this be combined with the previous general statement to generate: It is preferable to live anywhere and eat anything in cities we like than in cities we don't like? *It cannot*. Each sequence, as defined by the process just described, allows combination as the union of subsets. In the end the level of generalization of the comparison category has reached that of the preference category. The grouping is no longer acceptable. We must therefore change our comparison category.

Up to this point we have been operating with single-category preference classes (things to eat, places to live) compared to a single binary category (cities we prefer and cities we do not prefer). We have demonstrated the process of preference category formation, the process of single-category comparsion, and the limitations of both processes. The illustration is an example of "all else being equal" reasoning. Preferences may be used to eliminate whole categories of alternatives so that choice is simplified (see Section 5.2.3).

Consider the choice of a meal. Our highest priority preference is roast beef; we usually prefer browned potatoes with roast, but we would also like French onion soup, so we decide on potatoes au gratin. This creates a problem, as we'd rather fancied a Cabernet Sauvignon, but the amount of cheese would tend to overpower it, so we choose a Pinot Noir; we decide to forego cognac with our after dinner coffee. In order to choose a meal we attempt to establish a sequence of preferences that act as limiting conditions on subsequent choices.

We may generalize from this dining experience to a statement: In general, when we eat beef, we prefer a hearty soup, oven-cooked potatoes, a green vegetable, red wine, and cognac with coffee. We may decide to generalize further: We prefer meat with soup and vegetables. We still have not answered this multiple-category question: If we prefer meat to soup and meat to vegetables, do we prefer meat to soup and vegetables? We would say that it depends on the meat (or the soup and the vegetables). This illustration, lacking an overriding preference category, demonstrates that there is a level of generalization at which useful comparison can no longer occur.

We have illustrated two related issues. In the first case, the multiple-category comparison problem developed when the sets to be compared to the preference value reached the same level of generality as the preference value. In the second case, although the levels of generality of the preference value and the comparison sets remained the same, the multiple-category comparison problem developed when the level of generality became too great for specific comparisons. Both cases illustrate that relative preferences can be established only in reference to *some fixed standard* even though the value held constant may be free to vary in other comparisons.

6.3.5 Interactive Ethical Systems

This type of system is best envisioned as an artificial intelligence device (although at this point "theory" may be a more preferable label) that can pass Turing's test for ethical reckoning.[4] Obviously, unless we were to build a robot with totally human capabilities of action, the domain of what we mean by "reckoning" needs to be radically restricted.

In the simplest possible application of ethical/cognitive simulation, we can think of a single form of activity. That is, the output of our device should be restricted to some form of language. For the sake of easy illustration, a computer terminal connected to an electronic central processing unit will serve. One can interact with the device through a keyboard—through a "sense of touch" (e.g., the 256 ASCII character set), and it can respond in the same character set by activating its keys internally. We have called such a device a first-person device because it has to make ethical decisions with respect to its own behavior. Some of the questions it ought to be able to consider with reference to itself are listed in Figure 6.22.

Who is it I ought to talk to? (access)
Why ought I talk to him/her? (justification)
How ought I talk to him/her? (sociolinguistics)
What ought I talk to him/her about? (content)
How much ought I talk to him/her? (quantity)
When ought I talk to him/her? (time)
Where ought I talk to him/her? (location)

NOTE: These are with reference to "wants" and "oughts" of talking. Other verbs may be substituted.

Figure 6.22 Questions for a First-Person Discourse Model

The only theoretical devices that seems capable (at least potentially) of accounting for purposive questions are control systems (or control theory; Powers 1973). The simplest such everyday device is a thermostat controlling the temperature of a house. The system starts with a reference setting (signal) for the desired temperature. This is the value (temperature) that the whole system ought to maintain. We use for it the term "value" advisedly. Maintaining the temperature reading as close as possible to the set reference value is "good." All deviation of the reading from the reference setting is "bad," and the system will try to change the environment through its actions, which change the reading. Thus control systems with negative feedback are capable of imitating purposive behavior. The values are set, of course, from *outside* the system. In Powers's model each reference value is set by the next higher control system in the hierarchy.

Control Systems

A prototypical control system is represented in Figure 6.23. The perceptor function transmits the relationship of input quantities, including environmental feedback and disturbances, to a comparator. Here the perceptual signal and reference signal are compared and any error (derivation) is computed. The error signal activates the effector function, which emits an output quantity. The output quantity modifies the environment so that the error signal is kept at or near zero. This

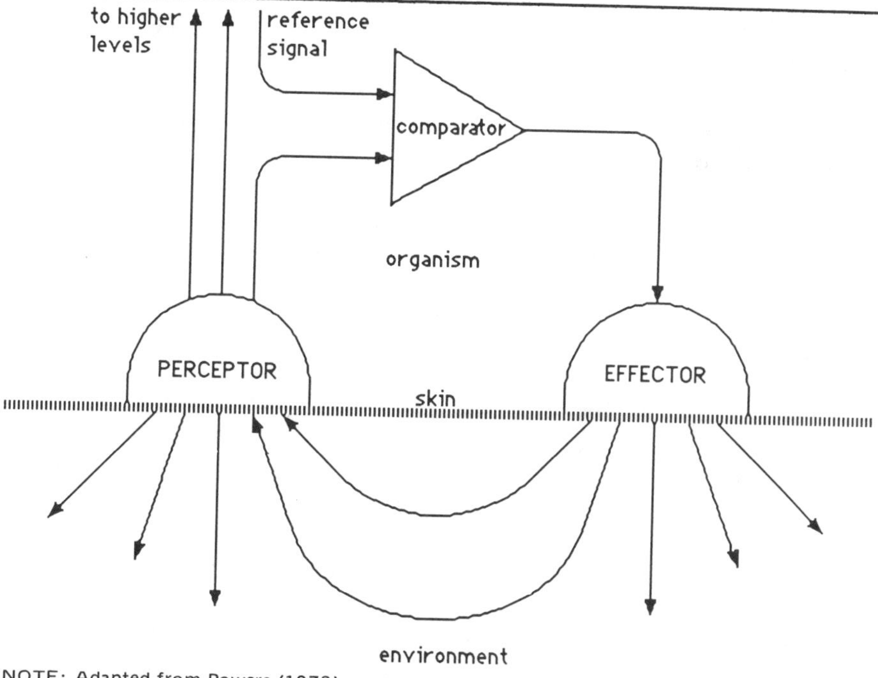

NOTE: Adapted from Powers (1973)

Figure 6.23 Control System with Negative Feedback

control is affected by changing the perceptual signal. In this sense, in a control system, "behavior" (the output quantity) controls perception. (For details see Powers 1973).

It is not our intention to explore all the ramifications this model has for a general theory of behavior. Our aim is to adapt it to the successful incorporation of values and evaluations into a first-person theory of ethnoscience. Before proceeding it may be worthwhile to repeat that the reference signal (in the above example) functions as a value. The comparator evaluates the state of the world (albeit limited in our example) to the value set by a higher order system. Keeping on the mark (within some set tolerance level) is "good," deviating from the reference level is "bad," and the system moves to compensate for the deviation until reference signal and perceptual signal are equal and the error disappears; that is, until we are in conformity with our values.

A control system must have certain prerequisites. We will discuss each in turn. In the process we try to speculate what these features mean when they are translated into the framework of a control device that intelligently responds to questioning in the manner indicated above. The prerequisites are as follows:

(1) Every control system must be able to output activities that affect the environment. Our first-person device has only one way of affecting the environment: by talking (or, more precisely, typing).

(2) It must have an environment that can affect the controlled quantity. The environment consists of whoever occupies the computer terminal that is interacting with the control system. The controlled quantity is a value that should change but does not, or one that is maintained when disturbed. We have to search for invariants in the verbal (typed) social interaction that respond to disturbances in such a way as to prevent changes. Changes, of course, are possible, but following the model of control systems they occur only if and when the reference signal is also changing.

One variable that remains static throughout a discourse is our intention(s) as speakers. These intentions are closely tied to the questions (Figure 6.22) we have raised as significant for a first-person ethical theory. Every language of the world has an extensive vocabulary of verbal intentions: For example if we scold or praise, our general intention is scolding or praising. We expect a desired effect—for example, greater effort—after scolding or praise. Only if this effort is not forthcoming do we change our reference level, which in turn changes our intentions. Human intentions are unbelievably complex. This complexity will have to be translated into theoretical considerations as well as some form of empirical confirmation.[5]

Powers (1973) postulated at least nine levels of control systems needed to describe human action. Intentions seem to coincide best with his level of programs or strategies. Strategies in turn are controlled by principles or values: If a given strategy comes to a point at which we begin to perceive that it violates our values, we will switch strategies (or much more rarely values).

(3) The environment of every control system contains disturbances that affect the controlled quantity. If intentions are controlled, the unexpected reaction of another (or an alter) to our intention would create such a disturbance. It is accommodated by reference to principles or values at the next higher level of the organization of control.

(4) It contains a perception affected by the controlled quantity. In Powers's sense our actions control our perception. The actions of the ethical first-person system are verbal (typed) acts. Our perceptions are the inputs to our assessment of how well our verbal acts comply with our intentions.

(5) In a control system, action and disturbance should approximately amount to zero. Our actions are the result of our assessment of the compliance of our verbal acts with our intentions. Unless the compliance is near perfect, as it tends to be, our control system is not functioning well. Our intentions are closely tied to our perceptions of a given context. Lack of compliance is the precipitation of a *context mistake*. If the mistake is severe, all communication may grind to a halt (Goffman 1959). The error signal becomes too great for correction. Only if the situation is redefined in some way acceptable to both participants to the mistake can communication resume. But first they must redefine each other's intentions.

6.3.6 Themes and Values

In the preceding sections we equated values with reference signals from the next higher level of a control system. By analogy, a thermostat setting is a value. Conformity with it is "good." Departure from the setting is "bad" and has to be corrected by appropriate action. Values can be seen in this light as high-level attributes attached to entire cultural domains and activities associated with them. In this sense, too, values are recurrent. A cultural domain has an associated universe of discourse. In this discourse value statements surface with regularity. Interestingly, disapproval (negative evaluations) seems to outnumber approval by about two to one (Werner and Begishe 1968).

The recurrent nature of value statements identifies them taxonomically as kinds of themes. Whether all themes are evaluative is open to debate. Certainly all evaluative statements that consistently pervade the discourse within a cultural domain are themes of that domain.

Both Spradley (1979) and Agar (1979), two recent proponents of thematic analysis, have stressed that in addition to recurrence, themes must recur across several domains. This statement is misleading if domains and themes are seen as structureless, undifferentiated lists. Both cultural domains and associated themes are hierarchical. That is, there are smaller cultural domains included in larger ones, and more general themes govern more specific ones in smaller cultural domains. The prerequisite for themes to cut across domains implies that these themes are on the next higher level of organization just as the reference signals of control systems.

In the past, anthropologists searched for themes and values always on the highest levels of society. They called this quest the search for values, value orientations, core values, core symbols, premises, ethos, eidos, worldview, and cognitive orientation (Spradley 1979: 186). All of these themes can be viewed from a societal point of view, but they can also be much more restricted. On each level a theme or value can be compared to the "organ tone." In music, this is a tone held steady while the melody moves up and down but always with reference to the steady drone in the background. Yet this musical analogy fails to account for the multilevel nature of themes and values in the cultural life of people.

We saw in Figures 6.19 and 6.20 that the ultimate value of John was his hedonism of success ("It feels good"). But this value and theme were only the highest in a series of intermediate values and themes. For example, at the lowest level, riding a bicycle in the rain contains the immediate value or theme that it is all right to subordinate some personal discomfort to the hedonism of success. Similar subvalues (sub-"organ tones") are invoked on all levels of the diagram. The strength of Colby's (1975) diagram is that its transition from activities "on the ground" to the highest themes follows a logical chain from manifest behavior to the most abstract principles underlying it. We can literally see how Colby moves from empirical statement to ultimate principles. This is a transition rarely made explicit in the anthropological literature.

In Volume 1, Section 1.2 we outlined the principle of epistemological windows. Simply restated, it says that we get to learn more about a social system by trying to resolve contradictions (explain them) than by siding with one issue or the other. The same principle applies here, as is demonstrated by Agar (1979). A theme or value is more thoroughly understood if we make a concerted effort to look for contradictions. Agar (1979) calls these the "unless" clauses of thematic analysis.

We are convinced that this aspect of themes provides the most important source of insights into the working of a social system (a human group). We are also convinced that "unless" clauses are very difficult to find in an ethnographer's field notes, including journal and transcriptions, without an efficient method for finding both supporting and contradictory evidence to any theme or any value statements made by consultants.

Thematic analysis is not yet very sophisticated. Even accepting that themes and values are high-level attributes attached to a whole domain of discourse, though important, is theoretically still a primitive assertion. We have only a vague idea of how these attributes attach. Even less clear is to what kinds of units they are attached. Plans, especially high-level plans, appear to be good candidates for attachment. Thus values and themes may be part of initial decision conditions.

More important at this stage in our knowledge of these structures is the ability to deal with many examples. This will be possible only if both values and themes and their contradictions in some contexts are easily accessible through efficient data management techniques.

6.3.7 Summary and Conclusions

We have explored the possibilities of incorporating values into a theory of ethnoscience. We have found that values form systems and are ethnoscience par excellence. We are less successful in incorporating values into ethnoscience theory. A number of field techniques and empirical considerations can be helpful; however, these help most with third-person models. Such models treat cultural knowledge and values as belonging to another person whose knowledge system we are *describing*. Third-person models are what we have done in ethnoscience so far. The incorporation of them into the MTQ lexical/semantic field schema seems relatively straightforward.

First-person models are another matter. Although they are infinitely more difficult (it seems), they offer rich insights. The most fruitful approach seems to be via control systems with negative feedback, as proposed in the hierarchical model of Powers (1973).

Values are kinds of themes. We suspect that all themes are also values. Both are hierarchical—that is there are low-level and high-level themes and values. Colby's (1975) diagramming technique has the advantage that it makes explicit the transition from low-level (mundane?) actions to high-level values, themes and causes. Hirschman's "required for" relation offers the same advantages.

Agar's (1979) recent recommendation to look not only for confirmation of themes but also for "unless" clauses demands sophisticated data management. In addition, it improves ethnographic analysis by leading more surely to the *resolution* of contradiction (see the discussion of epistemological windows in Volume 1, Section 1.2).

6.4 OTHER SEMANTIC SYSTEMS

Everything we know about semantic systems beyond those discussed so far are complex relations introduced in Volume 1, Section 2.3. These are relations of the form

(X) T ((C) M ((Preposition) M (Y))).

In this formula C is a constant—for example, "kind," "part," "cause," "required," "reason," "used," and possibly others. The prepositions seem to be limited most commonly to "of," "for," "with," "in," and "to" and possibly others. There exists a family of these complex lexical/semantic relations. Their full extent, however, is not known.

Of the well-known complex relations, only "part/whole," "cause," and "requires" seem to form fields large enough to be called cultural domains. Others have been used sporadically in the anthropological and related literature (see Evens et al. 1980). Most of these other complex relations define small lexical/semantic fields and may occur only in highly specific contexts. Their utility for summarizing complex ethnographic data seems limited.

Spradley (1979) lists the following relations applicable to this discussion:

X is a kind of Y

X is a part of Y

X is the result of Y

X is the reason for Y

X is a place to Y

X is a use for Y

X is a way to Y

X is a stage in Y

The first of these is special. Although it follows the canonical form shown above, this complex relation is a paraphrase of the atomic one. That is, the "kind of" phrase in the taxonomic relation is optional or emphatic. Most simply, it is usually "An X is a Y."

Similarly, at least one interpretation of "X is a stage of Y" is the relation of queueing Q. This relation is most simply expressed by "X and then Y." A more common interpretation of stages is developmental: Examples are stages of trees (sapling, tree), stages of animals (calf, heifer, cow) and, of course, human developmental stages. Frake (1964), who pioneered the use of some of these complex relations with Williams (1966), used the stage relation with descriptions of plants in Subanum agriculture.

Complex relations beyond the well-known set are useful in some cultural domains, but their utility seems severely restricted. However, interpreting Hutchins's (1980) relation "A has user rights to B" from the Trobriand Islands as "A is a user right holder to B" transforms this relation into the canonical form shown earlier. It is significant that Hutchins sees this relation as establishing an entire domain of discourse or cultural schematum. It remains to be seen if all cultural schemata are built on complex relations circumscribing a domain of discourse.

6.5 SUMMARY AND CONCLUSIONS

The final step in going beyond simple structural analysis is the application of other semantic systems. These are based on relations that go beyond taxonomies, part/whole classifications, folk definitions, plans, and decision models.

The "required for" relation was discovered by Hirschman in 1984. The analysis of causes and of causal chains is inspired by the work of Colby (1975), who also pioneered trying to automate (or semiautomate) the elicitation and acquisition of ethnographic data. "Require" mental and causal chains in our MTQ schema are complex relations derived from modification, taxonomy and the serial queueing relations. While we discuss an entire family of these complex relations (the part/whole relation is one of them), only the part/whole relation, the "required for," and causal chains seem to form large lexical/semantic fields that can be used to describe concisely complex ethnographic information. Most of the other complex relations appear only in isolated context, rarely (if ever) forming chains (or trees). Some complex relations may establish cultural schemata, or whole domains of discourse may evolve around them (Hutchins 1980).

Values are kinds of themes that deal with human wants and oughts. Just as themes and values are hierarchical, high-level values give rise to lower levels and ultimately to the lowest levels. What constitutes a level to which values apply remains unclear. However, it seems clear that values are similar (or identical) to high-level attributes (conditions). These attributes determine what is and is not appropriate within their domain. We used the analogy of the "organ tone" or drone that sets a musical background, coloring the melody unfolding in the foreground.

Values and evaluations are responsible for the most fundamental perceptions of every animate being: to determine what is good for it and what is bad. It is a fundamental characteristic of life that it introduces wants. The complexities of human social organization introduce societal wants that translate into individual action as oughts. Both wants and oughts are fundamental to human life. Ethnoscience ethnographies have grossly neglected values. This must change. Values are expressed in language, which puts them squarely into the realm of ethnoscience. As a research plan, the integration of values with lexical/semantic fields is an imperative for future research.

NOTES

1. This section is based on the work of Kim Hirschman, who discovered the "requires" relation in 1984 and applied it to Navajo agricultural decision making during the summer of 1985.

2. This section depends heavily on the collaboration of Judith A. Remington and Frank Pasquale: Werner, Remington and Pasquale's paper, "Prolegomena toward a Theory of Values in Ethnoscience," was presented at the meetings of the American Anthropological Association in November 1976.

3. We are indebted to Judith A. Remington for this argument.

4. Turing's test involves a human tester who communicates by terminal with an "intelligent" machine in one room and a human in another. There are no restrictions on possible conversations. If the tester cannot determine which room contains the human, then the machine has passed Turing's test.

5. We discuss problems of ambiguity of intentions in Volume 1, Section 1.4.5

Chapter 7

Analysis of Texts

Textual analysis is the least intrusive methodology available to the ethnographer. It has the advantage that the consultant is able to respond to questions in a natural and (at least to him or her) relatively unstructured or unforced manner.

7.0 INTRODUCTION

In taxonomic elicitation, for example, the consultant is constrained to produce new, lower taxonomic levels until he or she reaches terminal nodes that contain no further taxonomic structure. This is a type of behavior that is rarely encountered in ordinary discourse. Clarifications of the *proper assignment* of single taxons to a particular superordinate concept are, however, quite common in everyday speech—for example, "Father, are cherry tomatoes vegetables?" (actual request by Werner's six-year-old son). However, the more usual question, "What kind of X are there?" rarely occurs in ordinary discourse. We cannot recall such instances in discourse in any language.

Textual analysis frees the ethnographer to engage in very normal behavior. The separation of taxonomic and other types of semantic systems becomes part of the analytic process, rather than part of the elicitation process. Colby (1979) calls the family of ethnographies based on textual analysis "text ethnographies." In our view, ethnographies derived from texts are essentially ethnoscience ethnographies. Considering that all ethnographic data result in texts, the opposite is also true: All ethnoscience ethnographies are text ethnographies.

It is inevitable that in order to utilize textual analysis, the ethnographer needs to know his or her field well. This is most easily accomplished in a monolingual context (on monolingual native ethnography, see Volume 1, Sections 1.1 and 3.1). Since sentences in ordinary speech are often highly context bound (that is, incomplete from a more context-free point of view), analysis must provide the necessary but missing detail.

Case 7.1 Providing Context

> Interviewer: "What did the patient take?" Respondent: "I don't know. The doctor conjectures Ex-Lax." The question asked provides the necessary context for interpreting the opaque sentence, "The doctor conjectures Ex-Lax." That is, the "full" sentence is probably, "The doctor conjectures that the patient took the medication called Ex-Lax."

Case 7.1 also implies that analysis is best done *immediately* after the interview. The systematic distortion hypothesis applies here as well (see Volume 1, Section 1.2). Even in the best case the ethnographer will be unable to interpret part of the interview because he or she cannot recall the context. In the worst case he or she will make up a context on the basis of previous cultural experience in situations that may be more or less similar.

Even under good conditions with very articulate consultants, parts of various semantic structures may be missing. More formally constrained, so-called ancillary elicitation (Voegelin & Voegelin 1957, basically follow-up minitour questioning) is almost inevitably necessary. The aim of the ancillary elicitation is to make the semantic structures derived through analysis as complete as possible.

Thus textual analysis requires often indirect Grand Tour questions that elicit open discourse. However, since open discourse is *never semantically exhaustive*, structured minitour questions must be used to round out any knowledge system. The most appropriate procedure is as follows: open text elicitation (with indirect questions) → analysis → structural elicitation → analysis. Most usually several iterations of this sequence are necessary. This is especially true in the cultural domain focal to one's theoretical interests.

Perhaps the major advantage of textual analysis is that the consultant is free to explore his or her own mind with relatively little interference by the ethnographer. We assume, therefore, that the first (or immediate) answers are more accessible for recall (in a given questioning context) than are later answers, perhaps later in the interview or even in later interviews.

It is worthwhile to keep track of the order of elicitation and of what information was obtained only through ancilliary elicitation. At this time, however, the theoretical implications of such ordering are not entirely clear. More precisely, we are not as yet sure what to do with information that marks order in elicitation. See, however, Sanday (1968, also see Section 2.2.2) who conjectured, we think correctly, that the order in which a consultant retrieves some structural information may be a clue to its storage location in the brain.

It is therefore a good idea for any ethnographer to keep track of the order in which various items were elicited. In this an efficient data management system is a prerequisite. Although we cannot give a general rule of how to interpret such order, in the context of an ethnography it may provide the analysis with insights about salience that may be difficult to detect any other way. Most simply put, items readily recalled are probably more salient that items recalled only after some time and after some prodding. At this stage in our knowledge, cautious consideration of such data seems most appropriate.

The ethnographer should note, each time the conversation in an interview turns to the "same" topic, what topic preceded the discussion. The reason is simple. If the semantic network model has any validity, then each time a semantic domain is approached from a different direction the retrieval of information should also be different. In other words, salience of recalled characteristics may be influenced by the temporal context of elicitation.

Serial order is, of course, the fundamental organization of text, the result of open-ended discourse. The only place we do not destroy this serial order is in the use of plans and cases. Plans are more usually composite, constructed on the basis of several unique cases (descriptions) of the same activity. Cases are instances or parts of an interview preserved in their original order. They are usually reports on unique events that may be analyzed into recurrent events. Nevertheless, one of the most powerful uses of cases is to cite them in unedited form.

In the following sections we start with the elicitation of case and then proceed to more complete analysis of texts.

7.1 COLLECTION OF CASES

Collection of actual cases, of unique, though perhaps recurring episodes, is a very illuminating method (see "Case for Cases" in Volume 1, Section 3.2). We feel that actual collection of descriptions of historical events—the proverbial anecdote—is a sorely underutilized technique of data collection and presentation. This approach was recently pioneered by James Spradley and some of his students at Macalester College, but as we have shown in Volume 1, Section 3.2 that their use is as old as ethnography. The important thing to remember is that, just as with anything else, cases should be used systematically.

Cases can be used to illustrate the behavior of a certain class of individuals or certain groups. For example, one category of teachers we obtained from Navajo students is an "angry teacher." This is an Anglo teacher who wants to be nice to Indian students, usually in contract school (a kind of private school) settings, who therefore fails to enforce even minimal discipline and is then pushed by the students to the breaking point. Navajos tend to reject or feel very uneasy about uncontrolled emotion such as destructive anger.

To illuminate exactly what type of behavior Navajos consider "angry," it is best to ask for an example, or case. We asked for a story about a teacher actually getting angry. The following narrative was given in response. (The reference to "my door" implies that the doors, etc. in a community school belong to the community and hence also to the students.)

Case 7.2 Angry Teacher

"[The teacher] was trying to get them boys . . . into class and they were in the other room where they have a different class and they locked themselves in there and [the teacher] was trying to get in there and got mad and said, 'Some

> of these days I'm gonna kick the door down,' and a student said, 'Go ahead, kick the door. I don't care. It's my door, go ahead and break it.' The teacher really took his word for it and he kicked the door and made a big hole in it."

One caution is important: a case should rarely be long. It is easy to lose track of the central idea of a long case. It should therefore make a point and stop.

Cases can also be used to illustrate types of activities, such as methods of punishment. Two different cases, one collected at an elementary school and one at a high school, demonstrate the different types of behavior called "punishment" in different school cultures.

Case 7.3 Running on Stairs

> "About a week, or just a few days before Christmas vacation, Doris, Thelma, Karla, Sandra, Lloyd, Irving, and Methew were running down the lunch stairs on their way to lunch. The room is on the second level of the school and there is a flight of stairs which the children must go down to get to the lavatory where they wash their hands before eating and then go down the hall to the lunchroom.
>
> "After lunch, on the same day, on the way up to the room, Kimberley and Doris were 'running on the stairs playing tag.' On the way up to the room, the children take the gym stairs, a flight of steps without landing, which the lunch stairs possess.
>
> "Ordinarily Mrs. Jones can tell when people have been running down to lunch. She dismisses them at the door of the room, goes down the music stairs and meets them at the end of the hall by the lunch room door, 'They walk down like little angels and when they get to the doorway they run madly into the bathroom.' On this particular day, however, the lunch room ladies informed her that the class had been running down the stairs.
>
> "When Mrs. Jones returned to the room after lunch, she said, 'Line up.' And we said, 'Why?' and she said, 'You'll see.' She took us to the lunch stairs and we had to go up and down the stairs twenty times. She stood right there and watched us do it. We thought it was funny at first, but I got real tired!"

Here is the second case illustrating "punishment."

Case 7.4 Unfair Principal

> "He's hard on students and he knows this school is full of Indians and that most Indians don't like school and they'll be cutting class. So he'll be hard on students. . . . I cut class and he caught me. At the same time there were some boys that were caught ripping off supplies so [the principal] had to use us as witnesses. He got that out of the way and then he came back to the the case of our cutting class and he just suspended us from school. I was on probation for a whole year. I couldn't go to school activities; I couldn't join any school activities; I couldn't go home for lunch; I couldn't miss any classes unless I had a

> note from my parents; and I had to go right to the principal for his permission to leave the school grounds."
>
> Another girl continues about the same principal: "He put me on probation for being five minutes late for class. And then (we) went to DNA (Navajo Legal Aid), me and three other girls, and we filed a case against him."

We found cases to be greatly serendipitous. They often provide surprise information that is difficult to elicit by asking direct questions. One example is direct questioning of Navajo students about witchcraft. The case below emerged while we were talking with a student about a category of girls whom she described as "critical." This case illustrates the persistence of traditional beliefs about witchcraft among Navajo students. It was one of only two in over 100 interviews with Navajo students that mentioned witchcraft.

Case 7.1.D Witchcraft as Sanction

> "There's one certain girl that can really criticize. . . . She's the only one that got to be the enemy of all girls . . . because she . . . likes to gossip about girls and talks about [them] . . . She makes fun of your clothes . . . and she would get real jealous of [nice clothes] and tell her father to do something about it.
>
> One of my friend's mother came to school and she was dressed neat and this girl who was jealous came in while [the mother] was standing there. [The mother] was staring at the class and the girl just happened to go by and bumped into her. [The mother] turned and here the girl was standing. And the next day the mother passed away."

Cases are also very effective ways of illustrating generalizations: That is, one of their greatest uses is in the *presentation* of ethnographic data. In the analysis of data cases are used to arrive at generalizations. The following methods were adapted from suggestions made by Brenda Man (personal communication via J.P. Spradley) in a slightly different context. But her ideas can be expanded for ethnographic analysis:

(1) Data Acquisiton. Cases are collected. Some are singled out for special attention.
(2) The cases are annotated with comments by consultants (if possible) and sorted for particular instances or activities that are of interest.
(3) A generalization is made on the basis of a few cases. For example, on the basis of a few cases one might judge the punishment of students as excessively harsh.
(4) The generalization is tested on a wider sample of similar cases. A numerical tally is kept of all cases illustrating the same generalization. It is possible to use statistics on numbers of cases (e.g., Agar 1974).
(5) Further testing is conducted by collecting or identifying cases that *fail to support* the generalization. A numerical tally is kept of these as well. The cases supporting and those contradicting a generalization are compared, possibly statistically. If necessary, the generalization is accepted, amended, or rejected.

(6) Typical or representative cases supporting or contradicting a generalization are selected for the ethnographic write-up. These cases aptly illustrate the generalization through examples and counterexamples. This allows the ethnographer to capture variations in context or themes (generalizations across a variety of contexts) and their "unless" clauses when themes fail to apply (Agar 1979).

The case of the unfair principal was elicited when we asked about situations involving types of punishment. In the analysis of the case, first a category of "principal" and "unfair principal" was noted (the beginnings of a taxonomy of principals and other personnel at a school). It would have been appropriate for the ethnographer to return to the students and ask for elaborations of this category by asking for folk definitions or for more cases. It would be particularly interesting to establish what the students considered "fair" or "unfair," by whom (principal, teachers?), and toward whom "fairness" and "unfairness" was directed under what circumstances. The category "fair" or "fairness" also needs further elaboration. Cases should be collected in similar circumstances for positively and negatively evaluated episodes. The contrast between "fair" and "unfair" can be expanded further through ancillary elicitation— for example, folk definitions.

Although in the ethnographic report cases may be used for illustration, they should always be seen also as opportunities for understanding more about the social system or knowledge system in question. In this spirit cases should invariably lead to deeper ancillary questioning.

7.2 HYPOTHETICAL CASES

Often it is important to understand how well members of a cultural knowledge system or a social group can predict the behavior of the system as a whole or of parts of the system or of individual members. This type of information can sometimes be gathered by asking for hypothetical cases. "What would happen if . . . ? is a way in which to ask for this kind of case. Other possible ways to ask for hypothetical cases more indirectly are "Tell me under what circumstances would X happen?" or "What could cause X to (not to) happen?" The behavior described by X must be carefully identified in advance and must be meaningful to the consultants.

Nothing is more damaging to the fidelity of an ethnography, and nothing can be more misleading, than a hypothetical question put badly. Before such questions are asked, it is important for the ethnographer to understand a great deal about the social system of the consultants. This means that considerable ethnoscience elicitation and analysis must go into the process before it is safe to ask hypothetical questions.

The basic problem with hypothetical cases occurs when they are used to find answers to questions the ethnographer tried, without success, to ask. These questions may be related to interest or to deeper theoretical concerns. But such concerns need first to be translated into an idiom meaningful to the consultants. That translation cannot be done without considerable understanding of the social system in which the ethnographer operates. Such understanding can be gained only through hard work in elicitation and analysis. It is therefore safe to assume that no ethnographer should start fieldwork with hypothetical questions. Only after achieving considerable familiarity with the cultural system under investigation and after careful preparation—preferably with the help of a native collaborator—is this a safe and reliable method for gathering data.

Collecting hypothetical cases is generally an underutilized method of ethnographic elicitation (see Volume 1, Section 3.2). Nevertheless, causal statements—for example, long causal chains such as "The ceremony was performed because . . ."—can be ethnographically very illuminating. Colby (1975; see also Chapter 6) has developed a computerized schema which he uses to elicit hypothetical causal chains of the form "X occurred because of Y," "Y occurred because of Z," "Z occurred because of" . . . and so on.

Following is an example of a hypothetical case:

Case 7.6 Keep Them Sitting: A Hypothetical Case

The context is an ethnography describing a home for autistic children. The questioning turned to the maintenance of discipline. The ethnographer, Florence Kozak, asked the consultant, "What would you do if a child is totally noncompliant and just refuses to get in the shower?" The result was a hypothetical case:

"Well, of course, that depends on which boy it is. You handle each one a bit differently. You really try to get them to comply verbally, because it's too hairy trying to get physical with them in the bathroom. And if they are naked and wet, they're pretty slippery. If they are in the bathroom but refusing to undress or get in, I'd remove them and have them sit in the hall. Every minute or so I'd ask them: 'Are you ready to get up now and take your shower?' If so, fine; otherwise, I'd have them keep sitting, so they understand they're not going to get away with it. I would say most of the boys would be ready in 10 or 15 minutes. But if I had to wait even an hour, I'd wait out the hour, probably switching off with another staff member now and then."

Hypothetical cases such as this one may best be elicited through indirect questioning. However, rather that asking how the consultant would react given certain circumstances, one could ask how some class of people (established, for example, through taxonomic elicitation) would react given those circumstances. The advantage of speaking about hypothetical third persons is that consultants and ethnographer can utilize the "projective response." This idea is derived from psychological projective testing. Briefly, this is a method (the most usual response is to pictures e.g., Thematic Aperception Test, to inkblots (Rorschach test), or to samples of audio recording; see Werner, personal communication) in which respondents use fictitious third persons (e.g., the person in the picture) to talk about themselves and their own feelings. Hypothetical cases can be elicited under similar circumstances. For example, Werner used stick figure pictures to elicit possible happenings at a Navajo secular dance (see Volume 1, Figures 6.3 and 6.4).

The important thing to remember is that the ethnographer does not use the projective response for probing the psychological state of the consultants. The goal is to facilitate talk about hypothetical topics that may be too difficult, painful, or embarrassing to discuss directly. The goal of the resulting text is always to illuminate some ethnographic problem—that is, a problem of description.

7.2.1 Folk Probability (See also Chapter 5)

Hypothetical cases and elicited judgments of probabilities for the occurrence of certain events are closely related. This aspect of elicitation at present is also underutilized in ethnography. In fact, we cannot think of a single systematic instance of this type of elicitation in the literature (see Volume 1, Section 3.2 about the rare uses of hypothetical cases in some classical ethnographies).

It may be extremely important, especially for projects in applied anthropology, to obtain consultant's judgments of the probability of occurrence of certain events. However, the user of folk probabilities should be aware of the literature on the systematic biases that seem to underlie intuitive judgments of this kind. An article by Tversky and Kahneman (1974) summarizes these findings. It will suffice here to highlight their major conclusion. Systematic intuitive bias falls into three major categories (Tversky and Kahneman 1974):

(1) *Representativeness:* This implies that people will tend to predict outcomes in terms of their system of beliefs rather than in terms of actual, impersonally tabulated frequencies and probabilities.
(2) *Availability:* This implies that people are willing to estimate the probability of easily available (imaginable) information higher than information that does not come to mind as easily.
(3) *Adjustment and Anchoring:* This implies that, especially in numerical estimates, the starting point of an intuitive judgment seems to affect its outcome radically.

The above description of potential biases in folk estimates of probability is extremely superficial and is intended only to alert the reader to this field of inquiry. There is a sizable psychological literature on the subject. We hope to return to this subject from an ethnoscience viewpoint in subsequent editions of this book.

7.3 PROCEDURES OF TEXT ANALYSIS

Not counting translation, textual analysis is based on the following steps:

(1) Transcription of the interview.
(2) Identification of complex sentences.
(2ā) Translation of complex sentences (if necessary).
(3) Completion of complex sentences (usually the insertion of nouns and noun phrases in place of pronouns), such as replace "John and I (Bill) were talking and he hit me" by "John and Bill were talking and John hit Bill."

(4) Analysis of the complex sentences into constituent simple sentences; more accurately, "maximally complete simple sentences" (MCSS).
(5) Dispersal of the MCSS in concordance fashion to the files; one for every (major) concept within each sentence.
(Steps 2, 3, and 4 may be more or less simultaneous.)

Throughout the rest of Chapter 7 we discuss these six steps in detail: First, with a simple example from English, then with a more complex example in English, then with an example from Navajo, and finally with an English example including plans and decision tables.

7.3.1 Complex Sentences

Most texts consist of complex sentences. Simple sentences in the sense of the kernel sentences of early Chomsky (1957) are the exception rather than the rule. Thus identifying complex sentences in this context means separating all separable sentences from one another and assigning a number to each.

This sounds simpler than it usually is. For example, our transcription secretaries in Navajo often could not decide where to place a period ending a Navajo sentence. This was partly because spoken Navajo can string a virtually endless number of sentences together by *áádóó* (and then). When performing this kind of text analysis we let the sentence boundaries coincide with the word *áádóó*. This proved satisfactory for all purposes. Similar or analogous methods may have to be worked out for other languages in which placing a final falling tone (periods at sentence ends) may not be part of ordinary speaking style.

7.3.2 Completion of Complex Sentences

Many sentences in texts can be understood properly only in the context of those sentences preceding and following them. The most common information gathered from (usually) preceding sentences is the value of pronouns and pro-verbs. For example, the value of the pronoun "he" could be a person named John, the man on the corner, the generic ethnographer, or any number of other male or generic referents. Similarly, the English pro-verb "do" can stand for a large number of activities describable by English verbs. Similarly, ambiguous phrases must be appropriately disambiguated. The following case illustrates this with examples.

Case 7.7 Inserting Nouns or Noun Phrases

The ambiguous phrase "old men and women" must be replaced by "old men" and "women" or "old men" and "old women" depending on the sense that emerges from context. "The letter was written" must be replaced by "The letter was written by John" if it is clear from other sentences that John was the writer of the letter. Full verbs are inserted for the verb "to do": "Bill was done" is replaced by "Bill finished the chair." Replace pro-verbs by their appropriate contextual referent: Replace "John went to the store and Mary did so too" by "John went to the store," and "Mary went to the store." And so on.

7.3.3 Constituent Simple Sentences

In the following extended case we analyze a fairly large segment of an interview. In the process we illustrate the steps described so far and the analysis of textual (interview) material into maximally complete simple sentences (MCSS).

Case 7.8 Primary Nursing Interview

This is an example of an interview that was conducted in order to describe a particular model of primary patient care. One of the features of this ethnography was the description of the patient care model on a patient care unit from many different points of view: the nurse's, the nursing coordinator's (supervisor's), the physician's, the patient's, and so on. The transcription that follows is from an interview with the coordinator (formerly nursing supervisor), Sarah Xaviera Jones, abbreviated SXJ (coded name and initials). The interviewer's first question is long, attempting to encourage a long answer, as it was the first question of the interview immediately following introductions. Since we were also looking for potential sociolinguistic clues (for a later, more sophisticated, detailed analysis), the transcription is relatively fine grained, marking interruptions, hesitations, and other aspects of free discourse (E = Ethnographer, C = Consultant).

E: So, uh, what I am interested in is to get your viewpoint, uh, *vis-à-vis* primary nursing, but, uh, I . . . I'd . . . I mean I don't want to quite say it the way it's going to come out, you know, I'm not interested in the . . . uh . . . your evaluation of your, uh, attitude toward primary nursing as much, at this point, uh, . . . although I'm interested in that, I'm interested in how it fits into sort of your daily activities, how it relates to you directly, through the nuts and bolts aspect of it, you know . . .

C: Mmmm, uhuh.

E: The day-to-day basis, essentially. You know, from morning till . . .

C: How do I relate?

E: How do you relate, how do you relate to the head nurse? You know, how do you relate to the model?

C: OK, (breath) I don't relate to it as much as I'd like to.

E: Mmmm, uhuh.

C: Uh . . . I think . . . I believe in primary nursing as . . . the model has been set up. I think it's . . . it's a good way to deliver patient care.

E: Mmmm, uhuh.

C: I think it provides patients with the professional nursing skills that they need. (Irrelevant exchange about tape recorder.) Uh . . . I think that the . . . as a coordinator, my . . . I see myself as a support to the head nurse, to the staff nurse who's delivering primary care. I'd like to see myself taking primary patients.

E: Mmmm, uhuh.

C: Up until the present it hasn't really been possible. I had a couple of primary patients last fall . . .

E: While you were coordinator?

C: While I was coordinating.

In this example, steps 2, 3, and 4 cannot be clearly separated (apart from one exception, which will be discussed later). This seems to be because the consultant speaks in relatively simple sentences already and her response can therefore immediately be analyzed into maximally complete simple sentences. The list of MCSS below therefore includes the identification of complex sentences (step 2) and the completion of these sentences (step 3) in which completed or inserted parts are marked by placement between brackets ([]). Step 4 is applied only in the case of 1SXJ.7. (The first "1" refers to the first interview with SXJ, the coded initials of the consultant. ".7" is the seventh complex sentence. ".7.0" marks the complex sentence itself as an MCSS and ".7.1", and ".7.2", . . . as an MCSS derived from complex sentence .7 and is the first, second, . . . MCSS of the original complex sentence ".7".)

Maximally Complete Simple Sentences

1SXJ.2.0	I don't relate to [primary nursing] as much as I'd like to.
1SXJ.2.0	I believe in primary nursing as the model has been set up.
1SXJ.3.2.0	I think [primary nursing] is a good way to deliver patient care.
1SXJ.4.0	[Primary nursing] provides patients with the professional nursing skills that they need.
1SXJ.5.0	As a coordinator, I see myself as a support to the head nurse.
1SXJ.6.0	[As a coordinator, I see myself as a support] to the staff nurse who's delivering primary [patient] care.

(Note that the last sentence contains an additional assertion about the role of the staff nurse. This aspect will be important in the "dispersal" of the information in step 5.)

1SXJ.6.1	The staff nurse [is the one] who is delivering primary [patient] care.
1SXJ.7.0	I'd like to see myself taking primary patients [as a coordinator].
1SXJ.8.0	[Taking primary patients as a coordinator] hasn't really been possible until the present.
1SXJ.9.0	[As a coordinator] I had a couple of primary patients last fall.

Dispersal of MCSS

The basic idea is to place as many *copies* of each sentence as are necessary into places where they become most useful for the final ethnographic report—that is, files for major key words (nouns and verbs) and key phrases. Before the final write-up, the sentences may indicate the need for further, ancilliary questions, especially if the patterns are incomplete (see Chapter 2).

In this example, sentence 1SXJ.2.0 should be dispersed to two locations:

(1) One copy should go to the file entitled "coordinator," perhaps paraphrased and transcribed as follows:
1SXJ.2.0 The Coordinator does not relate to [primary nursing] as much as she'd like to [on this unit].
(2) A second copy should be placed with the general file on descriptions or attributes of primary nursing.

Sentence 1SXJ.2.0 will go to the same two locations, as will sentence 1SXJ.3.0. Sentence 1SXJ.3.0 is assigned to "primary nursing" and "delivery of patient care," which is a part of "patient care." Sentence 1SXJ.5.0 goes to "coordinator" and "head nurse"; 1SXJ.6.0 to "coordinator," "staff nurse," and "delivery of primary patient care," a subcategory of "delivery of patient care" and part of "patient care." Sentence 1SXJ.6.1 is actually more relevant to "staff nurse" than is 1SXJ.6.0; the latter may therefore be deleted. Sentence 1SXJ.7.0, again, is about the role of the coordinator; thus it gets assigned there, but it also goes to "primary patient" or, more precisely, to the part of "primary patient" that describes who can take primary patients. Sentences 1SXJ.8.0 and 1SXJ.9.0 are assigned or dispersed analogously. Which unit to disperse and which to ignore depends on the goals of the ethnography. The selection of entries to which sentences are dispersed can be very comprehensive during analysis. An appropriate reduction (for example, 1:10) can be undertaken at the time of writing (see Chapter 9).

At the time of dispersal MCSS should be inspected for lexical/semantic relation. For example, the above set of MCSS implies the folk classification shown in Figure 7.1.

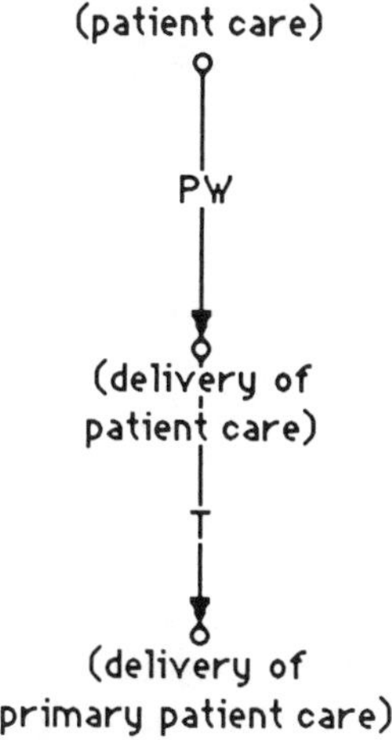

Figure 7.1 Classification of Patient Care

The dispersed MCSS accumulate in the files to which they have been assigned. Each MCSS is identifiable by interview, consultant and sentence within the interview. At the time of writing the ethnographic report salient key words are selected for description. Since the sources are identified it becomes easy to follow variations in meaning.

Case 7.9 Text Analysis from NEME Project

The following example is from elicitation for *The Navajo Ethno-Medical Encyclopaedia* (Austin-Garrison & Werner *et al.*, in preparation). Volume III deals with Navajo ideas about marriage, conception, pregnancy, and birth. The interview explores causes of complications that a woman may experience during the birth process.

Transcription

This step is adequately described in the section on *transcription* (see Volume 1, Section 13.6). In bilingual contexts, translation is usually necessary. Multistage translation is slow and painstaking but is preferable because of its superior accuracy relative to other more casual translation techniques (see Volume 1, Section 12.3.1).

Detailed translation at this point, or after complex sentences or completion of complex sentences, is advisable only if the ethnographer does not control the language of the ethnography. In all other cases it is preferable to translate the actual semantic systems only *after* the dispersal of the maximally complete simple sentences. The reason is simple: Dispersal of the MCSS is tantamount to constructing definitions from text. A much more accurate translation is possible after these definitions have been constructed and they become available in searching for the best translation equivalents. In other words, it is safer to do final ethnographic translation after constructing detailed folk definitions. The entire procedure we call "dispersal" is designed to enable the ethnographer to construct (folk) definitions from texts.

For ease of handling, temporary translation labels can be used, at first, to help identify an imperfectly known language. It is often appropriate to mark temporary translation labels. In our taxonomic presentation of the Navajo world (Werner *et al.* 1983)[2] we mark all translation labels with (TL). This warns the reader that these are temporary "crutches" to our understanding rather than carefully worked-out translation equivalents.

The example below is unique in another sense. Constructing a free translation from the original transcription was exceedingly difficult; so difficult, in fact, that we never attempted it. Only after we had analyzed the text into maximally complete simple sentences did we manage a successful free translation. The reason is that most of what we reconstructed in the following analysis was self-evident from the context of the interview and therefore left implicit by the consultant. For the ethnography we had to make these implicit parts fully explicit, so that the texts could be understood in minimally specified contexts.

(E = ethnographer; C = consultant: Note that translation labels and original Navajo are vertically aligned. In other words, the same items start in the same vertical column. 3ASA: third interview with Ann Sandra Ashi. The name is coded.)

E: Navajo original:	*Asdzání*	*yiltsą́ągo*	*heit'éego*
Literal translation:	A woman	when pregnant	in what way

bąąh dahoo'aah?
she becomes ill (she has complications)?

Free translation: How does a woman become ill, or have complications during pregnancy?

C: (the entire following text is sentence 1ASA.1)

. . . *Náánà díídí*	*ch'ééh*	*achí*	*wolyé*
. . . again this here	in vain birth		it is called

éí éí	*dinéhígíí*	*t'ááhó*	*ájít'íigo*	*índa*
that that	man he	alone	he does it-when	and then

asdzání	*jílínígíí*	*da*	*ha'át'íishíí*
the woman	the one who is it	or	whatever (it may be)

níjílhkadgo	*da baa nijigháago*	*t'áadoole'é*
she is sewing-when	or for him doing	something

níléí	*dahistl'óo*	*da*	*éí*	*t'áá*	*éí*
that	she is weaving	or	that	just	that

nílááhdi	*dahistl'ó*	*t'áá éí*	*wooltáád*
over there	she is weaving	just that	Unraveling Ceremony

ánaal'įįhgo	*áko doo*	*bik'í*	*diitsas*	*da*
when performed	thus not	on him	tangle	not

áko	*níléí kodóó*	*bits'ą́ądóó háát'i'gíí*
thus	there from here from it	the one that extends out

jó	*éí*	*bik'ídeesdiz*	*yileeh . . .*
well	that	it tangles on him	it becomes . . .

The first problem is to determine the boundaries of the answer.

Complex Sentences

Very often sentence boundaries must be drawn arbitrarily on syntactic and/or semantic grounds. In free speech, people generally do not talk in clearly bounded sentences, as in most writing. This fact is indicated in the above example by the elipses (. . .) at the beginning and end of ASA's answer.

The answer in this case is very choppy and without pauses or stops of any kind. Everything the consultant wanted to say on the subject is just added on, making a sensible free translation of the original answer difficult. The word-for-word translation is only minimally helpful at this stage. When an answer such as this one becomes too involved and complex, several expanded sentences can be developed. Each of the sentences is given an identification number.

Completion of Complex Sentences

Here are the sentences derived from the above text. First, an implied sentence: (Brackets are used to indicate implied parts that were made explicit through analysis—most usually from known context or, occasionally, through ancillary elicitation):

3ASA.1.1:	*[Asdzáni]*	*ch'ééh*	*ałhchíígo*	*[asdzání]*	*bąąh*
	Woman	in vain	she gives birth-when	woman	she is
	dahaz'ą́go	*wolye.*			
	sick-when	it is called.			

Free: When a woman has birth complications, then it is called "the women is sick."

3ASA.1.2:	*Ch'ééh*	*ałchíígo [ígíí]*	*[asdzání]*	*bąąh dahaz'ą́ągo [ígíí]*
	In vain	at birth-when	woman	she is ill-when
	[át'é].			
	it is			

Free: A complication [at birth] is [a kind of] woman's illness. (Note the taxonomic implication of this sentence)

3ASA.1.3:	*[Asdzání]*	*ch'ééh ałchíígo*		*éí*	*diné*	*bá*
	woman	in vain she gives birth-when		that	man	for him
	ootsánígíí	*t'ááhó*	*ájít'įį*	*łeh.*		
	there is pregnancy	just to her	he does it	usually.		

Free: When a woman has birth complications, it is usually the man who is responsible for it.

3ASA.1.4:	*[Asdzání*	*yilhtsáago]*	*ha'át'íishíí*	*néílkadgo*
	woman	pregnant-when	whatever (it may be)	she is sewing-when
	[awéé' yidá'ditl óóhgo]		*ch'ééh achíí*	
	baby gets tied up inside-when		in vain there is birth	

łeh.
usually.

Free: If a woman is sewing something while pregnant, then the baby usually gets tied up inside (causing) complications.

3ASA.1.5: *[Asdzání yilhtsą́ągo]* *níléí* *dahiistl'ǫ́*
woman pregnant-when there weaving (tools)

[yinaalnishgo *biniinaa]* *ch'ééh* *ałchíí łeh.*
she works on it when therefore in vain birth usually.

Free: If a woman works on her weaving while pregnant, then complications usually result.

3ASA.1.6: *Asdzání* *i'niiłchííhgo* *dahiistl'ǫ* *t'áá éí*
woman in labor-when weaving (tools) just that

wooltáád *anál'į́įhgo* *áko* *doo* *awéé' bik'i*
Unraveling Ceremony is performed thus not baby on it

deestasgóó *yichííh.*
tangle-when it is born

Free: If a woman is in labor, then the Unraveling Ceremony is performed over her weaving (tools) and the baby is born untangled.

3ASA.1.7: *[Asdzání ałchíigo]* *níléí* *[awéé']* *bits'ą́ądóó*
woman in birth-when there baby away from him

háát'i'ígíí *[bits'éé' bitl'óól] bik'i*
that which is extending his umbilical cord on him

deesdiz yileehgo *[ch'ééh alchíí łeh].*
tangled it becomes-when in vain birth usually

Free: When a woman is in labor and the umbilical cord that extends from the baby entangles it, complications of the birth result usually.

Constituent Simple Sentences

We now analyze the above complex sentences into MCSS. For example, from 3ASA.1.3, which we repeat first, we create the following MCSS:

3ASA.1.3: *[Asdzání]* *ch'ééh* *ałchíigo* *éí* *diné* *bá*
woman in vain she gives birth-when that man for him

ootsánígíí *t'ááhó* *ájít'į́į* *łeh.*
there is pregnancy just to her he does it usually.

Free: When a woman has birth complications, it is usually the man who is responsible for it.

The simplified MCSS:

3ASA.1.3.1:	*Asdzání*	*ch'ééh*	*ałchíigo*	*diné bá*
	woman	in vain	causing birth-when	man for him
	ootsánígíí	*át'įį*	*łeh*	
	there is pregnancy	he does it	usually	

Free: If the woman has complications, it is the responsibility (fault) of the man for whom she is pregnant.[3]

This sentence has been stripped of all emphatics (e.g., *t'ááhó,* "just for him") to its minimal sense. The relatively complex *ájít'į́,* stressing an emphatically human actor, is replaced by the "regular" third person form of the verb *át'į́* "he is it." We consider this sentence an MCSS because further reduction of the complexity becomes awkward for practical ethnography (encyclopediography). Taxonomically, there are three units involved here: (1) *Asdzání ch'ééh ałchíigo . . .* "When the woman has (birth) complications . . ." This is a time adverbial specifying the time of the man's responsibility—namely, when complications arise. This is therefore a kind of time period. (2) *Diné bá ootsánígíí,* "the man for whom there is birth." This is a kind of Navajo man (*diné*), her husband, for whose benefit the pregnancy is taking place. The third aspect (3) *át'í,* "he is the doer, he has the responsibility, it is his fault" is clearly an attribute of the man in item 2.

Dispersal of MCSS

The dispersal involves assignment of sentence 3ASA.1.3.1 to three (on closer analysis perhaps more) places in the growing file for an encyclopedia or an ethnography. In our case, the description of conception, pregnancy, and birth appeared to be best organized as a verbal action plan with a definite inception, history, and completion. This sentence could therefore be dispersed into (1) the entry concerning the time period of the birth when complications might appear, (2) the description (outside the plan structure) of the responsibilities of the males (and the females) toward the growing new life in the uterus of the mother, and (3) the responsibilities of the husband. This sentence is therefore placed among the attributes of the man mentioned in 2.

In this example, the second complex sentence (3ASA1.1) establishes the taxonomic relation of birth complications to illness (see Figure 7.2). The first sentence (3ASA.1.1) appears to be a paraphrase stressing the naming relationship rather than the taxonomic one specifically. The third sentence (3ASA.1.3) also yields but one MCSS. This is not always the case. More than one sentence (MCSS) may

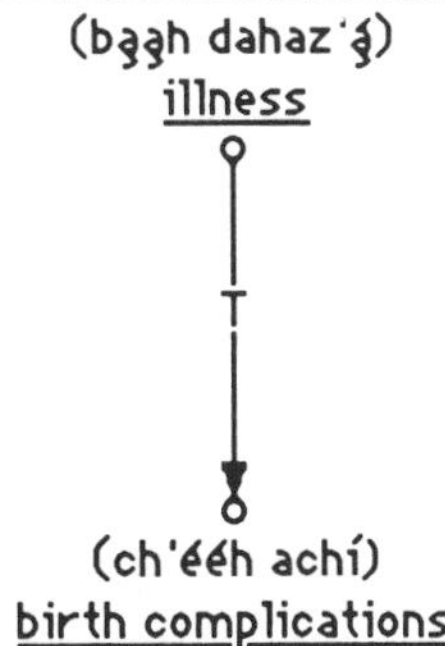

Figure 7.2 Taxonomy of Birth Complications

result from the analysis of a complex sentence (see, for example, sentences 1SXJ.6.0 and 1SXJ.6.1 in the preceding English example).

The above analysis can be facilitated with a form we have used for this purpose. The top of the form has space for entering the analyst's name, the source of the sentence, usually the number of the interview, and the coded initials of the consultant. Each analysis form contains one key word. In the above example we would make three copies to be filed (dispersed) in three different places, each under a different key word.

Further down on the form (see Figure 7.3) there is space for the sentence number and a listing of the entire complex sentence. In the final part, captioned "analysis," we write down the maximally complete simple sentence(s) derived from the complex sentence. These sentences receive the same sentence number as the complex sentence, but each constituent sentence is identified by a period and a running number. Thus sentence number 3ASA.1 was first divided into one of several complex sentences—for example, 3ASA.1.3. This sentence has only one MCSS, 3ASA.1.3.1. If there were more MCSS, the next sentence would be 3ASA.1.3.2, and so on. We present an empty form in Figure 7.3 to allow the reader to duplicate it and use it for his or her ethnography.

We present a final example of text analysis to demonstrate that at least simple texts can be *fully analyzed*. The purpose of this analysis is to show how an entire text is reducible to its underlying structure. This example should be viewed as suggestive rather than as definitive; many questions remain before all texts can be so completely reduced.

Perhaps the most important question is how this fine-grained analysis can be usable for reducing ethnographic complexity. The best explanation we can offer is the map analogy. The full analysis of this text can be compared to aerial photographs. Now that we know the full extent of the complexity, depending on ethnographic goals, we can reduce it. For example, if the ethnography's central focus is hognose snakes, we would use the entire text. For other purposes a natural boundary to follow for simplification is the taxonomic part that can be separated from the Verbal Action Plan. Other simplifications may emerge as the ethnographic writ-

ANALYST'S NAME	SOURCE REFERENCE	KEY WORD

SEN-TENCE NO.	

NO.	ANALYSIS

Figure 7.3 Sentence Analysis Form

ing progresses or, better, as the theoretical or practical goals of the ethnography (the map) are clarified.

Case 7.10 Analysis of "The Game of Death"

Following is a text analysis of a children's story according to the principles laid down above:

The Game of Death
(from Hornblow & Hornblow 1970)

1HH.1. The hognose is a gentle snake.
1HH.2. He has no rattle.
1HH.3. He has no venom.
1HH.4. He never bites.
1HH.5. When an enemy is near, he does a funny thing.
1HH.6. He puffs up his body, lashes his tail, and hisses.
1HH.7. If the enemy won't go away, the hognose tries a new trick.
1HH.8. He rolls over and plays dead.
1HH.9. Then he peeks to see if it is safe to move.
1HH.10. If someone flips him over, he flips right back.
1HH.11. He probably thinks he looks more dead upside down.

This is the text of a story. It consists of two parts. Sentences 1HH.1. to 1HH.4. are taxonomic and attributive; they set the stage by describing what a hognose snake is.

1HH.1 The hognose is a gentle snake.

The MCSS:

1HH.1.1	TAXONOMIC:	The hognose is a snake. (hognose) T (snake)
1HH.1.2	ATTRIBUTIVE:	The hognose is gentle. (hognose) M (gentle)

1HH.2 He has no rattle.

The MCSS:

1HH.2.1	ATTRIBUTIVE:	The hognose has no rattle. (hognose) M (has NO rattle)

1HH.3 He has no venom.

The MCSS

1HH.3.1	ATTRIBUTIVE:	The hognose has no venom. (hognose) M (has NO venom)

1HH.4 He never bites.

The MCSS

1HH.4.1 ATTRIBUTIVE: The hognose never bites.
(hognose) M (NO biter)

This sentence (1HH.4) of the text could be interpreted taxonomically by an ad hoc taxonomic node of nonbiters. However, taxonomy is a kind of attribution that is transitive (see Volume 1, Section 2.3), so whether we interpret the relation taxonomically or attributively does not seem to make much difference in this case and at this stage of our analysis.

The time reference of "never" is not fully treated here because the formalism of time references has not been worked out theoretically. There the word "never" is part of a temporal logic. It is the negation of the temporal existential quantifier "sometimes." The temporal universal quantifier is "always."

The taxonomic and attributive information contained in the first four sentences can be represented as shown in Figure 7.4. The same information can be represented in the convention of the MTQ schema (see Volume 1, Section 2.3). See Figure 7.5. This representation will become useful later when we present the complete semantic structure of this story.

Sentences 1HH.5. to 1HH.10. describe what a hognose does when an enemy is near. The behavior patterns are also attributes, albeit complex ones. We elaborate the details in the following analysis, turning now to the second part of the story.

1HH.5 When an enemy is near, he does a funny thing.

The MCSS:

1HH.5.1 CONDITIONAL: When an enemy is near.

1HH.5.2 PLAN: The hognose does a funny thing.

This set of sentences can be represented by the decision table in Figure 7.6. We continue our analysis:

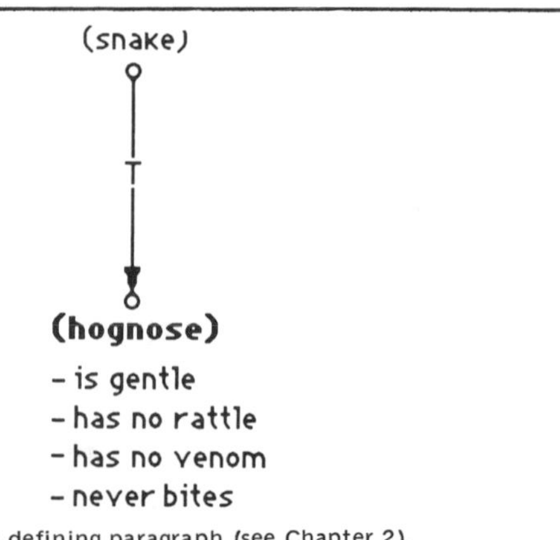

NOTE: The four attributes are a defining paragraph (see Chapter 2).

Figure 7.4 Taxonomy and Attributes of "Hognose"

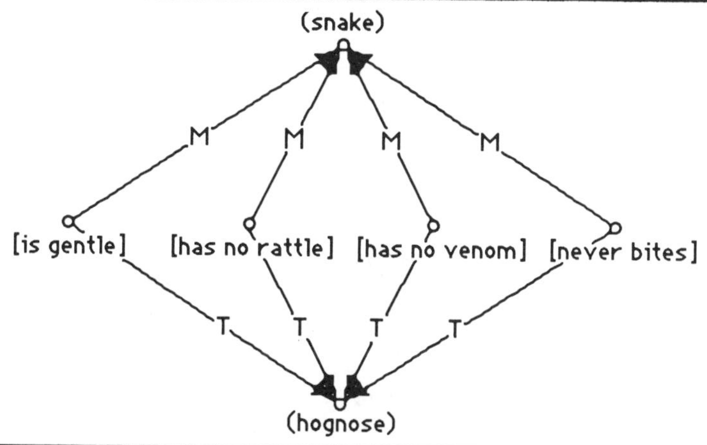

Figure 7.5 Taxonomy of "Hognose" in MTQ Schema

Name of Table :

D1 Enemy is Near	1	2
1. An enemy is near?	Y	N
1. The hognose does a funny thing	X	
2. The hognose does nothing special (business as usual) EXIT		X

Figure 7.6 Sentence 1HH.5: Decision Table 1

1HH.7 If the enemy won't go away, the hognose tries a new trick.

The MCSS:

1HH.7.1 CONDITIONAL:	If the enemy won't go away.
1HH.7.2 PLAN:	The hognose tries a new trick.

This sentence can also be represented by a decision table (Figure 7.7). In the process we change the negative condition, "If the enemy won't go away" to a positive one, "The enemy [does] go away" for better readability, especially in conjunction with the Y and N of the condition stub.

These two decision tables could be combined. However, in the process we would lose the ability to account for one of the resulting plans. The first decision table precipitates the plan "The hognose does a funny thing." After this plan, only if the enemy does not go away is the plan "The hognose tries a new trick" initiated. It is therefore clear that the two decisions are not simultaneous; one must follow the other. Therefore, they cannot be combined into one table.

Name of Table :

D2 Enemy Goes Away	1	2
1. An enemy [does] go away?	Y	N
1. The hognose tries a new trick	X	
2. The hognose does nothing special (business as usual) EXIT		X

Figure 7.7 Sentence 1HH.7: Decision Table 2

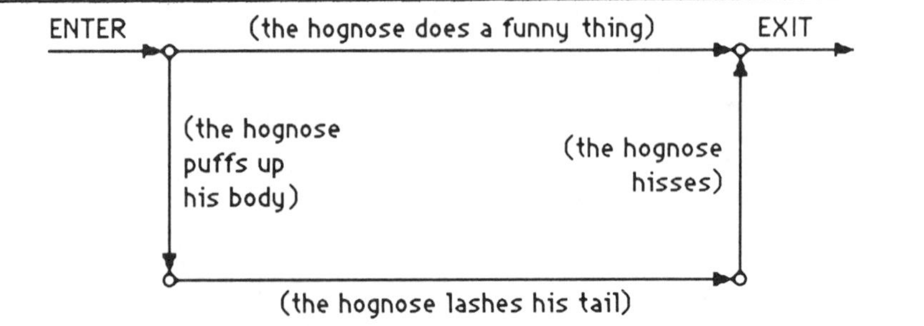

Figure 7.8 Sentences 1HH.5 and 1HH.6: Plan A

The first of these plans is elaborated in sentence 1HH.6. It is the description of the verbal action plan called (or titled) "The hognose does a funny thing."

1HH.6 He puffs up his body, lashes his tail, and hisses.

The MCSS:

1HH.6.1 PLAN: The hognose puffs up his body.

1HH.6.2 PLAN: The hognose lashes his tail.

1HH.6.3 PLAN: The hognose hisses.

This plan can be illustrated graphically in Figure 7.8. It is not clear from the text whether 1HH.6.1, 1HH.6.2, and 1HH.6.3 occur simultaneously or in the sequence shown in Figure 7.8. For example, 1HH.6.1, "puffing up," and 1HH.6.2, "lashing," could occur simultaneously followed by 1HH.6.3, "hissing"; or alternatively, 1HH.6.1, "puffing up," could occur, followed by the simultaneous occurrence of 1HH.6.2, "lashing," and 1HH.6.3, "hissing." The linear order of text syntax rules out the simultaneous mentioning of 1HH.6.1, 1HH.6.2, and 1HH.6.3 except by some device introduced by "meanwhile" or "while." The authors in this text do not employ such a device, possibly because simultaneity is plausible but grasping its precise nature is not essential to understanding the story. If it were important, ancillary questioning could resolve the problem.

Sentences 1HH.8 and 1HH.9 describe the verbal action plan B, called "The hognose tries a new trick".

1HH.8 He rolls over and plays dead.

The MCSS:

1HH.8.1 PLAN: The hognose rolls over.

1HH.8.2 PLAN: The hognose plays dead.

We represent this simple plan by the graph in Figure 7.9. Sentence 1HH.9, however, contains a decision.

1HH.9 Then he peeks to see if it is safe to move.

The MCSS:

1HH.9.1 PLAN: The hognose peeks.

1HH.9.2 ATTRIBUTIVE: (The peeking is) to see:

1HH.9.3 CONDITION: if it is safe to move.

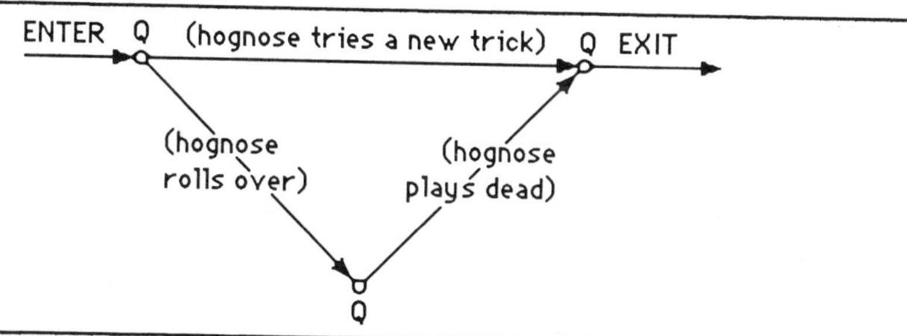

Figure 7.9 Sentence 1HH.8: Plan B

Name of Table :

D3 It is Safe to Move	1	2
1. It is safe to move?	Y	N
1. The hognose plays dead (this action may be repeated)		X
2. The hognose does nothing special (business as usual) EXIT	X	

Figure 7.10 Sentence 1HH.9: Decision Table 3

That brings us to sentence 1HH.10 and the decision contained in it.

1HH.10 If someone flips him over, he flips right back.

The MCSS:

1HH.10.1 CONDITION:	If someone flips the hognose over,
1HH.10.2 PLAN:	The hognose flips right back.

The decision table in Figure 7.11 represents this condition.

Decision Tables 3 and 4 can be combined: The peeking of the hognose or its being flipped over by an enemy can occur in any order. The combination of the two tables reflects this (see Figure 7.12). This decision table can be simplified with the first reduction rule given in Section 4.2.2 (see Figure 7.13).

Finally, only the last sentence of the text remains to be accounted for

1HH.11 He probably thinks he looks more dead upside down.

The MCSS:

1HH.11.1 PLAN:	The hognose probably thinks
1.HH.11.2 ATTRIBUTIVE:	(The thinking is that the hognose) looks more dead upside down.

Sentences 1HH.11.1 and 1HH.11.2 are a simultaneous activity of "thinking" taking place at the same time as sentence 1HH.8. We therefore assign 1HH.11 to this sentence (The hognose "thinks" while it plays dead). In other words, the arrow in Figure 7.9 marks the hognose's playing dead *and* his "thinking." In an actual ethnography, it may be useful to ask ancillary questions about the "thinking" of hognose snakes, or animals in general.

Discussion of "Game of Death"

The first four sentences of the story "The Game of Death," 1HH.1.2, 1HH.2.1, 1HH.3.1, and 1HH.4.1 are attributes of "hognose" and are unordered in the semantic structure of the story. The only order that *is* imposed is that of the linearity of the story text. That is, as soon as we make a decision as speakers to tell a story, we must decide on a linear order of unordered elements—here the attributes "gentle," which may be interpreted as a "title" summarizing the further attributes "has no rattle," "has no venom," and "never bites." This seems to be the prevailing style of the story: announcing a title and then filling it out with details.

The taxonomic relation (1HH.1.1) establishes a different order. This order is not left implicit in this text. Elaboration would involve a listing of the taxonomy either upward to the reptiles or downward to subspecies of the hognose. The preference of 1HH.1.1 over the attributes 1HH.1.2, 1HH2a, 1HH.3.3, and 1HH.4.1—that is, the taxonomic position of the hognose—is mentioned first be-

Name of Table :

D4 Hognose is Flipped Over	1	2
1.[An enemy] flips the hognose over?	Y	N
1. The hognose tries a new trick		X
2. The hognose [continues to] play dead	X	

Figure 7.11 Sentence 1HH.10: Decision Table 4

Name of Table :

D5 Flipping and Peeking	1	2	3	4
1. [An enemy] flips the hognose over?	Y	Y	N	N
2. It is safe to move?	Y	N	Y	N
1. The hognose flips right back	X	X		
2. The hognose peeks				X
3. The hognose does nothing special (business as usual) EXIT			X	

Figure 7.12 D3 and D4 Combined: Decision Table 5

Name of Table :

D6 Flipping and Peeking (reduced)	1	2	3
1. [An enemy] flips the hognose over?	Y	N	N
2. It is safe to move?	-	Y	N
1. The hognose flips right back	X		
2. The hognose peeks			X
3. The hognose does nothing special (business as usual) EXIT		X	

Figure 7.13 Decision Table 6: Reduced D5

cause introductions, usually definitions, proceed from general labels (genus, here taxonomic superordinate label) to specific attributes (differentiate).

The taxonomic part is followed by a complex plan that also illustrates a complex attribute of the hognose snake. It goes under the name of "The Game of Death," the title (name) of the entire story. Thus the story is a definition of hognose snakes with this complex attribute—the verbal action plan "Game of Death." This complex verbal action plan contains two subplans: (1) ". . . does a funny thing" and (2) " . . . tries a new trick." The entire story can be summarized diagrammatically as a story plan (Figure 7.14).

This story, like all stories, is organized sequentially. In the first part the taxonomic place of a hognose snake is given. This functions as an introduction to the topic of hognose snakes and fixes their position in the taxonomic field of snakes. Next, the general attribute "gentle" acts as a title for three specific attributes that establish the hognose as a known entity by differentiating it from other snakes.

The second part of the story contains plans and decisions. Figure 7.15 shows the complex interaction of these elements. We present the story of the hognose in two illustrations. In the first it appears as a sequence of plans and decision tables; in the second, as a flowchart with plans.

A flowchart representation is analogous.

The entire story can be viewed as a complex encyclopedic definition of the hognose snake. It consists of the following canonical forms:

A hognose is a snake which . . . (all attributes follow here).

Diagrammatically:

	hognose
TAXONOMIC:	(1a) . . . is a snake
MODIFICATION:	(1b) . . . is gentle
	(2a) . . . has no rattle
	(3c) . . . has no venom
	(4a) . . . never bites

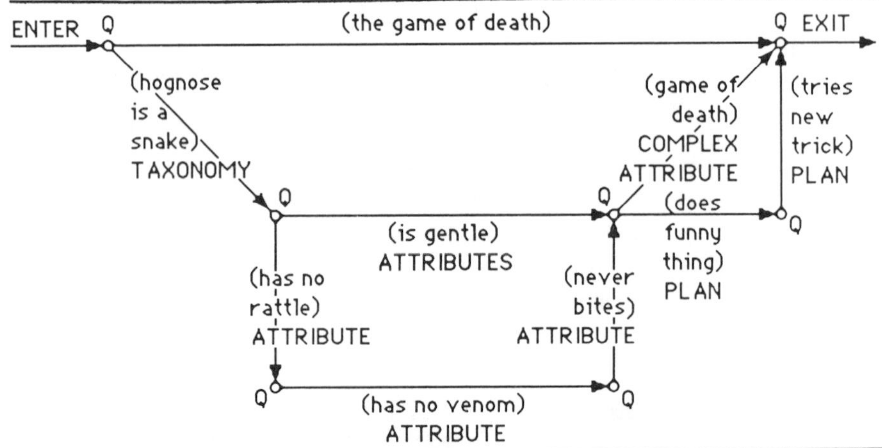

Figure 7.14 Plan of Story "Game of Death"

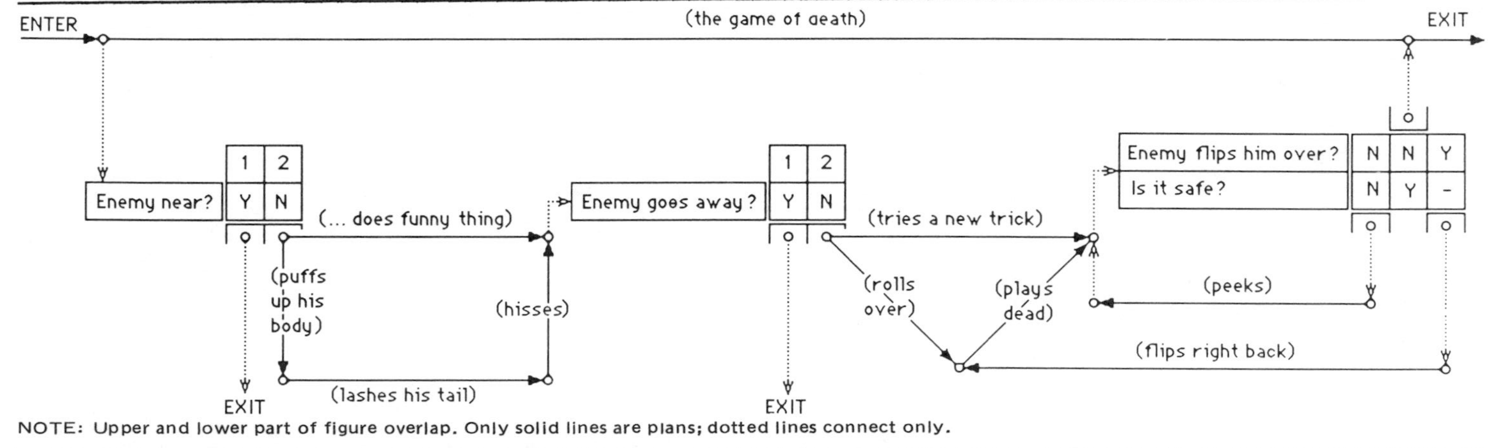

NOTE: Upper and lower part of figure overlap. Only solid lines are plans; dotted lines connect only.

Figure 7.15 "Game of Death": Decision Tables and Plans

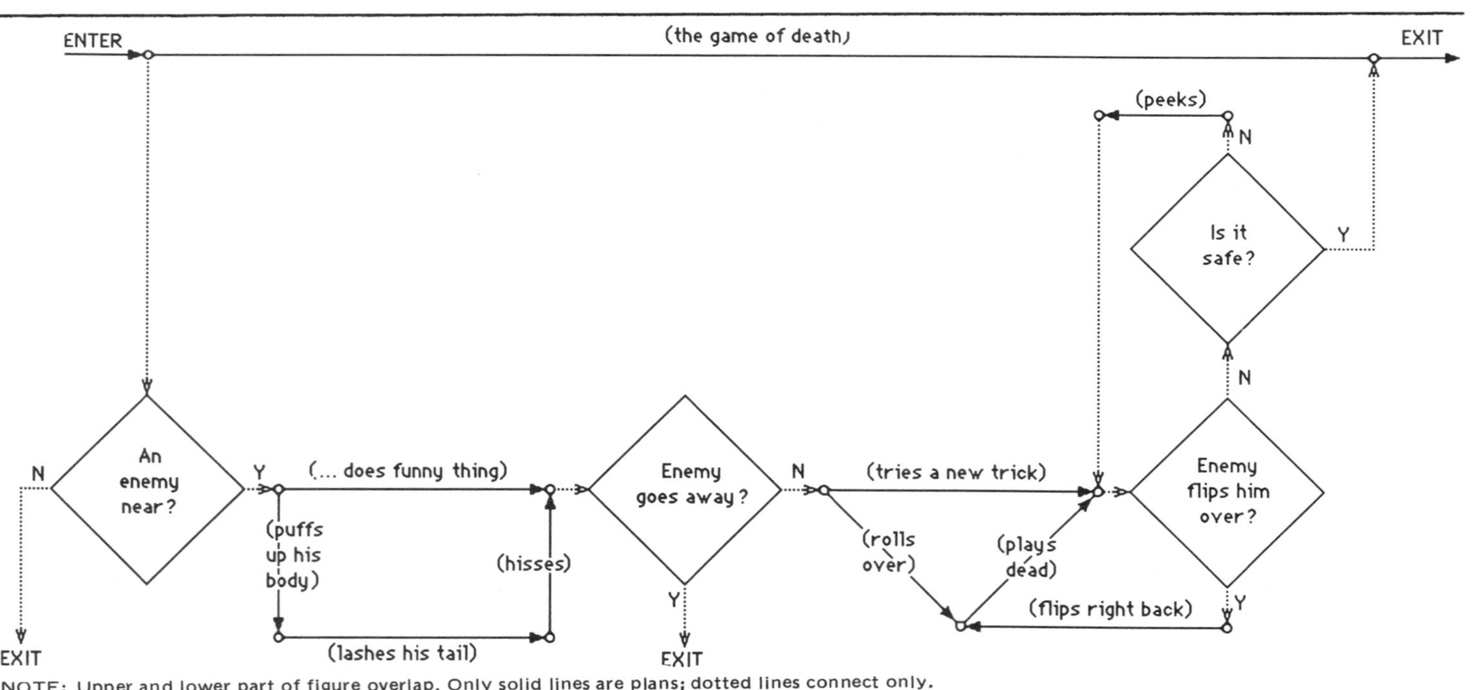

NOTE: Upper and lower part of figure overlap. Only solid lines are plans; dotted lines connect only.

Figure 7.16 "Game of Death": Flowcharts and Plans

MODIFICATION by a COMPLEX ATTRIBUTE:

PLAN . . . [plays] "The Game of Death"

Figures 7.15 and 7.16 provide a graphic representation of the complex attribute "The Game of Death."

7.4 SUMMARY AND CONCLUSIONS

In our own ethnographic work we prefer ordinary conversation, indirect questions, and the subsequent transcription of these conversations as texts. Only if the texts do not yield sufficient structural information (taxonomies, part/whole classifications, plans, etc.) do we resort to structural elicitation.

The main advantage of collecting texts is that they are the result of naturally occurring human interaction. In ethnoscience ethnographies all data (interviews, journal entries, protocols of observation, etc.) result ultimately in texts. Colby's (1979) point about text ethnographies is well taken. All ethnography is based essentially on the analysis of texts and all ethnographies are text ethnographies. The consultants' texts have a privileged position, but for proper analysis and comparison the ethnographer's texts must be analyzed following the same principles of lexical/semantic fields.

Textual elicitation and the analysis of texts places some emphasis on completeness of structural information and, by extension, on the order of acquisition of various data types. A good data management system is therefore essential. It is not clear what serial order of data acquisition means (at the simplest level of conjecture it has implications for how data are stored in memory); however, we are not going to discover what governs memory retrieval unless our data management allows us to identify easily what was obtained when and from whom.

The most obvious use of texts is in the collection of cases. These can be used for exemplification, for generalization, and for example by citing them in the ethnography. In addition, they can be systematically collected, sorted, counted, and further analyzed as texts.

Cases are textual fragments that often get into an ethnography with minimal editing or modification. If a set of cases supports a generalization, one may be enough to illustrate the point. But others become necessary for supporting the generalization.

Equally important is the collection of counterexamples. Just as we followed Agar's (1979) advice to collect "unless" clauses to themes, we consider it essential to collect counterexamples to cases as well. Hypothetical cases can be very helpful, especially if they can be combined with the projective response—attributing actions and statements to hypothetical representatives of a social group.

Cases are often a main source of further discovery. Consultants' generalizations can often be misleading. Cases are always specific and therefore more easily interpreted. Furthermore, when the habit of relating cases to the ethnographer becomes well established, consultants will often find new and unanticipated case material to tell the ethnographer.

Earlier we mentioned the importance for decision making of understanding estimates of folk probability and their associated common errors. A similar warning is appropriate when collecting hypothetical cases. These too may involve estimates of probability that tend to depart systematically from mathematical estimates.

The process of text analysis is based on a set of simple principles: (1) that most sentences in texts are complex; (2) that complex sentences can be analyzed into their constituent simple sentences; (3) that for ethnographic work a level or two before "kernel sentences" is adequate; (4) that such sentences are generally incomplete, so pronominal and pro-verb references must usually be inferred from preceding and following sentences; and (5) that each sentence contributes to the definition of its major constituents (nouns or noun phrases and verbs or verb phrases). The maximally complete sentences (MCSS) of steps 3 and 4 can therefore be dispersed to as many different files as there are major constituents in them of interest to the ethnographer.

During the early stages of the ethnography it may be better to disperse too many words or phrases to files than too few. Later, as the ethnographer begins to see his or her ethnographic goals more clearly, limitations can be imposed. Then the MCSS are dispersed only to those key word files that are salient to the ethnography.

The proposed procedures are lexicographic or encyclopedic in spirit (as is most ethnoscience). The lexicon or encyclopedia in alphabetical organization does not have to be presented that way in the final ethnographic report. However, it is useful to have detailed definitions of at least the key recurrent terms as a back-up to an ethnographic description.

We present several examples in this chapter showing that the analytical steps we propose can be applied (almost) exhaustively with very little unanalyzed or unanalyzable residue. The treatment of this residue awaits further research.

Our examples show how simple and complex attributes interact and how plans can form complex attributes. In the process we uncover the plan structure of texts.

Every ethnoscience ethnography is by necessity a text ethnography. There is almost no limit to how fine grained our textual analysis can get. The reduction of complexity (e.g., by at least 1:10) necessitates careful attention to the goals of the ethnography. However, a fine-grained analysis permits a more rational and systematic reduction than do ad hoc procedures. Such analyses usually fail to uncover (almost?) much of the data contained in the texts that the ethnographer has collected.

Our final plea is to speed up textual analysis through automated or semiautomated procedures. The bottleneck is the same in ethnography as it is for expert systems in artificial intelligence: the acquisition of analyzed data. In anthropology Benjamin Colby (e.g., 1979) has made some progress. More needs to be done (see Chapter 8).

NOTES

1. We are grateful to Florence Kozak for allowing us to use this case.
2. At least, this was the case in the manuscript version before the piece was edited for printing.
3. A Navajo woman gives birth *for* a man. Her children are *of* her clan, born *for* her husband's clan.

Chapter 8

Ethnoscience and Statistics

This section is by necessity brief and suggestive. One reason for this is that the major part of this book is devoted to structural methods and methods built on structural considerations. Ideally, we would like to see statistical and structural (ethnoscience proper) approaches frequently combined. At present few anthropologists cover both sides of the equation. This section and Volume 1, Section 5.1 are intended to encourage many more projects incorporating combined methodologies. Structural methods and statistics can validate each other. Although this is one of the main reasons for using both, it is not the only reason. In Volume 1, Section 1.2 we discuss epistemological windows. The qualitative/quantitative window is one of these. Evidence that different things can be discovered in structural/ethnographic investigations than in statistical ones is accumulating—all the more reason to use the two methods in combination. The aim of this section is to sketch out possibilities and to illustrate them with specific examples.

8.0 INTRODUCTION

In Chapter 5 we discussed some of the limitations of traditional ethnoscience ethnography and how these limitations are rooted in problems of shared cognition among natives. We see these limitations on at least two levels. First, people in any society have difficulty conceptualizing and describing stochastic or macroprobabilistic phenomena in their society (see Volume 1, also Section 5.1 and 5.2). Particularly in complex societies, for example, people are rarely (if ever) able to recognize long-term economic or demographic trends without modern data-gathering and data analysis techniques. Second, on the opposite end of the continuum, people also recoginize only with difficulty microbehavioral phenomena, particularly in the realm of nonverbal communication in small groups.

The difficulties carry over to the techniques and methodologies of ethnoscience ethnographies. A sensitive, insightful ethnographer cannot limit himself or herself to interviews alone any more that it is possible to limit oneself exclusively to observation. Nevertheless, we stress the primacy of verbatim transcribed texts and relegate observational data (text recorded in writing) to an ancillary position.[1] Most ethnographies are accommodations between the two approaches. As long as the boundaries between them are clear and the reader can determine *who contributed what,* no ethnocentric harm is done.

In Chapters 4 and 5 we discuss how ethnographers use decision models. This too requires a combination of conversation with the natives and observation that should always be further discussed with them. There are at least two good reasons for using this approach: (1) The ethnographer is able to move beyond taxonomies and folk definitions and can relate these to environmental constraints affecting the sequences of activities that the actors perform. (2) The combination of conversation and observation allows the ethnographer and the natives to set up quasi-experimental situations in which they can test plans by monitoring behavior. Therefore, through decision modeling ethnographers can simulate both the actor's view of his or her environment and behavior and the manner in which an ethnographer or any newcomer must learn this behavior. These two ways of advancing beyond traditional ethnoscience techniques to controlled observation/interview (and of processes) is to utilize macrobehavioral or stochastic levels *and* microbehavioral levels as sources of data.

In the first of these, social actors rely on various *heuristics* rather than calculating explicit probabilities. For example, Mfantse fish sellers look at the number of canoes along the coast in order to deduce the numbers of fish in the market, rather than directly obtaining the probabilities (Quinn 1978). The second case reflects how actors change their knowledge of nonverbal behavior. For example, in the description of simple activities such as wood chopping and shaving, actors and ethnographers can closely monitor behavior and bring into awareness items they would ordinarily fail to consider.

This kind of interplay—or, perhaps more accurately resonance—between cognition and behavior contributes to an ongoing revelation (making explicit) of the actor's cultural knowledge. These revelations change ethnographic reality. Moreover, the changes can be monitored systematically and can become one of the most important sources of hypotheses about the fundamental properties of cultural knowledge systems.

Decision modeling provides a way to systematize the relationship between the domain of verbalizable knowledge (TEXT (2)) and observation (more correctly, protocols of observation by the ethnographer—what in Volume 1 (Section 3.3) we called (TEXT (1)). Decision modeling is nevertheless subject to the same constraints and limitations as is any approach to ethnography. Some of these are the following:

(1) *Reduction of Complexity:* Given that any description must be less rich than reality or it becomes as useless as a 1:1 map, how can we systematically reduce the complexity of an ethnographic description?

(2) *Generality:* Given the fact that an ethnography usually describes only a small group of people (usually part of a larger group), how are the ethnographer's findings generalizable to the larger social context?
(3) *Cause and Effect:* Given the small group source of ethnographic information, how can an ethnographer infer the causal relations between various dimensions that are valid for an entire population? Generalization of cause and effect (3) is thus a corollary of generality (2).
(4) *Validation and Internal Consistency:* Given that there is variability of cultural knowledge even within small group cultures, how can data obtained in one way be validated by data collected by using different methods? How can an ethnographer distinguish between idiosyncratic differences and systematic, internally consistent differences?
(5) *Alternative Classification:* Given that ethnographic folk classifications (taxonomic, part/whole, componential analysis, etc.) have been elicited, how can an ethnographer infer, explain, and expand variation in classifications, plans, and decision processes?

These questions are central to mathematical anthropology and the application of statistical techniques to ethnoscience. In this section we provide examples showing how anthropologist-ethnographers have used ethnoscience and cognitive ethnography with various statistics to shift from ethnographic research to survey research, from replication to validation (Campbell and Fiske 1959), from ethnographic hypotheses to their confirmation, from folk classification to numerical classification and back.

In the following sections we discuss how ethnography is related to numerical methods, or, in other words, how ethnoscience ethnography is able to contribute systematically to survey and other statistical applications and vice versa.

First (as we have shown in Volume 1, Section 11.4), ethnoscience ethnography is a uniquely rich source of appropriate language with which to compare survey questionnaires. Second, it provides systematic distinctions or contrasts that facilitate the construction of all kinds of tests and elicitation instruments tailor-made for a speech community sharing cultural knowledge. Third, ethnoscience ethnography provides a source of statistically testable hypotheses. Fourth, it can provide background context for statistically derived patterns not necessarily derivable from survey data alone. Thus there is a reciprocal relationship between ethnographic techniques and statistical techniques that not only allows for mutual validation but expands insights and explanations (see Volume 1, Section 1.2).

8.1 REDUCTION OF COMPLEXITY

In various parts of this book we recommend ways of summarizing the rich detail provided by ethnographic data. Analysis was one method we used to reduce complexity by replacing the linear order of speech with nonlinear (often tree or lattice) structures usually understood "at a glance."

Here we briefly review a statistical technique (tabulating word frequencies) to decide which items in the total inventory of words (occurring in an elicited text) to pursue for further analysis. The empirical principle, called *hapax logomenon,* helps us to achieve this. It states that in every text (long or short) the majority of words occur exactly once.

If our interviews[2] are reasonably carefully focused on the topic(s) of interest to the theoretical goals of the ethnography, then words that occur only once are uninteresting. They are auxiliary to establishing the meanings of more central and therefore more frequently occurring concepts.

On the opposite end of the continuum are high-frequency words. Their membership can be gleaned from frequency counts based on a large corpus of texts. For example, *The American Heritage Word Frequency Book* contains 100 most frequently occurring words in a corpus of 5 million, shown in Figure 8.1.

If we count the word frequencies of an ethnographic data text, eliminate all words with a frequency of one and all high-frequency words, the remaining list of words is a highly significant reflection of the content of the text. We propose that this list of words, between the frequency of more than one and the high-frequency words, determines those concepts with which ethnographic analysis should begin. An example illustrates.

Case 8.1. *Hapax Logomenon*

The analyzed text comes from an interview of an ethnographic evaluation of a community-based family self-help organization. Most low-frequency words

1. the	21. be	41. which	61. into	81. made
2. of	22. this	42. their	62. has	82. over
3. and	23. from	43. said	63. more	83. did
4. a	24. I	44. if	64. her	84. down
5. to	25. have	45. do	65. two	85. only
6. in	26. or	46. will	66. like	86. way
7. is	27. by	47. each	67. him	87. find
8. you	28. one	48. about	68. see	88. use
9. that	29. had	49. how	69. time	89. may
10. it	30. not	50. up	70. could	90. water
11. he	31. but	51. out	71. no	91. long
12. for	32. what	52. them	72. make	92. little
13. was	33. all	53. then	73. than	93. very
14. on	34. were	54. she	74. first	94. after
15. are	35. when	55. many	75. been	95 words
16. as	36. we	56. some	76. its	96. called
17. with	37. there	57. so	77. who	97. just
18. his	38. can	58. these	78. now	98. where
19. they	39. an	59. would	79. people	99. most
20. at	40. your	60. other	80. my	100. know

NOTE: From *The American Heritage Word Frequency Book* (1971).

Figure 8.1 One Hundred Most Frequent Words

> have been eliminated. The high-frequency word "very" was left in for comparison. For the sake of clarity, only entries under the letter "v" are considered. The interview consisted of 8396 words. Figure 8.2 displays the frequencies.

It emerges clearly that in the domain of words beginning with the letter "v," the concepts of "volunteer(s), volunteering and volunteered" with a total frequency of 107, "values" with a frequency of 8, and "visitor" with a frequency of 6 clarify the target for ethnographic analysis.

Relatively inexpensive, fast word frequency programs for microcomputers are now readily available. Counting words and eliminating high- and low-frequency words significantly speeds up ethnographic analysis. This simple procedure also focuses analysis on the core issues that are important to the consultants.

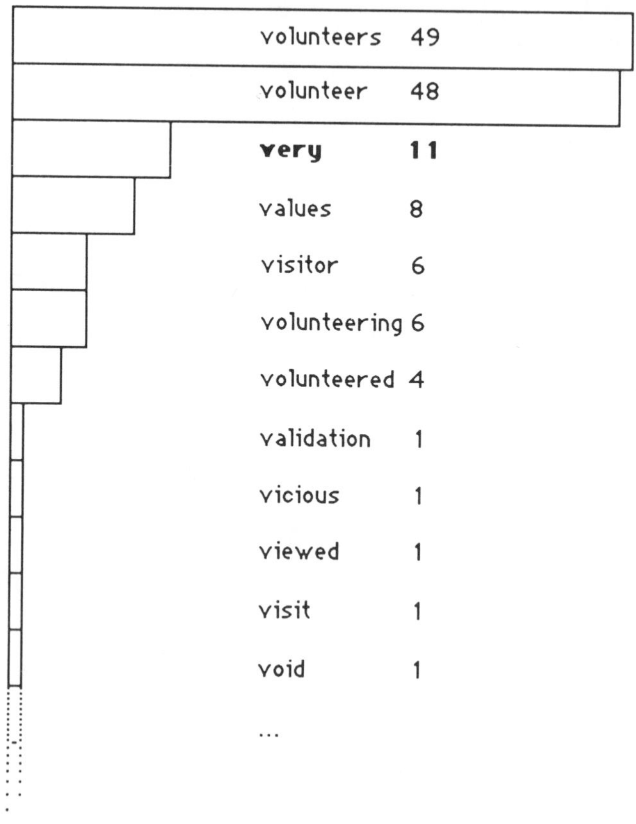

NOTE: The high-frequency word "very" is included for comparison. It is a word within rank 100 in **The American Heritage Word Frequency Book** (1971; see Figure 8.1). Five words ocurring with a frequency of 1 are also included for comparison.

Figure 8.2 Frequency of Words

	mean	nice
good	A	B
bad	C	D

Figure 8.3 Cross-Classification of Teachers

8.2 GENERALITY

The question of generality is simple. So far ethnographers have addressed this issue only occasionally. Perhaps the major contribution of ethnoscience ethnographies in this area is through ethnosemantically based questionnaire design. The semantic design (i.e., the wording of the questionnaire) is based on terminology explained (defined) in the ethnography. Generality can be achieved through the administration of such a questionnaire to a carefully sampled population. Thus it can be established whether parts of folk classifications, contrasting terms, folk definitions, plans, decisions, and other more complex schemata are extendable from a small ethnographic sample to a population at large (see Volume 1, Section 11.4).

Case 8.2 Ethnography Followed by a Survey

Schoepfle and Garrison (1977) based their work on the six ethnoscience ethnographies created by Werner *et al.* (1976), testing how ethnography and survey complement each other. They carefully selected a stratified random sample of 2,000 students drawn from a student population of over 50,000 across the Navajo Nation, and asked them about their lives as students in the Navajo educational system. For their questionnaire Schoepfle and Garrison utilized folk terms that the students used and defined and that had been collected the year preceding the survey.

According to the six ethnographies, all students distinguished between good and bad teachers. Older students (fifth graders) further refined their classification by distinguishing in addition "nice" and "mean" teachers. Thus the six ethnographies contained four definitions for each one of the four kinds of teachers. However, many students did not seem to distinguish "nice" from "good" and "bad" from "mean" teachers. This fact seemed to imply that many students were cross-classifying the four concepts along a mean-nice continuum and a good-bad one. This situation can be represented in a fourfold table (Figure 8.3).

Why students' definitions varied was not clear. The attributes of each cross-cutting label may be mixed in a student's definition, or students may simply differ depending on what importance they assign to the attributes in their definitions. Since the students' perception of teachers was considered an impor-

First fill out answers A through F. Then ask the child for the most important item and put a "1" beside it; ask for the next most important item and put a "2" beside it, and so on, until you have a complete ranking. Please make sure the "other" category is filled in (if appropriate) before ranking.

A. ______ A good teacher helps students who are having trouble with their work.

B. ______ A good teacher explains things real well, so we can understand.

C. ______ A good teacher is a nice teacher.

D. ______ A good teacher doesn't give a lot of work.

E. ______ A good teacher isn't a mean teacher.

F. ______ Other: ____

____

Figure 8.4 Question Testing Cross-Classification

tant issue to pursue, Schoepfle and Garrison (1977) tested the attributes of "good teacher" *versus* "nice teacher" by including parts of students' definitions in a multichoice question within a larger (50-item) questionnaire. The question appeared in the questionnaire as follows.

4. What is a good teacher? What kinds of things make a teacher a good teacher?

These questions were followed by directions to the person administering the questionnaire to each child individually. Figure 8.4 illustrates.

On the basis of students' folk definitions Schoepfle and Garrison hypothesized two dimensions to students' evaluation of teachers—first, according to their professional competence (responses A and B in Figure 8.4) and second, the interpersonal compatibility of students and teachers (responses C, D, and E).

In the next step Schoepfle and Garrison (1977) compared the students' responses according to:

(1) Age (i.e., second graders versus fifth graders).
(2) First, second- and third-ranked choice of the attributes of a good teacher.
(3) The school that the students attended (Bureau of Indian Affairs Schools operated by the federal government, public schools operated by the states, and community-controlled contract schools).

After all comparisons were made the following patterns emerged. (These complement and clarify the results obtained in the *Six Navajo School Ethnographies* [Werner et al. 1976]):

(1) Fifth graders tended to value the professional competence of a teacher more than other traits. That is, these students rated a teacher's ability to help them understand the curriculum more highly than his or her interpersonal compatibility with students.

> (2) Second graders tended to value a teacher's interpersonal compatibility more than his or her professional competence.
>
> However, when students were compared by the type of school they attended *and* by age, a different pattern emerged:
>
> (1) More Bureau of Indian Affairs fifth-grade students than contract school students considered "not being mean" more important than any other teacher attribute.
> (2) More contract school second-grade students than public school students considered "helping students" the most important attribute of a good teacher.
> (3) More contract school second-grade students than public school students considered "being nice" the most important attribute of a good teacher.
> (4) More second-grade students in both Bureau of Indian Affairs schools and contract schools compared to public schools considered "helping students" an important attribute of a good teacher.
>
> Considering that Bureau of Indian Affairs schools and contract schools attract more rural students and that the students in the bureau and contract schools tend to be less acculturated to Anglo ways, the results are important.
>
> The less acculturated students are more concerned with getting along with the teacher interpersonally than with the mastery of the curriculum.
>
> Intergroup differences between Navajo students, the contrast of age (between fifth and second graders) and levels of acculturation (rural versus relatively urbanized students) validates the ethnographic data but adds new insights into how Navajo students perceive their education. The survey also extends both of these insights to the entire Navajo student population.

Another example of generalizability involves the validation of decision models. Gladwin (1976) strengthened her decision model about Mexican farmers' adoption or nonadoption of fertilizer (see Section 4.5). She accomplished this first by making sure that the proposed model made sense to the people she interviewed in order to construct the model; second, she expanded her sample to a group of farmers in the same village but whom she had not interviewed before. Her second sample closely matched (within 90%) the hypothetical model based on her first sample of interviews and observations.

In general, the combination of intensive qualitative and extensive quantitative methods remains rare for both tests of generality and validation (same result with different procedures; see Campbell and Fiske 1959). Quantitatively oriented anthropologists tend to do only quantitative work. Ethnographers tend to do only ethnographies.

For example, the statistical investigations—along encyclopedic lines—made by Kirk and Burton (1976) on anatomical terms in three cultures (American English, Maasai, and Kikuyu), and their semantic similarity as shown by multidimensional scaling and other clustering techniques, demand ethnographic (encyclopedic) follow-up and validation. Furthermore, their scaling model could have been improved by preceding their statistical analysis with a carefully worked-out part/whole classification and possibly other folk classifications of the relevant anatomical terms. The 13 terms used in Kirk and Burton's analysis (limited because of the rapid growth of triads in tests of similarity) represent only a tiny subset of hundreds of available terms. They were selected ad hoc (i.e., the head and face, three parts of the face [mouth, cheek, and ear], arm and leg, hand, finger, foot and two joints [elbow and knee]) rather than in some principled way based on the hierarchy or other classification of the anatomical lexical/semantic field. In other words, native criteria of association (classification) could have been used for selecting the experimental sample of terms.

In general, Kirk and Burton's (1976) clusters support a part/whole classification, except that in the Maasai case the picture grows more complex. That other lexical/semantic relations (e.g., "A connects to B") interfere is not surprising. The term "body" appears to be problematic in all cultures. In this case, cross-cultural hypotheses (e.g., ". . . there appears to be a clear-cut [Kikuyu] mind-body dichotomy, whereas the Maasai appear to integrate body and mind . . ." (Kirk & Burton 1976: 298) are inferred from scalograms but are not supported by ethnographic evidence.

Woods's (1980) work on the socioeconomic classification of Navajo households provides another example of a missed opportunity. His multivariate analysis based on questionnaire data resulted in seven socioeconomic types of Navajo households. This highly suggestive numerical classification should have been followed up by at least seven detailed ethnographies, one of each type. This type of investigation could yield insights into the dynamics of Navajo poverty and Navajo adaptations to it. According to Woods (personal communication), such an ethnographic follow-up was planned but not funded.

Effective collaboration between anthropologists and other social scientists with quantitative interests and ethnographers has at least two advantages over each group working on its own: (1) Different kinds of insights are afforded by each method (see Case 8.2). Although we lack sufficient data to state this authoritatively, we suspect that there are systematically different ways in which the two approaches may complement each other. (2) The different insights emerging from each of these approaches constitute an important epistemological window (see Volume 1, Section 1.2). The "opening" of such epistemological windows can lead to still deeper understanding of the social system under study and contribute more scientifically validated generalizations cross-culturally. For now, all we can hope for is increased collaboration: that is, more ethnographic studies that plan for and explicitly utilize quantitative extensions of interpretation, validation, and generalization.

8.3 CAUSE AND EFFECT

The central theme of this book is cultural description. There is no doubt about the value of careful description based on sound assumptions about human cognition, especially its formal constraints. In applied research a validated ethnoscience formulation or a decision model is often adequate. However, specialists in the field of environmental impact assessment and other applied branches of anthropology have pointed out that the insights made available through in-depth ethnography cannot easily be duplicated through quantitative methods (Finsterbush 1977).

If various political or administrative entities within a population find ethnographic research results adequate, then they will approve and presumably use this research for their own purposes (Jorgensen 1981; Tonigan *et al.* 1982). We have called such validation of an ethnography "political validity." Often, however, ethnography is a first step toward formulating cause-and-effect hypotheses about a social system. Whatever case ethnographers can make for their findings, the ability to assert some cause-and-effect relationships and concomitant generalizability beyond small populations confers greater persuasiveness upon ethnographic findings.

Case 8.3 Production Function and Decision Model

Gladwin (1976) buttressed her decision model about Mexican farmer's adoption of fertilizer by comparing her model to "more objective" economic production functions. Economists use these formulas to measure the effectiveness of newly introduced agricultural techniques. The production model views the amount of corn produced per hectare on each farm as directly proportional to the sums of variables such as the amount of plowing time per hectare, the quantity of fertilizer used, the quality of the soil, and whether or not the farmer fertilized at the time of planting, planted beans with the corn, or alfalfa, or whether he planted the field with the proper seed density.

The purpose of Gladwin's comparison was not to establish the superiority of one model over the other but to exploit their complementarity. First, she maintained that the decision model could test the assumptions about human behavior that were left untested by the economists who used only the production function. For example, she found the economists' assumptions that farmers try to maximize production too simplistic. The decision model provided information about the conditions under which small Mexican peasant farmers felt they could safely try to maximize their production of corn.

The decision model, in addition, made explicit the circumstances under which these farmers would adapt new production techniques (in particular, a fertilizer schedule). The economists' production function could determine only whether the farmers did accept a new production technique as better for them.

"A production function cannot be used to answer [the question of when farmers will actually decide to adopt a new production technique], since it does not deal with farmers' decision processes. In accepted economic theory, the role of the production function has been clearly defined: it specifies the maximum output (e.g., corn yields) obtainable from a given set of variable inputs (e.g., land, labor, fertilizer, water, plant population). . . . However, a

> function can appropriately be used to answer the questions "What happened to the corn yields of farmers who did not try the new technology? Did the recommendations improve the corn yield of the farmers who tried them, holding quantities of other inputs constant?" . . .
>
> The present analysis differs from more traditional economic treatment of adoption only by replacing the economists' behavior assumptions about farmers' decision processes with a *model* of the adoption-decision process. This is done because farmers' adoption-decision rules observed during fieldwork were too complex to fit into one mathematical behavioral assumption" (Gladwin 1976:3).

The use of the production function also complemented the decision model because it provided a more "objective" means of evaluating farmers' judgment. This point requires amplification. Throughout this book we have downplayed the possibility that one system of knowledge is inherently more objective than another, and we continue to do so. However, the validity of any cultural description is strengthened by its comparison to an independent system of measurement. This is validation par excellence (Campbell & Fiske 1959). In addition, there is an unfortunate tendency, particularly in applied settings, for bureaucracies to consider their own data as inherently more objective (particularly if the data are numerical) than the knowledge of the people for whom the bureaucrats are responsible. It is therefore often up to anthropologists to address this assumption, but they must do so without being subject to the usual complaint of the agent of change that anthropologists complain about the inappropriateness of changes being implemented but have no better alternatives to them.

From her decision model Gladwin had already determined that the farmers tended to base their decisions to adopt or not to adopt new fertilizer techniques (i.e., whether to apply fertilizer after the first rainfall and to plant corn with greater and more uniform density; see Chapter 5) depending on whether they were properly informed about the technique, whether they found the new techniques worth the extra labor and time, and other similar factors. Using the production function inputs Gladwin was able to obtain reports from the farmers about whether their corn yields had increased significantly after the introduction of the new fertilizer.

In the end, Gladwin was able to establish the following conclusions:

(1) The production function validated (or at least strengthened the validity of) the farmers' perceptions of the new technique's *effects*.
(2) The decision model was further validated, at least by implication.
(3) The decision model could increase the explanatory power of the production function.

In another example, Young and Garro (1982) wanted to validate their decision model to determine under what conditions the Tarascan Indians of Central Mexico would seek Western versus traditional medicine. In particular they wanted to examine past theoretical explanations that maintained that Tarascans who were more Westernized chose Western medicine, whereas more traditional Tarascans selected traditional practitioners.

These explanations are difficult to test because of the interference of variables such as the accessibility of Western medical facilities: People who have no access to modern clinics may prefer a traditional practitioner to not using any medical system at all. These facts confound the testing of assumptions about native preference of traditional versus Western medical practices.

Case 8.4 Tarascan Medical Decisions

Young and Garro (1982) first chose two Tarascan villages: one near a modern clinic, the other far from modern facilities. Through this choice they hoped to control for the interfering variable of access.

They then designed a triad test (see Section 8.3) based on their decision model (Young 1980) and analyzed the results using multidimensional scaling. They found that the two-dimensional scattergrams for the two villages were nearly identical.

They next tried to validate the results of the multidimensional scaling with a different method of elicitation: the so-called term-frame interview technique. In this procedure of structured interviewing the respondent answers "true" or "false" to questions derived from attribute lists that form part of a definition of particular diseases.[3] The measure of similarity is not the correlation of responses but the number of attributes shared between terms. Here again the data were analyzed by multidimensional scaling. The scattergrams for the two villages were highly similar. Young and Garro (1982) concluded:

"This study finds scant support for the position [that people who frequent Western physicians have more Westernized values while those who see traditional help are less Westernized]. On the basis of the data from the triad test study and the term-frame interviews, we see little reason to reject the "null hypothesis" of no significant differences between the responses of the two groups of informants. This leads us to the conclusion that the substantial variation apparent in the use of physician's treatment between the two samples [i.e. the two villages] is a consequence of differential access to such treatment, occurs without corresponding degrees of variation in residents' attitudes and beliefs about illness" (Young & Garro 1982).

The implications of this kind of study are considerable because they force health care practitioners in Third World settings to consider the relationship between pragmatic considerations and culture change. The possibility that modernization does not necessarily imply greater Westernization deserves further careful scrutiny.

8.4 VALIDATION AND INTERNAL CONSISTENCY

Statistically testing folk classifications, plans, decision models, or complex relations (schemata; see Volume 1, Section 2.3 and Volume 2, Section 6.3) implies a validation of the internal consistency of a description. Decision models in particular easily lend themselves to validation because they explicitly articulate the interrelationships among their hypothetized elements.

Entailment analysis provides one possible link between ethnographic results and survey data. Here we can present only a thumbnail sketch of the method that, more than any statistical technique we know of, closely links qualitative and quantitative investigations. For a more detailed view, we refer the reader to the specialized literature (D'Andrade 1976; Burton 1977; White, Burton & Brudner 1977; White 1980; White & McCann 1981; White n.d.; and others).

8.4.1 Entailment Analysis

The principles of entailment analysis are simple, though the statistics can get quite complex. Many aspects of the latter are controversial (see, for example, White's [n.d.] restudy of D'Andrade [1976]. The uncontested steps to an entailment analysis proceed as follows:

(1) Through a survey questionnaire (though we could imagine deriving a list of attributes from extended folk definitions), attributes for a set of taxons are elicited. Taxons that have been used in the past include diseases (D'Andrade 1976), human societies with different forms of sexual division of labor (White, Burton & Brudner 1977), and types of Navajos who respond differently to relocation (Schoepfle *et al.* 1984b).

The elicitation process may be set up to yield dichotomies (presence or absence of an attribute), or scaled data may be later dichotomized by lumping categories in some principled manner (see Case 8.5).

(2) Every attribute is then paired with every other attribute, each pairing forming a fourfold table. The four cells of the table are filled with taxons (for example, named diseases; D'Andrade 1976) that exhibit, or fail to exhibit, each of the two attributes (see Figure 8.5).

(3) Out of the set of all fourfold tables, those having one or two empty cells are singled out for entailment analysis. In some applications empty cells may be rare. In that case cells with small numbers of taxons (e.g., less than 5%) are treated as "exceptions" and the cell is considered empty in further analysis (White & McCann 1981).

(4) Out of a total of six possibilities for the distribution of empty cells (four cases of one empty cell and three filled cells, and two cases of two empty and two filled cells) only the three shown in Figure 8.5 seem to contribute to entailment analysis. The entailment relation in this case is "Attribute A implies attribute B," or "Taxons with attribute A are a subset of taxons with attribute B." Figure 8.6 illustrates the inverse of Figure 8.5.

The entailment relation in this case is "Attribute B implies attribute A," or "Taxons with attribute B are a subset of taxons with attribute A." Finally, the last relation is that of contrast, exclusion, or complementary distribution (Figure 8.7). The entailment relation in this case is "No taxon with attribute A has attribute B."

		attribute A	
		present	absent
attribute B	present	some taxons	some taxons
	absent	0	some taxons

Figure 8.5 Relation of Inclusion

		attribute A	
		present	absent
attribute B	present	some taxons	0
	absent	some taxons	some taxons

Figure 8.6 Relation of Inclusion

		attribute A	
		present	absent
attribute B	present	0	some taxons
	absent	some taxons	some taxons

Figure 8.7 Relation of Contrast

	1	2	3	4	5	6
1. Caused by germs	o	>	>	/	/	/
2. Contageous	<	o	>	/	/	/
3. Children's disease	>	<	o	/	/	/
4. Runs in a family	/	/	/	o	>	>
5. Caused by emotion	/	/	/	<	o	
6. Sign of old age	/	/	/			o

NOTE: Symbols are as follows: A > B = "A implies B"; A < B = "B implies A"; and A/B = "A contrasts with B." Adapted from D'Andrade (1976).

Figure 8.8 Incidence Matrix of Relations

By tabulating all attributes against each other while keeping track of the relations between them, an "incidence matrix" can be constructed. For example, D'Andrade (1976) was able to construct the table in Figure 8.8. It shows an intersection of the taxonomic domain of named disease terms and the field of their attributes.

An "incidence matrix" implies a directed graph that can be constructed by drafting a graph of the relationships. In the case of Figure 8.8 a complex graph results. It can be simplified considerably by taking the effect of the transitivity of the implication (subset) relation and the contrast relation into account. That is, transitivity means that if A > B and B > C, then A > C is an automatic by-product and can be generated but need not be explicitly represented in the graph. Note that in Figure 8.8 the first three attributes form a transitive chain. That is, (1) > (2) and (2) > (3); therefore we can infer that (1) > (3).

Contrast is also subject to inference due to the transitivity relation. That is, if C > B and B/A then C/A, or the relation of contrast is automatically inherited downward.

Thus the matrix for Figure 8.8 can be represented as a simplified graph, shown in Figure 8.9.

The power of entailment analysis and the entailment diagram is in its partial exposure of a belief system. We saw in Section 2.5.5 that componential analysis can be viewed as the elaboration of structure on one level of a taxonomy. Similarly, entailment analysis further elucidates the relationship between taxons in a domain of cultural knowledge. However, the relative weakness of the relation of coocurrence of attributes in a componential analysis is replaced here by a powerful logical/implicational relationship between attributes and therefore between taxons.

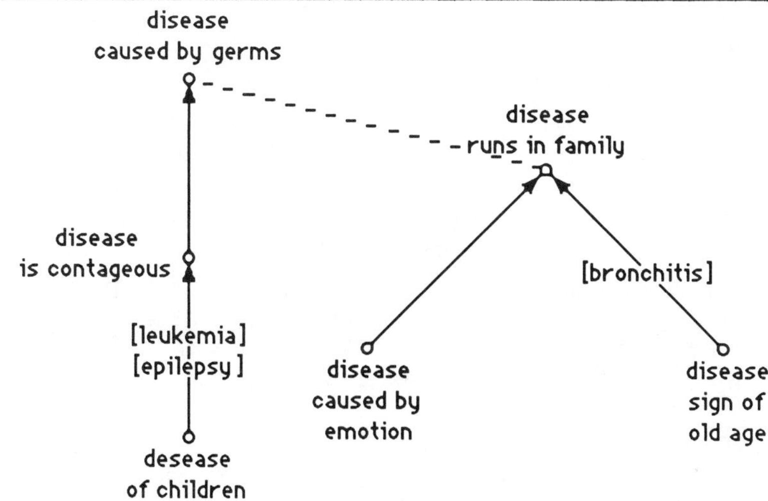

NOTE: Exceptions are listed in brackets. The dotted line is the relation of contrast. Because of the one relation of contrast (drawn), all other terms across the two unconnected figures contrast. Adapted from D'Andrade (1976).

Figure 8.9 Entailment Diagram

Case 8.5 Navajo Relocation

Schoepfle *et al.* (1984b) attempts to test the model proposed in Section 5.2 to determine whether or not it represents what Navajos living in the Four Corners area of (predominantly) New Mexico would do if faced with the same conditions and decisions represented in the flowchart (Figure 5.2). The question is, in other words, will a larger sample of Navajos support the flowchart based on a sample of interviews? In this case the conditions for relocation were far too uncertain; therefore direct validation of the model following Gladwin's example (1976; see also Section 5.1) proved impossible. The method Schoepfle *et al.* (1985) used for validation was entailment analysis. Their test proceeded in several steps.

First, Schoepfle *et al.* (1984b) designed a questionnaire containing the Navajo propositions and terminology contained in the ethnographic data base from which the flowchart (Figure 11.1) was constructed. The questions were then translated into English for easier comprehension by the non-Navajo investigators and readership.

The questions on the questionnaire were designed to validate (1) the socioeconomic background of the respondents, (2) the kinds of economic development they expected to take place in the area, (3) whether individual respondents expected to see themselves better off, unchanged, or worse off as a result of the anticipated development, and (4) whether respondents would change their attitude toward development depending on different possible outcomes. The latter was elicited in 23 attitudinal questions. The list of these 23 "variables" used to appraise Navajo attitudes toward relocation appears in Figure 8.10. The following items are translations from Navajo. This may explain some of the awkwardness of the English sentences.

This list of possible outcomes was presented to individual Navajos who had to evaluate the desirability of each item on a 5-point scale (favor, leaning in favor, undecided, leaning against, against). For the entailment analysis the variables were dichotomized by lumping the positive responses as the positive case and the undecided and negative responses as the negative case.

The entailment analysis followed. One example will illustrate. Pairing variable "5: Animals moved to feed lots" with variable "6: Reseed land" results in the table in Figure 8.11. For the clarification of the content of this table and the implicational structure it represents, a Venn diagram is helpful (see Figure 8.12).

The logic of entailment explained in Figures 8.11 and 8.12 and the beginning of this section, when consistently applied to all viable pairs (i.e.,

(1) General attitude toward change.
(2) Grazing permits will be sold.
(3) Livestock will be reduced or penned up at home.
(4) Grazing permits will be invalidated.
(5) Livestock will be placed on a range or in a feed lot away from the reservation or development.
(6) After development is completed, your grazing land will be reseeded for your use.
(7) Summer and winter camps will be kept.
(8) Kinship will be respected and you and your relatives will live together after relocation.
(9) You will be relocated in a new area among people you do not know.
(10) People that you do not know will move into or close to your land.
(11) You may not have a chance to live as you used to.
(12) You will move into mutual self-help housing project and you will be able to own your house later.
(13) You will be provided with homesites and assistance with housing materials.
(14) A house will be built for you at any place and you will not have to pay.
(15) Your relocation compensation money will be used for part of the cost of a house in a border town or any place off the reservation.
(16) The sacred places where you placed the sacred stones will be preserved.
(17) Burial places will be preserved.
(18) Lease your land to developers and land to move onto will be provided for your use.
(19) There will be development on your land. You will have to move even though land to relocate on has not been located.
(20) Your land will be reseeded after the development is completed.
(21) This land has been awarded to other people. You will have to move even though land to move onto has not been located.
(22) Locate your own land to move onto outside (i.e., on private, non-reservation land).
(23) Your land (in the Navajo-Hopi Land Dispute area) will be purchased from the new owners so that you will not have to relocate.

Figure 8.10 Navajo Attitudes Toward Relocation: List of Variables

		6. After development is complete your grazing land will be reseeded for your use.		
		in favor, or leaning in favor	against, leaning against, or undecided	
5 Livestock wil be placed on a range or in a feedlot.	in favor, or leaning in favor	19	4	23
	against, leaning against or undecided	50	108	158
		69	112	181

Figure 8.11 Interaction of Variables 5 and 6

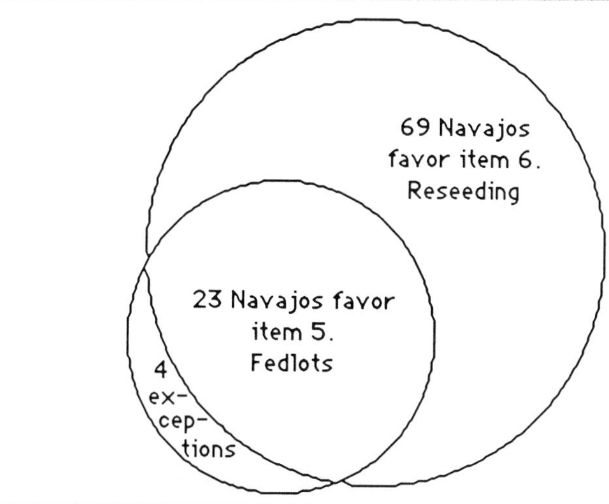

Figure 8.12 Overlap of Feedlots and Reseeding

0.5 × 23 × 23 = 0.5 × 529 – the diagonal(23) = 253 cases) of variables, results in the entailment or implicational structure illustrated in Figure 8.13.

Note the least desirable events on the left, so-called mitigating events in the middle, and the few events that are positively evaluated by most Navajos involved in the possibility of relocation at right. The percentages of positive responses to each variable (see Figure 8.10) are listed above or occasionally directly below

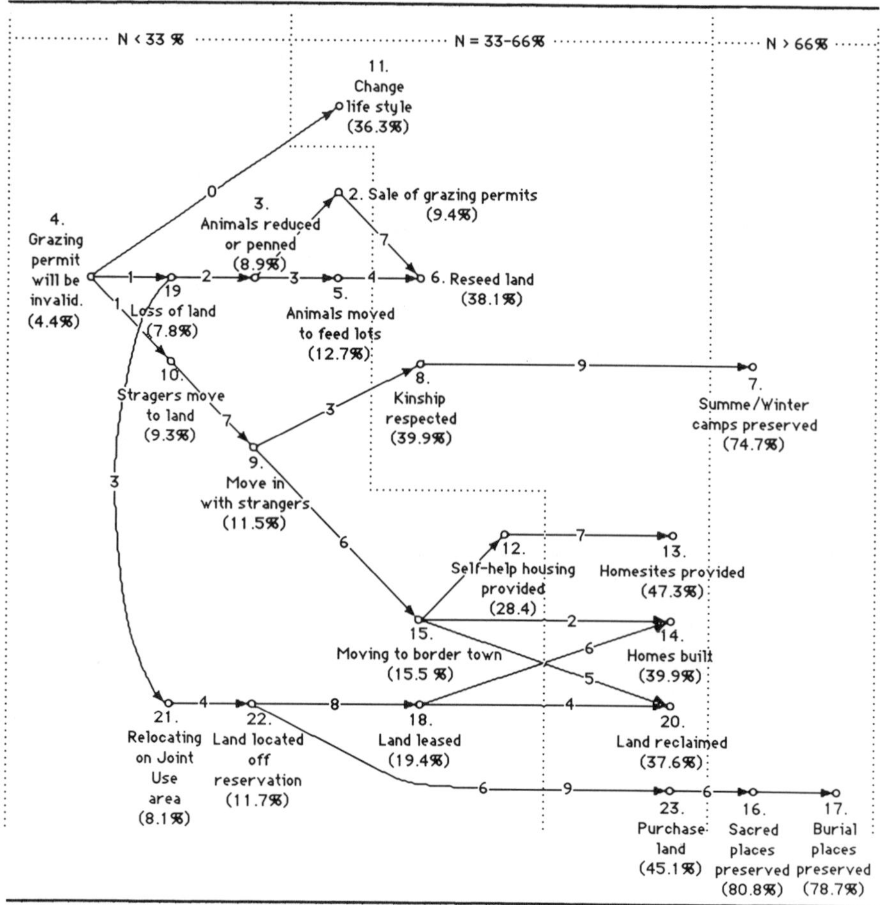

Figure 8.13 Entailment

each node. For example, in the computation of the pairing of variables "5: Animals moved to feed lots" and "6: Reseed land" the figures are 69:181 = 38.1% and 23:181 = 12.7%. The numbers attached to the arrows mark the number of exceptions to each entailment.

Entailment analysis elaborates a decision model in two ways: (1) it establishes implicational chains (see above), and (2) it can be used to rank order the outcomes.

The items in the middle are those we called in Section 5.2.5 "mitigations." These are possible future actions that no one is enthusiastic about. These middle variables came to be interpreted as mitigations through a review of the implicational chains in the entailment diagram (Figure 8.13). For example, the variable "4: Grazing permit will be invalid" is the source or point of departure for all implicational paths. This means that apprehension about the loss of grazing permits, shared by most Navajos in the sample, is a fear that serves as the point of origin for all other outcomes.

The rank ordering can in turn be used to establish which items are favored by fewer than 33% of the respondents, which items are favored by 33% to 66% of them, and which are favored by more than 66% of the people. We can thus assert that if people do not like items favored by less or equal to 33% of them, they will like only slightly more those favored by 33% to 66% and will like most those favored by over 66%. Thus it is apparent from Figure 8.13 that the Navajos in the sample do not like relocation. Item "11: Change in life-style" seems to imply that close to 40% of the Navajos are resigned to the inevitability of changes. However, if development and relocation are inevitable, then they would like to see the reclaimed land reseeded (items 6 and 20) for their later use after mining operations are completed. They would like to relocate with their extended kinship groups (item 8) and expect in general that new housing will be provided for them (items 13, 14, and 23). Almost three-quarters of the Navajos in the sample would like to preserve their winter and summer camps (item 7). Perhaps it seems inconceivable to many Navajos that one could live comfortably or keep sheep effectively in the same place throughout the year. An even higher percentage would like their burial grounds and sacred shrines left undisturbed by the open pit coal mines (items 16 and 17).

The entailment analysis clarified the ethnographic decision model in several ways. For example, summer and winter camps (item 7) are barely mentioned in the ethnographic interviews but turn out to be significantly valued. Sacred places and burial grounds (items 16 and 17) did not appear very important in the ethnographic interviews but in the entailment diagram moved to a position of great importance with an amazing degree of consensus. Schoepfle *et al.* (1985) interpret this discrepancy as sampling bias in the ethnographic data: A check of the ethnographic consultants' background shows a disproportionate number of Navajos who were Christians or members of the Native American Church. The sampling plan of entailment analysis controlled for that bias.

The importance of entailment analysis lies in the fact that whereas the decision model was logically articulated it was not easily validated. The reason for this lies in the hypothetical nature of the relocatees' dilemma. The people who were interviewed did not have the opportunity actually to implement their model. They were therefore never sure whether their assumptions were valid. It was necessary to test not only how the model worked but, more important, *whether the underlying assumptions are valid,* at least to the extent that the model can be assumed to exist in the minds of the population.

Entailment analysis is particularly useful in this instance because it tests the same kinds of relationships as does the decision model. The decision model too can be seen as an implicational chain because it combines taxonomy, attributes (conditions), and sequential organization (Werner and Topper 1976, see also Volume 1, Section 2.3). That is, any relation between elements A and B in a decision sequence can be restated, "If A, then B." For example, "If we are going to be relocated together, then land has been set aside for us." In this example B can be viewed as a *constraint* on A, or "A only if B is satisfied" (see Figure 5.2). Given the model, we can rephrase this as, "We will relocate together only if land has been set aside for us." However, if the condition is not met, the entire process stops and a totally different set of options must be considered.

Entailment analysis is of particular interest to cognitive ethnography because the method demands carefully designed questionnaires that only a prerequisite ethnoscience ethnography can provide. This ethnography then supplies, through its decision model, key propositions that are incorporated into the questionnaire. Analysis of the questionnaire responses leads to the entailments that validate and elaborate the ethnographic model.

8.5 ALTERNATIVE CLASSIFICATION

In Section 2.5.5 we discussed componential analysis as one method for investigating the internal structure of one taxonomic contrast set. To this end it was insufficient merely to know attributes in isolation. It was important to discover dimensions: that is, sets of attributes that belong together. For example, it is not enough to discover that there are male relatives; it is more important to know that all terms for relatives are classified according to the dimension of sex, which may take the values of "male" and "female."[4]

Many lexical semantic fields (apart from kinship terms and pronominal systems) involve dimensions that are often not easily verbalizable by the users of that cultural domain. Real-life situations are frequently similar to the problem Navajo students faced when they could not clearly distinguish between the dimension of "professional competence" versus "interpersonal compatibility" when they called a teacher "nice" or "good" (see Case 8.2).

The formulations of componential analysis (for example, the classic articles of Lounsbury [1956] and Goodenough [1956]) look promising until the issues of generalizability and variability emerge. Kin terms usage varies among individuals and groups (see, for example, the variability of the dimension of collateral distance in contemporary U.S. society and the concomitant variety of componential solutions in Romney and D'Andrade 1964) as much as the decision of how unambiguously to define a "nice" versus a "good" teacher.

Variability of components may occur even in the face of constancy of dimensions. For example, no one has questioned the dimension of collateral distance although its componential content varies from Goodenough's (Wallace and Atkins 1960) components of "lineal," "colineal," and "ablineal" through "close" and "distant," "nuclear" and "nonnuclear," or "monolexemic" and "multilexemic." The main thing to keep in mind is that *dimensions are attributes on a superordinate level of a taxonomy, whereas the manifestations of a dimension, its values, are attributes of a subordinate level.*

The fact that dimensions can remain constant while their values (i.e., components) vary harks back to the old anthropological issue of normative versus descriptive culture. Schneider (1968), in his description of Yankee kin terminology, does two things to address this issue. First, he restricts his ethnographic sample to East Coast Americans. Second, he proposes an idealized omniscient informant whose knowledge represents the essence of appropriate kin term usage in American society.

The idealized omniscient informant is a theoretical entity easily seen as an artifact of the ethnographer's position in the society he or she studies (see also Section 3.3 in Volume 1). The ethnographer's role differs in significant ways from the role of most natives of a culture. By definition, he or she spends much time gathering information in order to be able to make explicit statements about the nature of the natives' knowledge. Few natives have the luxury, opportunity, or time to look in on themselves as the ethnographer does. This means, however, that ethnographers, by describing what they see as normative in a culture, can make explicit various aspects of cultural knowledge that are only imperfectly shared and thus are statable realistically only in probabilistic terms. This is especially true once we leave behind small group cultures and move out to larger social units in which social network information and hence sharing of cultural knowledge is systemically impeded (see Volume 1, Section 1.3).

Romney and D'Andrade (1964) address these issues through a combination of recall testing, Osgood's semantic differential, and triads testing. They were confronted with the fact that a number of different componential solutions to the Yankee system can be generated. They wanted to see if this multiplicity was due to different people harboring different paradigms, to the same people harboring different paradigms, or to the interference of other psychological processes. More precisely, they wanted to see whether people classify Yankee kinship terms according to the referential or denotative meanings or according to some other psychological or emotive association.

They first performed recall tests (Romney & D'Andrade 1964) that required students to list all names of relatives they could think of. They then assumed that (1) the students listed only terms with which they were most familiar (i.e., close relatives), (2) terms recalled first would have a larger number of attributes than those listed later, and (3) more people would tend to list these more meaningful terms. With these assumptions in mind, they then ranked the terms (1) according to how often they were recalled, (2) to how often the terms appeared with modifiers (i.e., mother → stepmother; brother → stepbrother), (3) to how often terms within the same range set occurred with the same modifiers (e.g., half brother, half sister), and (4) according to the maximum number of modifiers used for close relatives. These facts both supported the Wallace/Atkins paradigm and the assumption that people did classify the kin terms of this domain by using components.

The application of Osgood's semantic differential was intended to help infer the relationship of this componential structure to other emotional associations. To apply it, Romney and D'Andrade had the respondent rate, on a 5-point scale, the terms "father," "mother," "brother," "sister," "man," "woman," "boy," "girl," and "myself" on the dimensions of good-bad, nice-awful, kind-mean, heavy-light, hard-soft, and fast-slow. Factor analysis of the results indicated two clusters that could be scored according to the composite dimension of "potency." The semantic differential once again supported the data that people rated the scored items according to components but, not surprisingly, did not do so clearly. This is most likely because the categories in the semantic differential are not consonant with native categories. It is here that the third approach, the triads test, proved most valuable.

In the triad testing students were asked to judge similarity between various triplets of terms in a cultural domain (that is, which single item is most different from the remaining two, or which two items among the three are maximally similar).

Multidimensional scaling is a form of factor analysis designed originally for analyzing triad test results (Romney & D'Andrade 1964). The scores are arrayed in clusters, usually in a two-dimensional Cartesian coordinate system. The Cartesian distance (roughly the intuitively shortest distance between two points) measures the degree of correlation and similarity between two terms. Closeness of terms in the plot means that they are semantically similar in some unspecified but often inferable manner. Inferences are usually made on the basis of external—that is, ethnographic—understandings.

The application of ethnographic judgment can be aided by specifying some arbitrary level of association as a cut-off point. If such a point is set at a correlation of, say .8, then all points within this range are considered members of the same cluster. Next, by considering higher and lower cut-off points, the investigator can establish clusters within clusters. If the distribution of all of these clusters and subclusters is plotted, then one can often infer a taxonomic structure much as one can infer it from Venn diagrams (see Section 8.4.1). This is just one possible form of numerical taxonomizing.

In the next step the ethnographer searches the native terminological system for suitable labels for each cluster. A tree diagram such as that used by Burton and Nerlove (1976) can complete the picture. The ethnographer can utilize some theoretically motivated terms that describe these hierarchies. Introducing outside terminology into native terminological systems must be done with extreme care in order to avoid undue ethnocentric biasing of the data. However, a combination of native terms and ethnographers terms may occasionally suffice.

The drawback of multidimensional scaling is the exponential growth of the number of comparisons that the ethnographer and consultants must make. For example, if a reasonably realistic 30-term domain is evaluated, one would have to consider 30!: (3! × 27!) or 8,120 triads.[5] Burton and Nerlove (1976) simplified the procedure by finding that if the test is restricted to triads so that all pairs of terms are represented only once, then in what they have termed a balanced design with 30 items only 435 (30!:2! × 28!) judgments need be made.

Romney and D'Andrade (1964) were confronted with 245 possible triad comparisons. To limit this number they used two questionnaires. The first ascertained that sex pairs (e.g., father-mother) were frequently classified together. Then they constructed a second questionnaire of only one sex, dealing with eight male terms (grandfather, father, brother, son, grandson, uncle, cousin, and nephew), or only 56 comparisons. The results show that after holding sex constant, generation, reciprocity, and collaterality were the three main dimensions. The test results also show that people respond to the terms "as if each term contained a bundle of distinct meanings" (Romney & D'Andrade 1964: 394). This is, of course, just like a folk definition.

Multidimensional scaling is but one method of numerical taxonomy (or numerical classification). New insights can be gained by using more than one of these methods whenever possible and comparing the results with ethnographic data.

8.6 SUMMARY AND CONCLUSIONS

In this part 1 of Volume 2 we considered the pursuit of intensive, in-depth ethnography combined with extensive, in-breadth statistical techniques. Each of these approaches offers new insights vis-à-vis the other. This makes the still rare explicit combination of cognitive ethnographic and quantitative methods an important epistemological window (see Volume 1, Section 1.2). This window can be further enhanced if it is possible to subject the same data set to several different statistical procedures.

In addition, the breadth of surveys helps to generalize ethnographically derived hypotheses to a larger population. Such generalization is especially valid if the survey questionnaire is based on a sound ethnoscience ethnography (see Volume 1, Chapter 11) and if an appropriate sampling plan takes into account native criteria for the classification of people.

Validation, the confirmation by one methodology of insights derived using another (Campbell & Fiske 1959), is another gain that can be realized by combining ethnographic data with quantitative investigations. Validation also provides checks on internal consistency—that is, answers to questions about the fit of ethnographic findings with statistical conclusions and vice versa. The reversibility is important: Validations and checks of internal consistency can go both ways—from ethnography to statistics and from statistics to ethnography. In the best of all possible worlds, the repetition of the ethnography-statistics cycle (iteration) may be highly desirable.

Inference of cause and effect is another important method for extending the reach and persuasiveness of ethnographic data. The test of ethnographically derived hypotheses on larger populations combines cause and effect with validation, internal consistency, and generalization.

Numerical classifications (derivable through multidimensional scaling and other techniques) introduce alternate arrangements to traditional folk classification. Attempts to interpret numerical classification in light of ethnographic understandings may also lead to new and better insights. In this case as well the application of a variety of statistical classification schemes can further enhance understanding.

Finally, this brief section barely scratches the surface of potentialities for interaction between cognitive ethnography and statistics. By relying on each other, both sets of understandings can grow stronger.

NOTES

1. Note, however, that for the utilization of epistemological windows (i.e., discrepancy) both are needed (see Volume 1, Section 1.2).
2. The procedure is equally applicable to the analysis of journal entries (i.e., TEXT (1)).
3. Note the similarity of the procedure for which D'Andrade used entailment analysis. At least one school of thought in statistics claims one should use multiple measures to learn about the data structure as much as possible from different viewpoints. That is, different statistical techniques can and should serve as epistemological windows.
4. It is equally significant that there are kin terms in the Yankee terminological system that are indifferent with regard to sex. The prime example is, of course, the term "cousin."
5. The formula is $n!/3!(n - 3)!$

Part II

POST-FIELDWORK

Chapter 9

Planning the Ethnographic Report

The final phase of fieldwork is writing the ethnographic report. Many books and articles have been written on writing. This chapter summarizes some proven guidelines for writing ethnographies. Ultimately the best way to improve writing and to make writing easier is to practice.

9.0 INTRODUCTION

Although this part of the book is called Post-Fieldwork, some very successful ethnographic writing has been done right in the field or very near the field site. Proximity to the original field site, rather than actually being "in" the field, has two advantages: (1) It allows the checking of data one may have missed or that assume their proper significance only after intensive analysis and/or during the process of writing. (2) Being near rather than in the field places the ethnographer far enough away to avoid the demanding aspects of day-to-day field relations (e.g., acting as a clinic or as a taxi service) but near enough to allow easy access to consultants if necessary.

There are two important aspects of writing the ethnographic report. The first is planning, which must precede all actual writing. The second is the process of writing itself. The first chapter in Part III deals with the preparation for writing; the following chapter with the writing process.

Writing an ethnography, just as with writing almost anything, requires preparation. The experienced ethnographer sets up the entire field operation so that every step in elicitation and analysis directly contributes to the ease of information retrieval and thereby to easier writing. Consequently, much of the preparation for writing—that is, data base management—should be planned before the field trip and kept up conscientiously in the field. The conventional figure that two-thirds of the time for writing a report is spent (or should be spent) in planning and preparation (Gould 1978: 1460) may be too low for ethnographies.

We think that writing ethnographies may require more time for preparation than other forms of report writing. One indication of this appears to be the fact that ethnographers who have put aside their data for some time (weeks, months, sometimes years) sometimes have extreme difficulty returning to writing. Ethnographic data tend to become unfamiliar very fast. The intensity of the ethnographic experience seems to alienate us from our data once we return home.

The need for warm-up time seems to increase as familiarity with the data decreases. Therefore, an ethnographic report should be written in or near the field, before the ethnographer leaves permanently. An added bonus to being near the field is the possibility of returning to check on data one may have overlooked.

Ideally, interviewing and data analysis should be done simultaneously. Only through analysis will the ethnographer know what data have been gathered and what data are missing and so need to be elicited through additional interviews. Not to analyze (organize) one's data is to work blindly. Unless an ethnographer has an unusually acute memory for ethnographic detail, omitting analysis is a sure way to let data get away—in other words, lose control of the ethnographic process.

The major problem of writing is the *linearization* of rich data that are available only in nonlinear form as taxonomic trees, part/whole trees, folk definitions, plans, decision tables, causal trees, and so on. By "linearization" we mean that data in different forms and shapes must be placed in a sequential order that can be discussed in discursive, linear language in the form of a book or paper. As Case 7.10, "The Game of Death," illustrated, the little story about the hognose snake is a linearization of a complex definition that involved simple attributes *and* complex attributes, including plans and decisions. The following example illustrates, in an elementary manner, the ethnographer's somewhat more voluble dilemma.

9.1 WHITE AND YELLOW CARD ANALYSIS

We have experimented with different arrangements for our analyses. The most efficient technique we found was used during the elicitation and analysis phases of our *Six Navajo School Ethnographies* (Werner *et al.* 1976). We found that 5 × 8-inch (127 × 203 mm) cards were the right size for our purposes. Smaller cards will not accommodate enough information and larger cards are not readily available in the United States. McBee cards or derived edge-punch cards are available in larger sizes. Whenever funds are available, these cards should be used (see Section 1.4.3).

9.1.1 White Card Analysis

Every structure that we are able to analyze out of raw data we put on white cards. We call this process the "white card analysis stage." A white card should always be assigned to a *particular consultant* (usually through a coded set of initials; see Volume 1, Case 12.3) and should include the interview numbers, added

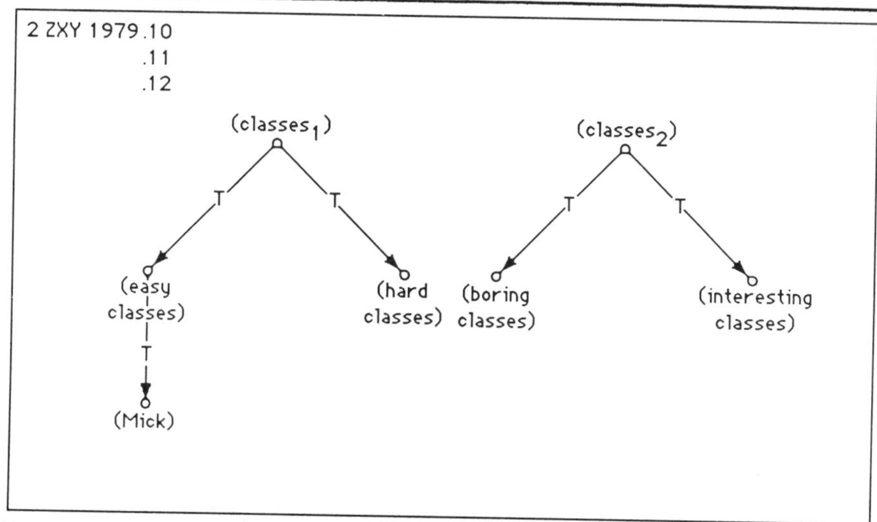

NOTE: From Figures 2.9 and 2.10 white card analysis. The upper left-hand corner identifies this card. The number of the interview is first. The initials XYZ are a code for each consultant (see text), which appear next, followed by the year of the interview. The last two numbers represent the page number in the data base (see Section 1.3) and the sentence number on that page, respectively.

Figure 9.1 Carol's Classes Revisited

initials, year, page, and sentence numbers relevant to the analysis. Figures 2.9 and 2.10, represented in white card analysis style, are shown in Figure 9.1.

"ZXY" stands for Carol Bournette (an actual name): "A" for Adamson Hall, where Carol lived. That is, the initials of Carol are ACB. We use geographical locations as additional identifiers if a middle initial is lacking. Generally, for identifying interviews and for maintaining confidentiality (it is almost always called for), we first use the actual initials of our consultants. Second, we scramble the initials according to some encoding schema (e.g., A = Z, B = Y, C = X, and so on through the alphabet); thus, Carol's initials ACB become ZXY. Each interview is numbered: Carol's first interview becomes 1XYZ. This is followed by the year of the interview, the page number in the data base (see the Bugos/Werner system discussed in Section 1.3), and a sentence number separated by a period. Sentence numbering is optional. The tenth sentence of Carol's second interview in 1979, which contains the taxonomic information shown on the card, is on page 7 of the data base and is encoded 2ZXY 1979: 7.10. In white card analysis we sometimes suppress the sentence number because information (e.g., taxonomic information) is often traceable to more than one origin in the interview text, and page number is therefore sufficient for unambiguous retrieval or double check.

There are two advantages to placing the results of analysis on card stock: (1) Cards can be organized in a card file and are more easily moved than slips of paper. This is important because analyses of the same topic with different consultants can easily be placed together. For example, if we interview a number of students, their classifications of classes can be placed together. (2) By preserving the identity of each individual consultant, the source of every piece of information is preserved. This is important for giving consultants proper credit for their statements and for keeping track of individual variation—who said what, and how differences in knowledge are distributed in the social system under study. In encyclopedic investigations, white card analysis efficiently keeps track of any controversies between consultants. One of our principles of understanding a system of cultural knowledge (see Volume 1, Section 1.2) is that a field is "well known" only if the ethnographer knows (has something to say about) the controversies and/or disputes that exist among consultants who are experts in their fields of specialization. In addition, white card analysis for each consultant is an excellent way of tabulating and documenting disputes and variations.

The actual white card may take different forms in one's data base. It may be an actual white filing card; it may be an edge- punch card specially coded to indicate source; it may be a "virtual" card in a computer-managed filing system; or it may be simply a page in one's general data base, perhaps marked or tagged in some special manner for rapid access. The essence of "white cards" is that they contain summarized and analyzed data for each consultant individually, as in our example, often a tree structure elicited from one person.

9.1.2 Yellow Card Analysis

Yellow card analysis is a natural extension of white card analysis. We use yellow cards as *summaries of the composite information* of several consultants. That is, whereas a white card is the result of the analysis of a single consultant (usually across several interviews), yellow card analysis contains the composite knowledge of the white card analyses of several consultants. Occasionally it may be necessary to have more than one yellow card analysis. This may be called for if there are two or more distinct groups of people in the social system with highly similar (or nearly identical) systems of knowledge within each group but very different knowledge systems across groups. A health maintenance organization provides a good example. Health professionals (doctors and nurses) may have expert medical knowledge, whereas support personnel (secretaries, receptionists) may have only slightly more extended medical knowledge than intelligent laypersons. It makes sense in such cases of contrasting knowledge to use two (or more) yellow cards to summarize the collective knowledge of each group.

It is advisable to keep track of particular individuals even on the yellow cards. We have used black ink for shared taxonomic tree structures (the intersection of all individual knowledge systems). We then assign ink of different colors to different consultants to show variations in how individuals elaborate the shared structure. Other coding schemes (e.g., numbering of subtrees or branches of trees) are also possible which do not require a large number of colored pencils. For example, each arrow in a tree diagram or plan that is not shared may bear the initials of the consultant who provided the verification.

Yellow card analysis has the advantage for the writer of the ethnography that the summaries of a set of yellow cards can be arranged in a specific order corresponding to the plan for writing. This procedure makes parts of writing the ethnography very easy because the ethnographer first arranges the yellow cards or their equivalent (pages in data base, or computer pages) in an order that makes sense for writing. As the ethnographer goes through the stack of yellow cards, the ethnographic report is written.

If the ethnographer has a large room available, he or she can spread the cards on the floor and visually inspect the entire sequence. This is a common technique called a "mock-up" used in magazine and newspaper editing. An entire issue is layed out (usually on cork-covered walls) for inspection. It is amazing how easy it is to detect inconsistencies, missing parts of patterns, and lack of continuity in a mock-up. This technique may be used not only in preparation for writing, but also, with equally rewarding results, each time the report is rewritten. In Section 10.2.2 we recommend five or more drafts. A mock-up phase may be used before each draft.

Occasionally yellow card analysis is unnecessary. In our *Six Navajo School Ethnographies,* we often skipped the yellow card analysis because the responses on each white card were relatively uniform and the relatively small stack of white cards could be handled as efficiently as a single yellow card. We arranged the stacks of white cards with related or identical information as if each stack was one yellow card. The actual yellow card analysis was done directly onto the pages of the first draft of the ethnographic report. We do not recommend this procedure for inexperienced ethnographers, however.

9.2 KEYSORT EDGE-PUNCH CARDS AND COMPUTER ANALYSIS (See also Section 1.4.3)

Computer analysis of ethnographic interviews and journal data offers similar advantages: Both allow easy access to cross-classification without requiring duplicate cards to be filed under different headings.

In yellow card analysis the order of the cards is fixed. If part of the content of a yellow card must be used in a later section, then it must be refiled in the new location immediately after being used the first time. With a few cross-classifications this is easy; with many intersecting classifications this may become an organizational nightmare.

Keysort card data retrieval techniques have the advantage that one deck of cards can be accessed through different systems of classifications. Since the relevant information is all encoded physically at the edge of the card, there is no need to refile. The cards may remain in random order. The principles of edge card encoding are explained in Section 1.4.3.

9.3 COMPUTERIZED ENCODING METHODS

With microcomputers shrinking in size, price, and power requirements almost daily, their use in the field will soon become as natural and commonplace as the use of tape recorder and camera is today. We and other ethnographers interested in the uses of computers for fieldwork are in the process of devising data management and retrieval systems that maximize the accessibility of data for analysis and writing. We hope to report on these developments in subsequent editions of this book.

Some uses of computerized text concordances for text analysis and the analysis of maximally complete simple sentences are discussed in Section 7.3.

9.4 SCRATCH LIST METHOD

Later we will suggest methods for combatting writer's block. The most effective way of avoiding writer's block, besides the gimmicks mentioned in Chapter 10, is to carefully lay out a plan of action. Every method for organizing data, thoughtfully applied, reduces the chances of writer's block.

The "scratch list" method is effective for writing entire ethnographies, though white cards and carefully ordered yellow cards or their equivalents (in the order of writing) may make this method more useful for writing sections and subsections. Several variations of this method are used in computer programs called "outline processors" or "spreadsheets for facts," which ease the organization and writing of reports. These programs are very new and we have had no chance to examine any of them in detail. In general they are organized along principles that more or less follow the scratch list method.

The scratch list method is very simple and uses the principles already established: (1) Obtain some relevant topics (e.g., a set of yellow card analyses) and (2) arrange the topics in a relevant and appropriate order. The latter may be accomplished through the mock-up method (physically laying out the product so it can be visually inspected in its totality). In fact, methods for establishing a writing order are very similar no matter what the topics are.

The scratch list method helps to obtain an initial list of topics. It can be broken down into the following steps:

(1) Everything that seems even remotely relevant to the topic of the ethnography is written down (as a scratch list or on cards). At this point, the writer of the ethnography has achieved the status of an "expert"—perhaps the world's foremost expert—on the culture in question. He or she should have no difficulty thinking of something to say about that culture. The random order is important: The problem of writing (and of writer's block) is caused by the overwhelming decision to commit to a particular order of presentation. With the scratch list method we postpone this step. Like a random memory "dump," we put down on paper one topic

Chapter 7: Writing the Ethnographic Report

Some issues to be included in this chapter

Writing for an audience
Writing encyclopedias or ethnographies
Taxonomy as the basis of organization
Plan-based organization
Part/whole-based organization
"Other"-based organization
White card analysis
Yellow card analysis
Order of presentation
Organization
Use of cases
How to start writing
How to overcome writer's block
Use of tape recorders
Cut and paste
Editing
Editing programs
Writing introduction last
Typing early drafts triple triple spacing
Co-authorship (and/with, footnotes)

Figure 9.2 First Scratch List for Part II

after another, in telegraphic style, as each pops into our head through random associations.

The list can be long or short, though longer lists are easier to manipulate and lead to better results.

Case 9.1 Scratch Lists for Part II (Chapters 9 and 10)[1]

Part II of this volume was written later than most of the chapters. The table of contents up to that point contained only a scratch list of topics to be included. Figure 9.2 shows the list as it appeared in the summer of 1979, just before the first draft of this chapter was written.

(2) The next task involved organizing the list into some cogent order. That is the major advantage of the scratch list method: It lets the writer put down the potential contents of the ethnography in *any order*.

Looking over the list in Figure 9.2, it is clear that with some additional input (from reading several books on writing, lecture notes on writing the ethnographic report, and an outline for writing ethnographies composed by Judy Abbott during 1978/1979), the major subdivisions of this chapter should be as shown in Figure 9.3. At this point, a scratch list for each of the two major sections was prepared (Figure 9.4).

The outline scratch list in Figure 9.4 served as the basic plan for writing. This was translated into the headings in Figure 9.5 on the first day of writing. The rest

Chapter 7. Writing the Ethnographic Report
7.0 Introduction
7.1 Planning
7.2 Writing
7.3 Summary and Conclusions

Figure 9.3 List for the Major Organization of Chapter 7

of this chapter was laid out in provisional form (at this point still unwritten), as shown in Figure 9.6.

Since for the revisions of this chapter we used the editing and formatting program for minicomputers called "Electric Pencil II" by Michael Shrayer Software, Inc., we went through several revisions or drafts. With electronic editing it is so easy to go through several drafts that, in the end, it is difficult to determine exactly how many drafts there were. We simply do not know. This is because many revisions and corrections can be made right on the cathode ray tube screen without going to a hard paper copy.

In the case of planned Chapter 7, the reader can inspect actual Chapters 9 and 10 and their current table of contents to see how the final product turned out.

9.5 CHECKLIST OF HEADINGS: ETHNOGRAPHIES AND ENCYCLOPEDIAS

In our experience we have found that with general and specialized ethnographic projects alike, many different types of information need to be presented. Judy Abbott (1979) greatly relieved the anxiety of beginning ethnography students by providing them with a checklist of items to include in their ethnographies. In our *Six Navajo School Ethnographies* (Werner *et al.* 1976) we also used the checklist method for key titles in order to maximize the comparability of the six ethnographies (see Case 10.4). A checklist of basic headings gives the writer of an ethnography a basic frame around which the white cards, yellow cards, or scratch list can be effectively organized.

A word of caution is necessary. No ethnography, especially one focusing on the "internal" view of a culture, should be forced into a checklist mindlessly. The proposed headings are suggestive of what information ought to be contained in the ethnography. The ethnographer must always be alert for any information relevant to the natives and not thought of in advance. This type of information is of the greatest value. The following example illustrates.

Case 9.2 Order of Navajo Anatomical Parts

We went through several drafts to produce *The Anatomical Atlas of the Navajo* (Werner *et al.* in press). In early drafts we presented the human body in an order that seemed to us "natural": We started with the head and finished with the toes. This happened because Kenneth Y. Begishe, who was Werner's col-

7.0 Introduction
7.1 Planning
  Planning takes two-thirds of composition (Gould 1978: 1146)
  White Card Analysis
  Yellow Card Analysis
  McBee Cards *OEdge-Punch Keysort Cards)*
  Computer?
    (These two sections were moved to Volume 1, Chapter 1 in 1983)
  Scratch list method (linearize)
  Relevant Headings:
    Ethnographies
      History (ethnohistory vs. documentary history, when?)
      Where (ethno vs. documentary)
      Props *(objects)*
      Who? (ethno vs. documentary?)
      Activities (when, what, cases)
      Repetitious patterns (themes, cases)
      How? Why? (really last??)
      Conclusions (what could have been done better)
      Appendices
    Encyclopedias
      Introduction?
      History (need)
      Where?
      Who?
      Organizational Principle
      Taxonomy
      Part/Whole
      Plans
      Cause
      Cases? ?
7.2 Writing
  Analytic vs. synthetic (systemic) approach
  Styles: building up to a climax (conclusion last)
    conclusion first
  Scratch list — planification (rerefer to "Game of Death")
  Writer's block — explain to friend,
    teach a class on topic, etc.
    tape record
    stimulus transcription
  Rough Draft (triple triple space) (red and blue pencil)
  1st draft: (John Wiley & Sons (1973:2-5))
    Is all there? Is too much there? (be ruthless)
  2nd draft: Clarity/organization
    Go by titles and subtitles and back
  3rd draft: Smoothing style/corrected writing
  4th draft: Reduce number of words
    Increase number of words???
  5th draft: Polish style ± Computer editing
  Know your audience
  Write as simply as possible
    (Coleman & Miller 1967: college sophomores learned more from material on 5th-grade level.)
  The more time for deciphering — the less time for understanding

Figure 9.4 Scratch List for 7.1 and 7.2 (Chapters 9 and 10)

The concreter your writing the better (cases)
Every passive is obscuring clarity unless proven otherwise.
Referencing sources from technical literature
from journal and transcriptions
Respect for authorship in literature and ethnographic data
Use of graphs and figures
Reduction of technical terms
(Comprehensive Conclusions and Summary)
Write Introduction last
Making several parallel versions uniform
(more than one ethnography)

NOTE: Items between *( )* were added later.

Figure 9.4 Continued

laborator, was then a young man only partially familiar with Navajo traditional culture. It was through his association with the Navajo Ethno-Medical Dictionary Project (later Encyclopedia Project) that he learned a great deal more about his own cultural tradition (see Volume 1, Section 6.7 about the training of consultants; also see Werner & Fenton 1970). It was only after we presented the first draft of the *Anatomical Atlas* to traditional Navajos that we discovered that the proper order of presentation had to proceed from foot to head (see Figure 2.15). We found that every ceremony contains a prayer about the human body—starting always with the foot and ending with the head. This is the direction of growth. Only in the Enemy Way ceremony (roughly equivalent to the "war dance") is the order reversed. Enemies are wished into the ground, the direction of death.

It is conceivable that too rigid an outline for studying anatomical classification and anatomical knowledge could have impeded our discovery of the appropriate order for describing the human body in Navajo.

The problem of mindless application of checklists does not stop with information that is overt or as easily elicitable as the order of body parts. There are often implicit or covert aspects of a domain of knowledge that are difficult to discover. Very often it takes hard work, luck, and an insightful consultant (or research collaborator) to discover such hidden principles. An example illustrates:

Case 9.3 Two- and Three-Dimensional Parts of the Body in Navajo

It was difficult to organize early drafts of *The Anatomical Atlas of the Navajo* (see below Case 9.6). The part/whole classification (occasionally interspersed with a taxonomy, e.g., the different fingers) did not fall easily into place. The part/whole tree structures just did not make sense. Then Begishe discovered that some terms in Navajo referred to two-dimensional surfaces of the body (e.g., in Navajo, the palm of the hand or, more literally translated, the *downward-directed surface of the hand,* or an area of the back called *"the*

Chapter	7.	Writing the Ethnographic Report
	7.0	Introduction
	7.1	Planning and Preparation
	7.1.1	White and Yellow Card Analysis
	7.1.2	Keysort Edgepunch Cards and Computer Analysis
	*(7.1.2.1	Direct Edge-Punch Coding)*
	*(7.1.2.2	Digital Edge-Punch Coding)*
	7.1.3	Computerized Coding Methods

NOTE: Items between *( )* were later moved to Chapter 1.

Figure 9.5 Chapter 7 Outline After the First Day of Writing

7.1.4	The "Scratch List" Method
7.1.4.1	Relevant Headings for Ethnographies
7.1.5	Relevant Headings for Encyclopaedias
7.2	Writing
7.2.1	Analytical vs. Synthetic (or Systemic) Approaches
7.2.2	Two Fundamental Styles: Climax First or Last
7.2.3	Know Your Audience
7.2.4	Combatting Writer's Block
7.2.5	Rough Draft to Finished Product
7.2.5.1	Computerized Editing and Formatting
7.2.6	Writing Comprehensive Summary
7.2.7	Writing the Introduction
7.2.8	Writing Several Ethnographies Simultaneously
7.3	Summary and Conclusions

Figure 9.6 Proposed Remaining Outline of Chapter 7

> *place that one cannot reach"*) and some referred to three-dimensional surfaces of the body (e.g., knee, liver, head). After the two- and three-dimensional part/whole classifications were separated, the whole system fell into place and became logically consistent. For the final versions of the *Atlas*, we put the two classifications back together again (for ease of presentation), but careful inspection of the part/whole trees reveals the separateness of the two- and three-dimensional parts of the body.

For a long time a rigid, non-Navajo interpretation of the parts of the body prevented our recognizing the "true" organizational principle of anatomical terms in Navajo.

There is a final problem that pervades the use of checklists. We take the answer to the "where" question, the description of the geographical location of the ethnography, as our example. It is relatively easy to describe the location of an ethnography in terms of Western geography. Every part of the globe is mapped to some extent. Certainly, it is easy to give the latitude and longitude of any geographical area in the world. This information is vital for readers who are familiar with geographical coordinates, globes, and maps. They need to be able to locate the site of any ethnographic research on the face of the globe.

It is equally important to find out where the "natives" think they are—the folk geography of the area. For example, do they consider themselves in the center of the universe or on the periphery of it? How do they see themselves in relation to other geographical entities in their universe? One of the best descriptions of the Navajo geographical/spatial universe appears in Pinxten *et al.* (1983).

Summarizing, it is not enough merely to fill in the suggested headings of any checklist. Some headings require only the native point of view, perhaps implemented by the ethnographer's observations and native comments on these observations. Many of the headings will, however, require two clearly distinct pieces of information: (1) the ethnographer's view or the view required by the ethnographer's professional culture (e.g., geographical coordinates), and (2) the native point of view. We comment on these problems in the next section as we discuss each proposed heading.

9.5.1 Checklist of Headings for Ethnographies

Every ethnography, to a greater or lesser extent depending on the problem orientation of the project, should cover the following topics.

History

Almost every problem (ethnographic or otherwise) has a past. This may include previous work done in the area (geographic or problem orientation) that needs to be reviewed. This requires a review of any such literature. Very often this review was (or should have been) completed (except perhaps for the latest titles) as part of preparation of the proposal for research. The relevant headings in the "wh" schema are the "What?" section, in the NIMH schema the "Background" section, in the NEH schema the "History" section (see Volume 1, Chapter 5). In the case of a good, detailed, thoroughly researched proposal, these sections can be easily inserted, often with little change. The only additional effort may be to cut, paste, and add a few new "connecting" sentences. With the help of electronic editing, if the section is already stored on tape or disk, a simple command will insert the relevant pages into an ethnography.

Some problems may also have an ethnohistory. It is imperative then to separate the "documentary" history prepared by the ethnographer from the ethnohistory as the natives see it.

Location

We have used the geographical location of ethnographic research as an important example. Geography can almost always be viewed "externally" and "internally"; that is, two standards must be satisfied:

(1) There is the standard of the profession for locating an ethnographic site on the globe. In some instances in which confidentiality must be maintained, there may be a problem with carefully coding such geographical information. This often

requires ingenuity: The code should give the reader some idea about the general culture area while protecting the identities of the participants and their exact locations. Unfortunately, many geographical pseudonyms are cracked with the greatest of ease. Some anthropologists consider all codes "inside" information and boast about their ability to break them or to wheedle them out of other ethnographers who happen to know them. It is important to understand that geographical locations are very difficult to disguise.

(2) There is the standard by which the natives themselves see their location in space. For example, some tribal societies may be unaware of the national societies in which they are a part. In other cases, if central control is minimal, they may be indifferent to the national state of which they are a part. In some instances, they may even ridicule their association to the national state. Equally important may be how the people think they arrived at their location, why they are there, who (if anyone) was there before them, how long ago they got there, who put them there, and so on. In short, a good ethnography will specify how the natives see themselves within the area in which they live, work, or play.

An ethnogeography may be a complex undertaking in itself if the ethnographer wants to work out all the details of place names and their histories. However, every ethnography should contain at least an ethnogeographic sketch—a broadly descriptive presentation of the native view of local geography. In some projects a detailed ethnogeography may be necessary (e.g., a project dealing with land use). A roughly sketched ethnogeography taken from a previous project can provide the nucleus around which to build a detailed ethnogeography.

The geography of an "area" need not be broadly geographic. Every human group uses space. People's ideas about the space they live in, the names of the locations, may be important in applied, urban, or even small group ethnographies (e.g., a jewelry store).

Props or Relevant Objects

An important aspect of any ethnography (closely related to space utilization) is props or objects that natives need to carry out their lives and activities. It is sometimes difficult to distinguish between a geographical location and a prop. A house, a boat, a tent, even a bed may be a place or an object that is crucial to the interaction and activities of the natives. The term "props" should generally be reserved for tools and utensils, though definitive separation from locations will often prove difficult. Perhaps the best advice is to describe locations and props together. They certainly constitute a continuum: We have previously suggested that locations can be subdivided following a filmmaking metaphor into locations, stages, and sets (see Volume 1, Section 10.2). "Scenes" take place on sets, and every scene has its contingent of "props." These are the objects the actors need to carry out their scenes.[2] Following this logic, the props appear much like still smaller spatial units below sets (for scenes).

It may be important also to view props in two ways. Some props are meaningful in the culture of the ethnographer. This needs to be stated because it will make the culture of the ethnography more comprehensible to readers who are natives of the ethnographer's culture. At the same time, it is crucial to obtain and present the view of the props *as seen by the natives*. It can never be taken for granted that the natives will see the world—or any, even minute, aspect of it—the same way as do the ethnographer and members of the ethnographer's culture. The only way to find out is through sensitive interviewing based on careful and systematic observation.

Actors (Life Histories)

Ethnographies are generally very casual about presenting their readers with a list of actors. Part of the problem may be that ethnographers are often embarrassed about the small size of their samples. They need not be. In an important paper on individual variation, D'Andrade (1970) showed that if three or more consultants agree on some ethnographic detail (in a relatively homogeneous culture), all (or most?) consultants will also agree. The problem is that the amount of sharing rarely (?) exceeds 60% and in less homogeneous societies may be well below 50%. Such lack of homogeneity may involve different age groups in a small community (Huff n.d.). Sixty percent of sharing (or less), however, still leaves much (following D'Andrade) that is unique to individual culture bearers. D'Andrade's examples of culture bearers are Navajo households and individual students at Stanford, both selected for maximal similarity.

Ethnographers should describe in their ethnographies the people who occupy the sets of their stages and locations; that is, some kind of "census" of collaborators is necessary. This census should be accompanied by a list of people who contributed information to the ethnography and a description of their role, status, occupation, sex, age, kin affiliation, and so on within the community or group. Only in very small groups with protracted fieldwork will the ethnographer talk to everyone; however, since this information reflects on the representativeness (sampling) of the ethnography, it should be made public in the ethnography. A section of names (usually coded)[3] and a description of each individual in as much detail as possible should precede the main body of every ethnography. In contrast to the dynamics of human interaction, this information could be viewed as a stationary map of the social universe. This list and description of participants in a culture serve a function comparable to character sketches written for a movie or play.

Just as in previous discussions, the native view of fellow actors may constitute another important part of this section. The depth and variety of such description—for example, that the same actor is viewed in many different ways by various factions of the group—may be dictated by the goals of the project rather than by general considerations.

Life histories (autobiographies) of various length (again depending on the goals of the study) can be included in the "static" map of actors.

Activities

The description of what consultants and other participants do can rightly be called the "meat" of an ethnography. Activities, consisting of actions and interactions, are the usual locus of the "problem" of an ethnography, be it an actual problem or the problem of a group's functioning in general. The ethnoscience approach is unequivocal in this area: *The native view of events must prevail.*

One approach is to focus on highly recurrent patterns such as daily activities (see Volume 1, Section 10.2). In some instances it may be useful to focus on units smaller than the whole day (e.g., a class) or on units larger than a day (e.g., weeks, months, years, and life histories). Of course, daily patterns of action and interaction better fit the heading on activities than do life histories. The latter may fit better in the section on actors because it gives one actor's view of his or her life.

The main vehicles of describing activities are verbal action plans, descriptions of participation by different actors in different action plans (see Section 3.1), and the decisions that the actors must make in order to negotiate their day's events (see Volume 1, Section 10.2 and also Figures 10.6 and 10.7; also Volume 2, Section 3.1). A human being's everyday activities require that he or she make very rapid taxonomic (Polanyi 1964) and other classificatory decisions. Thus it is clear that the lion's share of ethnoscience ethnographic techniques falls into the section describing activities and decisions. Taxonomies, part/whole structures, causal trees, and so on are all concerned with physical activities or verbal activities (conceptual activities) that human beings undertake while participating in their own daily cultures.

For a synthetic view of human activities, see section 10.1.2. We recommend the use of case material as an excellent source for cultural understanding.

Recurrent Patterns

Some activities and conceptual themes (perhaps described as "topics" of conversation) are all pervasive and recur continuously. Michael Agar (1979) has written perceptively on the extraction of themes from ethnographic materials. The key to such extraction is the frequent repetition and recurrence of activities or topics of conversation. These can also be called "preoccupations." Their importance is assumed because of the frequency with which they surface in everyday life. Whether these themes are conscious or largely ignored as topics in native focal awareness is an important datum but in either case should not preclude the need for discussing themes with consultants.

The boundaries between implicit (out of awareness) and explicit (retrievable and therefore in awareness) aspects of culture are not constant across its members. The differential distribution of cultural knowledge among natives argues for a different boundary for each individual. The act of acquiring some types of new knowledge may be viewed as moving previously implicit knowledge into the domain of the explicit. That seems to be one of the major distinctions between experts and laypersons: The former can make a lot more explicit than can the latter.

It is therefore imperative that all themes of a cultural system established by analytical methods (e.g., frequency counts of cases) be checked with native consultants. Some of them may be surprised, but they still may be able to comment cogently on a theme once it is pointed out. Others (and this is a reaction we have encountered often) may say that they tried to explain something to us several times before, but we apparently had to discover it for ourselves. Again, very useful discussions and rich additional supporting case material may follow.

Sometimes ethnographers have reduced entire complex cultures to a small set of key themes (e.g., Benedict 1934; C. Kluckhohn 1949; Hsu 1953). The practice in recent years has been more popular outside anthropology. We offer no analytical techniques that will uncover such sweeping thematic patterns. Our bias may err on the opposite side. It is inconceivable to us that the rich propositional knowledge about the world available in any culture will ever be strictly (deductively) derivable from a few (fewer than a dozen) fundamental propositions.

It may be useful to make a distinction here between two types of cultural knowledge. The first is *substantive cultural knowledge*—what most ethnoscience techniques are best suited for. This knowledge contains a description of what is actually known. It is very unlikely that such knowledge can ever be reduced to a few basic propositions. The second is meta-cultural knowledge, or knowledge about substantive cultural knowledge, and concerns how knowledge is acquired (styles of learning, e.g., Bateson's [1942] deuterolearning), how to interact with various people of different statuses and roles, and so on. It is much more likely that meta-cultural knowledge can be reduced to a few basic premises from which the entire system may be derived.

In Wallace's terms (1961), meta-knowledge resembles etiquette: "knowing how" (Ryle 1946) to do things, including verbally. This type of knowledge may be shared and may pervade a society. It is instrumental in organizing cultural uniformity and the transmission of this uniformity.

Substantive knowledge is "knowing that" (Ryle 1946). It is involved in the organization of cultural diversity—for example, the division of labor.

It is likely that themes are statements of meta-knowledge that emerge from repetitious statements of substantive knowledge. In other words, meta-knowledge, whenever not explicitly stated, can be gleaned only indirectly from themes through the frequency of their recurrence in one's data base.

Justification

It is not clear at which point in an ethnography one should justify (why? including how?) the very existence of the ethnography at hand. This could conceivably be done in the introduction, or could be placed near the end or even in an appendix. Certainly detailed discussions of methodology (how?) do not belong in the body of an ethnography. The average reader is not interested in how the ethnography was obtained as long as he or she retains a feeling for the quality, validity, and reliability of the monograph. On the other hand, for fellow ethnographers a methodological section may be of great importance. Under no circumstances should it be left out, but its placement should be dictated by the anticipated readership.

The justification of a project usually should be placed early in the work, perhaps in the introduction. The problem with many ethnographic projects is that they may have only two tenuously related justifications—first, that the ethnography is logical, timely, stresses importance, and so on in the culture of the ethnographer and/or in the profession. This could be called "external justification." A number of ethnographic projects can be justified on these grounds. There is a problem in anthropological theory (e.g., cultural evolution, theory of the origin of the state, a general theory of folk medicine, theories of migration, dispute settlements, etc.) that requires ethnographic data in order to test (validate, replicate) its generalizations.

These "professional" justifications will usually be inadequate for a justification of the project in the eyes of the natives. This is the second justification. The anthropologist's interest in the history or evolution of human-kind may leave the natives unmoved. They may face overwhelming problems of coping with their everyday lives and show little enthusiasm for humanity as a whole. Generally, eliciting useful information may be perceived as *taking things away* and often as a nefarious scheme by which the ethnographer gets rich at the expense of the natives. This may be especially true if the knowledge that consultants give to the ethnographer is considered valuable in their own culture. Even if the ethnographer pays for information, it may not place him or her above suspicion. If an ethnographer is willing to spend good money on such information, how much more valuable must such data be in the ethnographer's home culture? After all, he or she not only pays the going price but has also gone to great expense to get at the source of information.

It is inexcusable to undertake fieldwork in today's worldwide political situation without considering benefits that may accrue to the natives themselves. There is virtually no ethnographic project, no matter how obscure a theoretical point it tries to corroborate, that cannot by redirection or judicious choice of the field site actually contribute to the welfare of the natives. *The Anatomical Atlas of the Navajo* (Werner *et al.* 1984), though encyclopedic in conception, is a good example.

Case 9.4 Justification of* The Anatomical Atlas of the Navajo *(Werner* et al. *1984)

Our intention was to do basic research on the nature of lexical/semantic fields. It was clear that any domain of knowledge would have been appropriate as long as it was in the "focus" of Navajo culture. This focus is usually considered to be health and disease. A brief survey of the Western Reservation revealed that non-Navajo physicians and nurses considered the lack of anatomical terms in Navajo to be a major impediment to quality medical care for the Navajo. Interestingly, at this point in our research we had already collected over 200 anatomical terms from existing Navajo dictionaries. It was obvious that a great service could be performed for the quality of health care by providing health practitioners with an anatomical atlas of Navajo body parts. This was indeed the case.

To our surprise, the physicians and nurses acknowledged the existence of over 500 named anatomical parts in Navajo without much resistance. The ultimate surprise for us was that the *Atlas* proved to be a valuable reference work for Navajo driver-interpreters, Navajo nurses, and Navajo patient advocates.

Use of Graphs and Charts

This book is heavily biased toward the uses of graphs and charts, yet we recommend their use with great care. Graphs and charts can succinctly summarize complex data. However, no illustration can stand entirely on its own without some explanation. The decision to include charts and graphs is in large part based on these explanations. If a complex chart requires pages of prose to make it intelligible, it is best omitted. On the other hand, if a graph can be explained in a few lines, its use may be worthwhile.

Another factor affecting the use of graphs is the prejudices of the ethnography's consumers. If these people do not like graphs or charts, it is a waste of time and effort to include them. If they appreciate visual representations of information, graphs and charts can be used liberally.

It is important to remember that the graphs and charts we discuss in this book are aids, usually to assure as complete a coverage of a field of knowledge as possible. They show gaps in the patterns that may be significant for the culture under study. The ethnographer should use them liberally in his or her analysis. How much of a given graph and how many graphs to include in the final draft of the ethnographic report is a matter of carefully considered judgment.

Comprehensive Conclusions

Only unusual readers find every ethnographic tidbit presented in the pages of an ethnography of interest, especially in the case of ethnographic research for a "client" who may be totally indifferent to the details. A comprehensive conclusion often holds the answer. Busy administrators do not want to hear the minutiae of a problem area on which they require information. We have found a five-page executive summary and conclusions to be the most adequate size for abstracting a lengthy ethnography.

Case 9.5 Ethnography of the Tower Rock Community

> At the end of a summer's fieldwork, during which she discovered several major reasons for the strained relations between Lava Flow State Park and the Tower Rock community (Arizona), Julie Ahern produced a 35-page ethnography. It contained the causal tree we presented in Case 6.1. Both state park officials and the Tower Rock community felt it was important to read her report. We assumed that no one would read a 35-page report fully. A five-page comprehensive abstract was well received by park officials. Several commented that they "had learned something new from Julie's report." Whether the report will result in action to improve relations between park and community remains to be seen.

There may be instances in which even a five-page summary may be more than busy individuals are willing to read. In such cases our strategy has been to preface the ethnography with a five-page comprehensive summary and conclusions, and to preface that by a one-page summary of the comprehensive summary and conclusions. If a client will not read a well-composed abstract of one page, carefully edited for style and salient content, he or she will not read anything and the ethnographic study might have been a complete waste.

Often it may be important for the ethnographer to ascertain who, in fact, will read the ethnography or parts of it. Giving an ethnography and the comprehensive summary and conclusions to the right aide of a busy client may improve the chances of implementation of the ethnographer's recommendations. Since we assume that such recommendations will always be for the benefit of the natives, it is in the ethnographer's interest and is part of his or her ethical responsibility to ensure (as completely as possible) that beneficial recommendations reach responsible parties who can implement them.

Appendices

Not all clients or consumers of ethnographies will fail to read the entire ethnography. Yet the comprehensive summary remains important because it gives the reader a "cognitive map" of what to expect and may also direct his or her attention to particular sections that may be more important than others.

Ethnographers, on the other hand, have often obtained data under trying circumstances and frequently resist deleting data that required intense effort to acquire. In section 10.2.2, on drafting the ethnography, we will discuss the need for ruthlessly excluding unnecessary, repetitious, or otherwise distracting data. Such ruthlessness may be very painful to an ethnographer. In such situations we use the appendices as a solution. Anything that may be relevant to the ethnography but does not directly contribute to improved comprehension of it should be moved to the appendices. For example, methodological discussions of possible interest to other ethnographers should be stated, but not for the general reader. If such a reader wants to know more about methodology, the information is readily available in an appendix. Similarly, if one first-rate case clearly illustrates a generalization, any remaining similar cases belong in an appendix with proper cross-referencing (for example, "Seventeen similar cases are presented in Appendix I").

Thus the appendix assumes an important role in every ethnography: It saves the reader from having to wade through distracting detail. At the same time, it gives the suffering ethnographer a place to put marginally relevant, "pet" data. Appendices serve to maintain everyone's mental health.

9.5.2 Checklist of Headings for Encyclopedias

The organization of an encyclopedic ethnography is simpler than the headings for an ethnography. There are two reasons for this. First, an encyclopedia consists of an introduction and a body of encyclopedic knowledge. Second, the organization of encyclopedic data is governed by principles of native knowledge and cannot be prescribed in advance. Minimally, an encyclopedic ethnography should have the following headings and/or cover the following topics:

Need for the Study

No one should undertake an encyclopedic study unless some need for it exists. The need may be dictated by contributions to the native culture. For example, the need for *The Anatomical Atlas of the Navajo* (Werner *et al.* 1984) emerged out of the ignorance of non-Navajo health professionals about the richness of Navajo anatomical knowledge. Additional needs included the improvement of medical communication and a need that emerged during the elicitation and tests of the *Atlas* in Navajo health facilities: the need for a reference work by Navajo health personnel.

Equally legitimate needs are contributions to theoretical problems. For example, our work on the Navajo "psychological" vocabulary (still ongoing) has been seen as a contribution to the understanding of lexical/semantic fields of "abstract" terminological systems.

The best justification combines equal contributions to native culture and to theoretical knowledge. For example, we hope that our work on Navajo psychological terminology will contribute to theory in anthropology and to practice and application in the Navajo mental health system.

Again, the physical location the justification for a study is usually the introduction to the body of encyclopedic data.

History

To explain the need for a study to an audience of readers requires a historical account of what has already been done. This may appear as both a review of the relevant literature and other attempts to undertake research with similar aims and fulfilling (or trying to fulfill) similar needs. This historical section requires a discussion of why previous efforts were inadequate, what they did accomplish, and in what ways the current study supersedes its precursors. The physical location of the historical account of events leading up to the present study is usually placed in the introduction.

Geography

The introduction is probably the best place to discuss the study's physical location, which geographical areas were covered and how thoroughly. This topic should also include reasons for covering some areas less completely than others. The assumption is that it is usually impossible, impractical, or justifiably unnecessary to cover all areas equally. This section should also discuss sampling procedures that may have been employed to validate data, especially if different procedures were followed in different geographical areas.

Case 9.6 The Geography of **The Anatomical Atlas of the Navajo** *(Werner* **et al.** *1984)*

In our work on *The Anatomical Atlas of the Navajo* we did most of our elicitation on the Western Navajo Reservation because this area contains the most traditional Navajo population. A search for dialectical variation on the Eastern Reservation was conducted by sampling chanters (medicine men) and by presenting them with the lists of anatomical terms collected in the West for acceptance or rejection. Following classifications by ethnographic coworkers from the West, we used consultants in the East, but only as informants, to validate information and contribute Eastern variant terms.

Personnel

All the people who contributed to an ethnographic monograph (ethnographic or encyclopedic) should be acknowledged. This is best accomplished in the introduction. There are two types of personnel to be discussed.

(1) The ethnographer or ethnographers, including research collaborators who participated in gathering the data, should be acknowledged. If different personnel concentrated their efforts on different aspects of the monograph, this should be mentioned. Equally important, especially for a long-term project, are the dates of association of various contributors. Any other factors relevant to the personnel of a particular project ought to be included. Figure 9.7 illustrates the association of personnel with a multiyear project.

(2) The natives, especially consultants who contributed significantly to the project, should be mentioned. Whether to use their actual names or pseudonyms depends on the circumstances. If consultants want the credit, their real names should be used. If they prefer to remain anonymous, pseudonyms are called for. The use of *actual names or coded names* is something requiring discussion with each contributor/consultant. In the same population, some consultants may want to be associated with the project publicly, whereas others would rather keep their association out of the public eye. It is conceivable that a particular consultant may want his or her name mentioned on certain topics (usually if he or she is considered an expert in the area) while preferring anonymity in other areas, where he or she is less certain of the acceptance of his or her knowledge by the native population.

With the increasing awareness of native populations about what anthropologists do and how the academic community operates, the issue of publicly recognizing contributors needs to be openly discussed with each consultant. Our policy is to give public recognition whenever possible, but we are also sensitive to the protection of the privacy of some consultants if they so desire. We prefer ethnically or linguistically appropriate names to code letters or numbers. Names are easier to remember than opaque codes, and readers have an easier time following the same person or persons through the pages of the monograph. By using actual names the reader can also form a clearer idea about the extent of the ethnographer's sample without having to resort to time-consuming tabulations of coded names.

Organizational Principle of the Encyclopedia

From the point of view of presenting encyclopedic data, organization is a key issue. By consistently following the basic tenet of respect for native knowledge,

	Year								
	48	49	50	51	52	53	54	55	56
Alexander Leighton	X	X	X	X	X	X	X	X	X
John Adair	X	X	X	X	X				
Tom Sasaki*	X	X	X	X	X	X	X	X	X
Clifford Barnett			X						
Milton Barnett		X							
John Collier Jr.					X	X			
Howard French						X			
Elizabeth Green		X							
Ralph Leubben					X	X			
John Musgrave		X							
David Olmstead			X						
Seymour Parker							X		
William Ross*					X	X			
William Skinner	X								
Laila Shukry*					X				
Philip Sottong					X				
Gordon Streib			X	X					
Robert Textor			X						
Marc-Adelard Tremblay					X				
Total Participants/year	4	6	7	4	9	6	3	2	2

* = individuals who completed dissertation pertaining to Fruitland
NOTE: This table is adapted from Sasaki (1960:212-213). It shows the years and names of participants in the project. Note the start-up phase (1948), the major thrust (1949-1953), and the winding-down phase (1954-1956). Readers may obtain, an excellent view both of the personnel associated with the project and the duration of their associations. It also shows the peak in 1952, the rapid start, and gradual finish.

Figure 9.7 Participants in Fruitland Project

we insist that the organization of encyclopedic knowledge be based on principles endorsed by the natives. It hardly makes sense to seek out native knowledge if it is ignored in the final presentation. In other words, after the analysis of interviews and the discovery of native lexical/semantic structures, an equally vigorous effort should be directed toward the best *presentation of the data from the native point of view*. It was out of ignorance of Navajo organizational principles for anatomical knowledge that we first presented the human body from head to toe in *The Anatomical Atlas of the Navajo* (Werner *et al.* 1984). It would have been ethnocentric to persist in this presentation given the objection of our consultants and their insistence that the proper order of presentation is from foot to head.

Very often the organization of an encyclopedic project is an inevitable consequence of the structure of the data.

Case 9.7 **The Navajo Ethno-Medical Encyclopaedia,** ***Volume 3 (Austin-Garrison & Werner, in preparation)***

It seems self-evident now, but the best organizational principle was not at all clear to us when Martha A. Austin-Garrison compiled the first draft of Volume 3, *Marriage, Conception, Pregnancy, and Birth*. The organizational principle of this volume was obviously a plan. On the most general level the Navajo experts presented five major sections:

(1) marriage and how one contracts one appropriately;
(2) the Navajo theory of conception (this is in part a plan outlining the sequence of events leading up to conception and in part discursive theoretical knowledge);
(3) pregnancy and its complications (this section outlines the stages of pregnancy, such as the manifestation of the Little Spirit Wind [soul] when the fetus first moves. It also includes a discussion of the complications in pregnancy);
(4) birth and the difficulties associated with it, including cures and remedies (this section describes the events surrounding giving birth in a hogan, gives alternatives, and discusses the complications that may ensue during delivery. Subplans discuss the procedures for remedying some of the complications);
(5) the duties of women and men toward their children, the nature of child development, and the expectations of proper conduct by the child.

The last section is not in plan form at all; it is a theoretical treatise on the nature of children and what is required by the parents to promote the child to successful adulthood. Thus although the overall principle of organization is a sequential plan, it is interspersed with case material systems of classification (e.g., folk taxonomies) and folk-theoretical discussion.

In our current work with *The Navajo Ethno-Medical Encyclopaedia* we spend considerable effort with each volume (out of a total of ten) to make sure that the organizational principles are Navajo in spirit and letter. It is worthwhile to note that the division of Navajo ethnomedical knowledge into ten volumes also follows Navajo principles. The range of topics for the volumes was established by two conferences of chanters (medicine men) organized by Shonnie Allen and Martha A. Austin-Garrison, our Navajo researcher/collaborators.

The Anatomical Atlas of the Navajo is organized according to the ordering of body parts in Navajo ceremonials, songs, and prayers. Within this schema, the major principle of organization is the part/whole relation. Interspersed are folk taxonomies (e.g., the types of toes). Volume 3 of *The Navajo Ethno-Medical Encyclopaedia*, as with previous material, is organized following a plan with interspersed cases, classifications, and discursive theories. On the other hand, Volume 6, *Disease and Sickness*, is organized predominantly taxonomically. Diseases and their classification form the major focus of this volume.

Other principles of organization are conceivable. Julie Ahern's presentation of causes of Lava Flow State Park's infamy in the eyes of the surrounding Navajo community is a causal tree structure (see Case 6.1). Almost any atomic lexical/semantic relation (modification, taxonomy, or queueing), or any complex lexical/semantic relation (e.g., part/whole, cause or, reason for, etc.), if it is capable of forming the organizational principle of a lexical/semantic field or a domain of cultural knowledge, is a suitable principle for organizing and presenting encyclopedic data.

It is important to note that not all complex relations of the canonical form "A is the C OF B" (where the preposition "OF" is also variable, i.e., it may be replaced in some contexts by "for," "about," etc.) form large lexical/semantic fields. Relations that do not organize large cultural domains are not suitable as organizational principles for encyclopedic knowledge. For example, the relation "is used for" attaches to large numbers of useful objects without forming a cogent domain of cultural knowledge. The set of all objects that may be used for something is very large, but because it is such a disparate set, nothing is gained by using it as the principle of organization for any aspect of cultural knowledge. However, caution is appropriate. One of our consultants insisted that the best organizational principle for plants is not morphology (flexibility, woodyness, thorns) but their use for medicine (externally and internally), food, shelter, and so on.

NOTES

1. Chapter 7 later became Part 2 and 7.1 and 7.2 became respectively Chapters 9. 10. Here we will keep the old numbering schema.

2. Note our departure from Spradley's use of the term "scene" (see also Volume 1, Section 7.1.2, Note 2 and Section 10.2.1, Note 2).

3. We prefer plausible and appropriate code names to initials, letters, or numbers in the final ethnography.

Chapter 10

Writing the Ethnographic Report

10.0 INTRODUCTION

Once the data are analyzed and organized into a reasonable plan that outlines one's ethnography or encyclopedia in some plausible linear order, writing can commence. Before discussing the actual craft of writing, we need to review ethnographic writing styles.

10.1 STYLES OF WRITING

We discuss four styles: (1) analytic, (2) synthetic or systemic, (3) building to a climax, and (4) climax first. These four styles could be set up in the form of a cross-classification in a fourfold table, but this would not be very useful. Every good ethnography should have analytic and synthetic (systemic) parts. Whether to present one's conclusion (climax) first or last depends on the consumers of the ethnography or encyclopedia.

10.1.1 Analytical Style

In the analytical approach we take things apart and analyze them. Listing all locations, stages, and sets with appropriate props is an analytical procedure, as is listing all the actors and giving each a "job description." Listing activities is also an analytical procedure. The simplest analytical structure is a list; a more complex structure is a tree.

Analyzing data (from interview texts, for example) and presenting the result in list or "tree" form is clearly a valuable analytical procedure. Our educational system appears to be geared to analytical (usually part/whole or taxonomic) thinking.

This has also been called more generally the "taxonomic approach"—for example, as used by transformationalists in modern linguistics who speak of the earlier paradigm of structural linguistics as "taxonomic linguistics." Their usage is justified because structural (taxonomic) linguistics was highly analytical. The major task of the linguist was to identify the units of human language, first on the phonological (sound) level. The linguist specifies the phonetic properties (contexts, environments) of language specific sounds, its phonemes. Second, he or she specifies the minimal grammatical units (morphemes), inventories all of them, and gives the environments (language contexts) in which they occur. Because there was no explicit syntactic theory specifying (in sufficient, explicit detail) the co-occurrence possibilities and formal restrictions, the language under investigation was analyzed in a real sense but never wholly reconstructed.

Analytical procedures dismantle things. This is an important aspect of understanding them. Reassembling the parts to form a complete and functioning system is a much more difficult task.

10.1.2 Synthetic Style

There are a number of ways to achieve synthesis or, after an analysis, resynthesis; that is, to display a system (ethnographic or encyclopedic in this context) as a functioning whole. Before discussing possible methodologies for synthesis, we illustrate the contrast between analytical and synthetic (systemic) knowledge with an example.

Case 10.1 Pastoral Example of Synthesis and Analysis

Let us imagine a system that consists of four components: sheep, dogs, a corral, and logs. Let us also assume that there are two types of human beings: analytic people and synthetic people. Sets of objects, like the four items mentioned above, have been presented to varieties of human experimental subjects for classification. It appears that our educational system stresses analytical thinking (e.g., Manes 1976). Uneducated adults and children tend to give "functional" definitions (e.g., "A table is what we eat on"). We call this the synthetic style. Our educational system seems to discourage it, except on the highest levels where it reenters education (with difficulty) as some aspect of "systems theory." A tutored child or adult (after about eighth grade) gives "analytical" definitions (e.g., "A table is a piece of furniture which . . ."). The attributes of "table" (symbolized by the ellipsis) are most usually technical modifiers of "furniture" (e.g., rigid surface, pedestal of three or more legs, etc.) rather than "functional" attributes such as "eating on." If we submit our pastoral example to the two types of personalities, we may find the following:

(1) The analytic person will classify the four objects into two sets of two members each: (a) sheep and dogs and (b) corral and logs. This classification may be justified (correctly) on the grounds that sheep and dogs are animate and belong together, whereas corrals and logs are inanimate and therefore also belong together.

(2) The synthetic person is most likely to give a story: "The sheep are in the corral and are guarded by the dogs. The corral is made of logs."

The point of this case is that in order to understand fully the workings of a human group (culture) or of some system of cultural knowledge, both approaches—the analytic and the synthetic (systemic)—are important. It is not enough to take things apart; we must also show how things work together.

The analytic style is represented by lists (trees) or inventories. The synthetic (systematic) style is more difficult to capture. A short story or novel can sometimes give a reader a more complete synthetic view of a culture than an analytical ethnography.

Case 10.2 Clyde Kluckhohn versus Oliver LaFarge

In 1946 Clyde Kluckhohn and Dorothea Leighton wrote a well-known ethnography, *The Navaho*. It is highly analytic. Chapter titles include such topics as social organization, Religion, Economy, and "The Tongue of the People." One gets a very good feeling of what the parts of Navajo life were like before World War II. Yet the reader gets very little feeling for what Navajo life *as a whole* was like during that period.

Oliver LaFarge's novel *Laughing Boy* (1929)[1] is set in a similar period. It captivates the reader from the first page and gives readers (students) a better synthetic view of Navajo culture—a feeling for the functioning whole of traditional culture after "pacification" (1864-1868)—than the first-rate ethnography of Kluckhohn and Leighton.

Most ethnographies written in the past cover the ground between being extremely analytical and extremely synthetic. The most synthetic approaches in discursive language appear to be the short story or the novel. Life histories, or descriptions of daily activities, are another vehicle for presenting the synthetic view. Oscar Lewis's *Five Families* (1959) describes five typical days in the lives of five families; his *Children of Sanchez* (1961) describes one of the five families through the life histories of four of its members.

More contemporary methods for presenting the synthetic view may be achieved by designing a board game simulating a social system or an actual computer simulation of that system. For computer simulation of an encyclopedic knowledge system, Werner's (1977) Synthetic Informant Model shows how the system operates as a whole.

All of these newer synthetic techniques are underexplored in ethnography. The ideal approach appears to be analysis through synthesis. What this entails may be best illustrated through an encyclopedic example.

Case 10.3 Analysis Through Synthesis

It is conceivable to imagine a computer program that could, by asking appropriate questions (e.g., taxonomic questions), "automatically" analyze a sys-

> tem of cultural knowledge.[2] This program could be viewed as an "analytical" machine. It may be equally conceivable to imagine a computer program that could, by being asked appropriate questions (after information was somehow programmed into it), respond with appropriate answers. This program could be viewed as a "synthetic" machine: Given proper deductive power (deductive synthetic power) it could deduce answers to questions for which it did not have explicit, preprogrammed answers. It may also be conceivable to design a computer program combining the advantages of the two machines: It could give information appropriately (by synthesizing old knowledge); it could also absorb (learn) new knowledge and incorporate it in its memory. The resulting machine would do analysis by synthesis and/or synthesis by analysis; that is, it could output the data in either analytic or synthetic form.

Generative models of the grammar of human languages do for grammar what our "machine" could do for cultural knowledge, except that the analysis is done by hand (as opposed to by computer program). The linguist analyzes the grammatical units of a language and then proposes a generative grammar. This grammar generates sets of sentences that can be presented to consultants for acceptance or rejection. The quality of the analysis by hand is checked by the synthesis of the generative apparatus of the proposed grammar.

Building a synthetic/analytic machine for cultural knowledge may prove difficult; however, if we are serious about the systemic approach to ethnography and cultural knowledge, experimentation along these lines may advance the presentation of the synthetic (systemic) aspects of human cultures.

10.1.3 Building to a Climax

The synthetic style, especially if presented in the form of a novel or short story, usually has a plot, and a plot usually builds to a climax. This is a fine approach if the ethnographer is skilled enough to maintain suspense that will keep the reader reading. The conclusion is often seen as the climax of an ethnographic report. The same need for sustaining interest prevails here. Some writers insist on writing their conclusions (the systemic part of their ethnography) last. They do this in the face of common knowledge that the clever reader, who almost always is pressed for time, usually reads the introduction and the conclusions first.

Unless the ethnographer is a very clever and skillful writer, we cannot recommend building to a climax in ethnographies, and certainly not for encyclopedias. Especially when working for a client, the client will want the results first and the documentation later. Unfortunately, the world is full of editors who still insist on giving the conclusions last. They should be condemned to reading the midsections of ethnographies for eternity.

10.1.4 Climax First

C.F. Voegelin championed this style of writing in the *International Journal of American Linguistics*. All articles in *IJAL* are edited so that the introduction and conclusions are combined in the first section of the paper. The documentation follows. Some researchers find it distressing that the papers often end rather abruptly without "tying up loose ends." They overlook the fact that the "loose ends" come together in the introductory section.

We recommend this style of writing for ethnographies. Encyclopedias usually do not have a clear-cut temporal progression, so the "climax first" approach seems to fit them naturally. In ethnographies, the introductory remarks and the conclusion should form one section at the beginning or two separate subsections of the introduction, especially if the ethnography is intended for a client. Putting the reasons he or she wanted to do the ethnography first (the statement of the "problem") and what he or she actually obtained from commissioning the ethnography (the "solution") next seems to us good practice. We covered this topic also in the section on a comprehensive summary (9.5.1).

10.2 CRAFT OF WRITING

There are two fundamental prerequisites to good writing: First, the ethnographer needs to know who the audience is. Sometimes a brief ethnographic investigation to clarify who will read the ethnographic product can be very helpful. Second is the actual "nuts and bolts" aspects of producing a report of reasonable organization and polish.

10.2.1 Know Your Audience

Every manual on how to write well stresses that the writer had best know who he or she is writing for. A procedure generally accepted involves selecting one personally known representative of the group of potential readers and writing the report as if it were specifically for that reader. Spradley (personal communication) has recommended that students doing ethnographic exercises should address them to their mothers. "Dear Mom:" may be an appropriate beginning for any ethnography.

Spradley's approach covers another important aspect of writing: Never overestimate the technical knowledge of your audience. Coleman and Miller (1967) reported that college sophomores learn more from material written on the fifth-grade level than from materials written on "their" level. The general rule that the less time a reader needs for deciphering a sentence the more time he or she has for understanding the ideas should be taken seriously. This is not always easy; however, it pays off in almost every case. We have stressed this point in proposal writing (see Volume 1, Section 5.1): Write for the intelligent reviewer who has some good general knowledge at his or her disposal. Do not write for the narrow technical specialist. This is equally true for ethnographies and encyclopedias. It is even more true if the ethnographer is writing for a client who could not care less about social science and/or ethnoscience but who wants to discover something useful about a social system or a system of knowledge. It is unrealistic to assume that such a consumer will learn the latest wrinkle in, say, taxonomic theory. It is more important for a client to understand generally what is happening. That understanding must be presented in a language that he or she can understand and use in dealing with the "problem" that originally prompted the commissioning of the ethnography.

10.2.2 Nuts and Bolts of Writing

Before any writer can apply the tricks of the trade, writing must commence. The most serious problem that stands in the way of starting to write is "writer's block."

Combatting Writer's Block

Writer's block means staring at a white sheet of paper on a table or in a typewriter and being unable to begin writing. Often writer's block takes subtle forms of procrastination. Some writers will go to extraordinary lengths to avoid writing their first paragraph. They will sharpen all their pencils, arrange all papers very neatly, discover a sticking key that needs to be oiled or a type element that needs cleaning. There is an endless variety of preliminary activities that need to be done and that effectively postpone writing the first paragraph.

Part of the problem in confronting writer's block is that many beginning writers do not realize that a good piece of writing is inevitably the result of several drafts. It is usually the commitment to a given linear order that causes the reluctance to start; however, with several drafts (see the next section), there is no reason for fearing a rigid commitment. Perhaps the most important tools for writing are scissors and paste or tape. It is much easier to change the order of presentation if one has something on paper than to change it in the abstract on a blank page.

Good planning and preparation of data (Chapter 9) are the most important steps toward starting to write easily. With yellow card analysis completed (Section 9.1.2) or a stack of carefully encoded keysort edge-punch cards (Section 1.4.3) and/or a well-organized scratch list (Section 9.4) or a computer program that organizes one's outline, there should be no serious problem beginning. Good, preorganized data makes the start easy.

Sometimes even organized writers insist on starting their ethnographic report with the introduction. That is almost certainly asking for trouble. It is possible to write an introduction following a detailed outline of presentation of the major data. In our experience, however, writing the body of a report is full of surprises. The very act of writing may dredge up information from memory or reveal the relevance of data that were to be used elsewhere, making the experienced writer wary of any certainty about the exact nature of the finished product.

It also happens that the first few pages are written with difficulty. There is a warm-up period in writing after which the words will flow with greater ease. It is much better to leave such early awkwardness (which should be edited out later anyway) in the body of the ethnography rather than in the introduction.

The writer should put his or her best foot forward in the introductory remarks. A good introduction sets the stage for the entire written product. At the same time, it should serve as a true introduction that leads the reader into the ethnography. The best policy, therefore, is to write the introduction last.

Sometimes even the best of preparation, with yellow cards, keysorts, organized scratch lists, or computers, will not ease the ethnographer into writing. The very fact of commitment to paper can be paralyzing. The key to overcoming this paralysis is to outwit one's own psyche. Sometimes a fast-approaching deadline generates enough anxiety to penetrate the writer's block. Unfortunately, this is a last-minute measure and the writing may suffer from it due to lack of time for revision.

Another way of overcoming the blockage is to shift into another medium of communication. Writing a letter to a friend instead of Chapter 1 may get a writer started. The letter can be sent after duplicating it for cut-and-paste editing. There is no reason why a letter to a friend, spouse, or relative could not form the nucleus of an ethnographic monograph.

One of our favorite shifts of media is to give a lecture on the topic. This can be a formal lecture before an academic or professional audience or an informal report to one's friends, colleagues, or students. A couple of friends after dinner, with plenty of refreshments, can form an excellent audience with which to start. The key to the procedure is a tape recorder. It could be hidden or in plain view, as long as the writer's block is not replaced by microphone fright. Hanging the microphone in laveliere fashion around one's neck gets it out of view and tends to reduce anxiety.

Recording the ethnography presented from organized notes or from memory is the next step. It represents a potential core around which the rest (or the full version) of the ethnography can be constructed. It is conceivable that someone may want to give the recording of an informal report or a lecture to a transcription secretary. Those few who are able to speak in flawless prose may be able to get away with this and obtain reasonable results. A much more effective method (though at first more tedious) is for the ethnographer to do the transcription. But just as we recommended earlier for interviews in which initial recording is not possible (see Volume 1, Section 13.5), we suggest stimulus rather than verbatim transcription. That is, rather than writing down what was said word for word, the transcriber uses the recording as a stimulus for his or her own memory. If the ethnographer's memory is also supplemented by a carefully organized plan for the monograph, writing should begin to flow easily. If one gets stuck, it is always possible to continue the transcription verbatim. In our experience the writer is soon overwhelmed by the richness of his or her memory and the availability of a detailed data base and begins to elaborate on the original recording with the greatest of ease.

First Draft and Beyond

For the writer who must start an ethnography, the first draft looms large. It is actually the least important draft of all revisions prior to the final product. It is least important because it is only raw material from which a polished ethnography will, with hard work, emerge.

The first step in preparing a first draft is to make subsequent revisions as easy as possible. The most important aspect of first draft writing is to leave enough space for corrections, insertions, revisions, and cutting and pasting. Some typewriters can triple space. On IBM Selectrics, which have only double spacing, hitting the carriage return twice will give quadruple spacing. We have written first drafts triple-triple spaced, the main advantage being that there is usually no need to write in the margins. There is enough room between lines to insert full sentences or even longer passages. In subsequent cutting and pasting it is easier to cut lines—even inserted lines—than marginal insertions that may go all over the remaining white space on a page. Every writer should assume as a matter of course that cutting and pasting is essential to the production of any polished, well-organized final product. Word processors have made the editing process even easier.

The next step is to edit in two colors. Copy editors usually use a blue and a red pencil, but any combination of a dark color and red will do. There are two fundamental principles: (1) Everything in red is *instruction* to the typist; thus, balloons for insertions, deletions, and any other instruction (e.g., about paragraphing) should be written in red. (2) Anything to be typed should be in the dark color. Thus words or letters to be inserted, underlinings, and so on should be in a dark color. The little extra work of using two colors will pay off in ease of operation. Even when typing our own drafts, using only one color is confusing. The corrections are made, sometimes days apart from the actual typing of the draft, and a clear separation of instructions (meta-messages) from the actual messages to be typed is always helpful and speeds typing. A typist accustomed to the use of two colors will have a much easier time preparing a draft efficiently than one who is forced to interpret a maze of a single color.

There are a number of ways to cut and paste. A pair of paper scissors and paste are the minimum requirement, but paste is messy. Stapling cut pieces into their proper location is also possible, but sheets of typing paper full of staples are difficult to sort and stack. We prefer to use any kind of plastic tape on which one can type or write. It is often unavoidable to have to write across a piece of tape. Finding that a piece of tape does not take ink or pencil can be maddening.

There are several ways to facilitate cutting and pasting. The best method we have found (especially in the first draft) is to use as many different headings as possible. Almost every paragraph could have a title that summarizes its content for quick inspection. For smoother writing, the profusion of titles may be reduced in later drafts, but for getting organized nothing is more helpful than many detailed titles and subtitles.

A numbering system for titles is also helpful. If the numbers violate the style of the publication for which the manuscript is intended, they can be edited out in later drafts. The main advantage to numbered titles is that they allow a quick inspection of the level of a subtitle (such as the system used in this book): Single numbers are first level; two numbers (separated by a period) are second level; and so on.

After completing the first draft (of a section, chapter, or the entire ethnography), make a table of contents using the titles and subtitles introduced during typing.[3] One can regularly detect inconsistencies in the organization and sequencing of the titles.

The next step is to reorganize the titles. After this, we return to the text and reorganize it by cutting and pasting following the new arrangement. We sometimes do this several times. We reinspect the titles (some of which may have been rewritten during cutting and pasting) and cut and repaste the text if further changes are necessary.

Computerized editing systems make revising much easier. The first draft may be typed directly into the computer's memory. Some word-processing systems will automatically pull all titles, allowing the table of contents to be constructed with one simple command. Cutting and pasting is still more difficult because one cannot inspect the entire document at once; this is possible only in hard copy laid out as a mock-up. A livingroom floor or a classroom can be used for this purpose. It is amazing how much easier it is to edit an ethnography for organization if it is laid out and inspected as a whole. The CRT screens of computers allow only a "window" of a certain size (such as a page) for viewing a text; cutting and pasting (electronically moving portions of a text) is more difficult and strains the writer's memory more than physically handling paper pages. In computer editing, therefore, the procedure is often a recurring cycle of computer editing and inspection of hard copy.

Computerized editing, or just the cycle of editing, revising, and cutting and pasting, followed by an outline of titles tends to obscure the boundaries between successive drafts. The publishing house of John Wiley & Sons (1973) recommends five steps for arriving at a polished final draft, listed below. Keeping the purpose for each draft separate (as in the list below) has the advantage that the editor/writer can concentrate on *one* aspect of the ethnographic text at a time. Concentrating on *all* aspects of a text is difficult or impossible. It is like juggling too many balls at the same time. Some may get dropped and never picked up again.

> *First Draft:* Key questions are, Is everything there? Is too much there? We advise including what is missing and ruthlessly deleting repetitions or superfluous material. One of the most difficult aspects of editing one's own text is to discard what one has written with great effort. If the passage to be cut seems to have some merit, it may be moved to become a section of the appendix.
>
> *Second Draft:* Key questions are, Is the text clear? Is it clearly organized? Cutting and pasting will help organization. Clarity may be aided by editing out superfluous material that obscures the main point. Often, inexplicit or overly concise writing requires the addition of detail for clarity.
>
> *Third Draft:* Key questions are, Is the style smooth? Are there unexplained or unjustifiable "jumps"? Generally, short sentences are preferable to long ones; the active voice preferable to the passive. Sudden jumps may require either a section heading or the insertion of a transitional paragraph.

Fourth Draft: Key questions are, Are there too many words? Can what needs to be said be said more succinctly? Cutting down the number of words must be done carefully. A text can become so terse that it is difficult to read. The best advice is perhaps to check for the right number of words. There should be neither too many nor too few for clarity and ease of understanding.

Fifth Draft: Key question is, Is the style uniformly polished? It is difficult to maintain a uniform style throughout a long document. Various parts may have been written weeks or months apart, sometimes by different people. Reading the manuscript in one sitting may help. If several authors are involved, one (the most experienced writer) should be appointed "editor-in-chief" and his or her editorial word should be final.

Case 10.4 Editing Several Ethnographies

Occasionally a team puts out several ethnographies at once. The ethnographies in our book, *Six Navajo School Ethnographies* (Werner et al. 1976) were written at different times by different individuals but were presented to the client (the Navajo Division of Education of the Navajo Tribe) in one volume. Werner was selected as the editor-in-chief. Two important tasks had to be accomplished: (1) To make the ethnographies maximally comparable, the same headings were used in each. This was done by collating all headings from the six ethnographies and selecting from these a core list. Some of the ethnographies contained unique materials that were put under a set of unique headings. Making the table of contents of these ethnographies as uniform as possible solved (in part) problem 2, uniformity of style. Having an editor-in-chief whose editorial judgment was accepted by all authors helped smooth out the remaining inconsistencies of style.

10.2.3 Referencing

There are many different styles of referencing sources from the literature. We prefer a simplified form of the style used by the *American Anthropologist* and related journals. The advantage of this referencing system is that each time credit is given the author's name is typed (printed), making it easier to know *while reading* who was responsible for a particular statement. In all other, usually numbered systems, the source of a reference is available only at the bottom of the page or the end of the document.

The style of *American Anthropologist* is very straightforward: In the simplest case, it lists parenthetically within the text the name of the author followed by the year of publication (in parentheses or brackets), a colon and a page number or a range of page numbers—for example, Conklin (1962:72) or Frake (1969:12-14).

Two authors are listed with an ampersand (&), e.g., (Casagrande & Hale 1967). More than two authors are listed via "*et al.*" (e.g., Evens *et al.* 1980). In the bibliography, last name is listed first only for the first author. All other authors have their names listed in the regular order. Generally, first and middle names are not spelled out, though there is a tradition of spelling out first names for women. Perhaps that practice can now be abandoned.

References for articles within books should consistently follow this style. If an article appeared in Naroll and Cohen (1970), the reference to the article should only contain "in Naroll and Cohen (1970:17-75)," and there should be a full reference to Naroll and Cohen under the letter N in the bibliography.

10.2.4 Referencing Native Consultants

It is our firm conviction that consultants who have contributed to an ethnography deserve the same rigorous standard of referencing that scholars apply to referencing colleagues. It makes no sense to value the derived statement of a fellow ethnographer higher than the statements of native consultants who are the experts on their own culture.

No standard referencing style exists for consultants. We therefore make the following recommendations:

(1) Every reference to consultant's statements should contain the consultant's name. If necessary, the name should be coded. Using names (coded or not, but consistently) gives the reader an idea of who was quoted by the ethnographer more than others and/or how wide-ranging his or her evidence is.

(2) The name should be followed by the year in which a statement was made. This is crucial information. Sometimes if publication is delayed, it is extremely difficult to find out when particular fieldwork was conducted, or if the field trip lasted several years, or when exactly a particular statement was actually made.

Using these two simple conventions should expedite evaluation of the reliability of ethnographies. The argument that quotations from the ethnographer's journal (which should also be referenced) and quotations from transcriptions of interviews are not part of the public record and hence may be faked is beside the point. Fake evidence, no matter how perpetrated, is as serious a scholarly offense as plagiarism. That it does occur does not mean that it should be condoned. The highest standard of referencing native statements as well as other ethnographer's statements may make falsification of data more difficult and raise the standards of quality for ethnographies.

(3) Though we have not given year of statement in referencing consultant statements in the past, we usually treat each interview as a separate document. This may be useful where certain key consultants are interviewed more than once during a year or over several years.

(4) We paginate transcriptions of interviews. Following the analytical procedures of ethnoscience, individual sentences may be dispersed to different parts of the analyzed data. We recommend that the sentence number of quoted consultant's statement should also be given.

Thus a reference to a consultant statement may appear as follows:

Name: "John Begay"
or, if a code is necessary, a fully coded name replacement, e.g., James Benally or coded initials such as PML (arbitrarily coded)
Year: "1979"
e.g., the statement was made in 1979
Interview Number: ".5"
e.g., Mr. Begay's fifth interview of the year. (in order to reduce the string of numbers we have sometimes placed the interview number before the name)
Page Number: 361
e.g., this is page 361 in the data base
Sentence Number: ".23"
e.g., his twenty-third sentence in the fifth interview

The entire reference looks as follows: "quoted passage" (John Begay 1979.5:361.23) in which John Begay may be replaced by an appropriate code name or coded initials.

Being properly referenced is not a courtesy in scholarly publication but a right of the person being quoted. The same right should extend to native consultants.

10.3 SUMMARY AND CONCLUSIONS

Planning is the most important part of writing. Some writers plan before writing. Others fare better after they get words down on paper in any order and then radically reorganize their first draft.

A well-designed data base helps any writer. We recommended recording the analysis of an individual's knowledge on white cards and those of groups on yellow cards. These cards can be plain, edge-punched, or virtual cards in a computer system. They can be arranged according to the order of writing. The scratch list method of writing is a variant of this method. Any and all items that occur to the writer (or items of the data base index) are immediately written into a random list. The list is ordered logically afterward. Details are then filled in. There are computer programs that help expedite this process.

Writer's block can be combatted in many ways. The method we like best is switching media. Telling the ethnography to a friend in a letter, or recording it on tape, or giving a lecture on the topic (with concurrent tape recording) are our most successful methods. The tape is transcribed by "stimulus" rather than verbatim. In this manner, drawing on one's memory (very cautiously) and data base information, details can be filled in effectively.

There are two fundamental ethnographic styles: analytic and synthetic. The first describes all parts of a cultural knowledge system without telling how the system as a whole works. The synthetic approach describes the system's workings (most often as (pseudo)fiction) but rarely exhausts adequate ethnographic detail.

Ethnographies are expert systems: They should contain the potential of answering questions by deducing new knowledge from old. The ideal is "generative" ethnography that does analysis by synthesis and synthesis by analysis. Experiments by Colby (1979), Werner (1977), and artificial intelligence researchers have adapted variations of this view.

We recommend that experts contributing to our expert system/ethnoghraphies should be treated equally, whether they are natives or members of the professional community. We propose a referencing of native consultants in our ethnographies as rigorous as that currently used to cite fellow ethnographers.

The culmination of the ethnographic process is writing the final report. This report presents new knowledge to the public. Recent innovations seem to move toward shortening this feedback loop: Rather than waiting for the final report, ethnographers communicate their results to natives from the beginning. The procedure seems ideal whenever natives are involved in changing their own culture.

NOTES

1. The book is marred for today's reader by quaint references to "primitive" mentality. However, the descriptions of kinship behavior and its functioning in Navajo society, for example, are exemplary.
2. Colby's (1979) QUESTOR and related experiments are a beginning. Expert systems in artificial intelligence, especially systems capable of "learning," are additional examples (see e.g., Feigenbaum *et al.* 1982, *The Handbook of Artificial Intelligence,* Volume 3).
3. Some word processing programs automatically number and renumber as sections are moved in a document.

Part III

EPILOGUE

Chapter 11

Minimum Standards for Ethnography

Our goal is, first, to set standards any ethnographer can follow in order to ensure a minimally adequate ethnographic report. Two more goals are important. Second, we have remarked on several occasions in this book that every ethnography is a compromise between the ideally desirable and the realistically possible. Without minimal standards we have no way of assessing, neither as ethnographers nor as readers or "consumers" of an ethnography, in which aspects of an ethnography we encounter ideal conditions and where we find problems. Underlying this is, of course, our basic assumption that it is usually better to have an ethnography—any ethnography—than none at all. No ethnography will be perfect, but minimum standards serve as measures for gauging the ethnographer's success in attaining an ideal, minimally adequate ethnography. Third, we have stressed throughout this book that the ethnographer's toolkit requires continuous innovation and upgrading. Without minimum standards, improvement becomes difficult. We can continuously evaluate each minimal standard and estimate its adequacy in providing minimally adequate data sets. If an old standard violates current knowledge of human communication and cognition, or of our understanding of the dynamics of social interaction, then it is best revised, abandoned, or replaced with a better formulation.

11.0 INTRODUCTION: TOWARD MINIMUM STANDARDS

Minimum standards for ethnography and ethnographic data quality control are related but not identical. Whereas minimum standards for ethnography attempt to provide guidelines for the compilation of better ethnographies, data quality control does this only indirectly. It focuses chiefly on the evaluation of ethnographic reports *after* compilation. Naroll (1962), who pioneered in this area, summed it up succinctly: "Data quality control deals not with individual reports but with groups of reports compiled by various authors under various conditions" (1962:2). It is self-evident that principles derived from external quality control—derived from the use of ethnography for comparative purposes—affect internal quality control, the achievement of minimally adequate ethnographic reports.

Naroll's findings are directly applicable to minimal standards and can be summarized as follows (although the following propositions are strictly speaking applicable only to culture stress data, we feel safe to generalize them to the ethnographic enterprise in general):

(1) Professional ethnographers are no more trustworthy than lay-ethnographic reporters (e.g., missionaries; Naroll 1962:160).

This is a strong indictment of our profession and supports our conclusion that an ethnographer must learn a culture using different methods than would a casual visitor or an immigrant. The entire program outlined in this book attempts to raise the quality of ethnographic reports well above the casual level of competence. We feel this, the first of Naroll's conclusions, alone sufficiently justifies our concern about minimum standards of ethnographic practice. Three more that follow further amplify the need for standards.

(2) Ethnographers who control the native language are more reliable ethnographic reporters than those who do not (Naroll 1962:160).

To most ethnographers this conclusion is not surprising. In the past we have paid at least lip service to the importance of speaking the language of the natives. We have worried less about degrees of proficiency (e.g., does the ethnographer understand native jokes or conversation not directed at him or her?) or about what to do when a native language presents (given the time constraints of fieldwork) an insurmountable barrier to learning to use it with any degree of subtlety. Our minimum standards (listed below) address this problem, which receives extensive treatment in the preceding chapters (e.g., Volume 1, Section 6.3; also see Paredes 1977; Werner 1978).

(3) Ethnographers who stay in the field longer (e.g., a year or more) tend to report on sensitive topics (e.g., witchcraft), while shorter stays produce much less detail or no information (Naroll 1962:160).

Our interpretation of this finding follows several lines: First, any human being immersed into another culture as totally as ethnographers are after a while will acculturate and begin to act more like a native. The reverse culture shock upon reentry into the ethnographer's own culture substantiates our observation. Reports based on longer stays in the field are more nativelike than those based on short forays.

Second, we recognize the persistence of phonological accents. There is no reason to believe that semantic accent is less tenacious, because even the detection of semantic accent, let alone its elimination or reduction, is more difficult. Only systematic ethnoscience investigation of native meanings followed by a rigorous comparison with the ethnographer's meanings guarantees the reduction (or possibly elimination) of the ethnographer's semantic accent. In this book we discuss these methods in detail (e.g. Part I). The need for such comparison is expressed in our minimal standards as well (listed below).

Third, on several occasions we have stressed the need for ethnographers, especially in applied work in our own culture, to shorten the time lag between fieldwork and ethnographic report. The success of ethnography as a viable tool complementing other social science data-gathering techniques depends on improving the speed of ethnographic analysis. Naroll's conclusion (3) seems to contradict this need, juxtaposing quality and speed. This is certainly true if we pursue ethnography while ignoring the powerful tools of computerized ethnographic data base management. In the preceding sections of this book we devote an entire chapter (Chapter 1) to this problem. Some aspects of data collection can already be automated, as Colby (1979) has demonstrated; many more can follow. Efficient data base management is part of our minimal standards as well. We are convinced that such efficiency will vastly improve speed. At the same time, we must constantly search for additional ways to speed up ethnographic analysis without sacrificing quality. Herein lies the greatest promise of (micro)computerized ethnographic data management and analysis.

> (4) An ethnography that deals explicitly with a trait or trait complex represents a more reliable source on that trait or trait complexes than a report that mentions it only in passing (Naroll 1962:160).

The closer the topic of the use of an ethnography to the goals of the ethnography itself the better. Still, no ethnography can cover everything. The extent of human cultural knowledge is vast. In applied work the best ethnography is one tailored to the problem to be solved. We deal with this issue only indirectly in our set of minimal standards. The need for a theoretical orientation beyond a theory of cultural cognition comes closest to addressing the problem.

Naroll's conclusions concerning external quality control clearly have a direct bearing on the maintenance of internal quality. But we are just starting to formulate minimum standards of internal quality control. Our measures are primitive, and many of the standards we propose appear self-evident or relatively pedestrian. The beginnings of any quality control system always appear primitive—lists of do's and don'ts. Only later, if this is a reasonable goal for ethnography, can we hope to reach standards exhaustively stated as tolerance limits. For example, some day a statement of the following form may become possible: "An ethnographer's mastery of the native language with a minimum TEFOL score of 500 ± 50 tends to result in a better (more reliable, higher fidelity) final ethnographic report." In other areas it seems more difficult to think of minimum standards statable as tolerance limits. Whether we propose do's or don'ts for following minimum standards or are able to create more sophisticated versions, the journey will be long and arduous.

We raised the issue of fidelity in various parts of this book. Our lead metaphor is the comparison of a cubist portrait with a portrait photograph. The cubist's picture may be high art, but the culture may not be recognizable, especially by insiders. A photograph may be crafted competently, have only marginal pretensions to art, but be recognizable. Natives should be able to comment on its resemblance to their own perception of the system in which they live.

When ethnographic description is used for social intervention, preferably with the consent of the native population, fidelity becomes crucial. Many ethnographers (e.g., Lewis 1958) have remarked on the need for more rigorous standards when working closely with or perhaps even *for* the natives. It is this more stringent requirement for fidelity that motivates us to formulate minimum standards. We hope that application of minimum standards to the ethnographic process will improve not only ethnographic reporting but the credibility of our profession as well.

In discussing standards many ethnographers invoke the highly personal experience of fieldwork as argument against them. This is a red herring. There is no question that fieldwork is highly personal and each cultural immersion unique. But the product of ethnographic work is a public ethnography. The public deserves to know how we compile an ethnography and what standards we use to measure its minimum adequacy, not be given double-talk about fieldwork mystique.

In the following sections we go through the ethnographic process following the flowchart we presented in the Introduction (Volume 1, Figure 2). We discuss each minimum standard as we propose it. Next we summarize all standards of presentation in order in a master list. This list is augmented by a schematic presentation of each of the 28 minimum standards as they intersect with epistemology, theory, technology, ethics, and personal growth.

11.1 EPISTEMOLOGY AND THEORY

The theory and epistemology of ethnography are closely linked. Both answer the related questions: How is an ethnography done? Why is it done in this manner? Both are therefore answers to meta-ethnographic questions.

11.1.1 Journal and Transcription

On several occasions we have invoked the metaphor of "stereo" or "binocular" vision (Kluckhohn 1949). In this section it will provide our lead metaphor. Stereo vision involves two images: the image of the left eye (the ethnographer's) and the image of the right eye (the native's). There are many more paired images in this analogy. Our procedure in the case of each is the same. First, investigate each image separately using the same methodology, then combine them to resolve any discrepancies (see Standard 19 and Section 11.7). Kluckhohn's stereo vision metaphor, formulated more than 40 years ago, sets the stage for the first epistemological standard:

(1) The ethnographic record should consist of at least two texts that must be kept separate:

TEXT (1) is created by the ethnographer and includes any written part of the ethnographic record that is the product of the ethnographer's mind.

TEXT (2) is created by the native and includes any written part of the ethnographic record that is the product of the native consultant's mind.

This idea of separating journal (TEXT (1)) from transcriptions of interviews and conversations (TEXT (2)) occurs again and again in these books. It involves a separation of direct quotes by the ethnographer from direct quotes by the native consultant. It also leads to the separation of ethnographer's observations (protocols of observation are TEXT (1)) and the conversations with the natives that are TEXT (2) or a blend of TEXT (1) and TEXT (2) (Questions by ethnographer, answers by native consultant). It follows that in order to resolve the discrepancy between observation and conversation, native consultants must be asked to comment (TEXT (2)) on the ethnographer's protocols of observation (TEXT (1)). These comments are a check on the ethnographer's ethnocentrism and bring out the ethnocentrism of the native: the internal view. The double image of the ethnographer and native sets the internal view of a culture into sharper focus. This allows the ethnographer to comment (preferably in conclusions) on the native culture.

11.1.2 Epistemological Windows

The next step consists simply of generalizing Standard 1 and extending the principle of separation to any discrepant set of texts dealing with the "same" ethnographic reality. The goal remains the resolution of discrepancy. We call these extensions and the concerted search for "anomalous" sets of texts epistemological windows (see Volume 1, Section 1.2). This concept leads to the second epistemological standard for ethnography:

(2) *Any portions* of an ethnographic corpus of texts[1] that contradict each other ((TEXT (1) versus TEXT (2), or within TEXT (1) or TEXT (2)), should be analyzed separately and an attempt should be made to *resolve* all contradictions, anomalies, or discrepancies.

Our assumption is that discrepancy or contradiction is crucial to learning anything new. This applies in physics (see Kuhn 1962) as well as (or perhaps even more so) in the social sciences, particularly in the ethnographic process that must overcome heavy ethnocentric biases even in the case of the best-trained ethnographers. This is the result of Manheim's (1936) paradox: The investigator of culture is himself cultured. Therefore, special steps must be taken by an ethnographer to prevent his or her "culturedness" to interfere with the fidelity of the description.

Although ethnocentric bias is unavoidable, it is controlable by resolving discrepancies, especially if these are made explicit through a concerted search for epistemological windows.

The stereo vision metaphor applies therefore to any part or whole "ethnographic images" (text fragments) that are at odds. As in stereo vision, what is improved through the comparison of two discrepant images of the same ethnographic event is the perception of *ethnographic depth*.

The systematic use of epistemological windows leads us to a rigorous definition of "thick" ethnographic description: *Thick description is that which maximizes the use of discrepant ethnographic images for deeper ethnographic understanding* (Ward and Werner 1984).

There is an important corollary to Standard 2 and the use of epistemological windows. According to Festinger (1957), human beings tend to reduce discrepancy in their worldviews. However, reducing dissonance is the way an immigrant or naive participant observer learns a new culture: After a period of adjustment he or she forms a coherent image of the host culture. This simplified approach overlooks the fact that the dynamics of a culture lie in its controversies.

(3) An ethnographer should learn a culture systematically, focusing on both issues that separate *and* unite its members—that is, issues that are controversial and those beyond dispute within a social boundary.

11.1.3 Theory

An explicit ethnographic theory is indispensable to good ethnography. Such a theory constitutes a model of human knowledge, including the ways in which this knowledge is communicated from one human being to another. No matter how narrowly we restrict the domain of an ethnography, the ethnographic process ultimately boils down to obtaining knowledge from other human beings and then presenting this knowledge in an ethnographic report to readers. Even an ethnography written about the *social world* of a group of human beings is more like an expert system—the view of a knowledgeable participant—than any other kind of construct. It is therefore imperative that a theory of ethnography incorporate the best available knowledge for the construction of expert knowledge systems. This leads us to our next theoretical standard:

(4) Every ethnography should be based on an explicit theoretical construct incorporating the best available insights into the nature of human knowledge systems and the nature of human communication, including translation.

Our MTQ schema (see Volume 1, Section 2.3) and extensions, including complex relations, high-level attributes (contacts?), and logical operators (see Volume 1, Section 2.3), constitutes a beginning. This book is based explicitly on a cognitive/ethnoscience theory of lexical/semantic relations. We remarked at the beginning of Volume 1 that the proposed machinery (MTQ schema and logic) is the same for substantive cultural knowledge and for higher-level meta-knowledge (e.g., rules of the game). This last observation is based on the fact that language is its own meta-language. That makes commitment to an explicit theory even more imperative. But more development must follow.

11.1.4 Ethics

Cultured relativism predicates ethical standards. It is the root of the greatest insights of cultural anthropology: While studying a culture different from our own we cannot be blinded by our own ethnocentric judgments. In order to see another culture clearly, we must maintain a cultural relativistic outlook. As Bidney (1967) has shown, cultural relativism, though untenable as a value, is essential for method:

(5) An ethnographer should maintain a methodological stance of cultural relativism.

11.2 PERSONAL EQUATION

In Chapter 4 of Volume 1 we discussed the personal equation of the ethnographer. Here we touch only upon highlights relevant to the establishment of minimum standards. Two aspects of the personal equation are particularly important—self-awareness, or a knowledge of oneself, and training in the practice of ethnography.

11.2.1 Self-Awareness

A knowledge of oneself can be fostered in many different ways. Self-reflection goes back at least as far as Socrates' admonition to "know thyself." Yet despite over 2,000 years of methods for achieving self-reflection, none is very clear or very explicit. It is true that since its introduction into the Western world about 80 years ago, psychoanalysis and derivative methods based on "insight" have developed a sizable theoretical literature. Psychoanalysis was perhaps feasible in the 1930s when, by American standards, Viennese analysis was cheap. Kluckhohn is said to have availed himself of this opportunity. Although Powdermaker (1966) and other report improvements of ethnographic work after analysis, it has other drawbacks. Except for the analysis of students of psychoanalysis, few mentally healthy people have attempted analysis. This one-sided selectivity biases the sample considerably, although several ethnographers report that analysis helped them (see Agar 1980:42).

Still more important is the ephemeral nature of "insight." It is a mental state that we as human beings may have, but as with all mental states, it is subject to change over time as additional experiences and perhaps insights (by whatever means) accumulate. In other words, insight is part of human memory and as such is dynamic rather than a permanent, immutable phenomenon.

The goal for ethnography must include methods for acquiring and maintaining permanent insight that can be upgraded as our internal view of ourselves improves.[2] This leads us to another next minimum standard:

(6) An ethnographer should *maintain* a detailed autobiography that he or she periodically updates and revises.[3]

A personal journal kept over several years may prove a useful document in constructing one's autobiography. However, it is not sufficient in itself. A journal is more like protocols of events described as they were unfolding. They are therefore, following the systematic distortion hypothesis (see Volume 1, Section 1.2), more strongly tied to events themselves than to the writer's mental state. An autobiography therefore represents his or her reactions to events more credibly than an immediate daily journal.

We have no preconceived notions about the length of this autobiography. Future experimentation will have to establish this. It should certainly be detailed enough to give a reader a thorough view of the writer's formative experiences, personal accomplishments, biases, and (at least indirectly) his or her blind spots.

Essential to the documentation of an autobiography are periodic updates. The best procedure seems to be doing a major update *before* every major ethnographic project. These revisions or additions can help a reader perceive currents in the personal development of the ethnographer. To this end every version should be saved, and revisions should take the form of comments made in previous versions of the document.

It is unclear how public such a document should be. We are fully aware that in many autobiography projects the ethnographer-writer will also be the only reader. Anticipating who else will read these autobiographies during the ethnographer's lifetime is impossible. Making autobiographies available posthumously should perhaps be standard. Robert Lowie's "language maintenance testament" (Lowie 1945) is a very important document allowing a reader to better assess Lowie's contribution to anthropology. The document is particularly useful for understanding the controversy about the status of field languages by Lowie, Mead, and others (in the pages of the *American Anthropologist* 1939-1941).

The creation of a "language acquisition and maintenance testament" is an important step, but it does not go far enough. A document approaching "a testament of living"—in short, an autobiography published at the end of one's professional career—may be more important. There are still few documents like Margaret Mead's (1972) *Blackberry Winter* and Boas's (Rohner 1969) and Malinowski's (1967) diaries that allow one to assess the person behind the ethnographer. It is amazing how little we know about the nonacademic side of the lives of most great ethnographers.

11.2.2 Cross-Cultural Training

The second aspect of the ethnographer's personal equation is his or her education. We stated this minimum standard as follows:

(7) An ethnographer should expose himself or herself to the widest range of cultural variation available on our planet.

The reasons for this standard are obvious, yet it might be useful to look at it from a new perspective. The standard is based on sound psychological insight. In addition to exposure through reading, ethnographic experience, both in foreign cultures and in one's own, should also be included.

The main reason for cross-cultural experience can be paraphrased as "what you don't expect you can see or hear only with difficulty." The Brunner and Postman (1949) experiment (quoted by Kuhn 1962) amplifies this point. Test subjects experienced great discomfort when they had to deal with playing cards whose colors had been exchanged (e.g., black hearts and red spades). Yet some of the experimental subjects could never (after more than 40 trials) make explicit the reasons for their discomfort.

Different cultures are a lot like decks of cards with the colors confounded. If an ethnographer is attuned to cross-cultural variation through previous experience with different cultures, identification of exotic culture patterns may be relatively easy. Without such training identification may be missed completely.

Our expectations strongly bias what we can find or comprehend. It was perhaps the rich variety of human speech sounds and sound combinations that prompted early travelers to claim that some natives communicated by means of grunts and groans, if they communicated at all. Today we know that there are no "primitive languages" spoken anywhere in the world. All languages of our species (*Homo sapiens*) are at essentially the same level of structural complexity. This species emerged about 100,000 years ago. Human language as we know it today followed soon after. It is amazing that highly intelligent, well-read, well-traveled contemporaries often overlook these facts. For example, James A. Michener (1974) tells his readers in his novel *Centennial* The Paleo Indian flint napper, whom Michener describes in detail, in the year 9268 B.C., "had a working vocabulary of twelve to thirteen hundred words, few of which would be intelligible even a short time after his death, for in language swift change was in process" (1974:113). The Paleo Indians of 10,000 years ago were not significantly different from the villagers in Egypt and Mesopotamia who started our civilization at about the same time. It is unlikely that these Indians' language was very different from modern human languages. To translate the Bible requires a vocabulary of about 7,500 lexical items (Nida 1957). No natural language exists that cannot meet this requirement. Whether this was true of languages 10,000 years ago is anybody's guess. But a vocabulary of a mere 1,200-1,300 words is highly unlikely. That change was faster then than it is today is even less likely.

Cultural variation is usually more subtle than differences in language. Cultural subtleties may be harder to detect than relatively circumscribed subtleties of language. Extensive reading in the cross-cultural literature along with ethnographic experience abroad and near one's own culture are no guarantees for not missing anything. Yet they do increase the chances for better ethnographies.

11.3 RESEARCH DESIGN AND PROPOSAL

In Volume 1, Chapter 5 we discussed the problems of designing ethnographic research and writing a proposal for its conduct. Here we merely touch on a few highlights relevant to minimum standards. The first of these is the role of theory in general, and a plan for integrating theory with the conduct of research. Equally important is the design of an adequate data base management system. Finally, we deal with considerations about the human subjects whose lives we study and the importance of adjusting research goals to a personal style of working.

11.3.1 Theory

In cognitive ethnoscience ethnographies we must recognize at least two levels of theory. The first is ethnoscience theory, or a theory of human cultural cognition, which deals with the nature of cultural knowledge, including human memory. The memory component is crucial because it imposes the major constraint on eliciting information from human beings. The second aspect of theory is that which motivates a particular ethnographic project. If we consider the conceptual schema of ethnoscience bottom-level theory, then these project-related theories can be called mid-level theories.

These theories are intermediate between theories of memory and cognition, and perhaps grand theories of human society. Examples of mid-level theories are not difficult to find. In a study of small group cultures, everything known about group dynamics is relevant, particularly in synthetized form. In an ethnographic study of economic development, past experience with development must be considered. In an ethnographic study of the careers of Silicone Valley high-technology engineers, theories of career development cannot be neglected. These examples could be expanded without limit. Every ethnographic research project has an intellectual focus, and chances are that someone else has thought about it before. Developing a theoretical base means finding such thinking and, if possible, synthetizing or at least testing it in the current ethnographic effort.

Occasionally our ignorance of a social system may be so profound that a baseline ethnography must attempt to include "everything." But even in such cases there is usually some problem lurking in the background that initially stimulated interest in the acquisition of ethnographic knowledge.

The point is simply that even the most general ethnography benefits from being informed by theoretical knowledge related to a specific problem. This leads us to our next minimum standard:

(8) An ethnographer should consider the problem that motivates an ethnography. Every ethnography benefits from making the theory underlying the ethnographic problem explicit.

On the simplest level this means knowing what has previously been done in the problem area. On more complex levels it means designing a theoretical synthesis from past efforts, testing it through ethnographic fieldwork, and, if necessary, revising the theory in light of new knowledge.

Occasionally ethnography may be used differently. In encyclopedic projects the cognitive theory of ethnoscience may suffice. The goal is to build a knowledge base that can serve as background for the interpretation of native texts and therefore as background for further investigation of social problems. An ethnomedical encyclopedia represents an appropriate example. Understanding a native medical knowledge system, including native principles for organizing that knowledge, is an important and basic step toward understanding any folk medical system. Without this step native texts may remain only partially intelligible.

An extreme form of the encyclopedic approach is conceivable, although it has been rarely attempted. Its main feature is to collect an encyclopedia of *all knowledge* available within a cultural system. This body of data then serves as a general background for any problem requiring a special theory or a special ethnographic follow-up. An entire set of ethnographic projects can be started with an extensive encyclopedia. The encyclopedia then acts as an expert system, or a resource of comprehensive "translator's notes," informing any problem-oriented follow-up research (see Volume 1, Section 12.3).

A more economical and perhaps theoretically sounder approach involves commencing an ethnography with an encyclopedic first step learning about cultural domains that relate directly to a problem and to the theory that attempts to explain the problem. The encyclopedic data base then serves as background for understanding native texts elicited to illuminate the problem. A possible plan of research following this outline appears in Figure 11.1. Ideally preceding every ethnography should be an encyclopedic first phase. This would provide every ethnography with a knowledge base against which problem oriented texts could be interpreted and translated.

11.3.2 Theoretical Plan

A theoretical plan is the integration of ethnoscience theory and the theory of the problem within the conduct of specific ethnographic research. In other words, a research plan bridges theory (what we know or would like to know) with making certain that we know how to achieve these theoretical ends (method). This means making all our theoretical variables directly or indirectly (through other theoretical variables) operational. We need not rely too closely on a narrowly linear algebraic formulation of dependent and independent variables. Most ethnographic problems are far too complex for this kind of oversimplification. A better metaphor would be to view our task as matrices of starting conditions and end conditions. The latter should indicate whether certain key states of existence have been achieved. This is not unlike decision tables we introduced in Section 4.1. If at the start conditions C_1 through C_n are met, then outcomes O_1 through O_n are possible. At least some of these conditions and outcomes must relate to the problem under study.

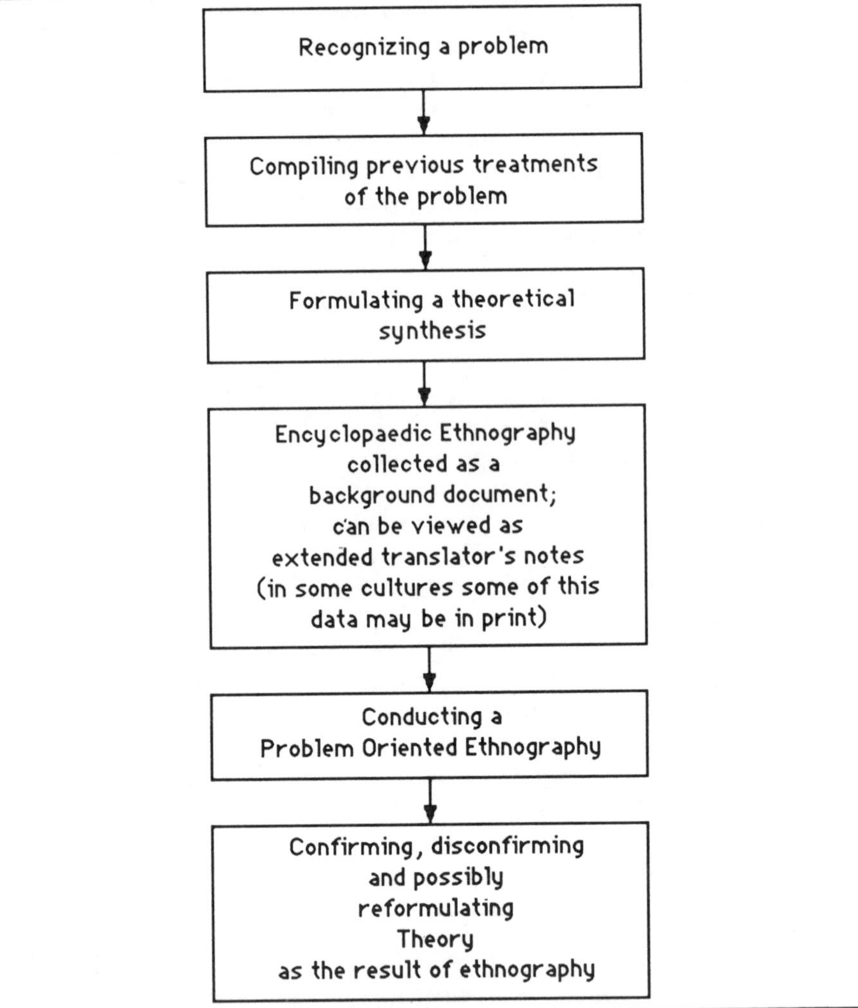

Figure 11.1 Theory and Encyclopedic Ethnography

We can now formulate a very general minimum standard.

(9) Any proposal for ethnographic research needs a theoretical plan and a plan of action—how to translate theoretical goals into ethnographic process.

Theoretical goals are twofold: ethnoscience theory, which contains assumptions about the nature of human knowledge Standard 4; and thematic theory, which informs and motivates the specific goals of the ethnographic undertaking.

11.3.3 Data Base Management

Our general epistemological Standard 2 and the more specific item 1 set stringent conditions for comparing different texts (text fragments) from different parts of an ethnographic corpus. Our data bases must be well organized, with easily accessible records so that the comparisons required between Standards 1 and 2 can be undertaken quickly and efficiently. The entire ethnographic edifice must be built on a sound data base management system. Given the nature of human memory and the dangers associated with unaided recall, no significant ethnographic contributions can be forthcoming without the efficient storage and retrieval of one's texts. This leads us to our next standard:

(10) Every ethnographer must design an efficient data management system for ethnographic texts and other documents. The data management system should be in place *before* the collection of the first texts or documents.

The last sentence is particularly important. Data base management is usually seen as part of analysis. We too have placed a detailed discussion of it at the opening of Part I on analysis. Yet it is crucial to remember that many ethnographic opportunities will be missed if the ethnographer does not set up an efficient storage and retrieval system *before* acquiring any data. Only with the aid of such a system can any ethnographer hope to stay in control of the ethnographic process, know what he or she has collected, and efficiently relate the collected material to some theoretical goal. In addition, a well-managed data base in the field allows an ethnographer to conduct interviews more efficiently by focusing on what is as yet unknown rather than on duplication through inadvertently redundant elicitation.

An efficient data base management is also important for the reduction of ethnographic complexity. Figure 11.2 illustrates. The first step in ethnographic reduction is aided by the "poverty of language" (Polanyi 1964); that is, language is less rich than reality. Creating a text reduces complexity. An explicit cognitive/ethnoscience theory (Standard 4) makes this reduction through language more systematic. Ethnoscience analysis and what we have called mid-level theory (Standard 8) informs the second step. This step requires an efficient data management and retrieval system.

11.3.4 Protection of Human Subjects

We subscribe to the American Anthropological Association's Statement on Ethics. We want to stress but one aspect of this document: *the right of all people who come in contact with an ethnographer to have their privacy and safety protected*. This means that upon preparing his or her proposal, an ethnographer should have thought through a schema that will protect the identification of particular texts with particular people. A coding schema for the protection of consultants is an integral part of any ethnographic data retrieval system.

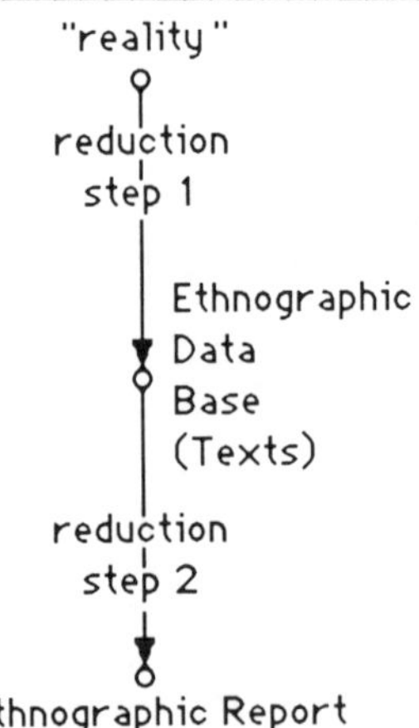

Figure 11.2 Steps in Ethnographic Reduction

(11) A plan to protect the privacy of all people whose statements enter the ethnographer's data base should be in place *before* the first texts are deposited in it.

Closely tied to the protection of consultants is our understanding of who they are. This effort should become an ongoing process. As our understanding of a culture deepens, so does our understanding of the particular biases of our consultants. There are two consequences to this. First, by knowing better who our consultants are, we understand better who could hurt them. This improves our ability to protect them. Second, knowing our consultants better improves our ethnography. We can better appreciate where their statements fit if we get to know who their friends and detractors are. If native controversies are at the heart of good ethnography (Standard 3), knowing one's consultant's location in the native social context is especially crucial.

Finally, there is an internal aspect to the protection of human subjects. This is internal in the sense that it allows consultants to assess better the risk they may be taking by associating with an ethnographic project. We state this as a minimum standard:

(12) An ethnographer should carefully formulate an explanation of his or her project for the natives in language (content and style) that they can understand and upon which they can base intelligent, informed judgments.

Explaining one's project in a language and culture very different from one's own is no easy task. Neither is it a task that can be accomplished once and for all. It is an ongoing process that can grow in sophistication as the ethnographer and his or her research collaborators gain familiarity with each other and with the project.

The first time to formulate a project in terms of native understandings is when proposing the project. Once the ethnographer "gets a foot in the door," subsequent explanations may become easier, but nothing is ever certain. New consultants may ask new questions or old questions with new interests. It is a good idea to work very hard on the explanation of one's ethnographic project while exposed to the field situation.

11.3.5 Ethnographer's Private Work Style

We all have personal strengths and weaknesses that are reflected in our style of work. Some of us feel more comfortable with pastoralists, others with agricultural people. Some of us prefer persons of action whereas others seek out philosophers. Some prefer to work in cities; others prefer villages or the wilderness. Some like lush vegetation; others prefer the subtleties of desert flora. Some prefer to work with women and others with men; still others are particularly good with children. Some of us are very good at translating qualitative data into numbers that can be statistically processed, whereas others are excellent at eliciting long texts even on extremely sensitive subjects. Any ethnographer who neglects his or her strength cheats himself or herself and the public. People should do what they do best.

It is true that the ability to perform many different ethnographic tasks well in diverse environments marks a good ethnographer. The less skilled or naturally endowed ethnographer requires narrower pastures. The important thing to remember is that because the human mind is the most crucial instrument in the ethnographic enterprise, the phenomena we have loosely grouped under the label "personal style of work" are critical to any ethnographic projects that we undertake. We formulate this as a standard:

(13) An ethnographer should take into account when proposing an ethnographic undertaking the interaction between the proposed research and his or her personal style of working.

Just as with awareness of one's own thought and behavior, one's personal work style is a matter of insight. It too can be helped by an autobiography. This record of past work may be more revealing for those who have conducted ethnographies before. In all likelihood autobiographical notes will disclose recurrent patterns in one's ethnographic work experience. These can be extracted and taken into account in the next project. Less experienced ethnographers may look for clues in their past. Questions such as what brought them to ethnography and what made them stay and enjoy certain aspects of it may provide some of the answers.

The personal rewards many of us feel are the result of a successful field trip (abroad or nearer to home), and the personal fulfillment that fieldwork offers seems to be dependent on our pursuing the kind of work we do best. It therefore behooves us to cultivate our sharpest talents.

11.4 FIELD RELATIONS

In Volume 1, Chapter 6 we discussed the problem of establishing and maintaining field relations. We touched upon the skills an ethnographer needs to have in order to make his or her way among people who are complete strangers. We talked about the importance of introductions, official sanctions of our entry, and similar problems. We also mentioned preparation for entry into the field—learning the language, taking previous literature critically but seriously, and similar problems. For minimal standards learning the language is most important. The rest of making contact and maintaining it contains just one important aspect: to keep the field open after one's study for others to follow.

11.4.1 Language

Learning the language of the natives is without doubt the single most important method for gaining rapport with any group of people. It is appropriately our next minimum standard.

(14) Every ethnographer should make a serious effort to learn the language of the people who are the topic of the ethnography.

In the ideal situation the ethnographer should learn to speak the language of the natives well rather than just make an effort. However, there are mitigating circumstances. In ethnographic fieldwork the stay of the ethnographer may prove too short to learn the language well. Functional language use for everyday tasks may be easy to acquire. To manage the subtlety of a language's humor or fine points of philosophy is another matter. To acquire that kind of proficiency may take years.

Non-Indo-European languages are notoriously difficult for Western ethnographers and may require extraordinary dedication. Sometimes in environments where the natives speak an Indo-European contact language, learning may be complicated by the native's impatience with the ethnographer's groping in their native language. Special time periods may have to be set aside dedicated entirely to language learning. In addition, some ethnographers do better at learning a new language than do others. This personal factor must also be taken into account.

Regardless of the situation in which the ethnographer finds himself or herself, the natives' language must be taken seriously. This means several things:

(1) No matter how difficult the language or how poor the ethnographer's ability to learn languages, he or she must attempt to learn it at least to the limit of natural ability. The natives will greatly appreciate the effort and forgive imperfections. (In fact, they may find some of the latter hilarious.) The point for the ethnographer is to grin and bear it while trying to avoid embarrassing mistakes the next time.

(2) Native texts should be transcribed *in the native language* and carefully translated afterward (see multistage translation discussed in Volume 1, Section 12.3.1). This may place a tremendous burden on an ethnographer who does not speak the language well. Transcription phoneme by phoneme is a tedious, slow, and often inaccurate process. Transcription is greatly facilitated by understanding the language. The only other alternative for an ethnographer is to learn to write the language well phonemically and teach native collaborators or assistants to transcribe (see Volume 1, Section 13.6).

(3) Part of literacy training must be devoted to training native collaborators or assistants to interpret for the ethnographer. This too is no simple task. The natives' knowledge of the contact language may be imperfect at best. The best safeguard here is for the ethnographer to know as much about the native language as possible so that he or she can aid the translation of native texts into smooth English (or whatever is ethnographer's language). What the ethnographer lacks in fluency he or she may make up through understanding the formal grammar of the language. This is possible only where a good grammar source is available or the ethnographer is willing to undertake writing one.

A second aspect of interpreter training is allowing time for the study of the domain(s) essential to the focus of the ethnography. A bilingual collaborator who speaks both languages well may be an expert interpreter on agricultural topics but need extensive time for retooling before becoming a minimally adequate interpreter on medical topics. This problem may be exacerbated by the bilingual collaborator's knowledge of different domains in different languages. For example, he or she may be excellent in Western technology in the contact language and equally excellent in medical topics in the native language with problems of translating medicine to medicine or technology to technology. The answer, as before, lies in retooling. The ethnoscience paradigm offers an efficient, fast way of exploring unknown cultural domains in any language, even one's own.

Making a serious attempt to learn the language of the natives reaps its greatest rewards in building rapport. Nothing will increase the acceptance of a Western ethnographer better than speaking the native language a little better than the average outsider. Ethnographers who manage to do considerably better than the average outsider are usually exceptionally well accepted. Few human beings can resist the ultimate flattery engendered by an outsider who takes them seriously by learning their language well.

11.4.2 Keeping Field Access Open

Systematic ethnography as we have tried to present it in this book claims to be more rigorous than classical ethnography. Part of this more systematic approach involves maintaining the public nature of ethnography. This means in particular that restudies should be welcomed. That brings us to the final minimum standard for field relations:

(15) An ethnographer should conduct his or her fieldwork and field relations in such manner that other ethnographers will be able to follow and do restudies.

There are too many events in today's world that close off field areas for ethnographers. We advocate that the ethnographer's conduct should not constitute an additional reason. Aside from condemning irresponsible personal conduct, we stress responsible professional conduct.

Every ethnographer should welcome restudies as part of our efforts toward improving the ethnographic process. We have far too few restudies, especially those in which the study is sufficiently controlled for understanding the vexing question of why so many restudies tend to turn out so differently from their precursors. Our tendency is to blame everything on the personal equations of the ethnographers involved. Explanations of different entry points for each new ethnographer also follow in part the personal equation argument. Yet there seems to be more to it. For example, in Section 11.1 we gave a rigorous definition of "thick ethnography." It is easy to imagine that an ethnographer's approach to the treatment of anomalies may significantly affect the outcome of the investigation. Systematic restudies are thus crucial for the advancement of the science and theoretical bases of ethnography.

11.5 OBSERVATION

The preceding four sections suggest several minimum standards for ethnography. They all apply to the time period we have termed pre-fieldwork. In the next three sections—observations, interview, and analysis—we move into the fieldwork phase. At this point very few degrees of freedom remain; many of the most important epistemological, theoretical, technical, ethical, and personal standards are in place. The standards for fieldwork—in this section specifically those for observation—are almost all based on previously introduced standards. Only fine tuning remains. We therefore change our format of presentation. In the sections that follow, all standards are listed in one section without subsections.

11.5.1 Standards for Observation

From an epistemological point of view, our treatment of observation is fixed by Standards 1 and 2. We carefully separated, following Standard 1, texts created by the ethnographer (TEXT (1)) from texts created by native consultants (TEXT (2)). This separation has immediate repercussions for ethnographic observation. The protocol of observations go into different files, or differently marked files, depending upon who reports the observation.

In addition, according to the systematic distortion hypothesis (e.g., Shweder & D'Andrade 1980) there is a predictable shift in content between observation reported "on the spot" and observation recalled some time after an event. Following Standard 2, every piece of information (text fragment) must be separable from every other piece that may potentially contradict it. This requirement is closely tied to Standard 10 on the quality of the ethnographer's data base management system. Every record of observation, be it recalled or reported on the scene, must be identifiable by date, time, place, observer, and actor(s) participating in the described event.

Looking at observation pretheoretically, everything from Spradley's (1980) cycles of global "descriptive observation" to localized "selective observation" may be set up as a minimal standard. However, before elaborating minimum standards for observation, a full-scale investigation of the uses of observation in ethnography is needed. (We are not ready at this stage of our theoretical understanding to undertake this study.)

There are many ways to impose interesting variations on ethnographic observation. For example, observational studies often operate with the ethnographer-social scientist's units of observation. More interesting results may emerge if we observe in native categories followed by a comparison of native's and ethnographer's categories. We are certain that there are many more innovative ways in which to conduct observational studies. Some of these innovations may be included into minimal standards at some future date.

We do not think that minimum theoretical standards should be formulated independent of Standards 4, 8, and 9. That is, observation is constrained by current theories about the nature of cultural knowledge and by the general, more mid-level theoretical aims of an ethnographic study. In other words, the application of observation to the collection of an ethnography must be based on its theoretical fit. Again, formulation of minimal standards beyond the preceding general statement may be premature.

Observation can be better aided by the latest technology than by any other part of the ethnographic enterprise, with the possible exception of data management by computers.

(16) An ethnographer should be on the lookout for applications of the latest technology to observation.

Photography, film, videotape and the ability to slow down or speed up motion have contributed dimensions to observation that were unheard of a century ago. More is to come, and much of it is already available, though usually beyond the budgets of ethnographic projects. For example, the technology linking computers and videodiscs will soon allow cross-referencing film images in the same way we can cross-reference texts today. This will enhance the efficiency of analyzing visual data by several orders of magnitude. Similarly, the image-processing techniques developed by the National Aeronautics and Space Administration will some day filter down to the social sciences. The management of huge picture data bases, electronic enhancement of low-quality images, and electronic separation of figures from background will soon allow for analyses of human behavior that were inconceivable only a few years ago. In this atmosphere of new technology moving rapidly from experimental applications to consumer products, ethnographers need to keep up with what is available within our budgets today, and perhaps more important, to look out for technology that we may soon utilize but today is just beyond our budgets. Being ready to apply technology as it becomes available may hold the greatest promise for advancement.

Among ethical standards, everything we have said about the protection of human subjects here applies perhaps even more. Quotations taken from a consultant during an interview may be denied by claiming the ethnographer did not understand correctly. It is more difficult to deny tape recordings and almost impossible to deny the veracity of visual records. We must look into technology that alters voices and into electronic means of protecting people appearing in pictures.

For the first time in our quest for minimum standards, observation introduces the collection of data. In a number of recent cases scientists have falsified data in order to advance their prestige; therefore an appropriate minimum standard has become appropriate.

(17) An ethnographer is never, for any reason, justified in altering or fabricating data.

We can think of personal, interpersonal, political, and theoretical reasons why an ethnographer might want to falsify data. There is no excuse for such behavior. In ethnography doctoring data is more difficult to detect than in a science, where experiments can be replicated. We as ethnographers are therefore more vulnerable and need to take every precaution to make even the temptation to alter data difficult.

Finally, we formulate a personal standard that should need no explanation or extended commentary:

(18) An ethnographer should keep current in his or her field.

In particular, ethnographers need to keep up on the epistemology of observation, the theoretical fit of observation into ethnography, the technical and technological aspects affecting observation, and the ethics of observational studies.

11.6 INTERVIEW

In this section we follow closely the precedent set in the previous section. Most of our discussion consists of fine tuning the application of previous standards.

11.6.1 Standards for Interviewing

From an epistemological point of view, our treatment of interviewing is based on Standards 1, 2, and 4. Standard 4 is theoretical with epistemological repercussions. However, a separation of 1 and 2 from 4 is possible. We follow this strategy, but separate Standard 4 from 8 more rigorously than in Section 11.5. Our reasons will become clear as we present the arguments.

The separation of texts generated by the ethnographer (TEXT (1)) from those generated by natives (TEXT (2)) affects interviews differently. In interviews an exchange occurs between two people—the interviewer and the interviewee. This makes the interview record more complex than the protocols of observation. In observation the stimulus for texts is based on some initial agreement to observe, but beyond that it is mostly the unfolding events that stimulate the creation of an observational protocol.

In an interview the most direct stimulus for an answer is usually the interviewer's questions. Thus an observational protocol is more clearly a TEXT (1) or a TEXT (2) depending on who created it. An interview is always a blend of the two types, usually containing longer speeches by the native and shorter interrogatives by the ethnographer. The ethnographer has control over the interview to the extent that the questions "lead" the interview through the content areas required by theory and the cultural domains under study.

The systematic distortion hypothesis is less relevant to interviewing when the interviews are audio recorded. An interview recorded in notes and, even more, an interview record based entirely on recall suffer from the same systematic introduction of biases as does recalled observation.

Interviews and interview questions display the same hierarchical structure we found in observation. The best interview style begins with Grand Tour questions. These usually elicit descriptive answers. The interview then proceeds to various levels of minitour questions, which require more selective responses. While the progression from Grand Tour to minitour is important, we are not prepared to formulate this progression as a standard. More research may uncover principles that lend themselves to such a formulation.

Learning the language of the natives (Standard 14) is crucial to interviewing. The whole point of an interview is to uncover native categories that natives use to talk about their experience. Eliciting cultural knowledge in anything but the native language is self-defeating. We can now formulate a corollary standard to 14:

(19) The language of the interview should be determined by the language that the natives use for conducting their business in the cultural domain(s) of interest to the ethnographer.

Theories about the nature of cultural knowledge (Standard 4) are important for interviewing. But it remains difficult to formulate explicit standards beyond the statement that no interviewing technique and no procedure applied in interviewing should violate theories of cultural cognition. A tremendous amount of research is needed in the area of efficiently translating interview texts into knowledge structures. At present this is the focus of interest in the design of expert systems as well. While we seem to begin to understand how knowledge is structured (for example, following our MTQ schema), how the knowledge of one person is effectively transferred into the knowledge of another person is much less well understood. Our theories of cultural cognition need to be expanded to incorporate the learning process more effectively.

The appropriate uses of technology are as important for interviewing as they are for observation. This assertion contains the idea for designing not only expert systems, or "ethnography machines" able to answer novel questions about a culture but also an *expert knowledge acquisition system,* or ethnography machines able to automate aspects of the ethnographic process. Benjamin Colby's QUESTOR (1979) is a move in the right direction.

In other words, Standard 16 applies to interviews with the same force that it applies to observation. The protection of interviewees follows directly from Standard 11. Everything we said on this subject in Section 11.5 applies here as well.

Standard 17 applies with equal force to interviewing. Falsification or unwarranted alteration of one's interview data is never justified. With textual data there is an additional factor that needs considering: quoting out of context. Precise guidelines are difficult to formulate, but the recognition that text fragments can assume a life of their own out of context should always be taken into account.

It is necessary to stress again the need to keep one's knowledge base current. For interviewing a better understanding of the dynamics of interviewing and the acquisition of knowledge must dominate the list.

11.7 ANALYSIS

In this section we follow the procedure of the two preceding sections. The major difference is that the theory of cultural cognition here is more important. Other than that, the discussion again focuses primarily on fine-tuning standards set up in the first four sections.

11.7.1 Standards for Analysis

From an epistemological point of view, there is little to add. At this stage in the ethnographic process all data are either already in the data base (the ethnographic corpus) or in the process of entering into it. Any analysis that follows must be based on the assumption that the collection of texts has been conducted according to Standards 1, 2, and 3.

The separation of TEXT (1) from TEXT (2) and, by extension the separation of any two discrepant textual fragments from the ethnographic corpus, requires a special analytical approach. We present the principle of analysis based on 1, 2, and 3 in generalized form, applicable to any two (or more) text fragments from the ethnographic corpus:

(20) The comparison of any pair of potentially discrepant text fragments should proceed by applying to each the *same* methods of analysis based on the *same* theory of cultural cognition.

Establishing this standard raises several issues. Potentially discrepant text fragments are any (two or more) pieces of text that come from different sources (e.g., ethnographer versus native), that originate from different time periods in the ethnographic record (e.g., early versus late), that originate from different methodologies (e.g., numerical versus qualitative), or that show any other differences that could lead to an epistemological window.

Standard 20 is a generalized extension of Spradley's (personal communication) solution to the analysis and comparison of TEXT (1) and TEXT (2). Each of these texts should be subject to the same rigorous ethnosemantic analysis based on the same theory of cultural cognition.

In some domains of analysis in which one text is compared with another, this standard may be easily implemented. Other situations—say, in comparing qualitative results with quantitative conclusions—may stretch the investigator's ingenuity. Perhaps because numerical results always require interpretation in natural language—that is, a text—the problem is less insurmountable than first appears. At this stage of our understanding of such comparisons, experimentation is the best policy. This need for experience is more general than the comparison of textual and numerical data. Comparison of ethnoscience structures urgently needs better methodology than those available today.

The implication of theoretical standards clearly has implications for analysis. Analysis must be conducted following the best available theory of human cultural knowledge (cultural cognition) and memory. We think that the MTQ schema and its extensions, including logical rules, provides a minimally adequate theory (see Volume 1, Section 2.3.2). There are several areas—for example, logical quantification—in which the extended MTQ schema needs further development. As better theoretical insights become available these should be incorporated or completely replace the old theory.

Much has been written about the inadequacy of "classical" ethnoscience (e.g., Keesing 1974, and Hutchins 1980, among others). Several recent developments have taken ethnoscience further. Among these are the introduction of plans (scripts), goals, decisions, schemas (systems of complex relations), folk theories and the analysis of meta-levels.

In Figure 1, Volume 1 we discussed the continuum of human knowledge, including self-referential or meta-knowledge. We used this illustration to claim that the structures of classical ethnoscience used to analyze (relatively) substantive object knowledge (and a few of the above-mentioned extensions) apply equally well to an infinite regression of meta-levels. This assertion implies that our models must *adequately cover analysis of all cultural knowledge systems*, regardless of the meta-level(s) upon which our ethnographic goals may depend. We can therefore construct another minimum standard:

(21) Any theoretical model underlying ethnographic analysis must be minimally adequate to cover analysis on the object level and on meta-levels of cultural knowledge.

We presented the need for a data base management system in Section 11.3 (Standard 10). However, it is during analysis that the adequacy of a data base management system truly pays off. The data base management system should be in place before the first texts and documents are collected. From the time the ethnographer begins analysis (preferably while still in the field) the data base management system must be upgraded as new insights or requirements become apparent.

We can only repeat our exhortation in Section 11.5 (Standard 16) that the best available (affordable) technology should also be utilized in the management of data bases.

Paralleling Standard 17, which we applied to observational interview, we offer the following standard applicable to analysis:

(22) An ethnographer is never justified in altering or fabricating the analysis of ethnographic data.

Finally, Standard 18, regarding keeping abreast of new analytical methods and of underlying theory, is equally appropriate here.

11.8 WRITING THE ETHNOGRAPHY

In this section we describe minimum standards for the post-fieldwork period, or the actual writing of the ethnographic report. We discuss briefly the role of theory in the write-up, a subject we touched upon in Section 11.1. We discuss the problem of making an ethnography acceptable to the constituencies of the ethnographer. This discussion returns us to the protection of human subjects and other considerations involving ethnographic consultants. Next we discuss the need to separate description from interpretation. We close this section with personal standards.

11.8.1 Standards for Writing the Ethnography

The first standard is an epistemological that applies specifically to writing the ethnographic report: Ethnography is first and foremost a description of a knowledge system (encyclopedia) or a social system (ethnography proper). The description should always come first, *followed by* interpretation and explanation. This leads to a further standard:

(23) Description should precede the ethnographer's interpretation and explanation. The two should be clearly separate.

The dangers of ethnocentric bias increase when description and interpretation are mixed. A reader never knows whether a text fragment describes an event from the natives' point of view or whether it is the ethnographer's commentary. Separation is absolutely necessary to being able to assess the quality of an ethnography.

Figure 11.1 states our case well. An ethnography, in addition to presenting some evidence for the fidelity of the description of a knowledge (encyclopedia) or social system (ethnography proper), also contains conclusions that include new knowledge:

(24) Every ethnography should contribute to the advancement of theoretical knowledge.

An ethnography's value as a source of empirical knowledge rests to a great extent upon the reader's ability to evaluate the quality of the work. Two items affect the evaluation of any ethnography. First is the reader's ability to assess the sources of the ethnographer's information. Consequently:

(25) Every ethnography should list consultants who contributed to the ethnography (appropriately disguised), their numbers, and demographic profiles. It is particularly important to specify how many interviews each consultant contributed and how each interview was recorded.

Every ethnography should contain a list of all consultants who contributed to the ethnographic corpus. It is important that readers know whether the knowledge system or social system presented in the pages of the monograph is based on a few key consultants, on key consultants and a wider sample, or some other formula that can be evaluated for adequacy and breadth of coverage.

Second, the reader must be able to form an opinion about the demographic representativeness of the ethnographer's sample. If proper protection of privacy can be assured, such information may be given for every consultant. If not, the average profile and its range of variation demands inclusion. If different populations are examined, the characteristics of each population must be independently specified.

The quality of information depends on the form of recording. As we showed earlier, structured, recorded data may be reproduced with the greatest accuracy but are more likely to be stilted by self-consciousness and/or fear of technology. Informal interviews utilizing recordings or note taking are intermediate in their accuracy of recall. Casual interviews are least reliable, especially when the recall of their contents comes some time after the interview itself. Yet casual statements may represent the most natural conversations. A blend of formal, informal, and casual interviews seems best because it guarantees a balance between accuracy and candor.

The final write-up is the "acid test" of the ethnographer's ingenuity in disguising the identity of his or her consultants. Sometimes more than names have to be changed. Place names, state names, the names of companies, and the nature of the industry are just a few disguises we have seen used by ethnographers in recent years. In all cases, concealing identities is a good idea if by the time of the preparation of the final written report all levels of coding are established and well tried. Confidentiality in data gathering must be maintained during the collection of the entire corpus. In many cases it is then, when fellow consultants could obtain sensitive data, that the security system is most needed.

Our next standard is crucially dependent on the appropriate protection of privacy and safety of consultants.

(26) After considering the privacy and safety of consultants, they should receive the same privileges of citation as do professional sources.

Safety and the protection of privacy must come first, but there are many instances in which particular consultants should be given citations similar to those acceptable in the case of fellow ethnographers and other colleagues in the social sciences. Two benefits follow from this practice. First, we recognize the expertise of native consultants. If they are quoted verbatim, the passage should be in quotes and reference should be made to the location of the quote in the ethnographic data base. In Section 10.2.3 we gave some examples. Second, practice improves ethnographies. From properly credited citations a reader can draw conclusions about the adequacy of the ethnographic data base. If the same consultant is quoted to the exclusion of others, this is an important clue to the ethnographer's working style. Quotations from many different parts of the corpus (for example, deduced from page numbers) give the reader clues about the extensiveness of the ethnographic data base.

Ethnographers have not generally considered the problem of presenting the final ethnographic report in sufficient detail. Usually a book, a monograph, or a report is considered the most usual end product. Ethnographers need to consider not only their readership but also whether they as ethnographers want to have an impact — that is, change peoples' behavior — and how such change is best accomplished. Writing a report sometimes may not be the most efficient way to be heard. Oral presentations with opportunities for audience response may be more effective. Direct quotes can be used effectively to convince bureaucrats, for example, that resentment of their conduct does exist. Styles of presentation represent a growth area in the ethnographic enterprise. We can formulate this as a standard:

> **(27) Because an ethnography is always intended for an audience, an ethnographer should weigh in every case the best medium and the best method within that medium for presenting ethnographic data and conclusions.**

For different constituencies it may occasionally be necessary to present a different final report to each constituency.

Finally, the ethnographer's personal standards reflect his or her style of writing. Without exception, the ethnographic style should be simple, matter-of-fact prose. We have advocated self-conscious awareness of the ethnographic process throughout this book. One's writing should be similarly part of self-reflection and self-improvement.

> **(28) An ethnographer should strive to improve his or her communicative skills, especially his or her writing.**

After collecting an ethnographic corpus in the best possible manner, communicating its findings becomes vitally important.

11.9 SUMMARY AND CONCLUSIONS

We opened this book with a flowchart outlining the steps that lead to an ethnography. We apply the same sequence to minimum standards and present them here in summary as a list. These are the steps that ascertain that our ethnographic picture meets *minimum standards of fidelity to the native cultural original.* Each ethnographer should elaborate this list with his or her own standards. This is not closed; more or better standards can be added any time by anyone.

The purpose of our list is to be minimal. We are led to these standard by the logic of our epistemology and the methods and procedures that we propose throughout the chapters that follow.

11.9.1 Standards of Epistemology and Theory

(1) The ethnographic record should consist of at least two texts that must be kept separate: TEXT (1) is created by the ethnographer and includes any written part of the ethnographic record that is the product of the ethnographer's mind. TEXT (2) is created by the native, or any written part of the ethnographic record that is the product of the native consultant's mind.

(2) Any portions of an ethnographic corpus of texts that contradict each other (TEXT (1) versus TEXT (2), or within TEXT (1) or TEXT (2)), should be analyzed separately and an attempt should be made to resolve all contradictions, anomalies, or discrepancies.

(3) An ethnographer should learn a culture systematically focusing on both issues that separate and unite its members—that is, issues that are controversial and those beyond dispute within a social boundary.

(4) Every ethnography should be based on an explicit theoretical construct incorporating the best available insights into the nature of human knowledge systems and the nature of human communication, including translation.

(5) An ethnographer should maintain a methodological stance of cultural relativism.

11.9.2 Standards of Personal Equation

(6) An ethnographer should *maintain* a detailed autobiography that he or she periodically updates and revises.

(7) An ethnographer should expose himself or herself to the widest range of cultural variation available on our planet.

11.9.3 Standards of Research Design and Proposal

(8) An ethnographer should consider the problem that motivates an ethnography. Every ethnography benefits from making the theory underlying the ethnographic problem explicit.

(9) Any proposal for ethnographic research needs a theoretical plan and a plan of action: how to translate theoretical goals into ethnographic process.

(10) Every ethnographer must design an efficient data management system for ethnographic texts and other documents. The data management system should be in place *before* the collection of the first text or documents.

(11) A plan to protect the privacy of all people whose statements enter the ethnographer's data base should be in place *before* the first texts are deposited in it.

(12) An ethnographer should carefully formulate an explanation of his or her project for the natives in language (content and style) that they can understand and upon which they can base intelligent and informed judgments.

(13) When proposing any kind of ethnographic undertaking an ethnographer should take into account the interaction between the proposed research and his or her personal style of working.

11.9.4 Standards of Field Relations

(14) An ethnographer should make a serious effort to learn the language of the people who are the topic of the ethnography.

(15) An ethnographer should conduct his or her fieldwork and field relations in such a manner that other ethnographers will be able to follow and do restudies.

11.9.5 Standards of Observation

(16) An ethnographer should be on the lookout for applications of the latest technology to observation.

(17) An ethnographer is never justified for any reason in altering or fabricating data.

(18) An ethnographer should keep current in his or her field.

11.9.6 Standards of Interview

(19) The language of the interview should be determined by the language that the natives use for conducting their business in the cultural domain(s) of interest to the ethnographer.

11.9.7 Standards of Analysis

(20) The comparison of any pair of potentially discrepant text fragments should proceed by applying to each the *same* methods of analysis based on the *same* theory of cultural cognition.

(21) Any theoretical model underlying ethnographic analysis must be minimally adequate to cover analysis on the object level and on meta-levels of cultural knowledge.

(22) An ethnographer is never justified in altering or fabricating the analysis of ethnographic data.

11.9.8 Standards of Ethnographic Writing

(23) Description should precede the ethnographer's interpretation and explanation. The two should be clearly separate.

(24) Every ethnography should contribute to the advancement of theoretical knowledge.

(25) Every ethnography should list consultants who contributed to the ethnography (appropriately disguised), their numbers and demographic profiles. It is

Chapter Title	Epistemological Standards	Theoretical Standards	Technical Standards	Ethnical Standards	Personal Standards
11.1 Epistemology and Theory	1. Separate TEXT (1) and TEXT (2) 2. Resolve contradictions 3. Focus on issues separating and uniting people	4. Use theory of cognition, communication, and translation		5. Maintain cultural relativism as methods	
11.2 Personal Equation	6. Know thyself				6. Know thyself 7. Get cross-cultural training
11.3 Research Design and Proposal		8. Utilize theory beyond 4 9. Plan theory (from 4 and 8)	10. Plan DBMS (from 1, 2, and 3)	11. Plan protection of human subjects 12. Explain project	13. Consider your own style of work
11.4 Field Relations	14. Learn the language			15. Keep field access open for others	
11.5 Observation	Follow 1, 2 and 3	Follow 4 and 8	16. Use available and appropriate technology	17. Do not falsify data Follow through on 11	18. Keep up to date

Figure 11.3 Minimum Standards for Ethnography: Schematic Chart

11.6 Interview	Follow 1, 2, and 3 19. Interview in a language relevant to cultural domain	Follow 4 and 8	16. Use available and appropriate technology	17. Do not falsify interviews Follow through on 11	18. Keep up to date
11.7 Analysis	Follow 1, 2, and 3 20. Analyze all texts by same method	Follow 4 21. Analyze object and meta-levels by same methods	16. Use available and appropriate technology Follow up on 10	22. Do not falsify analysis	18. Keep up to date
11.8 Writing the Ethnography	23. Separate description from interpretation	Follow 8 24. Contribute new theoretical knowledge		Follow through on 11 25. List consultants 26. Cite consultants 27. Consider your audience	28. Improve your writing

Figure 11.3 Continued

particularly important to specify how many interviews each consultant contributed and how each interview was recorded.

(26) After considering the privacy and safety of consultants, they should receive the same privileges of citation as do professional sources.

(27) Because an ethnography is always intended for an audience, an ethnographer should weigh in every case the best medium and the best method within that medium for presenting ethnographic data and conclusions.

(28) An ethnographer should strive to improve his or her communicative skills, especially his or her writing.

11.9.9 Schematic Chart of Minimum Standards

In order to show the interconnectedness of our 28 proposed minimum standards for ethnography more clearly, we summarize them in a diagram, shown in Figure 11.3.

Ethnography is description. Yet it must become description that transcends casual culture learning. Systematization of the ethnographic process presents the best way to overcome our limitations as human beings trying to understand other human beings. Three areas are focal to this endeavor:

(1) reduction of complexity
(2) reduction of ethnocentrism
(3) reduction of semantic accent

The reduction of complexity (a meta-language of description less rich than the object language of our data) is by far the ethnographer's most difficult task. Serendipitous insights simplify and clarify the picture of another culture. Systematic field procedures increase the chances of such insights while keeping these discoveries true to ethnographic reality. Few of our standards deal with simplification and clarification. Here good theory on the level of field methods and the level of field problems is crucial.

Most of our standards deal with ethnocentrism (or bias) and semantic accent (or the translation problem). These two concerns represent the core of these two volumes. A call for self-improvement, including of one's ethics, and the exploitation of technological advances for data gathering and management constitute the rest.

We close with standards because they point the way to better ethnographies. We hope other ethnographers will join us in the task of refining the standards offered here. Thus we end with a new beginning in the continued struggle to make the ethnographic endeavor more systematic and consequently of higher fidelity to the cultures we will attempt to describe in the future.

NOTES

1. An ethnographic corpus of texts is the collection of those texts that constitute the entire data base for one ethnography.

2. Our statement assumes that "insight" cannot or does not deteriorate over time. This may be an unwarranted assumption.

3. This minimum standard is both an epistemological and a personal standard. It appears on the summary chart in Section 11.9 in two columns, the epistemological and the personal.

References

Abbott, J.,1979, *How to Write an Ethnography*, m.s.

Aberle, D.F., 1961, Navaho, in Schneider and Gough 1961:96-201.

Agar, M.H., 1974, *Ripping and Running: A Formal Ethnography of Urban Heroin Addicts*, Seminar Press.

Agar, M.H., 1979, Themes Revisited: Some Problems in Cognitve Anthropology, *Discourse Processes* 2:11-31.

Agar, M., 1980, Stories, Background Knowledge and Themes: Problems in the Analysis of Life History Narrative. *American Ethnologist* 7:223-239

Ahern, J., 1979, *Results from the Tower Rock Community Study,* Northwestern University Ethnographic Field School, m.s.

American Heritage Dictionary (W. Morris ed.),1969, *American Heritage Dictionary,* American Heritage Publishing Company.

American Heritage (J.B. Carroll, P. Davies, and B. Richman eds.), 1971, *Word Frequency Book,* Houghton Mifflin and American Heritage Publishing Company.

Arbib, M.A., 1972, *The Metaphorical Brain: An Introduction to Cybernetics as Artificial Intelligence and Brain Theory*, John Wiley.

Austin-Garrison, M.A., O. Werner, *et al.*, in preparation, *The Navajo Ethno-Medical Encyclopaedia*, Volumes 1-10.

Barlet, P.F. (ed.), 1980, *Agricultural Decision Making*, Academic Press.

Basso, K.H. and H.A. Selby, 1976, *Meaning in Anthropology*, University of New Mexico Press.

Bateson, G., 1942, Social Planning and the Concept of Deutero Learning, in Bryson & Finkelstein 1942:81-97 (also in Bateson 1972: 159-176).

Bateson, G., 1972, *Steps to an Ecology of the Mind*, Ballantine.

Begishe, K.Y., 1982, *Nitsáhákees (Thought)*, Dine Bi'olta Association, m.s.

Benedict, R., 1934, *Patterns of Culture*, Houghton-Mifflin.

Bernard, H.R. and P.D. Killworth, 1973, On the Social Structure of an Ocean-Going Research Vessel and Other Important Things, *Social Science Research* 2: 145-184.

Bidney, D., 1967, (second edition), *Theoretical Anthropology*, Columbia University Press.

Bierman, A.K., 1964, *Logic: A Dialogue*, Holden-Day Inc.

Black, M., (ed.), 1961, *The Social Theories of Talcott Parsons*, Prentice-Hall.

Bohannan, P.J. and L. Bohannan, 1968, *Tiv Economy*, Northwestern University Press.

Brunner, J.S. and L. Postman, 1949, On the Perception of Incongruity: A Paradigm, *Journal of Personality* 18:206-223.

Bryson, L. and L. Finkelstein, (eds.), 1942, *Science, Philosophy, and Religion:* Second Symposium, Harper.

Burton, M., 1977, *Entailment Analysis: Applications to Anthropology,* m.s.

Burton, M. and B. Nerlove, 1976, Balance Design for Triad Tests: Two Examples from English, *Social Science Research* 5:247-267.

Campbell, D.T. and D.W. Fiske, 1959, Covergent and Discriminant Validation by the Multitrait-Multimethod Matrix, *Psychological Bulletin* 56:81-105.

Casagrande, J.B. and K.L. Hale, 1967, Semantic Relations in Papago Folk Definitions, in Hymes with Bittle 1967:81-105.

Casson, R.W., 1983, Schemata in Cognitive Anthropology, in Siegel *et al.* 1983:429-462.

Chambers, A., and R. Bolton, 1979, We All Do It, But How? A Survey of Contemporary Field Note Procedure, paper presented in the Symposium on Computers and Ethnoscience at the annual meetings of the American Anthropological Association.

Chomsky, N., 1957, *Syntactic Structures,* Mouton.

Colby, B.N., 1975, *Computer Aided Exegesis of Culture Patterns,* m.s.

Colby, B.N., 1979, Computer Assisted Text Ethnography and the Building of Knowledge, presented at the Conference for Cognitive Anthropology, m.s.

Conklin, H.C., 1962, Lexicographical Treatment of Folk Taxonomies in Householder and Saporta, 1962:119-141, (reprinted in Tyler 1969:41-59).

Conklin, H.C., 1972, (80), *Folk Classification: A Topically Arranged Bibliography of Contemporary and Background References,* Yale University, Department of Anthropology.

Cook, T.D. and D.T. Campbell, 1979, *Quasi-Experimentation: Design and Analysis Issues for Field Settings,* Houghton Mifflin.

Cruden, A., 1953 (1738), *Cruden's Unabridged Concordance to the Old and New Testaments and the Apocryphal,* Baker Book House. (First published as *A Complete Concordance to the Holy Scriptures of the Old and New Testament).*

D'Andrade, R.G., 1970, Culture Shared and Unique, paper read at the meetings of the American Anthropological Association, m.s.

D'Andrade, R.G., 1976, A Propositional Analysis of U.S. American Beliefs About Illness, in Basso and Selby 1976:155-180.

Devereux, G., 1967, *From Anxiety to Method in the Behavioral Sciences,* Humanities Press.

Direnzo, G.J. (ed.), 1967, *Concepts, Theory and Explanation in the Behavioral Sciences,* Random House.

Dorland's Illustrated Medical Dictionary, 1965, (fourth edition) *Dorland's Illustrated Medical Dictionary,* W.B. Saunders Co.

Dvorak, A., N.L. Merrick, W.L. Dealey and G.C. Ford, 1936, *Typewriting Behavior: Psychology Applied to Teaching and Learning Typewriting,* American Book Co.

Evens, M.W., B.E. Litowitz, J.A. Markowitz, R.N. Smith, and O. Werner,1980, *Lexical-Semantic Relations: A Comparative Survey,* Linguistic Research.

Feigenbaum, E.A., A. Barr, and P.R. Cohen,1982, *Handbook of Artificial Intelligence,* Volumes 1, 2 and 3, William Kaufman.

Fenton, J., 1974, *A Cultural Analysis of Navajo Family and Clan,* Dissertation, Northwestern University, Department of Anthropology.

Festinger, L., 1957, *A Theory of Cognitive Dissonance*, Row, Peterson.

Finsterbusch, K., 1977, The Potential Role of the Impact Assessment in Instituting Public Policies, in Finsterbusch and Wolf 1977:2-12.

Finsterbusch, K. and C. Wolf, (eds.), 1977, *Economic Development on Native Reservations,* University of New Mexico Press.

Fisher, L.E. and O. Werner, 1978, Explaining Explanation: Tension in American Anthropology, *Journal of Anthropological Research* 34:194-218.

Frake, C.O., 1964, How to Ask for a Drink in Subanun, in Gumperz and Hymes 1964:127-132.

Garrison, E.R., 1974, *Navajo Semantics: The Classification Verb,* Dissertation, Northwestern University, Department of Anthropology.

Garrison, E.R. and G.M. Schoepfle, 1977, Attitudes of Navajo Students toward Teachers and School Activities, paper presented at joint meetings of the Society for Applied Anthropology and Southwest Anthropological Association, m.s.

Garvin, P.L. (ed.), 1970, *Cognition: A Multiple View,* Spartan Books.

Gildersleeve, T.R., 1970, *Decision Tables and Their Practical Application in Data Processing,* Prentice-Hall.

Gladwin, C.H., 1976, A View of the Plan Puebla: An Application of Hierarchical Decision Models, *American Journal of Agricultural Economics* 59:881-887.

Gladwin, C.H., 1980, A Theory of Real Life Choice: Applications to Agricultural Decisions, in Barlet 1980:45-85.

Gladwin, C.H., n.d., Production Function and Decision Models: Complementary Models, International Fertilizer Institute, Guatemala.

Gladwin, H. and M. Murtaugh, 1980, The Attentive-Preattentive Distinction in Agricultural Decision Making, in Barlet 1980:115-136.

Goffman, E., 1959, *The Presentation of Self in Everyday Life*, Doubleday/Anchor Books.

Goodenough, W.H., 1956, Componential Analysis and the Study of Meaning, *Language* 38:195-216.

Greenberg, J.H. (ed.), 1963, *Universals of Language*, MIT Press.

Grossman, J., 1976, *Quickhand*, John Wiley & Sons.

Gould, J.D., 1978, Writing, Dictating and Speaking Letters, *Science* 201:1145-1147.

Gumperz, J.J. and D. Hymes (eds.), 1964, The Ethnography of Communication, *American Anthropologist* 66, Part 2.

Hohmans, G., 1950, *The Human Group*, Harcourt, Brace and Co.

Hornblow, L. and A. Hornblow, 1970, *Reptiles Do the Strangest Things*, Random House.

Householder, F.W. and S. Soporta (eds.), 1962, *Problems in Lexicography*, Indiana Research Center in Anthropology, Folklore and Linguistics, Publication 21.

Hsu, F.L.K., 1953, *American and Chinese: Purpose and Fulfillment in Great Civilizations*, Natural History Press.

Huff, J., 1969, *Individual Variation in Lexico/Semantic Classifications of Navajo Anatomical Terms*, m.s.

Hutchins, E., 1980, *Culture and Inference: A Trobriand Case Study*, Harvard University Press.

Hymes, D.H. with W.E. Bittle (eds.), 1967, *Studies in Southwestern Ethnolinguistics*, Mouton.

Iris, M.B., B.E. Litowitz, and M.W. Evens,1984, *The Part-Whole in the Lexicon: An Investigation of Semantic Primitives*, m.s.

Iris, M.B., n.d., *Navajo Clan Kinship: A Decision Model*, m.s.

Jaffrey, M., 1975, *An Invitation to Indian Cooking*, Random House.

Jordan, B., 1980, *Birth in Three Cultures*, Eden Press Women's Publications.

Jorgensen, J.L., 1981, Social Impact Assessment and Energy Developments, *Policy Studies Review* 10:66-86.

Katz, T., 1982, An Overview of SMARTKEY, *Lifelines: The Software Magazine*, 3.5:54-55.

Kay, P., 1971, Taxonomy and Semantic Contrast, *Language* 47:866-887.

Keesing, R.M., 1974, Theories of Culture, in Siegel *et al.* 1974:73-97.

Killworth, P.D. and H.R. Bernard, 1974, Catij: A New Sociometric and Its Application to a Prison Living Unit, *Human Organization* 33:335-350.

Kirk, L. and M. Burton, 1976, Meaning in Context: A Study of Contextual Shifts in Meaning of Maasai Personality Descriptions, *Social Science Working Paper 115*, School of Social Sciences, University of California at Irvine.

Kluckhohn, C., 1949, [1939] *Mirror for Man: The Relation of Anthropology to Modern Life*, McGraw-Hill.

Kluckhohn, C. and D. Leighton, 1946, *The Navajo*, Harvard University Press.

Kluckhohn, R., 1962, *Culture and Behavior: Collective Essays of Clyde Kluckhohn*, Free Press.

Kuhn, T.S., 1962, *The Structure of Scientific Revolutions*, University of Chicago Press.

Ladd, J., 1957, *The Structure of a Moral Code: A Philosophical Analysis of Ethical Discourse Applied to the Ethics of Navajo Indians*, Harvard University Press.

LaFarge, O., 1929, *Laughing Boy*, Houghton Mifflin.

Lazarsfeld, P.F., 1967, Concept Formation and Measurement in the Behavioral Sciences: Some Historical Observations, in Direnzo 1967:144-196.

Lewis, O., 1958, *Village Life in Northern India*, Vintage Books.

Lewis, O., 1959, *Five Families: Mexican Case Studies in the Culture of Poverty*, Basic Books.

Lewis, O., 1961, *Children of Sanchez: Autobiography of a Mexican Family*, Random House.

Litowitz, B. and S. Novy, 1984, Expression of the Part/Whole Semantic Relation by Three to Twelve Year Old Children, *Journal of Child Language* 11:159-178.
Loflin, M.D. and J. Silverberg, 1978, *Discourse and Inference in Cognitive Anthropology: An Approach to Psychic Unity and Enculturation,* Mouton.
Lombardi, L.A., 1963, A General Business-Oriented Language Based on Decision Expressions, paper presented at a working conference on mechanical language structures, Princeton, NJ.
Lounsbury, F.G., 1956, A Semantic Analysis of Pawnee Kinship Usage, *Language* 32:158-194.
Lounsbury, F.G., 1964, The Structural Analysis of Kinship Semantics, in Lunt 1964: 73-93 (reprinted in Tyler 1969: 193-211).
Lounsbury, F.G., 1965, Another View of Trobriand Kinship Categories, *American Anthropologist* 67, Part 2:142-185.
Lounsbury, F.G., 1969, A Formal Account of Crow- and Omaha-Type Kinship Terminologies, in Tyler 1969:212-254.
Lowie, R., 1945, A Case of Bilingualism, *Word* 1:249-259.
Lunt, H.G. (ed.), 1964, *Proceedings of the 9th International Congress of Linguistics,* Mouton.
Luschei, E.C., 1962, *The Logical System of Łešnievski,* North-Holland.
Malinowski, B., 1967, *A Diary in the Strictest Sense of the Term,* Harcourt, Brace, and World.
Manes, J.I., 1976, *Semantic Relationships in American English Folk Definitions,* Dissertation, University of Pennsylvania.
Manheim, K., 1936, *Ideology and Utopia,* Harcourt and Brace.
McCormack, W.C. and S.A. Wurm (eds.), 1977, *Language and Thought: Anthropological Issues,* Mouton.
McDaniel, H., 1970, *An Introduction to Decision Logic Tables,* John Wiley & Sons.
McNeley, J.K., 1979, *Progress Report,* Minority Biomedical Research Project, Navajo Community College, Shiprock, NM.
Mead, M., 1972, *Blackberry Winter: My Earlier Years,* Morrow.
Miller, G.A., E. Gallanter, and K.H. Pribam, 1960, *Plans and the Structure of Behavior,* Dryden Press.
Michener, J.A., 1974, *Centennial,* Random House.
Morgan, M.W., 1973, *Navajo Suicide: Cultural Etiology of Suicide Behavior and Variant Patterns of Cultural Knowledge About Suicide,* Ph.D Dissertation, Northwestern University, Department of Anthropology.
Murdoch, G.P., 1960 [1938], *Outline of Cultural Materials,* Human Relations Area File Press.
Naroll, R., 1962, *Data Quality Control: A New Research Technique,* Free Press.
Naroll, R. and R. Cohen, 1970, *A Handbook of Method in Cultural Anthropology,* Natural History Press.
Nida, E., 1957, *Learning a Foreign Language: A Handbook Prepared Especially for Missionaries,* Friendship Press.
Ortiz, A.(ed.), 1983, *Handbook of North American Indians,* Volume 10, Smithsonian Institute.
Paredes, A., 1977, On Ethnographic Work Among Minority Groups: A Folklorists's Perspective, *New Scholar* 6:1-32.
Parsons, T. and E.A. Shils (eds.), 1951, *Toward a General Theory of Action,* Harvard University Press.
Pinxten, R., I. van Dooren, and F. Harvey, 1983, *Anthropology of Space: Explorations into the Natural Philosophy and Semantics of the Navajo,* University of Pennsylvania Press.
Pirsig, R., 1974, *Zen and the Art of Motorcycle Maintenance,* Bantam Books.
Polanyi, M., 1964, *Personal Knowledge: Towards a Post-Critical Philosophy,* Harper Torchbooks.
Polanyi, M., 1969, *Knowing and Being* (edited by M. Grene), University of Chicago Press.
Pollack, S.L., 1963, *How to Build and Analyze Decision Tables,* Memorandum 2829, Rand Corporation.
Pollack, S.L., 1971, *Decision Tables: Theory and Practice,* John Wiley & Sons.
Pollack, S.L., 1974, *Conversion of Limited Entry Decision Tables to Computer Programs,* Memorandum RM-4020-PR, Rand Corporation.

Polya, G., 1957 [1945], *How to Solve It,* Doubleday/Anchor Books.

Powdermaker, H., 1966, *Stranger and Friend: The Ways of an Anthropologist,* W.W. Norton.

Powers, W.T., 1973, *Behavior: The Control of Perception,* Aldine.

Quinn, N., 1976, A Natural System Used in Mfantse Litigation Settlement, *American Ethnologist* 3:331-351.

Quinn, N., 1978, Do Mfantse Fish Sellers Estimate Probabilities in Their Heads? *American Ethnologist* 5:206-226.

Rameh, C. (ed.), 1976, *Semantics:Theory and Applications,* Georgetown University Round Table on Language and Linguistics, Georgetown University Press.

Roberts, J.M., 1956, *Zuni Daily Activities,* Laboratory of Anthropology, University of Nebraska, Notebook 3, Monograph 2, (also in Human Relations Area File).

Rohner, R.P. (ed.), 1969, *The Ethnography of Frank Boas,* University of Chicago Press.

Romney, A.K. and R.G. D'Andrade, 1964, Cognitive Aspects of English Kin Terms, in Romney and D'Andrade 1964:146-170 (reprinted in Tyler 1969:369-418).

Rosenthal, R. and L. Jacobson, 1968, *Pygmalion in the Classroom,* Holt, Rinehart & Winston.

Ryle, G., 1946, *Knowing How and Knowing That,* Proceedings of the Aristotelian Society, Harrison and Sons.

Sanday, P.R., 1968, The "Psychological Reality" of American-English Kinship Terms: An Information-Processing Approach, *American Anthropologist* 70:508-523.

Sapir, E. and H. Hoijer, 1942, *Navajo Texts,* Linguistic Society of America.

Sasaki, T.T., 1960, *Fruitland, New Mexico: A Navajo Community,* Cornell University Press.

Schank, R.C and R.P Abelson, 1977 *Scripts, Plans, Goals and Understanding,* Lawrence Earlbaum.

Schneider, D.M. and K. Gough (eds.), 1961, *Matrilineal Kinship,* University of California Press.

Schneider, D.M., 1968, *American Kinship: A Cultural Account,* Prentice-Hall.

Schoepfle, G.M., 1977, *Nogales High School: Peer Group and Institution in a Mexican American Border Town,* Dissertation, Northwestern University, Department of Anthropology.

Schoepfle, G.M., K.Y. Begishe, R.T. Morgan, J. John, and P. Reno, 1979, *A Study of Navajo Perceptions of the Impact of Environmental Changes Relating to Energy Resource Development,* Environmental Protection Agency, Contract 68-01-3868.

Schoepfle, G.M., K. Nabahe, A. Johnson, and L. Upshaw, 1982, *Navajo Perceptions of Land Use and Conservation in Modern Ecological and Economic Contexts,* Report to National Science Foundation *re* Grant NSF/ISP-82015.

Schoepfle, G.M., M.L. Burton, and F. Morgan, 1984, Navajos and Energy Development: Economic Decision Making Under Political Uncertainty, *Human Organization,*3:265-276.

Schoepfle, G.M., M.L. Burton, and K.Y. Begishe, 1985, Navajo Attitudes Toward Development and Change: Unified Ethnographic and Survey Approach to an Understanding of Their Future, *American Anthropologist* 86: 885-904.

Schoepfle, G.M. and E.R. Garrison, 1977. "Navajo Attitudes Toward Teachers and Classes." Paper presented at the joint meetings of the Society for Applied Anthropology and Southwest Anthropological Association. San Diego, CA.

Shweder, R.A. (ed.), 1980, *New Directions for Methodology of Social and Behavior Science,* Jossey-Bass.

Shweder, R.A. and R.G. D'Andrade, 1980, The Systematic Distortion Hypothesis, in Shweder 1980:37-58.

Schoepfle, G.M. and E.R. Garrison, 1977. (ref forthcoming)

Siegel, B.J., R. Beals, and S.A. Tyler (eds.), 1974, *Annual Review of Anthropology,* Annual Reviews.

Siegel, B.J., R. Beals, and S.A. Tyler (eds.), 1983, *Annual Review of Anthropology,* Annual Reviews.

Snyder, D.P., 1973, *Model Logic and Its Applications,* Van Nostrand Reinhold.

Spradley, J.P., 1979, *The Ethnographic Interview,* Holt, Rinehart & Winston.

Spradley, J.P., 1980, *Participant Observation,* Holt, Rinehart & Winston.

Stedman's Medical Dictionary, 1966, *Stedman's Medical Dictionary* (21 ed.), Williams and Wilkins.

Tarski, A., 1937, Appendix to J.H. Woodger, *Axiomatic Method in Biology.*

Terkel, S., 1972, *Working*, Avon Books.

Tonigan, R.F., 1982, *Report on the Impact of the Proposed Separation of the Kirtland School District from Consolidated School District No. 22*, Central Consolidated School District No. 22.

Topper, M.D., 1972, *The Daily Life of a Traditional Navajo Household: An Ethnographic Study of Human Daily Activities,* Dissertation, Northwestern University, Department of Anthropology.

Topper, M.D., J.D. Nations, R. Detwiller, and J.A. Stovall, 1974, *The Ethnography of the Day: Some New Developments,* m.s.

Tversky, A., 1972, Elimination by Aspects: A Theory of Choice, *Psychological Review* 79:281-291.

Tversky, A. and D. Kahneman, 1974, Judgment under Uncertainty: Heuristics and Biases, *Science* 185:1124-1131.

Tyler, S.A. (ed.), 1969, *Cognitive Anthropology*, Holt, Rinehart & Winston.

Voegelin, C.F. and F.M. Voegelin, 1957, *Hopi Domains: A Lexical Approach to the Problem of Selection*, Indiana University Publications in Anthropology and Linguistics, Memoir 14.

Von Foerster, H., 1970, Thoughts and Notes on Cognition, in Garvin 1970: 25-48.

Wallace, A.F.C., 1961, *Culture and Personality,* Random House.

Wallace, A.F.C. and J. Atkins, 1960, The Meaning of Kinship Terms, *American Anthropologist* 62: 58-79.

Ward, J. and O. Werner, 1984, Difference and Dissonance in Ethnographic Data, *Communication and Cognition*, 17:219-243.

Webster's New Collegiate Dictionary, 1953, *Webster's New Collegiate Dictionary* (second edtion), G.C. Merriam Co.

Weinreich, U., 1963, On the Semantic Structure of Language, in Greenberg 1963:114-171.

Werner, O., 1966, Pragmatics and Ethnoscience, *Anthropological Linguistics* 8:42-65.

Werner, O., 1977, The Synthetic Informant Model: On the Simulation of Large Lexical/Semantic Fields, in McCormack and Wurm: 131-170 (also in Loflin and Silverberg 1978:45-82).

Werner, O., 1982, Microcomputers in Cultural Anthropology: APL Programs for Qualitative Analysis, *BYTE* 7.7:250-280.

Werner, O. and K.Y. Begishe, 1968, Styles of Learning: The Evidence from Navajo Thought, prepared for the Conference on Styles of Learning, m.s.

Werner, O. and J. Fenton, 1970, Method and Theory in Ethnoscience, in Naroll and Cohen 1970:398-420.

Werner, O., G.M. Schoepfle, D. Bouck, L. Roan, and K. Yazzie, 1976, *Six Navajo School Ethnographies,* Navajo Division of Education, Navajo Tribe.

Werner, O., J. Remington, and F. Pasquale, 1976, Prologomena Toward a Theory of Values in Ethnoscience, paper presented at the meetings of the American Anthropological Association, m.s.

Werner, O. and M.D. Topper, 1976, On the Theoretical Unity of Ethnoscience Lexicography and Ethnoscience Ethnographies, in Rameh 1976:111-144.

Werner, O., A. Manning, and K.Y. Begishe, 1983, A Taxonomic View of the Traditional Navajo Universe, in Ortiz 1983: 579-591.

Werner, O. and M.A. Austin-Garrison, in preparation, *Navajo Ethno Medical Encyclopaedia* project, n.d.

White, D.R., 1980, Material Entailment Analysis: Theory and Illustration, School of Social Sciences, Research Reports 15, University of California at Irvine.

White, D.R., n.d. *Implication and Variability in Cultural Systems,* m.s.

White, D.R., M.L. Burton, and L.A. Brudner, 1977, Entailment Theory and Method: A Cross-Cultural Analysis of the Sexual Division of Labor, *Behavioral Science Research* 12:1-24.

White, D.R. and H.G. McCann, 1981, Material and Probablistic Entailment Analysis: Multivariate Analysis of "If . . . Then" Statements in Cultural Systems. School of Social Sciences, University of California at Irvine, m.s.

Williams, G.E., 1966, Linguistic Reflection of Cultural Systems, *Anthropological Linguistics* 8.8:13-21.

Woods, J.J., 1980, Rural Western Navajo Household Income Strategies, *American Ethnologist* 7:493-503.

Young, J.C., 1980, A Model of Treatment Decisions in a Tarascan Town, *American Ethnologist* 7:107-121.

Young, J.C. and L.Y. Garro, 1982, Variation in the Choice of Treatment in Two Mexican Communities, *Social Science Medicine* 16:1453-1465.

Name Index

Subject Index

About The Authors

Oswald Werner was born in 1928 in Rimavska Sobota, Czechoslovakia. After World War II he attended the Technische Hochschule in Stuttgart, Germany. Werner has an M.A. degree in anthropology from Syracuse University and a Ph.D. in anthropology and linguistic anthropology from Indiana University. In 1980 he was elected a fellow of the American Association for the Advancement of Science. Werner's major fieldwork has been with the Navajo Indians in Northern Arizona; this book is based on his experiences with several research projects sponsored by the National Institute of Mental Health among the Navajo. Each summer since 1974 he has directed Northwestern University's Ethnographic Field School in New Mexico and Arizona. Werner has also conducted fieldwork on Easter Island in the South Pacific, and in 1974 he was Fulbright Professor at the Universidad Catolica in Valpariaso, Chile. Currently he is Professor of Anthropology and Linguistics at Northwestern University.

G. Mark Schoepfle is affiliated with the Dine Bi'Olta Association in Farmington, New Mexico. He holds a Ph.D in cultural anthropology from Northwestern University. Since the completion of his dissertation in 1974, he has conducted research on the Navajo Reservation for the Navajo Tribal Division of Education, for the U.S. Environmental Protection Agency, the National Institute of Education, and the National Science Foundation. His ethnographic work has included educational policy, philosophy, and planning social environmental impact assessment, natural resource use, and medical decision making. Present research interests include the combination of systematic ethnography to quantitative approaches and applied fields of rural development in education, agriculture, and health care delivery. Currently he is Associate Director of Planning and Legislation for the Navajo Tribe's Division of Health Improvement Services.

NOTES

NOTES

NOTES

NOTES

NOTES